FEEDING THE RUSSIAN FUR TRADE

FEEDING THE RUSSIAN FUR TRADE

PROVISIONMENT OF THE
OKHOTSK SEABOARD AND THE
KAMCHATKA PENINSULA

1639-1856

James R. Gibson

THE UNIVERSITY OF WISCONSIN PRESS

Madison, Milwaukee, and London   1969

Published by
The University of Wisconsin Press
Box 1379, Madison, Wisconsin 53701
The University of Wisconsin Press, Ltd.
27–29 Whitfield Street, London, W.1

Printed in the United States of America by
Kingsport Press, Inc., Kingsport, Tennessee

LC 79–81319
SBN 299–05230–3

To MY PARENTS

The history of Russia is the history of a country being colonized. . . . migration and colonization of the country have been fundamental facts of our history . . . .

V. Klyuchevsky, *Kurs russkoy istorii,* I, 20–21.

CONTENTS

ILLUSTRATIONS
AND MAPS

ILLUSTRATIONS

following page 156

MAPS

TABLES

INTRODUCTION

The importance that Klyuchevsky, one of nineteenth-century Russia's foremost historians, attributed to Russian expansion when he called the history of Russia "the history of a country being colonized" is noteworthy. In both the Old World and the New, European colonial expansion extended trade and settlement. Two prominent theaters of settlement were Siberia and Canada, which at the same time were the main sources of furs, a staple of trade. The lucrative trade in furs for the European market was the primary object of Russian expansion eastward from the upper Volga River over the Urals and through Siberia in the sixteenth and seventeenth centuries and of French and English expansion westward from the upper St. Lawrence River and Hudson Bay through Rupert's Land in the seventeenth and eighteenth centuries. Russian *promyshlenniks* (fur hunters) were drawn across Siberia by the sable and into Alaska by the sea otter; French *coureurs de bois* and their English counterparts were drawn across the Canadian West by the beaver. Both movements utilized well-developed drainage networks, founding posts at strategic river junctions and portages. In the early nineteenth century the two movements, in the forms of the Russian-American Company and the Hudson's Bay Company, met on the Northwest Coast (Map 1).

Although the two occupations were thus similar in several respects, there were fundamental differences. Because of Siberia's larger size and higher latitude, the climate, especially in Eastern Siberia, was

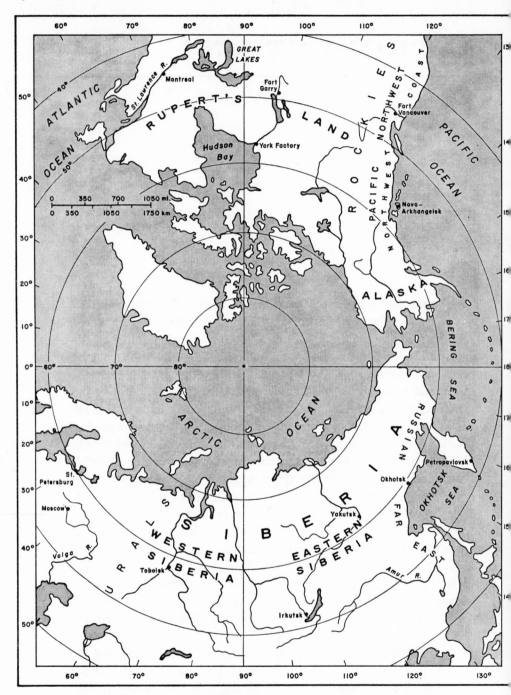

MAP 1. Siberia vis-à-vis Canada.

more continental and hence more severe than that of Western Canada—
a circumstance which created much greater difficulties for agriculture.
Also, the buffalo, the primary source of pemmican, which to a large degree provisioned the Canadian fur trade, had no Siberian equivalent. Indian corn (maize), an item in the diet of the Canadian fur traders around
the Great Lakes, was also lacking in Siberia. Reindeer were far fewer
in number and much more limited in range than the bison of North
America. Thus, the fur traders of Siberia could not depend upon game
as a major source of food, although they did utilize the abundance of
fish, especially on the shores of the far North Pacific. In addition, Siberia, even without Alaska (Russian America), had a much greater
longitudinal extent than Western Canada; hence it was more remote
from European Russia than was the Canadian West from the St. Lawrence Valley.*

Together, then, these circumstances created for the occupation
of Siberia in general and for the fur trade in particular a serious problem
of food supply, especially on the Pacific littoral. Here on the Okhotsk
Seaboard and the Kamchatka Peninsula the Russians were beset with
a chronic question of how, in such a harsh and distant region, to provision not only fur traders but also state servitors,** missionaries, convicts, serfs, and scientific expeditions. For the first time since Muscovy
had begun "gathering lands" in the fifteenth century, Russian expansion
faced a critical situation of food supply.

Thus the problem of provisionment profoundly conditioned
Russian occupation and exploitation of the Russian Far East and clearly
distinguished it from French-English occupation and exploitation of the

---

* In terms of the Canadian fur trade of the Hudson's Bay Company one
should properly speak of England as the home base. Even so, the distance
from London (headquarters of that company) to the westernmost post of
the Pacific Northwest was substantially less than the distance from St.
Petersburg (headquarters of the Russian-American Company) to the
easternmost post of Alaska. Moreover, it was possible to communicate
between England and Western Canada by sea via the direct, rapid, and
cheap route from London across the North Atlantic to York Factory on
Hudson Bay, whereas the Russians were unable to use the Northern Sea
Route off the Arctic coast of Siberia effectively until the advent of the
modern icebreaker.

** State servitors (*sluzhilie lyudi*) were mainly military personnel (especially Cossacks) but also noblemen and others who owed civil or military
service to the state in return for land.

Canadian West. The matter was vital to Russia's success in the North Pacific sphere of international rivalry, as well as to pursuit of the fur trade.

This book concerns the food supply problem primarily as it affected the Okhotsk Seaboard and the Kamchatka Peninsula from the beginning of Russian settlement in the mid-seventeenth century until the decline of the region in the mid-nineteenth century. "Russian Far East" or *Primorye* here denotes that portion of the eastern coast of Siberia which drains to the Pacific Ocean, and excludes some Arctic drainage that is normally included in the terms. "Okhotsk Seaboard" (*Priokhotskomorye* or *Okhotskoye poberezhye*) signifies that part of the coast of the Okhotsk Sea lying between the Penzhina River on the north and the Uda River on the south and draining to the Pacific Ocean. The regions north and south of the seaboard—Chukotka (Anadyr Basin) and Amuria (Amur Basin)—are not focuses of our attention here. The former was long only tenuously occupied by Russia (indeed, its chief Russian settlement, Anadyrsk, was abandoned in 1771), and its affairs were more closely connected with Yakutia than with the Kamchatka Peninsula or the Okhotsk Seaboard. The left bank of the Amur River and the right bank of the Ussuri River did not become Russian territory until 1858–60. And Sakhalin did not become Russian property *de jure* until 1875.

The Okhotsk Seaboard and the Kamchatka Peninsula from the seventeenth into the nineteenth centuries had their own changing geography, i.e., their own changing stamp or landscape, tangible and visible, created by the interaction of the region's physical and cultural elements. To reconstruct and interpret this landscape—verbally, cartographically, statistically—constitutes the task of the historical geographer. A salient feature of the changing geography of the Okhotsk Seaboard and the Kamchatka Peninsula from the advent of Russian settlement was the expression in the landscape of Russian attempts to solve the region's food supply problem through overland provisionment and local agriculture. This book tries to analyze this episode in the development of the region. It does not pretend to be a sophisticated or complicated analysis in economic history; rather, it is intended as simply a detailed. systematic, empirical study in historical geography, one that, it is hoped, elucidates a crucial problem (provisionment) in one of the most influential processes (expansion) in the development of Russia's Pacific frontier.

I am indebted to the following libraries and archives for assistance in locating, supplying, and duplicating much material: Archive of the Miklukho-Maklay Institute of Ethnography in Leningrad; Bancroft Library in Berkeley; British Museum, especially the Photographic Department; Central State Archive of Ancient Acts in Moscow; Central State Historical Archive in Leningrad; Gorky Library of Moscow State University; Helsinki University Library; Irkutsk State University Library; Lenin State Public Library in Moscow; Library of Congress, especially the Photoduplication Service; Memorial Library of the University of Wisconsin, especially the Interlibrary Loan staff; New York Public Library, especially the Photographic Service; Olin Library of Cornell University; Saltykov-Shchedrin State Public Library in Leningrad; and the State Historical Society of Wisconsin.

I am also grateful to the Centre for Russian and East European Studies of the University of Toronto for an exchange grant, and to the Department of Geography and the Russian Area Studies Program of the University of Wisconsin for research and travel grants.

Additional thanks go to Professors Andrew H. Clark (especially), Michael B. Petrovich, and Robert N. Taaffe of the University of Wisconsin for valuable criticism and patient encouragement, to Hania Guzewska and Gerry Fradsham for their diligent mapwork, and to Roberta W. Yerkes for her assiduous editing. Assistance is gratefully acknowledged, too, from Fyodor Aleksandrovich Kudryavtsev of the Faculty of History of Irkutsk State University, Georgy Andreyevich Novitsky of the Faculty of History of Moscow State University, and Fedot Grigoryevich Safronov of the Yakutsk Branch of the Siberian Division of the Academy of Sciences. None of these individuals is responsible for interpretation, which reflects the biases of the author alone.

Transliteration follows the system of the American Council of Learned Societies.

JAMES R. GIBSON

Toronto, Canada
November, 1968

PART I

Perspective and Context

1

HISTORICAL BACKGROUND: OCCUPATION AND EXPLOITATION OF THE RUSSIAN FAR EAST

> "The Russians sought in Siberia first sables and then Kamchatka beavers [sea otters]. These animals were the reason for the opening and conquest of Siberia, just as gold and silver were for America."
> K. F. German, "Statisticheskiya svedeniya," pp. 82–83.

Russian Expansion across Siberia

It is sometimes forgotten that European colonial expansion proceeded overland to the east as well as overseas to the west. While the maritime nations of Western Europe were advancing westward across the Atlantic Ocean to the New World, continental Russia of Eastern Europe was seeking its own new world by moving eastward across the Great Russian Plain. This expansion, whereby Muscovy grew from a principality of several hundred square miles into an empire spanning three continents and encompassing one-sixth of the earth, is certainly one of the cardinal features of modern history. In the words of a seventeenth-century Russian tale, "What man ever divined that Moscow would become a kingdom? What man ever guessed that Moscow would be accounted an empire? Once by the Moskva there stood only the goodly hamlets of a noble."[1]

Russian expansion to the east dates from the very dawn of Russian history. As Lantzeff has remarked, "in the beginning of Russian history, two Russian principalities, Novgorod and Rostov-Suzdal, were engaged in exploring, conquering, exploiting, and colonizing the area west of the Ural Mountains."[2] Bands of Novgorodian *ushkuiniks* (river brigands) raided "the country beyond the portage" (i.e., the basin of the Northern Dvina River) from the eleventh century, even crossing the

"Iron Gate" or "Stony Belt" (Urals). The Chronicle of Novgorod mentions its citizens traveling "beyond the portage" as early as 1079.[3] Novgorodians also ventured to Pomorye, the "summer [southern] coast" of the "Cold [White] Sea," in search of fish, salt, and furs.[4] Their booty, which also included honey and wax, silver and copper, river pearls and walrus tusks, was readily marketed in the Hanseatic trade of Novgorod the Great.

Muscovy, in annexing Novgorod Land in the 1470's, fell heir to the Novgorodian policy of commercial expansion to the northeast. This legacy, coupled with Muscovy's own aggressive policy of "the gathering of the Russian lands" in order to consolidate the absolute rule of the Grand Prince of Moscow, resulted in the intensification and extension of Russian eastward expansion, especially after Ivan the Terrible's conquest in the 1550's of the roadblocks of the Tatar khanates of Kazan and Astrakhan astride, respectively, the middle and the lower Volga. These victories secured the direct central route to Siberia, which the chronicles first mention in 1407. Novgorod's river pirates were succeeded by the soldiers and Cossacks* of Moscow. Their policy of periodic raiding to punish marauders and to exact tribute was climaxed in 1583 by the capture of Kuchum Khan's capital of Sibir (Isker), near the junction of the Tobol and Irtysh rivers, by Yermak, a renegade Cossack in the hire of the mercantile Stroganov family. This conquest of the Siberian Khanate removed the last serious obstacle to Russian expansion across Siberia.

Thereafter the policy of sporadic raids was replaced by the "planned domination of rivers and portages through the building of ostrogs [forts]."[5] Bands of Cossacks and promyshlenniks, on their own initiative but with official sufferance, horsed, boated, skied, and trudged farther and farther east of the Urals from one river basin to the next, subjugating and taxing the natives. In this manner Western Siberia was

---

* Cossacks, whose name is probably derived from a Turkish word meaning "adventurers," were pastoral frontiersmen originating from fugitives and refugees who fled to the steppes of southern European Russia in the late fifteenth and the early sixteenth centuries. Here they established military villages (*stanitsas*) with elected officers and herded, traded, and raided. Eventually they were employed by Moscow as frontier guards in return for certain privileges (e.g., tax exemption). They were largely responsible for the conquest of Siberia, which contained some 2,000 Cossacks by 1631 (George V. Lantzeff, *Siberia in the Seventeenth Century,* "University of California Publications in History," vol. 30 [Berkeley and Los Angeles: University of California Press, 1943], p. 69).

conquered by Tobolsk Cossacks, Eastern Siberia by Yeniseisk Cossacks, and the Russian Far East by Yakutsk Cossacks.* Following the interlocking river systems of the Ob, Yenisey, and Lena, the Russians erected *ostrogs* (forts) and *zimovyes* ("wintering places") at strategic confluences, along key portages, and near native villages. In such a manner there quickly arose a network of Russian posts spanning the Siberian taiga from the Urals to the Pacific: Tobolsk (1587) at the confluence of the Tobol and Irtysh rivers, Obdorsk (1595) on the site of the Ostyak (Khanty) village of Nosovoy, Mangazeya (1601) near the mouth of the Taz River, Yeniseisk (1619) at the eastern end of the Makovsk Portage between the Ket and Yenisey rivers, Yakutsk (1632) on the "big bend" of the Lena, and many others (Map 2). Close behind the pathfinding Cossacks and promyshlenniks came officials, merchants, churchmen, peasants, convicts, dissenters, exiles, fugitives, adventurers. By 1662, eighty years after Yermak's campaign, the Russian male population of Siberia had reached 70,000.[6]

The rate of advance across vast Siberia was extremely rapid. Only half a century separated the founding of Verkhoturye (1598) on the eastern edge of the Urals and Dezhnev's navigation of Bering Strait between Asia and America in 1648. Even the turmoil of the Time of Troubles (1598–1613) failed to slow this Russian *Drang nach Osten*. The natives of the taiga and tundra offered little resistance, being neither numerous nor well organized. The factious and scattered aborigines numbered only about 200,000 in 1662.[7] The superiority of Russian weapons was also a telling factor; indeed, it can truthfully be said that gunpowder conquered Siberia. The well-armed Cossack expeditions often comprised only several dozen, and seldom more than a hundred, men. Gifts (especially vodka) and promises, as well as force, induced the natives to pay *yasak* (fur tribute) and allegiance to the Tsar; compliance was strengthened by the practice of keeping several hostages from each tributary group of natives.

The Russian advance was further facilitated by the dense net-

---

* Throughout this book "Western Siberia" refers to that part of Siberia lying between the crest of the Ural Mountains and the left bank of the Yenisey River and draining to the Arctic Ocean. "Eastern Siberia" refers to the area lying between the right bank of the Yenisey and the Yablonovoy-Stanovoy-Dzhugdzhur-Kolyma Ranges and draining to the Arctic; it is thus distinguished from the "Russian Far East," which we have defined as that portion of the eastern coast of Siberia that drains to the Pacific.

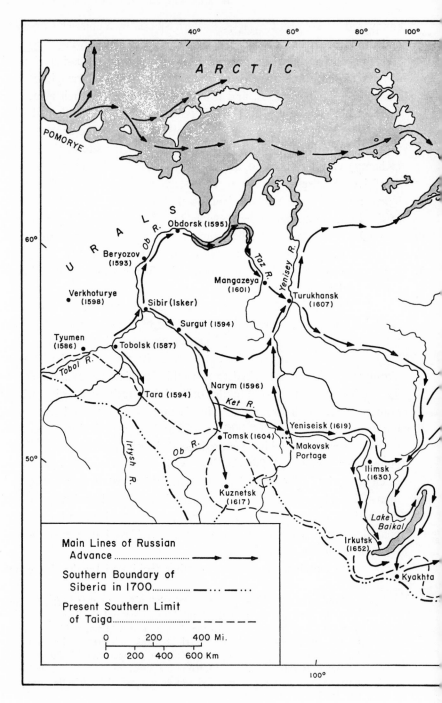

MAP 2. Russian Expansion across Siberia.

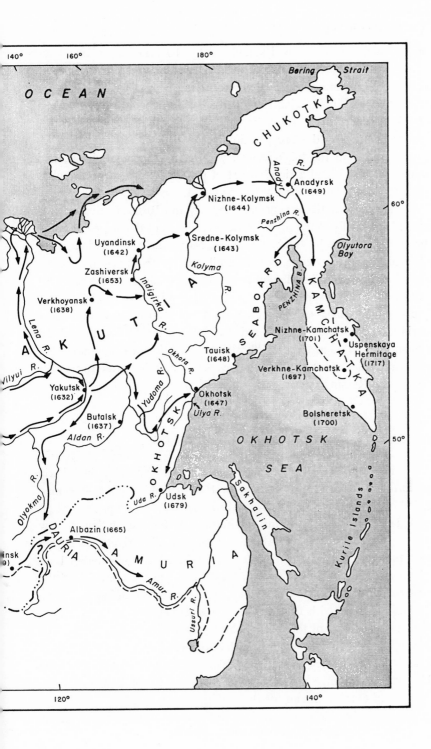

work of navigable rivers and stimulated by the insatiable demand for furs. The multibranched and dovetailed river systems of Siberia, closely linked by short portages, provided an intricate mesh of river roads for intruders. Observers invariably extolled Siberia's matchless waterways; a Swedish prisoner-of-war, for example, declared that "there is hardly any Country in the World more plentifully provided with Rivers than *Siberia. . . .*"[8] And the taiga teemed with sables, foxes, squirrels, and ermines, which yielded a rich harvest of pelts that seemed nevertheless unable to glut the voracious European market.

Throughout the seventeenth century the Russian advance was confined essentially to the forest zone. The taiga, not the steppe, was the source of furs, Siberia's main attraction. Moreover, the Russians were restricted to the forest zone, at least until the eighteenth century, by the stiff resistance of warlike Mongol and Turkic nomads along the southern flank of the taiga, especially the Kirgiz. Excepting the Chukchi, only these nomadic tribes seriously challenged the Russian advance across Siberia. Thus, fortified lines or strips (like the Roman *limites* and the German *marken*) and Cossack "hosts" were established only along the southern frontier of Siberia, just as they were along the southern frontier of European Russia against the Crimean Tatars.

Conquest and Settlement of the Russian Far East

The rapid rate and easterly direction of expansion in Siberia soon brought Russia to the Pacific. In 1639 a band of thirty-one men headed by the Tomsk Cossack Ivan Moskvitin was sent from Butalsk on the Aldan River "to the Lama [Okhotsk Sea] for the finding of new lands."[9] Proceeding via the Aldan, Maya, and Ulya rivers, in eleven weeks they reached the ocean at the mouth of the Ulya, where they built a zimovye (Map 2). For two years Moskvitin's party reconnoitered the southern half of the Lama Coast, finding the forests abounding in sables, the rivers teeming with fish, and the land peopled by numerous Tunguses. The members of this party, which returned to Yakutsk with 440 sable pelts and 323 fox pelts, were the first Russians to see the Pacific Ocean.[10] Then another Cossack, Semyon Shelkovnik, "in 154 [1646] with forty serving men was sent to the Ulya and to the Okhota for the collection of Our yasak and for the finding of new lands. . . ."[11] In the summer of 1647 this band reached the mouth of the Okhota River, where they battled "1,000 and more" Tunguses and "established a zimovye three verstas [two miles] from the mouth. . . ."[12] This event marked the beginning of Okhotsk.

Following this initial spate of activity, however, the Russians of "New Siberia" (Eastern Siberia) for the next half century paid little attention to the Okhotsk Seaboard, apart from the 1650–57 expedition of yet another Cossack, Stadukhin, which complemented Moskvitin's work by exploring the northern half of the coast of the Okhotsk Sea. Instead, interest was focused partly on Baikalia but especially on Amuria, which Tungus rumors from the Uda River credited with a wealth of sables, gold and silver, and grain. Throughout the last half of the seventeenth century Russian efforts in the Far East were concentrated on the occupation of the Amur Valley, directed mainly from Yakutsk via the Aldan and Olyokma rivers and highlighted by the founding of Albazin in 1665 in the heart of Dauria, homeland of the agricultural Daur natives (Map 2). But these efforts represented only a temporary distraction. Along the Amur Russia came into conflict with China, which had just been conquered by the powerful Manchu (Ching) Dynasty; this dynasty resolutely resisted Russian encroachment upon the frontier of its Manchurian homeland. The conflict culminated in the Treaty of Nerchinsk of 1689, which excluded Russia from the Amur Valley. Subsequently, the Russians greatly regretted the loss of this river valley, considering it the best source of foodstuffs for their Pacific possessions, as well as the best route both for shipping supplies to them from Baikalia and for shipping furs from them to the Chinese market at Kyakhta south of Lake Baikal.

With the loss of Amuria attention was again turned to extreme northeastern Siberia, but already by 1680 its fur trade had abated considerably, and new sources of furs were being sought around the Okhotsk Sea. The conquest of Kamchatka soon followed. Significantly, the peninsula was known to the Russians as early as the middle of the century and was depicted in Godunov's Russian atlas of 1667, but preoccupation with Amuria delayed its conquest for half a century. Within a decade of the signing of the Treaty of Nerchinsk, Kamchatka was subjugated by the expedition (1696–99) of still another Cossack, Vladimir Atlasov, the "Yermak of Kamchatka." His expedition returned to Anadyrsk with 3,862 furs (3,422 in tribute), including 3,640 sable pelts.[13] According to the naturalist Steller, Kamchatkan sables were the largest of all Siberian sables; "they are distinguished by portliness and have long fur, not especially dark, however, so they are more often exported to China, where they are dyed, than to Russia."[14] Steller rated Kamchatka "the richest place in the world for sables and foxes. . . ."[15] He asserted that at first one man could easily collect sixty to eighty and more sable pelts in one winter in the peninsula.[16] This bounty quickly attracted promyshlenniks to the peninsula; and soon Kamchatka was consolidated with the ostrogs of Verkhne-Kamchatsk (1697), Bolshe-retsk (1700), and Nizhne-Kamchatsk (1701) (Map 2). By 1712 Kam-chatka contained 198 state servitors and promyshlenniks.[17]

At first Kamchatka's Cossacks were simultaneously soldiers and traders, but from 1730 numerous merchants with all kinds of commodi-ties arrived from Russia. They sold their goods to the Cossacks at public shops for at least four times their cost price, and the Cossacks resold them to the natives for up to three or four times as much again. Axes, for example, which cost the merchants ten to twenty kopeks each at Irkutsk, were sold for one ruble each to the peninsula's Cossacks, who then resold them to the Kamchadals for two to three rubles each. In the early 1740's Steller estimated in Irkutsk prices that annually 10,000 rubles worth of European and Asian goods from Russia, Siberia, and China, 2,000 rubles worth of local goods, and 800 to 1,000 rubles worth of goods from Okhotsk were sold in Kamchatka and 60,000 rubles worth of goods were exported from the peninsula.[18]* Private entrepre-neurs evidently prospered, while state revenuers exacted handsome du-ties (10 percent) on imports and exports.

The Okhotsk Seaboard was momentarily overshadowed by the opening of Kamchatka. The seaboard contained only two Russian settle-ments of any importance—Okhotsk and Udsk (Map 2), which together comprised but seventy state servitors in 1690. Okhotsk in 1682 was a forlorn outpost of thirteen buildings (including eight dwellings).[19] Rus-sian control remained precarious until the end of the century. The unruly Tunguses around Okhotsk were not quelled until the 1690's, with the Russians losing fifty to seventy-five men per year during the hostili-ties. Such losses threatened the very existence of the post, which was chronically undermanned. In 1653 Okhotsk was burned by the Tun-guses;[20] and in 1679 state goods could not be sent from Okhotsk to Yakutsk "because many reindeer [nomadic] Tunguses stand on the road above the Urak River and on the Yudoma Portage."[21]

* Throughout this book all monetary figures are stated in terms of silver rather than paper rubles.

Then, as a direct result of the opening of Kamchatka, the Okhotsk Seaboard, especially Okhotsk itself, was rejuvenated. At first the route from Yakutsk, the administrative center of northeastern Siberia, to Kamchatka went as follows: Lena River–Arctic Ocean–Indigirka and Kolyma rivers–Anadyrsk–Penzhina or Olyutora Bays–Kamchatka (Map 2). Two to three years were often spent traveling this circuitous route. It was soon replaced by a slightly shorter, all-land route via the ostrogs and zimovyes of Verkhoyansk, Zashiversk, Uyandinsk, Sredne–Kolymsk, Nizhne–Kolymsk, and Anadyrsk (Map 2). This new route, which measured some 2,800 miles from Yakutsk to Nizhne–Kamchatsk, was still excessively hazardous, fatiguing, and costly, and took six months to a year to travel. The hostile Koryaks and Chukchi along the Anadyrsk–Kamchatka section were especially troublesome; from 1703 through 1714 some two hundred Russians were killed on this stretch, a serious loss to the small Russian population.[22]

Dissatisfaction with this situation prompted the authorities to seek a shorter and safer route between Yakutsk and Kamchatka. In 1710 Peter the Great ordered the Yakutsk Cossack Vasily Savostyanov "to find a route from the Kamchadal ostrogs across the Lama Sea to Touisk [Tauisk] and Lamsk [Okhotsk] Ostrogs with Russians and tributary natives. . . ."[23] This order, however, was not fulfilled. In the same year the Governor of Yakutsk was instructed by the Tsar "to find a route across the sea from Lama [Okhotsk] to Kamchatka."[24] Consequently, in 1711 Gutorov, Commandant of Okhotsk, was ordered by Yakutsk to reach Kamchatka by sea, but he failed for lack of seaworthy ships and expert mariners.[25] In 1712 one Tatarinov was sent to Kamchatka to quell Cossack and Kamchadal unrest; he was instructed "to try to discover a route to Kamchatka by sea,"[26] but he too failed. In 1713 the Yakutsk authorities were again ordered by the Tsar to find a sea route between Okhotsk and Kamchatka.[27] This water passage was preferable to the land route around the northern littoral of the Okhotsk Sea, which was not only long and roundabout but was exposed to Koryak hostility around Penzhina Bay.

At last, in the summer of 1714, sailors and shipwrights, including Swedish prisoners-of-war, arrived at Okhotsk, and the following year built a seaworthy vessel named *Vostok*. In this ship the Cossack Kozma Sokolov, Russia's so-called "Vasco Da Gama," opened the sea route to Kamchatka in 1716–17 by sailing across the northern part of the Okhotsk Sea. The land route between Yakutsk and Kamchatka via

Anadyrsk was then virtually abandoned in favor of the route via **Ya-kutsk, Okhotsk,** and **Bolsheretsk.** Okhotsk now became an embarkation point of some importance.[28] For the next 135 years it was Russia's chief Pacific port; its longitude even became a prime meridian for Russian navigators in the North Pacific. The significance of the discovery of the sea route to Kamchatka impressed Pushkin, who wrote in 1837: "The opening of the route across the Penzhensk [Okhotsk] Sea had important consequences for Kamchatka. Ships with Cossacks arrived annually; expeditions followed one after the other. The savages dared not revolt."[29] In addition, the northern half of the Okhotsk Seaboard gained some importance as an alternate route between Okhotsk and Kamchatka, particularly in winter. Post communication by this route was established in 1741.[30] All these developments were reflected in the removal of Kamchatka from the jurisdiction of Yakutsk and its subordination to Okhotsk in 1731.

Nevertheless, the Okhotsk Seaboard and the Kamchatka Peninsula still occupied a rather insignificant place in Siberian development. State revenue and control were equally slight. The annual tribute in furs exacted from the natives of Kamchatka was small. Sable yasak from the Kamchadals averaged only 2,500 to 3,000 pelts annually during the first two decades of the 1700's and decreased to 700 to 750 pelts annually during the most active Kamchadal uprisings, the decline being especially marked after 1720.[31] Russian occupation of the peninsula remained tenuous for over three decades. The Cossacks of Kamchatka were in a state of mutiny from 1707 through 1717, and during their mutiny of 1711 three officers, including Atlasov, were killed; the Kamchadals were from the beginning in a state of open revolt, terminating in the "great rebellion" of 1731, when Nizhne-Kamchatsk was burned and 120 Russians and 150 Kamchadals were slain.[32] Russian settlement on the peninsula and the seaboard was negligible. In 1726–28 Bering's first expedition found a total of only 96 to 110 Russian households at Okhotsk (10 to 11), Bolsheretsk (14 to 17), Verkhne-Kamchatsk (17), Nizhne-Kamchatsk (40 to 50), and nearby Uspenskaya Hermitage (15), compared with 300 at Yakutsk (Map 2). In 1731 there were but 40 Russian households at new Nizhne-Kamchatsk (70 just before its razing by Kamchadals in the same year), 30 at Verkhne-Kamchatsk, and 15 at Bolsheretsk.[33] When Captain Spanberg, a member of Bering's second expedition arrived at Okhotsk in 1735, he found that "the place was so to speak more a wilderness than anything else, and there were almost no other people than the Tungus and Lamuts [local natives] that have their dwellings here."[34]

This condition of dormancy was soon altered, however, by the scientific expeditions mounted by Russia in northeastern Siberia and the far North Pacific in order, in the words of Peter the Great, "to find glory for the State through art and science."[35] While the First Kamchatka Expedition (1725–29) of Bering revealed the underdeveloped state of the Okhotsk Seaboard and the Kamchatka Peninsula, the Second Kamchatka Expedition (1733–42) of Bering and Chirikov ameliorated this condition through the construction and peopling of new facilities and the discovery of new fur resources. This second expedition was unquestionably one of the most ambitious ventures yet undertaken in the history of exploration. Some two thousand men were employed to transport the expedition across Siberia to Yakutsk in 1733–34; and its thousand members included not only reputable seamen like Bering, Chirikov, Spanberg, and Waxell, but also respected scholars like Muller, Gmelin, Krasheninnikov, and Steller, who left invaluable accounts of their activities.

In order to accommodate the second expedition, living quarters, storage depots, port facilities, administrative offices, and conscripted laborers were established at Okhotsk in the middle 1730's; and in 1740 the port of Petropavlovsk was founded on Avacha Bay on Kamchatka's eastern coast (Figure 1). By a Senate decree of May 2/13* of 1732 it was ordered "at Okhotsk, which is near the Kamchatka Sea, to augment with people and to establish grain [cultivation] and a landing with a ship wharf, as well as several ocean vessels, for the transport of state furs and merchants with goods to Kamchatka and from there to Okhotsk."[36] The same decree ordered the sending of three hundred state servitors with weapons, ammunition, and gunpowder from Yakutsk to Okhotsk, Udsk, and Kamchatka. Actually, this decree was a reiteration of several edicts promulgated in 1731, which also ordered the settlement of three hundred state servitors, fifty Russian peasant families, and thirty Tunguses on the Okhotsk Seaboard and the Kamchatka Peninsula, the conscription of twenty shipwrights and four carpenters for Okhotsk, the building of a wharf, a shipyard, and four to six ships at Okhotsk, the exemption of Okhotsk's merchants from the payment of duties for ten

---

* Until 1917 Russia used the Julian calendar (Old Style), which in the seventeenth, eighteenth, and nineteenth centuries, respectively, was ten, eleven, and twelve days behind the Gregorian calendar (New Style).

years, the establishment of grain cultivation at Okhotsk, and the sending of grain seed and breeding stock from Yakutsk for distribution at Okhotsk, Udsk, and the ostrogs of Kamchatka.[37] In 1731, 153 persons were sent to Okhotsk, and seventy Cossack families reached there in 1734. Commandant Skornyakov-Pisarev, an exile, arrived belatedly in 1735 with eighty more Cossack families and sixty Yakut families.[38] By 1737 Yakutsk had sent "to Okhotsk for settlement four hundred and forty-three persons," and, by 1738, 292 state servitors and fourteen carpenters had been sent to the Okhotsk Seaboard and the Kamchatka Peninsula.[39] In 1738 Okhotsk comprised eighty-four Russians and twenty-seven buildings (including twenty houses) (Figure 2), and there were 111 Russian households altogether: at Udsk, 18; Tauisk, 10; Bolsheretsk, 30; Verkhne-Kamchatsk, 20; and Nizhne-Kamchatsk, 33[40] (Figure 3).

In 1744 a "large crowd of clerics" was sent to Kamchatka, and by 1750 there were "a company of soldiers and 300 Cossacks" at Nizhne-Kamchatsk alone.[41] Yamsk was founded in 1739, and in 1741 it comprised six Russians and six buildings.[42] Gizhiga (also called Izhiga) was established in 1752–53 in order to secure the land route between Okhotsk and Kamchatka against the rebellious Koryaks, whose hostility had closed this route since 1743. From 1755 through 1759 Gizhiga contained sixty-nine Russians.[43] Like Gizhiga, Tigilsk was founded in 1752 to protect the land route around Penzhina Bay. Significantly, Gizhiga and Tigilsk were the only settlements on the Okhotsk Seaboard and the Kamchatka Peninsula to be given the designation "fortress" (*krepost*). Finally, a saltworks was established several miles south of Okhotsk in 1737, and it employed twelve Yakuts and three Russians from 1747, although salt extraction from sea water had been initiated in 1733 at the joint mouth of the Okhota and Kukhtui rivers. The saltworks operated from December into April and produced an average of over fourteen tons annually from 1763 through 1770; yearly output subsequently averaged eighteen to thirty-six tons. In 1827, ten years before its closure, the saltworks comprised almost 150 exiles and approximately 100 guards and overseers.[44] Not infrequently convicts escaped from the saltworks, and menaced traffic between Okhotsk and Yakutsk. There were smaller saltworks in Kamchatka: in 1794 salt boilers at Tigilsk, Nizhne-Kamchatsk, and Petropavlovsk were each operated by twenty men.[45]

There was another Russian settlement in Primorye—Anadyrsk —but it was not within the confines of the seaboard or the peninsula,

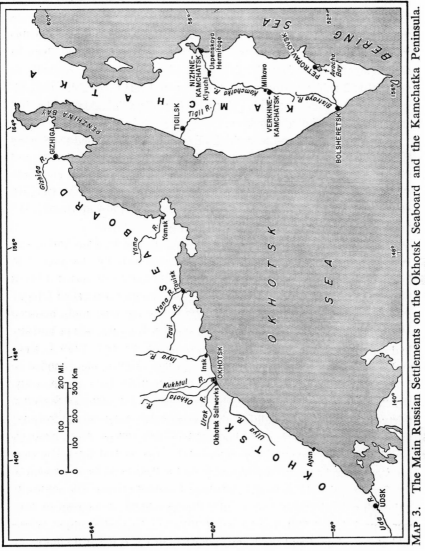

MAP 3. The Main Russian Settlements on the Okhotsk Seaboard and the Kamchatka Peninsula.

having been founded in 1649 on an island in the middle Anadyr River by Deshnev following his navigation of Bering Strait. Established to tap the forbidding Chukchi country, it consisted of a poplar fort with five towers and one gate, a church, and 130 houses in 1764 when its abandonment was ordered by the Senate after it had earned revenues of only 29,152 rubles and incurred expenses of 1,381,007 rubles (including 841,760 rubles for supply) since 1710, while a "notable number" of state servitors had died of hunger.[46]

Thus, the Second Kamchatka Expedition (also called the Second Bering Expedition, the Second Academy Expedition, or the Second Siberia-Pacific Expedition) wrought considerable settlement on the Okhotsk Seaboard and the Kamchatka Peninsula (Map 3). Okhotsk alone, which was moved two miles downstream in 1736 to a spit at the "new mouth" of the Okhota, swelled from ten dwellings in 1726 to seventy-three dwellings in 1741, even though the construction of Okhotsk Port proceeded "slowly and disorderly" from 1732 through 1740 because Commandant Skornyakov-Pisarev did not arrive until 1735 and because carpenters and navigators were conscripted by Bering for expeditionary work from 1736 through 1739; for example, by autumn of 1737 Okhotsk was supposed to have three hundred men but actually had only half this number, and in two years (1737–38) only two izbas and a church were built.[47] In 1742, according to Commandant Devier, Okhotsk contained fifty-seven buildings (including forty houses), while the "expedition settlement" nearby had forty-five buildings (including thirty-three houses); in addition, there was a fleet of eight vessels forming the Okhotsk or Siberian Flotilla[48] (Figure 4). Thereafter Okhotsk's population was progressively enlarged by the arrival of more state servitors, merchants, promyshlenniks, and exiles. In 1747, for instance, the Senate ordered the sending of three hundred Cossacks to Okhotsk, although only ninety-seven arrived.[49] By the middle of the century there were probably 1,500 (perhaps 2,000) Russians altogether on the Okhotsk Seaboard and the Kamchatka Peninsula, compared with probable totals of one to two hundred at the beginning of the century and four to five hundred at the end of the first quarter of the century.

The Second Kamchatka Expedition not only generated more settlement but also uncovered new resources of furs. The remnants of Bering's crew, after sighting the "big land" (American mainland) and subsequently wintering on Bering Island in the Commander archipelago, returned to Petropavlovsk in 1742 with the pelts of 600 to 900 sea otters; Captain Chirikov had already returned the previous year in the expedition's second ship with 900 sea otter pelts. These 1,500 to 1,800 pelts were worth 80 to 100 rubles each at Kyakhta, so that they would have defrayed 8 to 12 percent of the entire cost of the expedition, which incurred expenses of no less than 1,500,000 rubles.[50] The expedition's bounty triggered a "fur rush" to the Commander, Kurile, and Aleutian islands. Meeting some Russian promyshlenniks on the Alaskan coast in 1778, Captain Cook found that

> never was there greater respect paid to the memory of any distinguished person, than by these men to that of Bering. The trade in which they are engaged is very beneficial; and its being undertaken and extended to the Eastward of Kamtschatka, was the immediate consequence of the second voyage of that able navigator, whose misfortunes proved to be the source of much private advantage to individuals, and of public utility to the Russian nation. And yet, if his distresses had not accidentally carried him to die in the island which bears his name, and from whence the miserable remnant of his ship's crew brought back sufficient specimens of its valuable furs, probably the Russians never would have undertaken any future voyages, which could lead them to make discoveries in this sea, toward the coast of America.[51]

Cook added that "their great object is the sea beaver or otter" and that he "never heard them inquire after any other animal. . . ."[52] A year later the naturalist Pallas wrote that "the favourite navigation & trade carried on by Sea is now with our Merchants, the going to the Islands situated between Kamtshatka & America for hunting Sea-otters & black foxes, wherewith to trade on the Chinese fronteers."[53]

From 1743 through 1800, 101 ventures were outfitted by the Russians to the Commander and Aleutian islands and the Alaskan coast in search of furs, primarily sea otters but also fur seals. In 1787 alone twenty-five Russian vessels, manned by 1,000 men and owned by five merchants, pursued this fur trade.[54] These Siberian Argonauts reaped a rich harvest of golden fleece. The catch of sea otters from 1743 through 1798 amounted to 186,754 pelts, or almost ten pelts per day. From 1741 through 1797 at least forty-two different companies acquired ten million rubles worth of furs. These enterprises often realized profits of 100 to 200 percent and sometimes 500 to 700 percent.[55]

Even in Kamchatka fur traders commonly made profits of 200 to 300 percent before 1740. At the time of the Second Kamchatka Expedition, profits were such that within six or seven years petty traders from Russia became rich merchants in Kamchatka worth 15,000 and more rubles. However, from 1740 the fur bearers decreased and the fur trade declined in the peninsula, and by the middle 1740's trade in general there was rendering scarcely one-tenth its former profits.[56] But this commercial setback was very short-lived, for with 1745 there began regular ventures after priceless sea otters.

As a result of this commercial boom, the Okhotsk Seaboard and the Kamchatka Peninsula grew considerably in importance. Okhotsk in particular became a busy springboard of further commercial expansion to the east. Its population increased from between 70 and 84 persons in 1738 to 529 in 1775 and 921 in 1809[57] (Figure 5). In the autumn of 1806 its bustle impressed Academician Redovsky, who wrote, "It is a remarkable place of the Russian Empire, since navigation and trade with the harbors of the Eastern [Pacific] Ocean proceed from here. The town itself is a rarity in all Russia, if one considers its peculiar location in relation to Siberia and Kamchatka Oblast, for which it plays the role of a storehouse of goods. From here go all goods to the farthest localities."[58] In 1821–22 Okhotsk struck the English traveler Cochrane as being second only to Barnaul as the neatest, cleanest, most regular, and most pleasant of all the towns that he had seen in Siberia.[59] These impressions certainly show improvement since Spanberg's cheerless description of 1735. The other settlements also grew apace. Table 1

TABLE 1

Approximate Population of the Main Settlements of the Okhotsk Seaboard and the Kamchatka Peninsula, for Various Years between 1647 and 1865

Year	Persons[a]
Okhotsk	
1647	54
1649	26
1651	35
1662	61
1665	30
ca. 1670	44
1671	26
1675	150
1682	(8)
1690	40
1726–27	(10–11)
1738	70–84 (19)

[a] Figures in parentheses indicate families or households.

TABLE 1 (*Continued*)

Year	Persons[a]
1741–42	(73)
1775	529
1776	598
late 1790's	(80)
1809	921 (136)
1812–13	1,400–1,500
1817	847
1821	1,500–1,600
1825	1,002
1839	1,660
1841	875
1842	800
1846	884
1855	207 (32)
1864	170
1865	100 (32)

Udsk

Year	Persons[a]
1690	30
1738	(18)
late 1790's	53 (14)
1800–1809	200 (34)
1812	200 (34)
1865	164 (18)

Nizhne-Kamchatsk

Year	Persons[a]
1719	120
1728	(40–50)
1731	(40)
1738	(33)
1792	548
1813	400–500
1821	150
1829	141

Bolsheretsk

Year	Persons[a]
1724	142
1728	(14–17)
1731	(15)

[a] Figures in parentheses indicate families or households.

TABLE 1 (*Continued*)

Year	Persons[a]
1738	(30)
1773	(41)
1792	235
1821	116
1829	86

Verkhne-Kamchatsk

1724	128
1728	(17)
1731	(30)
1738	(20)
1829	60

Gizhiga

1755–59	69
1766	189
1767	171–174
1774	247–248
1776	301
1788	500–600
late 1790's	(93)
1803	770–773 (83)
1808	534
1813	900
1816	696 (78)

Tigilsk

1773	78
1792	338
1821	250
1831	192 (43)

Petropavlovsk

1779	75–80
1787	100
1789	35
1792	85

[a] Figures in parentheses indicate families or households.

TABLE 1 (*Continued*)

Year	Persons[a]
1804–5	180
1807	300–400
1825	938
1857	250
1865	300

Kamchatka

1792	1,687
1818	1,346
ca. 1819	1,027
1820	1,329
1823	1,393
1829	1,481
1831	1,375

SOURCES: Ya. P. Alkor and A. K. Drezen, eds., *Kolonialnaya politika tsarizma na Kamchatke i Chukotke v XVIII veke* [*Colonial Policy of Tsarism in Kamchatka and Chukotka in the XVIIIth Century*] (Leningrad: Izdatelstvo Instituta narodov severa TsIK SSSR, 1935), pp. 7–8 and doc. 7, pp. 45–46; Anonymous, "Chernovie opisi kazyonnikh stroyeny g. Gizhiginska i svedeniya o chisle zhiteley" ["Rough Inventories of State Buildings of the Town of Gizhiga and Information about Number of Inhabitants"], TsGADA, f. 1,096, op. 1, d. 53, fols. 1–3; Anonymous, "Iskhodyashchy zhurnal Gizhiginskoy kreposti za 1767 god" ["Outgoing Journal of Gizhiga Fortress for 1767"], TsGADA, f. 1,096, op. 1, d. 24, fols. 112, 138ᵛ, and 280ᵛ–281; Anonymous, "Iskhodyashchy zhurnal Gizhiginskoy kreposti za 1774 god" ["Outgoing Journal of Gizhiga Fortress for 1774"], TsGADA, f. 1,096, op. 1, d. 29, fols. 76ᵛ–77, 184ᵛ; Anonymous, "Okhotsky kray" ["Okhotsk Kray"], *Vostochnoye Pomorye*, no. 22 (November 6/18, 1865), p. 135; Anonymous, "Opisanie Irkutskoy gubernii" ["Description of Irkutsk Province"], TsGIAL, f. 1,350, op. 312, d. 239, fols. 46ᵛ, 51ᵛ, 53; Anonymous, "Reyester s vedomostyami o kazyonnykh veshchakh, nakhodivshchikhsya pri Gizhiginskoy kreposti (ne polnoye delo) 1766 goda" ["Register with Lists on State Belongings at Gizhiga Fortress (Incomplete File) 1766"], TsGADA, f. 1,096, op. 1, d. 14, fol. 11; Anonymous, "Vkhodyashchaya kniga Gizhiginskoy kreposti s priobshchyonnymi k ney vedomostyami o sostoyanii Gizhiginskovo proviantskovo magazina . . ." ["Incoming Book of Gizhiga Fortress with Attached Lists on the Condition of the Gizhiga Provision Magazine . . ."], TsGADA, f. 1,096, op. 1, d. 56, fols. 127–172ᵛ [*sic:* 134ᵛ]; S. V. Bakhrushin and S. A. Tokarev, eds., *Yakutiya v XVII veke* [*Yakutia in the XVIIth Century*] (Yakutsk: Yakutskoye knizhnoye izdatelstvo, 1953), pp. 307–308; I. Barsukov, *Pisma Innokentiya mitropolita Moskovskavo i Kolomenskavo 1828–1853* [*Letters of Metropolitan Innokenty of Moscow and Kolomna 1828–1853*] (St. Petersburg: Sinodalnaya tipografiya, 1897), bk. 1, p. 59; [Vitus Bering], "Donesenie flota kapitana Beringa ob ekspeditsii yevo k vostochnym beregam Sibiri" ["Report of Fleet Captain Bering about his Expedition to the Eastern Shores of Siberia"], *Zapiski Voyenno-topograficheskavo depo*, vol. 10, pt. 1 (1847), 2d suppl., pp. 71–73; Vasily Berkh, *Pervoye morskoye puteshestvie rossiyan . . .*

TABLE 1 (*Continued*)

[*The First Sea Voyage of a Russian* . . .] (St. Petersburg: Imperatorskaya akademiya nauk, 1823), pp. 12, 24, 26–27; F. Bocharov, "Neskolko slov ob Udskom kraye" ["Several Words about Udsk Kray"], *Vostochnoye Pomorye*, no. 20 (October 16/28, 1865), p. 118; Capt. John Dundas Cochrane, *Narrative of a Pedestrian Journey through Russia and Siberian Tartary* . . . (Philadelphia: H. C. Carey, I. Lea, and A. Small, 1824), pp. 251, 266, 273, 278; M. De Lesseps, *Travels in Kamtschatka, during the Years 1787 and 1788* (London: J. Johnson, 1790), 1 : 15, 2 : 76–77; Peter Dobell, *Travels in Kamtchatka and Siberia* . . . (London: Henry Colburn and Richard Bentley, 1830), 1 : 49, 159, 296; [G. Golenishchev], "O sostoyanii Kamchatskoy oblasti v 1830 i 1831 godakh" ["Concerning the Condition of Kamchatka Oblast in 1830 and 1831"], *Zhurnal Ministerstva vnutrennikh del*, pt. 10 (1833), pp. 2–3; A. A. Ionina, *Noviya danniya k istorii Vostochnoy Sibiri XVII veka* [*New Data on the History of Eastern Siberia of the XVIIth Century*] (Irkutsk: Tipo-litografiya P. I. Makushkina, 1895), p. 199; P. K., "O vozmozhnosti uluchsheniya Selskavo Khozyaistva v Kamchatke i bliz Tigilskoy kreposti" ["Concerning the Possibility of Improving Agriculture in Kamchatka and Near Tigilsk Fortress"], *Zemledelchesky zhurnal* . . . , no. 2 (1833), p. 300; Khersonsky, "Neskolko slov o proshlom i nastoyashchem g. Okhotska" ["Several Words about the Past and the Present of the Town of Okhotsk"], *Priamurskiya vedomosti*, no. 39 (September 25/ October 7, 1894), p. 12; Kapitan-Leitenant Minitsky, "Nekotoria izvestiya ob Okhotskom porte i uyezde onavo, dostavlennia Kapitan-Leitenantom Minitskim v 1809 godu" ["Some Information about Okhotsk Port and Its Uyezd, Supplied by Captain-Lieutenant Minitsky in 1809"], *Zapiski, izdavayemia Gosudarstvennym admiralteiskim departamentom*, pt. 3 (1815), pp. 88, 91, 93; Rear-Admiral Minitsky, "Opisanie Okhotskavo porta" ["Description of Okhotsk Port"], *Syn otechestva i severny arkhiv*, 5 (1829) : 139; G. F. Muller, "Geografiya ili nyneshnoye sostoyanie zemli Kamchatki 1737 goda" ["The Geography or the Present Condition of the Land of Kamchatka"], TsGADA, f. 199, port. 527, d. 3, fols. 25–26; N. N. Ogloblin, *Obozrenie stolbtsov i knig Sibirskavo prikaza (1592–1768 gg.)* [*Survey of the Rolls and the Books of the Siberian Office (1592–1768)*] (Moscow: Universitetskaya tipografiya, 1895), pt. 1, p. 119; Pervy sibirsky komitet, "O predpolozheniyakh Nachalnika Kamchatki ob ustroistve sevo kraya" ["Concerning the Proposals of the Commandant of Kamchatka on the Organization of This Kray"], TsGIAL, f. 1,264, op. 1, d. 167, fols. 2, 8, d. 168, fols. 147–147ᵛ; Russia, Arkheograficheskaya kommissiya, *Dopolneniya k Aktam istoricheskim* . . . [*Supplements to Historical Acts* . . .] (St. Petersburg: Tipografiya Eduarda Pratsa, 1846–72), vol. 3, doc. 86, pp. 320–321, doc. 91, pp. 330–332, vol. 4, doc. 122, pp. 278–279, vol. 5, doc. 11, pp. 68–73, vol. 6, doc. 136, pp. 401–408; Martin Sauer, *An Account of a Geographical and Astronomical Expedition to the Northern Parts of Russia* . . . (London: T. Cadell, Jr. and W. Davies, 1802), pp. 293–294, 306; Savin, "Okhotsk," *Zapiski Gidrograficheskavo departamenta Morskavo ministerstva*, pt. 9 (1851), pp. 154–155, 161; A. Sgibnev, "Istorichesky ocherk glavneishikh sobyty v Kamchatke" ["Historical Sketch of the Main Events in Kamchatka"], *Morskoy sbornik*, 103 (August, 1869) : 37; A. Sgibnev, "Okhotsky port s 1649 po 1852 g." ["Okhotsk Port from 1649 to 1852"], *Morskoy sbornik*, 105, no. 11 (November, 1869) : 32, 53; A. Shakhovskoy, "O nachale postroyeniya Gizhiginskoy kreposti" ["Concerning the Beginning of the Construction of Gizhiga Fortress"], *Vestnik Yevropy*, no. 24, pt. 102 (December, 1818), p. 283; I. V. Shcheglov, *Kronologichesky perechen vazneishikh dannykh iz istorii Sibiri 1032–1882 gg.* [*Chronological List of the Major Facts from the History of Siberia 1032–1882*] (Irkutsk: Tipografiya Shtaba Vostochnavo Sibirskavo voyennavo okruga, 1883), p. 465; N. S. Shchukin, "Udskoye selenie" ["Udsk Settlement"], *Russky invalid*, 35, no. 114 (May 25/June 6, 1848) : 456; N. S. Shchukin, "Udskoye selenie" ["Udsk Settlement"], *Zhurnal Minister-*

TABLE 1 (*Continued*)

stva vnutrennikh del, pt. 22 (1848), p. 177; Timofey Shmalev, "Kratkoye o Kamchatke obyasnenie uchinyonnoye Kapitanom Timofeiyem Shmalevym" ["Brief Explanation about Kamchatka Made by Captain Timofey Shmalev"], TsGADA, f. 199, port. 539, pt. 1, d. 8, fols. 1, 2ᵛ; Timofey Shmalev, "Statisticheskiya i Geograficheskiya Primechaniya Kapitana Tim. Shmaleva ob otdalyonnykh onykh mest krepostyakh, o khlebopashestve i pr. s pribavleniyami" ["Statistical and Geographical Notes of Captain Tim Shmalev about the Fortresses, Grain Cultivation, etc. of the Aforementioned Remote Places with Supplements"], TsGADA, f. 199, port. 528, pt. 1, d. 19, fols. 66–67; *Sibirskie goroda. Materialy dlya ikh istorii XVII i XVIII stolety. Nerchinsk. Selenginsk. Yakutsk.* [*Siberian Towns. Materials for Their History of the XVIIth and XVIIIth Centuries. Nerchinsk. Selenginsk. Yakutsk.*] (Moscow: Tipografiya M. G. Volchaninova, 1886), p. 101; Sir George Simpson, *Narrative of a Journey Round the World* . . . (London: Henry Colburn, 1847), 2 : 249; Grigory Skornyakov-Pisarev, "Promemoriya is kantselyarii Okhotskovo porta blagorodnomu Gospodinu Akademii Nauk professoru Gerardu Fridrikhu Milleru . . ." ["Memorandum from the Office of Okhotsk Port to Professor of the Academy of Sciences Noble Mr. Gerhard Friedrich Muller . . ."], TsGADA, f. 199, port. 528, pt. 7, d. 481, fol. 335; Archibald Campbell, *A Voyage Round the World from 1806 to 1812* (Honolulu: University of Hawaii Press, 1967), p. 25; Perry McDonough Collins, *Siberian Journey: Down the Amur to the Pacific, 1856–1857*, ed. Charles Vevier (Madison: University of Wisconsin Press, 1962), p. 341; Richard J. Bush, *Reindeer, Dogs, and Snow-Shoes* . . . (New York: Harper & Brothers, 1871), p. 36; James Kenneth Munford, ed., *John Ledyard's Journal of Captain Cook's Last Voyage* (Corvallis: Oregon State University Press, 1963), p. 163; G. A. Sarychev, *Puteshestvie po severo-vostochnoy chasti Sibiri, Ledovitomu moryu i Vostochnomu okeanu* [*Journey through the Northeastern Part of Siberia, the Arctic Sea and the Eastern Ocean*] (Moscow: Gosudarstvennoye izdatelstvo geograficheskoy literatury, 1952), p. 118.

indicates the growth in population of the region's main Russian settlements, as well as that of Kamchatka as a whole. Even Yamsk and Tauisk grew from 50 and 12 persons, respectively, in 1774 to 112 and 117 persons in 1806.[60]

The search for sea otters resulted, too, in a rapid extension of Russian eastward expansion to America via the Commander and Aleutian stepping-stones. In this advance "the sea was like a river; the key island, guarding passages between islands or dominating chains of islands (or the coast), was an ostrog."[61] Within only three years (1756–58) a single promyshlennik discovered thirteen of the "Eastern Islands" or "Newly-Discovered Islands" (Aleutians).[62] Kodiak Island in the Gulf of Alaska was reached in 1763. However, no permanent Russian occupation existed until 1784, when the Golikov-Shelekhov Company founded a settlement at Three Saints Harbor on Kodiak Island.* The Russian-American Company, which monopolized the fur

* However, in 1937 the remains of a European settlement of thirty-one dwellings dating back some 300 years were discovered on the Kenai Peninsula. This site may have been settled by the missing companions of

trade of Alaska from its formation in 1799, established a number of forts and redoubts, most of which were situated atop promontories at the mouths of rivers or at the heads of bays along the continental and insular coasts. Alexander Von Humboldt fittingly described these posts as "merely collections of sheds and huts, that serve, however, as emporiums for the fur trade."[63] By 1817, besides its headquarters at St. Petersburg, its branch offices at Moscow, Irkutsk, Kyakhta, Yakutsk, and Okhotsk, and its agencies at Kazan, Tyumen, Tomsk, Gizhiga, and Petropavlovsk, the Russian-American Company had five hundred Russian trappers and twenty-six sailors at sixteen posts in Russian-America, including the colonial capital of Novo-Arkhangelsk (1799) on Baranov Island.[64] Fort Ross (called simply Ross by the Russians), founded in 1812 on the coast of New Albion only about fifty miles north of the Spanish *presidio* of San Francisco, represented the easternmost point of the Russian Empire. Here on the Northwest Coast the Russians finally encountered their westbound imperialistic counterparts from Western Europe, and the eastward expansion of Russia came to a halt.

The Continental Fur Trade of Siberia and the Maritime Fur Trade of the North Pacific

This spectacular eastward expansion on the part of Russia, which carried the double-headed eagle more than halfway around the globe, was motivated primarily by lucrative trade and tribute in furs. The tempo of advance was regulated largely by the rate of depletion of successive fur bases, a mechanism that Fisher has termed "the basic factor in the eastward advance of the Russians across Siberia."[65] By the seventeenth century the number of fur bearers in European Russia had declined drastically as a consequence of rapacious hunting,[66] causing Russian traders to seek new fur sources ("suitable sable places") to the east. Furs ("soft gold") were plentiful in Siberia, prompting the adage

---

Dezhnev, who lost four vessels while rounding the northeasternmost cape of Siberia in 1648 (A. V. Yefimov and S. A. Tokarev, eds., *Narody Ameriki* [*Peoples of America*] [Moscow: Izdatelstvo Akademii nauk SSSR, 1959], 1 : 99). Thus, the Alaskan coast was not only probably sighted by Russians almost a century before the 1732 voyage of Gvozdev and Fyodorov and the 1741 voyage of Bering and Chirikov but also perhaps settled by them nearly one and a half centuries before the founding of Three Saints Harbor.

"Siberia is a gold mine." Other motives certainly induced the movement across Siberia, such as the desire for personal freedom and adventure and the search for gold and silver and for mammoth and walrus ivory, but furs represented the overriding incentive, especially in Eastern Siberia, the Russian Far East, and Russian America, where the finest furs were found and where alternate sources of wealth, particularly agricultural land, were very limited. Pallas wrote from Russia in 1779 that sables "grow more common the more eastward you go; & at the same time their furr is more valuable, the more to the north & east or in the highest mountains they are bred."[67] It has been said, with little exaggeration, that the conquest of Siberia was one continuous hunt for sables. With even less exaggeration it can be said that the conquest of Russian America was one continuous hunt for sea otters. Fisher concluded from his study of the Russian fur trade of the sixteenth and seventeenth centuries that "other sources of wealth existed in Siberia and the tsars did not ignore them, but furs, by virtue of their abundance, stood first and foremost as the practical purpose of conquest, paying not only the costs of conquest, but yielding a profit as well."[68] Just as furs from the east helped Novgorod to reach its peak of power and fame in the thirteenth and fourteenth centuries, so the ascendancy of Moscow in the sixteenth to eighteenth centuries was aided by the rich harvest of Siberian furs.

Furs were obtained through state tribute and taxation and through private trapping and trading. The Russian Government collected an annual tribute in furs from the Siberian natives, amounting to an average of five to seven sables per man in the seventeenth century. In addition, the state collected a tax of 10 percent of the catch of private trappers and traders and exercised its right to buy their best furs. It has been estimated that during the seventeenth century Siberian furs contributed almost one-tenth of Russia's state income. The state's share of the fur harvest was taken to Moscow, whence most was exported abroad and the rest sold or bartered or donated locally. Most of the furs procured by private trappers and merchants were exported via Arkhangelsk and Novgorod to the markets of Western Europe. Leipzig, the foremost European fur mart, was dominated by Russian furs.[69]

The sable (*Martes zibellina*), an arboreal marten native to the taiga of Eurasia, was the mainstay of the Siberian fur trade. Its fur, ranging in color from gray to brown to black, is prized for its combination of softness and durability. Sables grow a dense, silky undercoat in winter, moult in spring, and have short fur in summer and fall; the pelts of those caught in winter were preferred by buyers.[70]

Sables are omnivores, feeding mainly on rodents (especially squirrels), birds (particularly grouse), insects, berries, and nuts (especially "cedar" [pine] nuts).[71] Since squirrels were hunted for their pelts almost as avidly as sables, the more squirrels that were killed the more limited became the sable's food supply. Man, too, competed with the sable for sustenance, for Siberians were very fond of cedar nuts and also relished game birds and wild berries. But sables are rather solitary and largely nocturnal creatures, and these traits, plus the fact that their annual spring litters number two to five or more offspring, helped to prevent their extinction by intensive hunting over several centuries.

In the fifteenth century sables were found as far west as Finland, Courland, and Belorussia; by 1674 they were limited to Siberia, and only mediocre sables were available in Western Siberia, the best being found farther east. Around 1750 the best sables were trapped along the Uda River in extreme southeastern Siberia.[72] Hunting of sables (and foxes), which usually occurred from November through February, when they are easier to track and their fur is long and thick, did not conflict temporally with farming, but spatially the two pursuits did clash. Agricultural settlement in Siberia usually entailed forest clearance, which removed the habitat of fur bearers. This clash was especially marked in Eastern Siberia and the Russian Far East, where unforested plowland was scarce and where the best sables were found.

Such were the main features of the fur trade of seventeenth-century Siberia. During the eighteenth century the Russian fur trade changed substantially. Promyshlenniks and state servitors (especially Cossacks) remained the chief instruments of the Russian advance, but in the fur trade of the far North Pacific the basis shifted from land to sea, from sables to sea otters (unknown to the Russians before the conquest of Kamchatka), and the market shifted from Europe to China. The maritime fur trade presented the continental Russians with the unfamiliar problem of acquiring seaworthy ships and competent sailors to navigate the uncharted waters of the extreme North Pacific, waters further imperiled by frequent fogs and gales and by numerous rocks, reefs, and bars. It took them only sixty years to go from the Urals to the Pacific but a full century to reach the American mainland from the Okhotsk Seaboard.

The shift in the fur market, on the other hand, was an improvement. Active Russian trade with China in furs had begun in the last half of the seventeenth century, and in the eighteenth century China became the leading market for Russian furs, especially for sea otter skins, which were used mainly for trimming. Unlike sable fur, sea otter fur was not suitable for whole garments; it was not warm and it hardened in severe cold.[73] Nevertheless, it became the royal fur of China; other furs, especially squirrel and fox, were worn by the masses. A Jesuit missionary observed during the 1710's that winter clothes in North China were made mostly from sable, fox, and ermine furs.[74]

During the eighteenth century furs constituted 85 to 100 percent of Russia's trade with China. Trade was particularly stimulated by the revocation in 1762 of the Russian state monopoly on commerce with the Celestial Empire. The large Manchu upper class of North China constituted an insatiable market for furs, and the route from Okhotsk to Kyakhta on the Russia–China boundary (the sole official port of entry to China for Russian goods), though lengthy and laborious, was shorter and easier than the Okhotsk–Moscow or Okhotsk–Arkhangelsk routes. Moreover, sea otter furs commanded higher prices in China than in Russia.[75]

Furs from the Russian Far East and Russian America were conveyed to Irkutsk, where they were sorted on the basis of quality; the few best were sent to European Russia and the remainder partly to the fairs of Western Siberia but mostly to Kyakhta for Chinese buyers. The Chinese even preferred cheaper pelts of lower quality, for they were very artful at coloring furs.[76] Consequently, they also preferred lighter furs, so that "black Sables are not carried to *China,* but only the pale ones; Nor black Fox-Skins, but the red only . . . ,"[77] darker furs (such as most sable pelts) being marketed in Russia and Europe. Besides, China had its own source of sables in the Amur Valley, which Russia had lost in 1689 by the Treaty of Nerchinsk. Thus, sea otters, being lighter and scarcer than sables, dominated the Chinese market. In 1772 Pallas reported that furs, especially sea otter pelts, were by far the chief item of trade at Kyakhta.[78] A sea otter pelt there brought three to four times its Kamchatka price in the early 1740's, seven to eight times its Kamchatka price in the early 1750's, and two to four times its Kamchatka price in the late 1750's. In the 1770's red fox pelts and mediocre sea otter pelts were worth, respectively, ten times and almost four times as much at Kyakhta as in Kamchatka. Such price differentials meant sizable profits for Russian entrepreneurs, despite the halving of profits between Kamchatka and Kyakhta by transport, maintenance, and tariff charges.[79] For furs the Chinese at Kyakhta exchanged tea, cloth, porcelain, and other goods. During the 1780's—when state (though not private) trade between the two countries had been suspended—up to 10,000 Russian carts, handled by some 3,000 men, annually hauled Chinese goods from Kyakhta to Irkutsk. State trade was resumed in 1794, to become one of Russia's most lucrative sources of state income. The Russian Government as well as Russian merchants profited handsomely from the Kyakhta trade by levying duties of 20 to 25 percent on exports and imports; during the early 1770's these duties amounted to some 550,000 rubles annually.[80]

The sea otter (*Enhydra lutris*) or *kalan* was the cornerstone of the Russian maritime fur trade. Called "Kamchatka beaver" or "sea beaver" by the Russians because of the resemblance of its fur to that of the beaver, the sea otter was found only along the shore of the North Pacific from northern Japan to southern California, frequenting the kelp and shellfish beds of the shallow coastal waters in schools of seventy-five to one hundred. The waters between Kamchatka and the Commander Islands so abounded in sea otters in the middle of the eighteenth century that the Russians dubbed them the Otter Sea.[81] Sea otters, which eat mainly sea urchins and mollusks in winter and crabs and fish in summer, had to be hunted at sea, since they spend most of their lives in water, coming ashore only to rest (primarily at night) on steep, rocky shores. This circumstance compelled the Russian landsmen to develop sea legs. In foul weather sea otters stay close to shore, and in fair weather they swim far asea, where they sleep afloat.[82] Thus, under the climatic conditions of the far North Pacific the best time for hunting sea otters was from May through June. Such hunting did not, of course, clash spatially with farming, but temporally there was some conflict, and this conflict was crucial because agriculture on the Russian shores of the far North Pacific was so marginal that the slightest distraction could mean crop failure.

Sea otters were eagerly hunted and readily marketed, for theirs is the most beautiful and the most valuable of all furs, superb in its softness and fluffiness.[83] Among the Indians of the Northwest Coast the sea otter was esteemed as a symbol of wealth and prestige. A prominent Yankee merchant from Boston, Captain William Sturgis, described its pelt thus: "A full grown prime skin, which has been stretched before drying, is about five feet long, and twenty-four to thirty inches wide, covered with very fine fur, about three-fourths of an inch in length, having a rich jet black, glossy surface, and exhibiting a silver color when blown open. Those are esteemed the finest skins which have some white hairs interspersed and scattered over the whole surface, and a perfectly white head."[84] The fur was unmatched in value, even by precious sable. In 1737 in Kamchatka one sea otter pelt was worth two sable pelts, one sable pelt was worth two fox pelts, and one fox pelt was worth one ruble, so that a sea otter pelt was worth four rubles, while at Irkutsk sea otter pelts then sold for twenty-five to thirty rubles, sable pelts for four to five rubles, and fox pelts for three rubles. At the Okhotsk fair in 1775 sea otter pelts brought fifty to eighty rubles, compared with two and one-half rubles for sable pelts and two to two and one-half rubles for fox pelts. To the Russian-American Company in 1817 a prime sea otter pelt was worth twice as much as a prime silver fox pelt, six times as much as a prime fur seal skin, ten times as much as a prime beaver pelt, and forty times as much as a prime sable pelt.[85] So prized were sea otters that they were hunted to the verge of extinction. Their depletion was hastened by the facts that females bear but one pup yearly, that the pelt of the dam was more valuable than that of her mate or offspring,[86] and that they sleep so soundly afloat (more soundly than fur seals) that hunters can approach within striking distance fairly readily.

At first the Russian maritime fur trade was conducted by a number of small, private companies headed by Siberian merchants with substantial capital, as hunting at sea necessitated considerable outlay for building, outfitting, and manning ships. The ventures were in effect artels, since the crewmen commonly received shares in the enterprises rather than wages.[87] The ships were usually outfitted at Nizhne-Kamchatsk or Okhotsk with provisions and equipment imported via Yakutsk. They were generally built in Kamchatka from 1745, but after 1768–69, when smallpox killed most of the peninsula's inhabitants, they were constructed at Okhotsk; it was easier to obtain workers there, and more workers were needed by then for the longer and more dangerous voyages to the Alaskan coast.[88] Also, the longer voyages demanded better ships, which required iron, and iron was cheaper at Okhotsk than in Kamchatka. Moreover, by 1768 Steller's sea cow, which had initially been an important source of food for the Russians, was extinct, so that more grain was needed, and grain too was less costly at Okhotsk, which was only half as far as Kamchatka from the supply point of Yakutsk.

The vessels were built hurriedly from green timber—at first flimsy coasters and later light one- or two-masted barks and galiots of pine, birch, or larch (tamarack), forty-two to fifty-six feet in length and almost devoid of iron. These clumsy craft were cheaply and badly built, although some improvement was noticeable after 1760, probably in response to the longer voyages; with high sides, short and heavy masts, narrow sails, and long rudders, they averaged only about two knots.[89]

They were also poorly manned, the crew of forty to fifty or even sixty to seventy men being "all better hunters than seamen."[90] Many of them had never before been to sea or even seen the sea, and they lacked both navigational knowledge and marine maps. As many as half of the crew consisted of Kamchadals because of the cheapness of their labor, their skill in hunting, and their resistance to malnutrition. Russians, however, were more enterprising and more reliable. These were usually obtained in Irkutsk, Kirensk, or Yakutsk and sent to Okhotsk or Kamchatka; there they were employed in outfitting and in other necessary tasks until embarkation. A pilot was usually obtained from the port authorities, and sometimes a foreman was appointed from the crew. Before sailing, a list of shares was compiled, which was then signed by all shareholders. The crew's shares exceeded the number of crewmen by five to eight, since the pilot received three shares and the foreman two, while one share was donated to a church or a school.[91] A typical outgoing cargo comprised 550 pounds of tobacco, 100 pounds of glass beads, a dozen hatchets, some knives, assorted textiles, liquor, numerous traps, and a minimum of provisions, mostly salted and dried fish but also some rye flour for making *kvas* (cider). Everything except timber and fish was imported at great cost from Yakutsk and beyond.[92]

After receiving permission from the port authorities, the vessels left Okhotsk in late summer, rounded the southern tip of Kamchatka (Cape Lopatka), and made for the east coast ports of the peninsula or directly for the Commander Islands, where the winter was spent hunting sea cows (manatees) for their meat and sea lions and hair seals for their hides. The next summer the ships continued eastward to the Aleutians. Here the Russians sought the few short stretches of sandy beach, where they built earthen huts for shelter and took hostages from the natives, forcing them to net or harpoon sea otters and to trap foxes in small parties, each party under a Russian leader. Half of the ship's crew hunted, while the other half guarded the vessel and the camp and sought and prepared food.[93] Sometimes the Russians hunted in *baidaras* (umiaks), made from the hide of sea cows and holding six to eight men each;[94] but the use of Aleuts, with their exceptional skill in hunting sea otters by *baidarka* (kayak) and harpoon, was essential to the success of the hunt. In this respect the maritime fur trade of the Aleutians contrasted with the continental fur trade of Kamchatka, where "the Russians know this business ten times better [than the natives]. . . ."[95] The Aleuts, who had hunted sea otters before the advent of the Russians, could kill or wound the animals from as much as 105 feet. The Russian promyshlenniks tried in vain to emulate the skill with baidarka and harpoon of these "marine Cossacks," who, moreover, learned European seamanship faster than the Russians. Consequently, the indispensable Aleuts were exploited more than most Siberian natives by the Russians. Compulsory labor was exacted together with tribute, although the latter was banned in Russian America in 1788.[96]

When the Russian vessels returned to Kamchatka or Okhotsk with a full load of furs, their cargoes were first inspected and taxed one-tenth by customs officials and then divided among the shareholders in kind or in money; half went to the entrepreneurs and half to the crews, who either sold their pelts to local merchants or shipped them to Irkutsk. A crewman's half-share on a lucky voyage might amount to 2,000 to 3,000 rubles, but it usually came to fifty to sixty sea otter pelts (1,000 to 1,200 rubles), while an unsuccessful voyage indebted him to the ship's owner.[97] Such voyages lasted no less time than one to two years and might last as many as six years, depending upon how long it took to procure a full load of furs that would return at least twice the cost of shipbuilding and outfitting, a total of 10,000 to 30,000 rubles. Around 1760 in Kamchatka the cost of building and outfitting a ship measuring forty-nine feet in length totaled 10,000 rubles, and its fur catch averaged 5,000 sea otter pelts, which brought 100,000 rubles in the peninsula; thus the government's 10 percent tax was worth 10,000 rubles and the half-shares of owner and crew were each worth 45,000 rubles (1,000 rubles each for forty-five crewmen).[98] The business was very hazardous. From one-quarter to one-third of the crew was generally lost through disease, accident, or warfare. Shipwrecks were commonplace, and vessels that accomplished as many as a couple of voyages were fortunate. A small company usually undertook no more than three voyages before its ship was wrecked, spent, or sold.[99] But the lucrative prospects were evidently worth the high risks.

During the last quarter of the eighteenth century the declining population and receding range of the sea otter necessitated longer voyages and brought lower returns to the Siberian companies. Sea otters had disappeared from the coast of Kamchatka by 1750 and from the shores of the Kuriles by 1780. By 1789 they were rarely seen around the Aleutians—where the pelts in any case were not as valuable as those from Kamchatka or especially those from the Kuriles, which were distinguished by long and dark hairs and a silvery beard. From 1760 the Russians had to sail farther east to find suitable hunting grounds.[100] In the first decade of the nineteenth century this progressive depletion took them as far as the coast of California, which marked the end of both the sea otter's range and Russian eastward expansion.

Whereas at first the voyages (to the Commander Islands) lasted one or two years, towards the end of the eighteenth century voyages (to the Gulf of Alaska) of five to seven years or even more were the rule.[101] Pallas wrote in 1779 that "there is scarce a year without at least one vessel going out from Okhotsk on this errand, & none return under 3 or 4 years."[102] In 1786 Captain Sarychev, a member of the Billings Expedition (1785–94), learned that round-trip ventures between Okhotsk and Alaska sometimes lasted ten years.[103] By contrast, around 1800 it usually took New England vessels only three years or less to round Cape Horn, trade on the Northwest Coast for two seasons, market their furs at Canton, and return home with Chinese goods. The worst example of the Russian trend was the voyage of the *St. Michael,* belonging to the Golikov-Shelekhov Company, which, because of the incompetence of its captain and the willfulness of its crew, took 999 days in the middle 1780's to sail from Okhotsk to Kodiak, a voyage normally accomplished, even with adverse winds, in 70 days in the early 1820's.[104]

The longer voyages entailed not only higher expenditures but also greater risks, for the natives of the American mainland, especially the Kolosh (Tlingits), proved more hostile than the Aleuts. Indeed, the Kolosh, like the Chukchi of Chukotka, were never fully subjugated by the Russians. The greater risks, plus the diminishing rookeries, engendered vicious competition among the promyshlenniks. Captain Billings, the leader of the Secret North-East Geographical and Astronomical Expedition (1785–94), reported to Empress Catherine II in 1790 that the Russian fur companies in Alaska sometimes fought openly over hunting grounds.[105] At the same time foreign competitors, Englishmen and Americans, appeared on the scene in the middle 1780's, alerted by the findings of Cook's voyage to the North Pacific. In 1786 the East

India Company alone sent five ships to Alaskan waters to procure furs.[106] The small and contentious Russian companies, unable to cope with such conditions, either disbanded or united to form larger organizations capable of meeting the new requirements.

By 1795 three companies dominated the Russian maritime fur trade: the Golikov-Shelekhov or American Company on Kodiak Island, the Lebedev-Lastochkin Company at Chuvash Bay on the Alaskan mainland, and the Kiselev Company on the Aleutian Islands.[107] In 1798 the American Company of Golikov and Shelekhov and the Irkutsk Company of Mylnikov and his partners merged into the United American Company, which formed the nucleus of the Russian-American Company, chartered in 1799. This joint-stock company, modeled upon England's East India and Hudson's Bay Companies, was a commercial monopoly. The third and tenth articles of its first twenty-year charter authorized it to exploit Russian America "without competition from others."[108] Founded under the aegis of the Russian Government, the Russian-American Company was also an instrument of Tsarist policy from its inception in 1799 until its dissolution in 1868.

2

GEOGRAPHICAL BACKGROUND: PHYSICAL AND CULTURAL SETTING OF THE OKHOTSK SEABOARD AND THE KAMCHATKA PENINSULA

"The climate [of Eastern Siberia and the Russian Far East] is every-where extremely cold but in the so-called summer it is somewhat warmer."

> Stewart Culin, ed., "Wonderful News of the Circum-navigation," p. 507.

"Siberia may be cold, but it is a warm and a cosy place for the serv-ants of the government."

> F. Dostoyevsky, *Notes From A Dead House,* p. 9.

Severity of the Physical Environment

We have seen that the problem of provisionment of the Okhotsk Seaboard and the Kamchatka Peninsula was largely a problem of the fur trade, which was the basis of Russian eastward expansion. And just as this problem cannot be fully understood without some knowledge of the region's history of occupation and exploitation, so is some awareness of the physical and cultural makeup of the region essential to complete comprehension.[1]

The physical environment of the Okhotsk Seaboard and the Kamchatka Peninsula is severe in physiographic, climatic, pedologic, and vegetational terms. Physiographically, the predominance of moun-tains and plateaus of moderate elevation and steep slope impeded agri-culture and transport alike. At least nine-tenths of the region is moun-tainous. The seaboard comprises an extremely narrow coastal plain bounded gradually on the east by the cool, shallow Okhotsk Sea and abruptly on the west by rugged mountains and plateaus with summits of

2,000 to 3,000 feet. Numerous short, swift rivers have cut deep, narrow, devious valleys through this rampart, allowing difficult movement between the coast and the interior. Marshy floodplains along the lower courses of several of these rivers constitute the only sizable lowlands, apart from the negligible coastal strip. The southern half of the seaboard is regular; the northern half is well indented with headlands, peninsulas, bays, and islands that make movement along it difficult. Along the entire seaboard there are few good harbors; Magadan's fine harbor on Nagayev Bay was not developed until the Soviet period.

Kamchatka, too, has little lowland. The peninsula is dominated by two parallel mountain ranges averaging 3,500 feet in elevation: the Western or Central Range running unbroken up and down the middle of the entire peninsula and the Eastern Range intermittently abutting the eastern coast. Both ranges drop steeply to the Kamchatka River Valley, an intervening graben, but slope gradually to either coast; both, too, are highlighted by picturesque volcanic peaks capped with glaciers and snowfields. Kamchatka is one of the world's foremost regions of volcanic, seismic, and geyseric activity. Earthquakes have especially threatened settlement; Petropavlovsk, for example, has averaged one tremor per year since 1790.[2] There are three lowlands: open, boggy marine plains along the western and northeastern coasts and a somewhat marshy alluvial plain along the Kamchatka River, the peninsula's foremost watercourse. The Kamchatka River Valley afforded virtually the only suitable agricultural land in the peninsula, thanks partly to the protection of the surrounding mountains; at the same time, however, these lofty ranges, as well as the widespread marshiness, hampered transport, particularly in summer. With the exception of Petropavlovsk on superb Avacha Bay, Kamchatka's coasts offered the Russians very poor harbors in the form of exposed, shallow roadsteads. Even Avacha Bay, though spacious, deep, and sheltered, was handicapped, for its entrance was so confined and so hidden by the surrounding mountain rim that it was difficult to find; in addition, the steep mountain walls hindered access to the interior of the peninsula.

The climate of the Okhotsk Seaboard and the Kamchatka Peninsula is harsh, owing to the region's high latitudinal position (51°–63°N.) on the eastern coast of a huge land mass washed by cool ocean waters. The Okhotsk Sea, with its cold water, masses of ice, frequent fogs, and constant winds, as well as the cool Oyashio Current off Kamchatka, markedly condition the regional atmosphere. Strong, cold, and dry northwest winds blow from the center of high pressure over the superchilled interior of the continent from October through February; sometimes these winds have been so strong that men and horses could not walk against them.[3] From May through July weaker southeast winds blow from the center of high pressure over the North Pacific, bringing warm and dry air to the peninsula but, after passage over the Okhotsk Sea, cool and damp air to the seaboard, which is notorious for the cold, foggy drizzle of summer called *bus*. Rain or snow, cloud, and fog prevail throughout the year but especially in summer and autumn; indeed, the region is one of the most overcast places in the world. Snowfall occurs from early autumn through late spring and, like rainfall, is heaviest along Kamchatka's mountainous eastern coast, where cyclonic precipitation is orographically intensified; here snowfall sometimes reaches depths of up to ten feet and covers all but the roofs of houses at Petropavlovsk, so that doors there were built to open in rather than out.[4] In the middle 1830's an observer commented that "the most frequent and the most usual phenomenon is rain and snow, so that Kamchatka can be called the land of snow and rain."[5]

Regional temperatures remain low all year, averaging in the 50's in summer and around zero in winter. The growing season is consequently short (despite fifteen to eighteen hours of daylight per day), seldom exceeding three months. Night frosts may occur anytime during this period, especially in the "basins of freezing," that is, in the valleys, which act as catchment basins for cold air descending from the surrounding mountains. Indeed, the weather is so variable that the Mayor of Vladivostok told the writer Anton Chekhov in 1890 that "there is absolutely no climate" in the Russian Far East.[6] The only exception to most of these conditions is the sheltered Kamchatka River Valley, where the climate is more continental, being colder in winter, warmer in summer, drier, and clearer and thus more favorable for agriculture than any other part of the peninsula or seaboard; however, even here the growing season averages only two to three months. This execrable climate, apart from making everyday life quite unpleasant, was instrumental in thwarting local agricultural efforts by the Russians. The inclement weather also endangered shipping, already restricted by an ice-free season of only six months at Okhotsk.

The soils of the Okhotsk Seaboard and the Kamchatka Peninsula are generally infertile, with the exception of the shallow alluvium of the Kamchatka River Valley. Elsewhere mostly podzols prevail. With thin surface layers of organic matter that are heavily leached and strongly acidic, podzols are moderate to low in fertility. Under cultivation they require organic and mineral fertilizers. Even the alluvium of the major river valleys is podzolic or boggy. This soil infertility further limited Russian agriculture. In addition, transport was hampered by excessive surface moisture resulting from permafrost, which underlies the entire seaboard and most of the peninsula.

The vegetation of the Okhotsk Seaboard and the Kamchatka Peninsula is not very diverse; the peninsula's flora, for example, includes no more than 800 to 850 species.[7] The entire region is dominated by the Okhotsk taiga, comprising mainly spruce, fir, birch, and larch, with considerable undergrowth. These trees are largely confined to the uplands, except birch and larch, which also grow intermittently on the lowlands of the peninsula and seaboard, respectively. The park-like vegetation of the river valleys consists of bogs of moss, meadows of grass, and groves of birch or larch. The grassy meadows offered limited natural pasture for livestock, while the timber stands provided adequate wood for heating and building purposes. The Russians especially utilized birch for firewood and larch for shipbuilding. Larch, however, was brittle; and its best stands were rapidly depleted. The vegetation also supplied various kinds of edible berries, nuts, roots, and bulbs, which were gathered by Russians and natives alike.

The region contains few faunal as well as floral species; in Kamchatka, for instance, there are under two hundred species of birds, most of which are aquatic, and no reptiles whatsoever.[8] Nevertheless, the animals that mattered—the principal fur bearers—were present in large numbers. Several species of animals, however, proved anything but beneficial. In Kamchatka livestock were often killed by sled dogs and by bears and wolves, which abounded in the peninsula; bears and wolves also frequently attacked the convoys of horses and droves of cattle on the supply route from Yakutsk to Okhotsk. Among the few species of fish on the seaboard and the peninsula, salmon are very plentiful; their abundance was occasionally instrumental in preventing starvation.

Thus, the region's contorted physiography and harsh climate severely limited agricultural development, while the ruggedness of land and sea restricted the transport of supplies, including provisions. This severity was partially offset by the abundance of salmon, but there was no counterpart of the buffalo, whose pemmican long sustained the Canadian fur trade. Reindeer meat was little used by the Russians, largely because reindeer were neither as numerous nor as widespread as bison were in Canada.

Meanness of the Cultural Environment

Upon entering the Okhotsk Seaboard and the Kamchatka Peninsula the Russians found not only inhospitable physical conditions but also unfavorable cultural conditions in the form of hostile and primitive native tribes: Tunguses on the southern half of the seaboard, Koryaks on the northern half of the seaboard and in the northern half of the peninsula, and Kamchadals in the southern half of the peninsula. The Mongoloid Tunguses of the Okhotsk Seaboard, called Lamuts by the Russians, were mostly nomadic reindeer herders and hunters, but some were seminomadic or sedentary fishers and sealers with dogs instead of reindeer. The Lamut reindeer provided milk, meat, and hide but were used mainly for riding and packing. In winter on reindeer or skis with firearms and dogs the nomadic Lamuts hunted wild reindeer, elk, mountain sheep, and bears for meat and squirrels and foxes for fur, while in summer they fished the rivers. Salmon fishing at the river mouths and sealing in the coastal waters formed the livelihood of the seminomadic and sedentary Lamuts, who supplied their nomadic brethren with sealskins in exchange for reindeer meat and hide. The Lamuts practiced some metallurgy (forging of weapons and armor).[9]

The Paleo-Asiatic Koryaks, who comprised nine territorial groups, were primarily herders and secondarily fishermen. The seasonal round of the Koryak nomads corresponded to the movements of their reindeer, which were their main source of meat, clothing, roofing, and thong and their sole means of transport. In winter the herd grazed in the lowlands by the camp, which was moved four to five times in the course of the season as pasture was exhausted. In April the does were separated from the rest of the herd in preparation for calving in May, which was an extremely busy period for the herders, who had constantly to guard the newborn calves against cold and predators. In summer the herd was driven upland to graze the rich alpine pasture, with the camp usually being placed along a fishable stream. In early autumn the herders drove the reindeer to camp for slaughtering, and with the first snowfall herd and camp were moved to winter quarters along the seacoast or in the river valleys. The sedentary Koryaks, who commonly owned some reindeer, stayed year round in the lowlands, where they fished in summer and sealed and whaled in both spring and autumn. For transport they used dogs in winter and umiaks and kayaks in summer, whereas the nomadic Koryaks did not keep dogs because they attacked reindeer. The coastal Koryaks exchanged the skins and the fat of sea mammals with their nomadic kin for furs and reindeer meat. All Koryaks, however nomadic or sedentary, hunted bears, marmots, wild reindeer, and mountain sheep for meat and foxes, wolverines, otters, hares, and ermines for fur. They were also avid gatherers of wild plants—edible roots, grasses, and berries. Metallurgy was practiced by only one Koryak group, whose forged iron knives were renowned throughout the territory of the Koryaks and even beyond.

The Paleo-Asiatic Kamchadals (Itelmen) inhabited the seacoasts and the river valleys of southern Kamchatka, especially the Kamchatka River Valley, in permanent settlements comprising winter residences called *yurtas* (timbered and thatched dugouts) and summer residences called *balagans* (thatched, pyramidal huts elevated on piles). The Kamchadals were mainly fishermen. Salmon, especially, were netted in the rivers and stored in dried or fermented form; and hair seals, fur seals, and sea otters were caught in the coastal waters. Land animals, including sables, were hunted primarily for their meat rather than for their fur or hide. Gathering was more important among the Kamchadals than among any other tribe of northern Siberia. The women collected bulbs of lilies, stalks of sweet grass, leaves of club moss, cedar nuts, and various berries. The sole domesticated animal was the dog, which supplemented the dugout, snowshoes, and skis as means of transport. The Kamchadals did not know metallurgy, working only stone and bone.

Thus, all the aborigines of the Okhotsk Seaboard and the Kamchatka Peninsula were hunters, fishermen, gatherers, and/or herders; none were farmers. They did not cultivate crops, and their only domesticated animals were dogs and reindeer, which were half-wild; moreover, not all Lamuts and Koryaks were reindeer herders. In addition, only some Lamuts and Koryaks practiced a rudimentary sort of metallurgy. The absence of aboriginal agriculture, apart from extensive reindeer herding, deprived the Russians of ready-made native fields and experienced native husbandmen. This lack contrasted with conditions elsewhere in Siberia, where some native tribes had practiced agriculture before the

Russian conquest; for example, the Yakuts of the middle Lena Basin bred cattle and horses; the Daurs and the Dyuchers of the middle Amur Basin grew various grains, vegetables, and fruits; and the Buryats of Baikalia cultivated grain and tended livestock. Such tribes expanded their agricultural activities with the arrival of the Russians by adopting new crops, animals, and techniques from their conquerors; and some native agriculturalists eventually surpassed their Russian neighbors in productivity. The Russians were able to exact tribute from some tribes in the form of grain, cattle, husbandry, fish, or metal instead of furs, such tribute in kind being called "Yermak's method" after its first practitioner. But on the Okhotsk Seaboard and the Kamchatka Peninsula the Russians, unlike the pioneers of the Atlantic Seaboard of America, found no "Indian old fields," and the natives could not supply the promyshlenniks with "Indian corn." Moreover, the mostly semisedentary natives adopted agriculture very slowly. They did quickly adopt horses for transport; but it was not until the nineteenth century that the Kamchadals, for example, the most sedentary of the region's aborigines, accepted cattle breeding and vegetable growing. This resistance was an outgrowth of the initial hostility of the natives, and this hostility further hampered the Russians, costing both life and property. The Lamuts were not pacified until the end of the seventeenth century and the Koryaks and Kamchadals until the middle of the eighteenth century.

On the other hand, in living off the land by hunting and fishing the natives proved valuable to their Russian conquerors as hunters of fur bearers, the raison d'être of the conquest; as providers of fish, which helped to support the fur trade; and as guides and haulers. However, these roles diminished with the decimation of the native population by contact with the alien Russian culture. The cumulative impact of the language, religion, diet, social structure, economic system, and political organization of the Russian intruders on the native inhabitants was disastrous. Liquor and disease were particularly harmful; in 1768–69, for instance, smallpox from Okhotsk ravaged Kamchatka, killing 5,368 Kamchadals in 1768 alone.[10] Such depopulation substantially reduced the number of native laborers and the amount of tribute collections.

The well-being of the Okhotsk Seaboard and the Kamchatka Peninsula was also subverted by the Russians themselves. The region's state servitors (the sluzhilie lyudi) were commonly political or criminal exiles ("unfortunates"), for Siberia, with its reputation for unrelenting cold and ubiquitous savagery, attracted few volunteers, save those who wanted to "get rich quick" or to "get away from it all." These exiles, whose fate aggravated the notoriety of Siberia by making that land synonymous with banishment, were demoted or deported to the seaboard and the peninsula, where they repeated or redoubled rather than repented their misdeeds. Moreover, the worst offenders, such as traitors and murderers, were banished to the northern and eastern extremities of Siberia, including the seaboard and the peninsula, while lesser offenders were exiled to less remote and more civilized parts.[11] Officers were offered a promotion in rank and a doubling in salary for three to five years of service in Siberia; nevertheless, real salaries remained low, thereby inducing fraud, graft, extortion, and bribery, which were added to drunkenness and lechery. This situation struck Chekhov, who, while traveling the length of Siberia in 1890, exclaimed that "if it were not for the cold which deprives Siberia of summer, and were it not for the officials who corrupt the peasants and exiles, Siberia would be the very richest and happiest of territories."[12] Administrative corruption was proverbial in Siberia; and the Okhotsk Seaboard and the Kamchatka Peninsula were no exception to this rule. Some officials neglected their posts, regarding the region "merely as a soldier regards his winter quarters in war, or a traveller his temporary resting-place."[13] Others made the most of their terms by profiting at anybody's expense, even buying their positions, which they considered lucrative sinecures. At the beginning of the nineteenth century the Commandant of Kamchatka observed that abuses in the peninsula's administration resulted from "having appointed officials there from the very lowest, worst bred, most mercenary, and least competent people, such as Senate couriers, provincial servitors, and the like, who nominally buy their places for money."[14] The chief concern of such functionaries was obviously their own interests, not those of the seaboard and the peninsula. Most laborers, too, were exiles—such as the convicts at the saltworks near Okhotsk—who did their forced labor perfunctorily and frequently tried to escape. The region's Crown peasants also worked indifferently, for they were involuntary settlers whose backward methods produced meager crops that belonged mostly to the state. Thousands of free peasants did voluntarily migrate to Siberia, mainly to escape seignorial serfdom, but most of them settled in Western Siberia, since it entailed less travel from European Russia and promised better agriculture than Eastern Siberia. The fewest and the worst tended to go to the Russian Far East. This fact, together with native backwardness and resistance, retarded development of the Okhotsk Seaboard and the Kamchatka Peninsula.

Remoteness of the Location

The remote location of the seaboard and the peninsula also hindered their development. The region constituted a classic example of extreme location. Significantly, it was long classified administratively as a *kray,* i.e., a "borderland," derived from *krainost,* meaning "extremity." Siberia, especially its Far Eastern portion, was commonly deemed the *ultima Thule* and the *finis mundi.*[15] The seaboard and the peninsula represented, to most Russians, a "bear's corner," i.e., a godforsaken hole. They were exceedingly remote from the political, economic, and cultural core of Russia. Over 8,000 miles of travel, or one-third of the earth's circumference, separated St. Petersburg, the Imperial capital (after 1713), and Nizhne-Kamchatsk, the onetime administrative center of Kamchatka. From Irkutsk, the administrative center of Eastern Siberia and the source of many of the directives and personnel and of much of the materiel sent to the seaboard and the peninsula, it was 2,400 miles to Okhotsk and 3,400 miles to Petropavlovsk[16] over swampy, mountainous, and forested terrains and across stormy, foggy, rocky seas, with small, slow carriers and often inept drivers and pilots. Even the everyday stoical optimism of the Russians, expressed by the phrase *kak ni bud,* meaning "somehow or other," was unable to help the situation, although John Cochrane, an English traveler of the early 1820's in Siberia, asserted that "any thing can and will be done in Russia when the order is accompanied with those almighty words. . . ."[17] An old Russian tale relates that six Kamchadal maidens who were sent from Bolsheretsk to St. Petersburg at the command of Empress Elizabeth (1741–62) became mothers before reaching Irkutsk and noticeably pregnant again before reaching St. Petersburg, despite the dismissal at Irkutsk of the officer accompanying them.[18] Late in the century it still usually took half a year to travel from the peninsula to St. Petersburg.[19] During a farewell audience with Nicholas I following his appointment in 1847 as Governor-General of Eastern Siberia, Muravyov was reportedly warned by the Tsar that he would learn in Irkutsk of any attack on Kamchatka only six months after its occurrence.[20] Not surprisingly, the implementation of governmental decisions concerning the Okhotsk Seaboard and the Kamchatka Peninsula was often delayed. For example, after seven years of wrangling, permission was finally obtained in 1828 to move Gizhiga to a new site, yet this move was not accomplished until 1840.[21]

Remoteness especially affected administration, not only of the Russian Far East but of all Siberia. The great distances separating the Imperial capital from the Tsar's far-flung possessions in Asia prompted the central government to grant wide powers to the authorities in these remote regions in order to lessen the frequency of distant and expensive communications. In 1736 the Vice-Governor of Irkutsk Province became independent of the Governor of Siberia at Tobolsk "since there is great incapability in administration because of the remote distance of towns and villages [in Irkutsk Province]."[22] The authority of the central government in Eastern Siberia was thereby weakened. De Lesseps, the sole survivor of the ill-fated La Pérouse Expedition (1785–88), remarked, while returning to France from Kamchatka via Siberia with the expedition's journal, that "experience has too clearly demonstrated, particularly in the extensive empire of Russia, that authority becomes weak, in proportion as it is farther removed from the centre."[23] Muravyov received almost unlimited viceregal powers as Governor-General of Eastern Siberia, and during the Crimean War (1853–55) he was empowered to conduct all diplomatic negotiations independently of the Ministry of Foreign Affairs, owing to the unreliability of contact between European Russia and the Russian Far East.[24]

Remoteness of the Okhotsk Seaboard and the Kamchatka Peninsula not only diluted central control but also worsened local administration. D'Auteroche, a French astronomer sojourning in Western Siberia in 1761, observed that "as we get farther distant from St. Petersburg coming near to Kamtschatka, the people are under less subjection, not only on account of the difficulty of sending troops and provisions towards the eastern part of this empire, but also because the troops which are sent, being not within reach of the sovereign, the army, the governors, and all persons in office, abuse the authority they are invested with."[25] This point was echoed around 1800 by the Russian writer Radishchev, who noted that "the land space [of Siberia] is immeasurable, and almost everything is removed from the eyes of the government. For this reason [Siberia] was always a gold mine for those officials who were more concerned about their purse than about their conscience."[26] The scandalous situation at Okhotsk in particular was decried by the

Russian naval historian Veselago: "The commandants at Okhotsk, with rare exceptions, taking advantage of the remoteness of the higher authorities, abused their power and, it is possible to say, robbed the treasury, their subordinates, and private individuals. . . . At the same time they indulged in all kinds of licentiousness and cruelty, approaching tyranny."[27] When Devier succeeded Skornyakov-Pisarev as Commandant of Okhotsk in 1740, he found that there were only 12 rubles, 22 kopeks in the treasury and only 108 pounds of provisions in the magazines; that for three years the state servitors had received no salary from Yakutsk; that no horses had been sent to Kamchatka for plowing; and that the peasants sent to Udsk in 1735 had planted no grain.[28] Ivan Koch, Commandant of Okhotsk from 1789 through 1794, was so notorious that "God is in Heaven, but Koch is in Okhotsk" became a saying throughout Siberia. Other "Siberian satraps" also became infamous; for instance, the very first Governor of Siberia, Prince Gagarin, was hanged for abusing his office. During his stay of eleven years (1732–42) in Siberia, Heinrich Fick, who had been one of Peter the Great's favorites, met only one tax collector who "walked the straight path."[29] Another sojourner thought "every district assessor figures that he is not for the people but the people are created for him."[30] In the words of one inspector, "hungry officials serving in those krays want not to be just satisfied but rich, too. When we often see impudent dare-devils who, not fearing exile to Siberia, abuse the power given them and enrich themselves in the very capitals, robbing the immediate treasury, then what is to be expected from similar men many thousands of verstas distant from the supreme government in lands where they rule peoples having almost no understanding of laws and not even knowing reading and writing?"[31] Victims of such corruption could personally petition the Tsar, but there was that long trip to St. Petersburg from the seaboard or the peninsula. Officials defrauded, embezzled, extorted, and bribed unchecked, secure in the knowledge that "God is high above and Tsar is far away." In Kamchatka this adage had in the early 1820's "the sanction of a proverb, now become almost a principle. . . ."[32] Governor Simpson of the Hudson's Bay Company likewise found in the early 1840's that "the favourite maxim of most of the public officers, great and small, in Siberia, is that 'God is high, and the Emperor far off'. . . ."[33] Thus, in Siberia, as in New France and in New Spain, remoteness facilitated administrative corruption, with distance acting as a protective buffer between local maladministration and central authority.

This situation was enhanced, of course, by dishonesty and/or incompetence on the part of Siberian officials, who were commonly banished to their remote posts for offenses committed in European Russia; for instance, the first and the second commandants of Okhotsk, Skornyakov-Pisarev and Devier, were exiles from St. Petersburg.

Maladministration was further aggravated by the overlapping of powers between officials, especially between civilian and military authorities. Overlapping had been designed to check arbitrary and corrupt conduct, but the resulting conflict hampered the implementation of governmental policies. The development of Okhotsk during the 1730's, for example, was delayed by wrangling between Skornyakov-Pisarev, Commandant of Okhotsk, and Bering, leader of the Second Kamchatka Expedition. Such conflict of authority was further augmented by traditional class antagonism between noblemen and merchants and between servicemen and civilians.

Altogether, the forbidding physical environment, the primitive and hostile native culture, the corrupt, inept, and bureaucratic administration, and the remote location of the Okhotsk Seaboard and Kamchatka Peninsula contributed to the creation of an unattractive and inaccurate "psychological environment"; Russians perceived the region not as it really existed but as they thought it existed. The circumnavigator Vasily Golovnin, who inspected Kamchatka in 1810–11, remarked that "from time immemorial Siberia has been a land of slanders and denunciations."[34] In the middle 1830's an anonymous Russian observer commented that "it seems that just the name 'Kamchatka' one associates with at least some kind of miserable and unpleasant, if not horrible and terrible, feeling. . . . Even in Siberia the word 'Kamchatka!' is not uttered without exclamation. There it seems as dismal and as terrible as Siberia in Russia. . . ."[35] This attitude was reflected in Chekhov's line: "even in Siberia people can live." Kamchatka's ignominy was such that in Russian schools misbehaving pupils were punished by being "sent to Kamchatka," i.e., to the back of the classroom. This unfavorable impression of Siberia in general and of the Russian Far East in particular persisted until the late nineteenth century.

3

THE PROBLEM OF
PROVISIONMENT

"The main difficulty consisted of securing these remote places [the
Okhotsk Seaboard and the Kamchatka Peninsula] with provisions."
D. Romanov, "Prisoyedinenie Amura," p. 337.

Provisioning Siberia

The problem of food supply on the Okhotsk Seaboard and the
Kamchatka Peninsula was not a new experience for *Sibiryaks* (Russians
of Siberia). Provisionment was long a chronic problem throughout
Asiatic Russia. From the beginning of the Siberian conquest the government was faced with the task of feeding its various agents scattered east
of the Urals, and this matter was one of the main concerns and weakest
points of government policy in Siberia.[1] The problem was particularly
acute during the first century of the Siberian occupation; until the
eighteenth century the Russians were confined more or less to the
nonagricultural taiga, which abounded in fur bearers but not in arable
land, being too marshy (Western Siberia) or too rugged (Eastern
Siberia), as well as too cold, for agriculture. For instance, the ostrog of
Pelym (1592), situated on the swampy upper reaches of the Tavda
River, complained to Moscow in 1602 of a lack of arable land.[2] Significantly, Krasnoyarsk, founded in 1628 in the wooded steppe astride the
upper Yenisey River, reported that its site was suitable for cultivation.[3]
Siberia's ostrogs were normally established with a view to tribute collect-
ing, defense, and transportation rather than to agriculture.* In addition,
the great east-west extent of the taiga zone slowed the shipment of
foodstuffs from European Russia by land, while the Northern Sea Route
remained impracticable until the twentieth century. Because of the

* Having been founded mostly along rivers, the ostrogs were sometimes
inadvertently situated on fertile alluvium, which, however, was subject to
seasonal flooding.

dearth of fresh fruits and raw vegetables in northern Siberia scurvy was very common. According to Von Strahlenburg (Tabbert), a Swedish prisoner-of-war of the 1720's, "at Beresow, not far from the River *Oby,* you will meet with few *Russians,* whose Noses, or some other Members, do not bear the Marks of this raging Distemper."[4] Half a century later D'Auteroche even asserted that "all the Russians, in general, are much addicted to the scurvy. . . ."[5]

Provisioning the Okhotsk Seaboard and the Kamchatka Peninsula

Thus, provisionment of the Russian Far East was simply an extreme form of a familiar Siberian problem. But here this problem did not become acute until after the Second Kamchatka Expedition (1733–42). Before this venture the Russian population of the region was negligible, so that the demand for food was small and could be accommodated by the plentiful fish and game and by the occasional shipments of foodstuffs from Yakutsk. Following the Second Kamchatka Expedition, however, the region's burgeoning Russian population created a much greater demand for victuals, a problem that had to be resolved if Russian occupation and exploitation of the Pacific littoral were to be secure.

Satisfactory figures on the amount of provisions (mainly grain) required are available only for the early 1820's, when, having reached its population peak of the 1639–1856 period, the region needed some 639 tons of grain annually.[6] Also in the early 1820's, according to the English traveler Cochrane, Okhotsk, Gizhiga, and Kamchatka annually required 722 tons, 500 pounds of flour alone[7]—but Cochrane tended to exaggerate. At any rate, it is clear that large amounts of provisions, especially grain, were needed.

Much salt was also needed, mainly for preserving fish. From 1818 through 1826 Okhotsk required eighteen to twenty-seven tons of salt annually and Kamchatka and Gizhiga together required fourteen and a half tons. Commandant Golenishchev of Kamchatka reported in 1827 that altogether fifty-four to ninety tons of salt were needed yearly for the Okhotsk Seaboard and the Kamchatka Peninsula.[8]

The state servitors who administered the region in the name of the Tsar were paid annually in kind as well as in money. This traditional payment in kind, called "grain salary" (*khlebnoye zhalovanye*), commonly included grain, salt, and liquor. The amount varied from rank to rank, from time to time, and from place to place. In 1773 at Bolsheretsk the salary in kind amounted to 351 pounds of flour and 54 pounds of groats* for each soldier and 360 pounds of flour for each Cossack. When these rations failed to arrive, the soldiers and Cossacks were reimbursed in money at the rate of 1 ruble, 15 kopeks per pud (thirty-six pounds) of flour and 2 rubles per pud of groats.[9] This rate of compensation, however, was usually less than the local cost of private grain and consequently was a chronic source of discontent. Clerics, too, as representatives of the state church, were paid in kind as well as in money. Under a decree of May 11/22 of 1744 each of Kamchatka's ten missionaries received 262 pounds of flour and 48 pounds of groats per year. The flour ration was increased to 720 pounds by an edict of 1758.[10]

Promyshlenniks under contract were paid partly in kind. Around the middle of the eighteenth century, when the vessels of the maritime fur trade ventured no farther than the Commander Islands, the owners supplied the crews with provisions for two months, and each promyshlennik received seventy-two pounds of flour, a few casks of fresh water, and some dried and salted meat and fish at the time of hunting. With the extension of the voyages beyond the Commander Islands, the promyshlenniks were given enough provisions to enable them to reach "without need" some part-way island; there, while wintering, they prepared and stored enough meat to last at least a year through the hunting of sea animals, especially sea cows, whose flesh was considered healthful and, in dried form, served in lieu of bread.[11] In this manner the stock of provisions was replenished at each halting place, so that there was always a reserve supply on board. In the continental fur trade promyshlenniks not under contract supplied their own provisions, including flour, groats, and meat and sometimes dried goat's milk, cow's butter, and fish fat, and even less often, hemp seeds. Contracted promyshlenniks in the late 1730's in the basin of the Vitim River in Eastern Siberia received either free supplies and one-third of the catch or free provisions only and one-half of the catch. The season's provisions comprised 1,116 pounds of flour, 9 pounds of groats, and 36 pounds of salt for every party of three to four hunters, plus 252 pounds of food for each hunting dog.[12]

* Groats are dried grain, hulled and often ground. They are coarser than grits.

Salaries in kind, then, accounted for most of the food requirements of the Russians of the Okhotsk Seaboard and the Kamchatka
Peninsula. But natives also became consumers. Originally, none of the
natives of the region ate beef, grain, or vegetables, since they tended
neither cattle nor crops. Lieutenant Waxell of the Second Kamchatka
Expedition found in the early 1740's that "bread is something quite
unknown among them [Kamchadals]; many of them even say that it
makes them ill and, therefore, they do not ask much for it."[13] Eventually, however, some natives, especially Lamuts and Kamchadals, acquired a taste for Russian foodstuffs, and by the middle of the nineteenth century the Kamchadals were accustomed to bread.[14]

The Russian Diet[15]

The Russians did not rely on bread alone, but, as Simpson noted,
bread "to a Russian, is peculiarly the staff of life. . . ."[16] "Bread before
everything," says a Russian proverb. The diet of the Russian masses was
overwhelmingly dominated by cereals, especially rye, from which the popular "black" ("brown") bread was made. Wheat bread was eaten mainly
on festive occasions. Cereals were also used to make soups, porridges,
and pasties. *Burda* or *burduk* was a popular Siberian thick soup of rye
flour and water, first soured and then boiled. The kitchen garden was a
ubiquitous feature of the Russian landscape, and the common vegetables
in it were cabbages, turnips, beets, carrots, radishes, cucumbers, peas,
beans, mushrooms, dill, garlic, leeks, onions, gourds, and pumpkins.
Though seldom eaten separately, being used mainly for ragouts, soups,
and pasties, vegetables were especially prominent on the numerous fast
days. Cabbage soup (*shchi*) was a daily dish, and beet soup (*borshch*)
was also very popular. The usual fruits were apples, pears, peaches,
apricots, plums, cherries, grapes, melons, and berries, used principally
for making beverages and preserves. Beef, pork, and mutton were the
common meats, but less and less meat was being eaten by the peasantry
after the seventeenth century. Veal was avoided by the religious and the
irreligious alike. Meat was normally boiled or marinated, and it was
rarely served separately. The consumption of fowl was confined largely
to fasts. Fish was a prominent food, particularly during fasts, which were
strictly observed by Russians. Nuts were very popular in Siberia; cedar
nuts were even imported from Irkutsk by Kamchatka.[17] Salt was a vital

preservative, as well as a welcome condiment and a necessary comestible. Meat and fish were usually preserved by salting, while milk and butter were soured.

Kvas, the staple beverage made from grain, was used as a foundation in all soups and sauces. *Saturnan* was a popular Siberian beverage concocted from wheat grain, flour, butter, and tea.[18] Mead, vodka, wine, beer, and tea were all standard drinks. While grain was required largely for groats and flour for making gruel and breadstuffs, not a little was needed for brewing alcoholic beverages, especially kvas and vodka ("grain wine"), which were derived mostly from rye (above all), barley, and potatoes. Whatever the reasons, Russians were very fond of liquor; indeed, drunkenness was a chronic problem throughout the Empire. Although it is impossible to say exactly how much of the grain consumed on the Okhotsk Seaboard and the Kamchatka Peninsula was taken by liquor, it must have been considerable.

These, then, were the foods desired and required by the Russians of the seaboard and the peninsula. Bread was especially in demand, although it was allegedly dispensable. In 1745 the Yakutsk authorities asked Steller whether the Russians in Kamchatka could live without bread and, if so, what could replace it. Steller replied that his party had spent two breadless seasons (winter of 1743–44 and spring of 1744) on Bering Island without any ill effects. This experience convinced him that abstention from bread was neither difficult nor harmful and that the Russians of Kamchatka could use fish and *sarana* (Kamchatka lily) instead.[19] Nevertheless, essential or unessential, bread was desired by these people; consequently, it had to be provided. Meanwhile, there were various "wild" foods—fish, game, berries, and roots—that mitigated the problem of provisionment.

Hunting, Fishing, and Gathering

Even if the Russians had been ignorant of fishing, hunting, and gathering, they undoubtedly would have emulated the Lamut, Kamchadal, and Koryak practitioners. Certainly the region's unfavorable agricultural conditions induced the Russians to live off the land more there than around their ancestral homes in Pomorye, Baikalia, and elsewhere. Fortunately, the Okhotsk Seaboard and the Kamchatka Peninsula, as if compensating for their agricultural limitations, abounded in fish, game, wildfowl, berries, herbs, and nuts. Fish could be especially plentiful. Krasheninnikov asserted that Kamchatka's chief wealth was furs but its main abundance was fish.[20] Both Krasheninnikov and Steller described the summer runs in Kamchatka as so dense that the rivers overflowed their banks and cast ashore more fish than were found in most rivers elsewhere; such a stench arose that allegedly a plague was averted only by the incessant winds.[21] Dogs and bears could catch more fish with their paws than people elsewhere could with their nets, and they could afford to eat only the tasty heads. Nets were broken by the heavy runs of fish.[22] Around 1815 an observer asserted that it was difficult to cross the teeming Kamchatka River during a run, when its level was raised by the multitude of fish.[23] The waters of the rivers around Okhotsk tasted fishy; fish could easily be caught barehanded, and fishermen no sooner cast their nets into the Okhota River than they retrieved them lest they burst.[24]

The fish caught were mainly several varieties of salmon (*chavycha,* quinnat or king salmon; *nerka,* red or blueback salmon; *keta* or *khaiko,* dog salmon; *gorbusha,* pink or humpbacked salmon; and *malma* or *golets,* Dolly Varden trout), as well as herring, cod, and loach. Russians and natives fished from spring until autumn. In Kamchatka fish could also be caught in winter in some lakes and rivers kept ice-free by warm spring water. They were salted (especially), smoked, dried, fermented, and frozen. If prepared well and checked often, fish would keep two years and longer. Preserved and fresh fish became one of the chief nourishments of the Russians of the Okhotsk Seaboard and the Kamchatka Peninsula. In front of every Cossack dwelling in Kamchatka in the early 1740's stood three to six *baraks* (fish storehouses on stilts). The chavycha, which reached fifty-six inches in length and seventy-two pounds in weight (salted), was the best food fish. *Yukola* (dried fish) was a staple dish throughout the region. In Kamchatka yukola made from dog salmon was called "rye bread" or "Kamchatkan bread," and in the early 1740's yukola and *kislo* (fermented fish) were the mainstays of the peninsula's inhabitants. *Porsa* (fish flour) was also common. *Balyk,* smoked filet of nerka, was sometimes even shipped from Okhotsk to Yakutsk and Irkutsk.[25] Fish fat was used in place of butter.

Sea mammals, especially sea cows, whales, and hair seals, were also caught for food.* The promyshlenniks were responsible for the

---

* Erman found in 1829 that the Russians on Kamchatka and the Aleutians often argued the lawfulness (in the eyes of the Church) of eating seals and whales (Adolph Erman, *Travels in Siberia . . . ,* trans. W. D. Cooley [Philadelphia: Lea and Blanchard, 1850], 2 : 236*n*).

extermination of Steller's sea cow, whose "flesh was very savoury like the best beef; that of the young ones, was like veal."[26]* A sea cow measuring twenty-eight feet in length and six to seven feet in breadth and height and weighing three to four tons (including 5,400 pounds of lean and 2,160 pounds of fat) could feed a crew of fifty men for two weeks.[27]

Hunting was much less important than fishing. Wild reindeer and "stone sheep" or mountain sheep (*argals* or *musimons*) were plentiful in Kamchatka, but they were seldom hunted.[28] Steller noted in the early 1740's that reindeer "are found throughout Kamchatka in a wild state in enormous numbers. However, nobody, neither Russians nor Itelmen, is interested in them, partly because of the value and rarity of gunpowder and partly because of negligence, since the Cossacks and the Itelmen are satisfied with fish. . . ."[29] Fish were not only more plentiful and easier to procure but nutritionally superior. Only at Gizhiga and Tigilsk were some reindeer occasionally slaughtered for meat. From 1815 through 1817, 5,000 Koryak reindeer were butchered at Gizhiga to offset the shortage of fish and grain, but this occurrence was unusual, even though there were up to 12,000 reindeer in Kamchatka in 1818. Every winter during the 1830's, however, the inhabitants of Tigilsk bought 800 to 1,600 reindeer from the Koryaks, each beast averaging eighty-one pounds of meat.[30] Wild sheep were much more limited in both number and range, being confined mostly to the peninsula. Steller wrote that "these animals are encountered throughout Kamchatka in abundance" and that their flesh was "very tasty."[31] In 1742–43 Waxell noted that Kamchatka's mountain sheep, each of which weighed 120 to 150 pounds, were delicious in taste but difficult to hunt.[32]

Waterfowl were also hunted. At Okhotsk *turpans* (sea ducks) were bagged regularly in summer by Russians and Lamuts alike.[33] On

---

* This opinion was corroborated by Krasheninnikov (S. P. Krasheninnikov, *Opisanie zemli Kamchatki* [*Description of the Land of Kamchatka*] [Moscow and Leningrad: Izdatelstvo Glavsevmorputi, 1949], p. 288). Waxell found that "their flesh is quite free of any bad smell or taste" and "tastes like really good reindeer meat . . ." (Sven Waxell, *The Russian Expedition to America,* trans. M. A. Michael [New York: Collier Books, 1962], p. 157), and a promyshlennik declared that "the meat and fat are very tasty and . . . healthful . . ." (A. I. Andreyev, ed., *Russkie otkrytiya v Tikhom okeane i Severnoy Amerike v XVIII veke* [*Russian Discoveries in the Pacific Ocean and in North America in the XVIIIth Century*] [Moscow: Gosudarstvennoye izdatelstvo geograficheskoy literatury, 1948], p. 115).

July 15 of 1786 the Billings Expedition watched the inhabitants of Okhotsk catch some 6,500 turpans grounded by moulting.[34] In Kamchatka it was claimed around 1815 that a marksman could shoot more than three hundred ducks in a single day during the hunting season from May through August.[35]

Both the Russians and the natives did much gathering, especially in Kamchatka. Various kinds of berries (such as bilberries, cloudberries, cowberries, cranberries, and whortleberries), nuts (especially those of the Siberian "cedar" [stone pine]), roots and bulbs (particularly the sarana or Kamchatka or yellow lily), eggs, and even bark were collected for food. Vasily Golovnin found in 1810 that cloudberries grown at Bolsheretsk were shipped throughout Kamchatka.[36] Both cloudberries and cranberries were sometimes shipped from Okhotsk to Kamchatka, and it was reported in 1830 that even Yakutsk received cloudberries from Okhotsk.[37] The Cossacks of Kamchatka drank a concoction boiled from cowberry leaves in place of tea and made a homebrew from "sweet grass" in lieu of vodka. Both the meat and the oil of the pistachio-like cedar nut were used for food. Cedar nuts were even shipped to Okhotsk and Kamchatka from Yakutsk and Oimyakon.* Roots and bulbs were taken from the ground and from mouse nests, just as cedar nuts were sometimes taken from the nests of mice, squirrels, and sables. *Cheremsha* (wild garlic or "bear's garlic") was used as an antiscorbutic, and even exported from Kamchatka to Okhotsk and Yakutsk. Sarana or "Tsar's curls," pounded and dried, was used in place of flour and groats; it was to the Kamchadals what bread was to the Russians. Like the cheremsha, the sarana was also used in soups, hashes, porridges, and pasties, as well as mixed with berries to form a much relished confection. Around 1740 one pud of prepared sarana sold for four to six rubles, as much as one pud of imported rye flour.[38] Krasheninnikov opined that sarana could completely replace bread if there were enough for daily consumption.[39] Roots and herbs were used for want not only of bread but also of fish on the peninsula. The eggs of wildfowl, especially of murres (guillemots), were gathered by the thousands. Around 1815 "several thousand" gull eggs were collected annually on the islands at the mouth of the Kamchatka River. They were preserved in fish or train

* Erman found in 1828 that the Siberian passion for cedar nuts threatened the very existence of the plantations of stone pine in the Central Urals, since trees were sometimes felled for the sake of the nuts alone (Erman, *Travels in Siberia,* 1 : 177).

oil. Various "sea vegetables" (such as sea cabbage for jam) resembling cabbages, cucumbers, and turnips were collected for food, although they were sour and salty in taste. Finally, the dried bark of poplar and pine was used as food, just as it was in Russia.[40]

Thus, "wild" foodstuffs were used both as supplements and as substitutes for "tame" foodstuffs. However, fish, game, berries, roots, and the like could not completely replace agricultural products as provisions, for they could not supply all the gastronomic wants of the Russians. Besides, wildlife was not an inexhaustible source. Steller's sea cow, for instance, whose meat sustained much of the Russian maritime fur trade around the middle of the eighteenth century, was exterminated by 1768, just as the dodo bird and the great auk were hunted to extinction by hungry seamen. Fish, the foremost source of "wild" food, were not always plentiful, as the inhabitants of Kamchatka unhappily discovered in 1769, when a severe shortage of fish caused widespread starvation. From 1815 through 1820 the Okhotsk Seaboard, particularly Gizhiga, as well as Kamchatka, suffered the same plight.[41] Fish were usually scarce at Verkhne-Kamchatsk, since, "on account of its long distance from the sea, few fish reach there and very late. . . ."[42] Okhotsk Kray suffered starvation for want of fish in 1832, 1836, 1842, and 1843. Sometimes in Kamchatka, where fish failures were termed *golodovkas* ("hunger strikes"), heavy rains caused the rivers to flood, resulting in the stranding and death of multitudes of fish.[43]

Also, the preservation of fish was problematical. On the one hand, because of the lack of sunshine, fish were dried with difficulty, especially at Bolsheretsk on the peninsula's murky western coast.[44] Waxell found in the early 1740's in Kamchatka that the winter supply of fish had to be caught three or four times over because of the difficulty of drying fish in the damp climate;[45] sometimes not one fish in ten could be dried.[46] The Mayor of Nizhne-Kamchatsk reported in 1794 that because of this difficulty every spring "people suffered much" in some places.[47] Some fish, like the chavycha, were too plump for drying.[48] Sometimes, especially in Kamchatka, there was not enough salt for salting fish. The peninsula's chief lacks around 1740, in Krasheninnikov's opinion, were iron and salt; a pud of salt was worth almost as much as a pud of rye flour.[49] At some places, such as Bolsheretsk, there was a scarcity of firewood for smoking fish and for evaporating seawater to make salt. Nowhere else in Kamchatka was the preservation of fish so difficult as at Bolsheretsk.[50]

Moreover, much of the fish catch on the Okhotsk Seaboard and especially the Kamchatka Peninsula was needed for feeding sled dogs, which were indispensable for winter travel and transport. Dogs were to Kamchatka what horses were to Russia.[51] Steller declared that "nobody can do without them, just as nobody elsewhere can live without horses and cattle," since "nowhere in all of the Russian Empire . . . are summer and winter travel so onerous and dangerous as in Kamchatka."[52] What one horse could carry in Siberia required in Kamchatka the labor of thirty men on foot in summer or of five sleds with twenty-six dogs and five men in winter. A loaded sledge, carrying three adults and fifty-four pounds of baggage, could in one day be pulled by four Kamchatka dogs twenty to twenty-seven miles over a bad trail and fifty-four to one hundred miles over a good trail.[53] Kamchatka dogs, which rarely lived beyond ten years because of their arduous labor, were considered the hardiest and fastest canines in Siberia, and they were prized, too, because they were easily fed (with fish). Not infrequently a Kamchatka dog with harness brought sixty to eighty rubles around 1740.[54] Kamchatka contained 50,000 to 60,000 dogs around 1807, according to the naturalist and academician Von Langsdorff; but in 1818 there were officially only 1,535 dogs in the peninsula,[55] the discrepancy probably being attributable to exaggeration by Von Langsdorff and to the impact of the severe fish shortage of 1815–20. At Okhotsk in 1821 there were 1,200 to 1,500 dogs, and in Kamchatka in 1821–22 there were 2,208 dogs.[56] De Lesseps observed in 1787 that every Russian and Kamchadal in Kamchatka had no fewer than five dogs.[57] One man required at least six dogs, and they consumed some 20,000 fish per year, or enough to feed twelve persons. At Gizhiga in 1819 one *nart* (sled) of five to thirteen (usually ten) dogs required as much fish as twenty persons; and during the famine of 1815–20 Gizhiga's 1,500 dogs ate enough fish, meat, and fat to feed more than thrice the human population of the settlement.[58]

Finally, fish, game, berries, and the like simply did not satisfy the Russians of the Okhotsk Seaboard and the Kamchatka Peninsula; the state servitors, promyshlenniks, and others all wanted and needed foodstuffs from cultivated plants and tended livestock—rye bread, cabbage soup, cow's butter, etc.—which were nutritionally superior to "wild" foodstuffs. Fish did provide protein, calcium, iron, vitamin A, and the vitamin D that was vital in preventing rickets by compensating for the lack of sunshine. However, fish is lacking in vitamin C and low in vitamin B, fat, and carbohydrate. Although nuts provided additional fat, and berries, roots, and bulbs some vitamin C, grain was needed to supply more vitamin B and carbohydrate, and fruits and vegetables to supply more vitamin C and supplemental vitamin A. The deficiency of vitamin C (ascorbic acid) occasioned scurvy, especially in spring, while the dearth of vitamin B may have induced beriberi and pellagra; the debility resulting from these diseases may have contributed to the "indolence" remarked by many observers. Thus, customary foodstuffs were desirable on both psychological and physiological grounds.

Approaches to Provisionment

Wildlife, then, was precluded as a prime and reliable source of sustenance for Russians on the Okhotsk Seaboard and the Kamchatka Peninsula. There remained five possible, though not mutually exclusive, approaches to the problem of provisionment. One was the shipment by land and by water of foodstuffs from Eastern Siberia. This approach was both the first and the foremost response of the Russians, and throughout the period from 1639 to 1856 it was a sort of continuum that fluctuated in accordance with the success or failure of alternative approaches. One of these alternatives, and the only important one, was the striving for agricultural self-sufficiency in the Russian Far East through the local production of foodstuffs. This approach, first instituted in Kamchatka in the late 1710's, underwent its greatest development in the last half of the eighteenth century, particularly in Kamchatka. There were three other approaches: trade for foodstuffs with foreign countries, colonies, and companies, attempted toward the end of the eighteenth century and during the first half of the nineteenth; the shipment of provisions from European Russia by sea around the Horn or the Cape, tried during the first half of the nineteenth century; and the founding of extraterritorial agricultural colonies (in New Albion and on the Sandwich Islands) as food bases near the Russian Far East, also attempted during the first half of the nineteenth century. However, these three approaches, especially the last, were of minor importance to the Okhotsk Seaboard and the Kamchatka Peninsula, since their implementation was belated and their success was negligible. Overland provisionment and local agriculture remained the prime Russian responses to the region's problem of food supply.

PART II

Overland-Oversea Provisionment

4

INTRODUCTION

> "The Ilimsk Plowland was the chief supplier of all of northeastern Siberia, including Yakutsk, Okhotsk, and Kamchatka. It was the very foundation on which rested the holding of northeastern Siberia by the Russians."
>
> V. N. Sherstoboyev, "Zemledelie severnovo Predbaikalya," p. 281.

The principal response of the Russians to the food supply problem of the Okhotsk Seaboard and the Kamchatka Peninsula was overland (Irkutsk–Yakutsk–Okhotsk)-oversea (Okhotsk–Gizhiga–Kamchatka) provisionment.* At times this approach was supplemented but never supplanted by alternative responses, chiefly local agriculture; and the Russians invariably resorted to overland-oversea provisionment whenever other approaches failed. As late as 1788 neither the State Council nor the Ruling Senate could see any way of meeting the food needs of the region other than overland-oversea provisionment via Yakutsk.[1] From the very beginning of the Russian conquest of the region Cossacks and promyshlenniks subsisted largely on provisions that they carried from Yakutsk. In the seventeenth century grain was transported from Yakutsk to Okhotsk incidentally as part of the assortment of supplies accompanying state servitors and promyshlenniks, but with the opening of Kamchatka larger amounts of grain were sent separately.[2]

---

* Large amounts of state supplies other than grain (weapons, ammunition, military regalia, naval stores), as well as private merchandise (textiles, hardware, trinkets, tea, liquor, sugar, tobacco), were also conveyed overland-oversea to the Okhotsk Seaboard and the Kamchatka Peninsula. Around 1820 tobacco, tea, and sugar usually comprised one-third to one-half of all goods transported from Yakutsk to Okhotsk (Anonymous, "Vzglyad na torgovlyu, proizvodimuyu chrez Okhotsky port" ["A Glance at the Trade Conducted through Okhotsk Port"], *Seversny arkhiv,* pt. 7 [1823], p. 34). This merchandise was sold and bartered at summer fairs held at the major settlements; some Siberian merchants became wealthy from such fairs.

"Siberian Deliveries"

Overland-oversea provisionment was no innovation in meeting the food requirements of the Russian Far East; we have already seen that the problem of provisionment had been serious elsewhere in Siberia before Russian occupation of the Pacific Coast. During Yermak's campaign against Kuchum Khan in the early 1580's "the dearth of foodstuffs among the Russians in Siberia was so great that many of them died, and the rest ate the bodies of their dead comrades. . . ."[3] This situation prompted Moscow to send provisions regularly to Siberia from Russia proper, and for a century following Yermak's opening of Siberia the shipment of "Siberian grain supplies" from European Russia across the Urals by land and by water was one of the government's chief means of provisioning Siberia.

These "Siberian deliveries" involved the annual requisition by the government in winter of "cultivated supplies"—whole grain, groats, and flour—from the taxable peasants of certain settlements in Pomorye (northeastern European Russia), who also were obligated to cart these provisions in winter via Cherdyn to Verkhoturye on the eastern slopes of the Urals. They were further obligated to provide carpenters for building vessels for the spring shipment of the provisions to the rest of Siberia via the river network as far as Obdorsk and Mangazeya to the north, Anadyrsk and Nizhne-Kamchatsk to the east, and Udsk and Nerchinsk to the south[4] (Map 4). Large amounts of provisions were thus transported from Pomorye across the Urals into Siberia. For example, in 1596 the Siberian deliveries totaled 950 tons, 260 pounds of flour and groats, plus 71 tons, 1,100 pounds of flour and groats for Tara, Surgut, and Beryozov for use at "siege time"; in addition, 122 Cossacks and archers were sent to Siberia with 71 tons, 920 pounds of flour and groats as grain salary, as well as 36 tons of salt, 1,800 pounds of gunpowder, 1,800 pounds of lead, 540 pounds of wax, 14 reams of writing paper, 15 rolls of cloth, 28 gallons, 7 pints of wine, 25 pounds, 3 ounces of frankincense, 32 pounds, 6 ounces of caraway, and 5,340 rubles, 45 kopeks of money salary.[5] In the early 1600's ninety river boats, each carrying up to 36 tons of grain, left Verkhoturye every spring. In 1660 it was ordered to send 281 tons of flour and groats from Pomorye to Siberia and to build forty vessels annually at Verkhoturye, but actually 548 to 657 tons of flour and groats were sent on thirty vessels. During

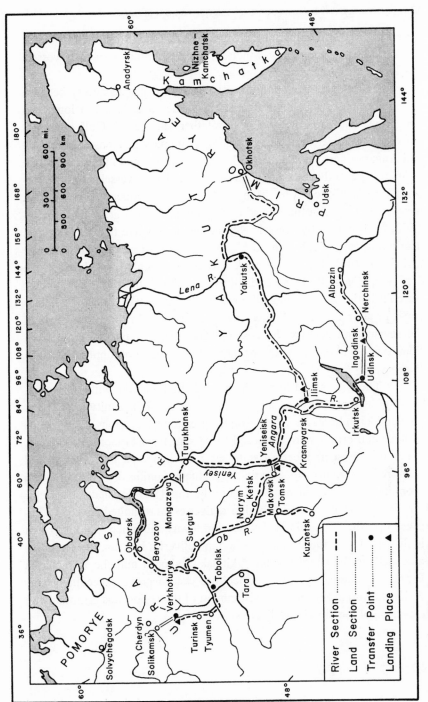

MAP 4. The "Siberian Deliveries."

the early 1670's the Siberian deliveries averaged 528 tons, 744 pounds of flour and groats annually, which required the building of forty vessels yearly at Verkhoturye.[6]

This system of supply eventually proved unsatisfactory because of human abuses and natural obstacles. The route was too long, too dangerous, and too costly. "Great weather" in the Ob Gulf often destroyed vessels, personnel, and cargoes, while passage along the Yenisey and Angara rivers was hampered by swift currents and many rapids.[7] In 1666–67 the authorities at Tobolsk reported that vessels went "carelessly" from Tobolsk to Mangazeya and consequently were often wrecked at sea, with the loss of many men and much grain and salt; in 1663, for instance, five vessels with almost ninety-five tons of flour and nearly four tons of salt were lost.[8] The transport of grain from Pomorye to Primorye (Pacific Coast) took five years, reaching Verkhoturye the first year, Yeniseisk the second, Ilimsk or Irkutsk the third, Yakutsk or Nerchinsk the fourth, and Okhotsk and Kamchatka the fifth; delays could prolong delivery another one or two years. In the second half of the seventeenth century the cost of transporting a pud of grain from Pomorye to Yakutia was ten or more times the price of a pud of grain in Pomorye.[9]

The delays and losses threatened the Sibiryaks with starvation, causing them at times "to suffer every want and impecunity, and to eat pine and larch bark. . . ."[10] In 1609, for example, 118 tons, 520 pounds of flour and groats were supposed to be sent from Pomorye to Siberia, but none was sent; Siberia's state servitors hungered in 1609–10 and clamored to return to Russia with their families.[11] This situation prompted the government to promote the rapid development of agriculture in Siberia itself, and Siberian deliveries were halted in 1685 "because now they till grain in the Siberian towns and much grain is grown in Siberia."[12] But the system of Siberian deliveries had already served as a model for the supply of the Okhotsk Seaboard and the Kamchatka Peninsula, where, moreover, agriculture was to prove exceedingly precarious. Overland-oversea provisionment of the region was essentially an extension of the Siberian deliveries.

Sources of Supply

Eastern Siberia was the general source of foodstuffs shipped overland-oversea to the Okhotsk Seaboard and the Kamchatka Peninsula. More specifically, there were four major regions of supply: (1) Yeniseisk *Uyezd* (District) around the confluence of the Yenisey and Angara rivers; (2) Ilimsk Uyezd astride the Lena (Ilimsk) Portage between the upper Lena and the middle Angara rivers; (3) Baikalia, comprising Prebaikalia, the uppermost reaches of the Angara River, and Transbaikalia, the lower basin of the Selenga River and the upper tributaries of the Amur River; and (4) the "big bend" of the Lena River, i.e., its middle reaches around Yakutsk, especially the Central Yakut or Vilyuy–Lena–Aldan Lowland. Yeniseisk and Ilimsk Uyezds and Baikalia were primarily sources of grain, while the Yakutsk region provided mainly livestock.

Yeniseisk Uyezd was the earliest source of supply. The district centered on the town of Yeniseisk, founded in 1619 just below the junction of the Yenisey and Angara rivers (Map 5). The number of state peasants and the amount of state plowland in the uyezd during the seventeenth century are shown in Table 2.

TABLE 2

Number of State Peasants and Amount of State Plowland in Yeniseisk Uyezd for Various Years between 1621 and 1699

Year	Number of State Peasants (Persons)	Amount of State Plowland (Acres)
1621	20	54
1630	53	143.1
1641	98	259.2
1654	207	356.4
1664	347	440.1
1674	423	469.8
1676	494	669.6
1699	928	1,193.4

SOURCE: A. N. Kopylov, "Yeniseisky zemledelchesky raion v seredine XVII v. i yevo znachenie dlya snabzheniya Vostochnoy Sibiri khlebom" ["The Yeniseisk Agricultural Region in the Middle of the XVIIth Century and Its Significance for the Supply of Eastern Siberia with Grain"], *Trudy Moskovskovo gosudarstvennovo istoriko-arkhivnovo instituta*, 10 (1957) : 117.

During the seventeenth century the proportion of state plowland to private plowland was 1 to 4.5, meaning that for every 4.5 *desyatinas* (12.15 acres) of their own plowland the state peasants were obligated to cultivate 1 desyatina (2.7 acres) for the state. Grain production (mostly rye and oats) from state plowland totaled 8,898 bushels in 1639, 8,548 bushels in 1651, 14,182 bushels in 1664, and 19,016 bushels in 1674. From the early 1640's considerable amounts of local grain began appearing on the Yeniseisk market, and in the middle 1640's Yeniseisk Uyezd began provisioning Krasnoyarsk, Ilimsk, and Yakutsk, as well as Yeniseisk itself. Yeniseisk last imported grain from Tobolsk in 1645. In 1646 Moscow decided to provision Yakutsk from Yeniseisk instead of from Tobolsk, although the frequent harvest failures and the small scale of agriculture in Yeniseisk Uyezd postponed full operation of this policy until the 1660's. In the middle of the century the *Sibirsky Prikaz*

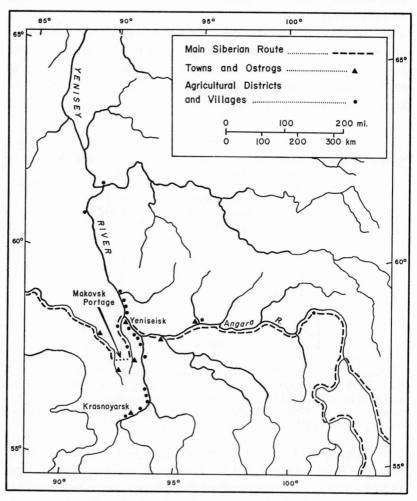

MAP 5.   Yeniseisk Uyezd.

(Siberian Office) regarded provisionment of Yakutia and Amuria as the chief task of the Yeniseisk Plowland, and during the last half of the century Yeniseisk Uyezd was the center of grain supply for Eastern Siberia.[13]

By the last quarter of the seventeenth century, however, northeastern Siberia was being provisioned by Ilimsk Uyezd (the Angara–Ilim–Lena district), established in the 1630's on the very eve of Russian penetration of the Okhotsk Seaboard (Map 6). For a hundred years the Ilimsk Plowland surpassed all other regions of Eastern Siberia in peasant population and cultivated acreage. Around 1700 it comprised 280 settle-

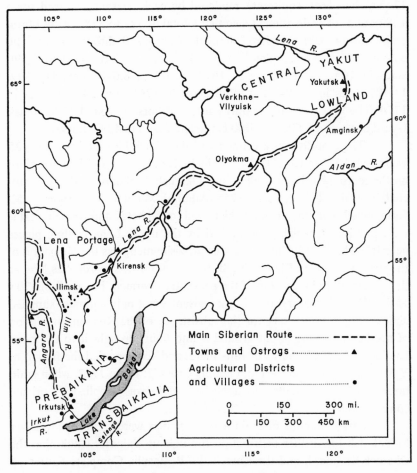

Map 6.   Ilimsk Uyezd, Baikalia, and the Yakutsk District.

ments, including seven ostrogs. Settlement size was small but household size was large; in 1710, 40 percent of the "villages" contained only one household, but 46 percent of the households included more than ten persons. Mixed farming (grains, livestock, vegetables) apparently prevailed, with rye being the chief cereal crop. During the 1640's the Ilimsk peasants had to cultivate one desyatina of grainland for the Tsar (using state seed) for every four desyatinas of grainland that they tilled for themselves; in addition, they had to surrender to the Tsar one-tenth of the harvest from their "extra" plowland, i.e., plowland exceeding the acreage allotted to them. During the 1730's, when Ilimsk Uyezd probably contained 6,000 to 7,000 peasants (5,236 in 1722 and 7,605 in 1745), the *obrok* (quitrent) rendered by each peasant averaged some 108 pounds of grain annually, so that a total of 324 to 378 tons of obrok grain was probably rendered annually from 1730 through 1739. The amount of peasant cropland in Ilimsk Uyezd totaled 4,050 to 4,590 acres in 1652, 5,916 acres in 1672, 8,100 to 8,640 acres in 1699, 11,497 acres in 1719–22, 17,798 acres in 1765, and 24,219 acres in 1774. The livestock were mainly cattle and horses; around 1720 Ilimsk Uyezd contained 5,600 to 6,000 cattle and 3,800 to 4,000 horses.[14]

The crop-livestock economy of the Ilimsk Plowland was for 125 years (ca. 1675 to ca. 1800) the principal source of provisions for all of northeastern Siberia, including the Okhotsk Seaboard and the Kamchatka Peninsula.[15] Around 1755 Admiral Myatlev, Governor of Siberia, noted that "the first and chief need [of Okhotsk and Kamchatka] is . . . provisions, which are supplied by the upper Lena landing places near Irkutsk. . . ."[16] Until 1772 this provisionment was the obligation of the state peasants of Ilimsk Uyezd. In Sherstoboyev's words, "as long as the system of grain taxation of the peasantry operated, i.e., until the 70's of the XVIIIth century, the Ilimsk peasantry not only annually supplied almost all grain necessary for the subsistence of the Russian population of northeastern Siberia but ground it into flour, brought it to the Lena landing places, built barks or rafts there, and accompanied the freight to Yakutsk and now and then to Yudoma Cross."[17] From 1772, when grain taxation of the peasants was abolished, grain was supplied by private contractors.[18]

Large amounts of grain and vegetables were shipped downriver to Yakutsk for further distribution throughout Yakutia, Chukotka, the Okhotsk Seaboard, and the Kamchatka Peninsula. Complete figures on such shipments are unavailable, but Table 3 indicates the quantities of

TABLE 3

State Grain Shipments Received by Ilimsk from Yeniseisk and Dispatched by Ilimsk
to Yakutsk for Various Years between 1652 and 1714

Year	Amount Received from Yeniseisk		Amount Dispatched to Yakutsk	
1652	155 tons, 1,652 lbs.		247 tons, 1,288 lbs.	
1653	31	28	unknown	
1654	22	640	188	740
1656	0	0	129	516
1657	84	12	125	848
1658	0	0	100	880
1663	231	420	107	992
1671	0	0	97	184
1675	41	368	78	1,248
1677	47	608	85	64
1691	0	0	67	1,026
1692	0	0	53	231
1693	0	0	73	1,188
1694	0	0	78	1,106
1695	0	0	48	314
1696	0	0	31	699
1697	0	0	64	641
1698	0	0	36	1,427
1699	0	0	110	1,331
1700	0	0	194	1,498
1701	0	0	209	440
1706	0	0	413	1,640
1709	0	0	432	864
1714	0	0	445	1,360

SOURCES: V. N. Sherstoboyev, *Ilimskaya pashnya* [*The Ilimsk Plowland*] (Irkutsk:
Irkutskoye oblastnoye gosudarstvennoye izdatelstvo, 1949), 1 : 571; Sibirsky prikaz,
TsGADA, f. 214, st. 1,424, fols. 169–175.

state grain Ilimsk received from Yeniseisk and dispatched to Yakutsk
("Yakutsk delivery" or "Lena delivery") in various years of the last
half of the seventeenth century and the first quarter of the eighteenth
century. From 1685 through 1688, 108 tons of rye flour alone were sent
annually to Yakutsk from Yeniseisk and Ilimsk. During the last quarter
of the seventeenth century Ilimsk Uyezd shipped 234 to 252 tons of
grain per year to Yakutsk.[19] The relatively small shipments during the
last half of the seventeenth century, as shown in Table 3, are probably
due to the concentration of expansion by the Russians of Yakutsk in the
Amur country, where grain could be exacted from the agricultural
natives. The sudden increase in the amount of grain shipped to Yakutsk

from Ilimsk at the end of the century probably reflects the needs of the Russian conquerors of Kamchatka, where native cultivation was nonexistent. During the eighteenth century 360 to 540 tons of grain from Ilimsk Uyezd were shipped down the Lena River to Yakutsk every year.[20]

Some fragmentary figures further illustrate the quantities of foodstuffs shipped to Yakutsk from the upper Lena. In 1701 the Siberian Office ordered the Governor of Ilimsk to collect from his jurisdiction and ship to Yakutsk 8,940 bushels of rye; about 7,500 bushels were collected and shipped.[21] In one month (April) of 1704 one village (Biryulsk) of Ilimsk Uyezd sent almost fifty-seven tons of grain to Yakutsk.[22] Some notion of the volume of vegetable shipments is gained from an incident around 1767 involving a late shipment of vegetables from Kirensk, long famous for its export of vegetables to Yakutsk and beyond; two barges headed for Yakutsk became ice-bound, and over nine tons of vegetables were lost, including 2,420 heads of cabbage, 124 buckets of cucumbers, 83 sacks of carrots and beets, 60 sacks of turnips, 10 sacks of radishes, 7,000 heads of garlic, and 12,000 onions.[23]

Ilimsk Uyezd began to decline as a source of provisions with the rise of Baikalia, where the Buryat natives were finally pacified during the last half of the seventeenth century. This subjugation rendered secure the strategic Angara–Ilim–Lena route between Western and Eastern Siberia and opened up Baikalia, which was climatically and pedologically more suitable for agriculture than the Ilimsk Plowland. Russian settlement in Eastern Siberia soon became concentrated in Baikalia, centered on Irkutsk (1652), especially during the consolidation of Russian power there following the expulsion of Russia from the Amur Valley in 1689. With the opening of the celebrated Nerchinsk silver mines in 1701 in Transbaikalia, some of the Ilimsk peasants were transferred there to provision the miners. A few others were resettled on the Okhotsk Seaboard and the Kamchatka Peninsula in the 1730's and 1740's. Then a series of severe crop failures during the second and third quarters of the eighteenth century further depreciated the Ilimsk Plowland, resulting in the abandonment of considerable farmland. The last important function of the Ilimsk Plowland was its supplying of Bering's first and second expeditions with men and materiel; for the second expedition it supplied over 1,753 tons of grain and nearly 132 tons of salt from 1733 through 1741.[24] By then the Angara–Ilim–Lena passage had been replaced by the Krasnoyarsk–Nizhne-Udinsk–Irkutsk route as the main link between Western and Eastern Siberia. Some agricultural settlement remained along the upper Lena, and this settlement even expanded downriver with the construction of the post road along the upper Lena in 1773 between Irkutsk and Yakutsk. By the end of the eighteenth century this agricultural settlement had reached Olyokma, but it remained patchy and unproductive, except at Kirensk, which continued to export surplus vegetables downriver.[25]

Baikalia, especially Prebaikalia, thus became around the middle of the eighteenth century the major source of supply (chiefly of grain) for the overland-oversea provisionment of the Okhotsk Seaboard and the Kamchatka Peninsula (Map 6). Thereafter, "most of the provisions needed for Okhotsk and Kamchatka krays were prepared at Irkutsk."[26] In Prebaikalia Russian agriculture was based on the limited but fertile wooded steppe, an extension of the southern steppe of Western Siberia. Originally an outlier of the Ilimsk Plowland, this agricultural tract developed steadily from the middle of the seventeenth century. It comprised numerous agricultural villages along the lower course of the Irkut River and the upper reaches of the Angara River, and by 1700 there were more than 470 peasant households.[27] Meanwhile, the wooded steppe of Transbaikalia was also being settled by Russian peasants. Russian agricultural production in Transbaikalia especially, but also in Prebaikalia, was augmented by the output of the agricultural Buryats. Chiefly cattle herders, the Buryats expanded their agricultural activities following the Russian conquest, and in 1802 they furnished Irkutsk with 83,440 bushels of grain.[28] Together, Russian and Buryat farmers produced sizable surpluses of grain for shipment to the Russian Far East. An 1806 "Project for Improving the State of Agriculture in Irkutsk Province" stated that "a large proportion of it [grain grown in Irkutsk *Okrug* (Township)] is sent in spring along the Lena to Kirensk, Olyokma, Verkhnevilyuisk, Yakutsk, Okhotsk, Nizhnekamchatsk, Zashiversk, and Zhigansk, to Utsk [Udsk] Ostrog, Gizhiga, Bolsheretsk, and newly discovered America," while an 1812 report on "The State of the Spread of Grain Cultivation in Irkutsk Province" declared that "all of vast Yakutsk Oblast [County], as well as Okhotsk and Kamchatka, are provided with the grain of Irkutsk and Nizhneudinsk uyezds."[29] A resident of Irkutsk recorded that in the early nineteenth century from Irkutsk "to Yakutsk are sent goods received from Russia, as well as various kinds of tea, sugar candy, rum and various wines, rye flour and wheat flour, rusks, cakes, groats, waxen candles, cow's butter and low-grade vegetable oil, tobacco, soap, grease candles."[30] She added that "many women [in Irkutsk] bake rye and wheat rusks of two sorts for Yakutsk, Okhotsk, and Kamchatka: plain and fancy."[31] Around the middle of the nineteenth century such shipments of provisions from Transbaikalia alone amounted annually to "a few thousand poods of rye, wheat, butter, cheese, tallow, and honey. . . ."[32]

The Yakutsk district was always the source of cattle (and horses) for the Okhotsk Seaboard and the Kamchatka Peninsula, supplied not by Russian but by Yakut stockmen (Map 6). Before the Russian conquest of Yakutia the Yakuts were primarily herders of cattle and horses and secondarily hunters, fishermen, and gatherers, but not cultivators. They had no sheep, goats, pigs, or poultry before the arrival of the Russians. In Russian documents of the seventeenth century the Yakuts are termed "horse people"; nevertheless, then and later they were chiefly herders of cattle. They did gradually adopt cultivation from the Russians, but it remained a minor occupation.[33] Some Russian peasants, centered at Amginsk, undertook cultivation, but with little success. The numerous lakes and streams of the Central Yakut Lowland teemed with fish and waterfowl, while the lush grasslands afforded abundant pasture and hay. Cattle rearing was especially pre-eminent in Aldan Okrug, which in 1784 contained more cattle than any other okrug of Yakutsk Province.[34] The Yakut livestock grazed year round, although during the winter (when the cold sometimes reaches −50° F. and lower) cattle and colts were stabled and hayed, but usually only overnight. The winter stables were small, cold, dark sheds, usually attached to the Yakut dwellings, and the hay was often low in quality. As a result of such harsh conditions, the small Yakut cattle and horses were hardy, but they yielded little milk. A Yakut cow produced an average of 780 quarts of milk a year, and for two to three winter months she gave no milk at all; mares were normally milked only in summer.[35] Both cattle and horses were eaten by the Yakuts,* but horses were used mainly for packing and riding, and cattle for milking. Horseflesh and *kumys* (fermented mare's milk) were the favorite meat and beverage of the Yakuts. Packing and riding by horse were the usual methods of Yakut travel, although oxen were used more than horses for drawing sledges bearing hay and wood in summer and winter.[36] It was common for observers to state that the wealth of the Yakuts consisted of cattle and horses.[37] Large

* Russian Orthodoxy proscribed the eating of horse meat by the faithful.

herds were not uncommon; in the 1820's many Yakuts owned up to a thousand and more horses and as many cattle. Around 1820 there were some 100,000 horses and about 125,000 cattle in Yakutsk Uyezd alone. Yakut horsebreeding declined in the nineteenth century, but at the end of the century Yakutia still contained 115,000 to 130,000 horses and 220,000 to 260,000 cattle.[38] Unfortunately, as in the case of grain shipments from Baikalia, figures are not available for the number of cattle and horses and the amount of butter and cheese sent from Yakutia to the Okhotsk Seaboard and the Kamchatka Peninsula.

Grain and livestock were bought from peasants or contracted from merchants when obrok and *barshchina* (*corvée*) grain was insufficient. Private contractors first supplied Yakutsk with grain in 1684, and from 1688 through 1697 one contractor supplied 108 tons of grain yearly. Most private contractors, however, were small traders who sold 3,600 to 10,800 pounds of grain each. Contracted provisionment was exceptional rather than usual; at the end of the seventeenth century only 10 percent of the state's acquisition of some 4,544 tons of Siberian grain came from contractors, while 90 percent came from peasants.[39]

5

ROUTES AND CARRIERS

"The Lena River is in all respects the national road to Yakutsk, Okhotsk, Kolyma, Kamchatka, and America."
N. Shch., *Poyezdka v Yakutsk,* p. 106.

From Irkutsk and Ilimsk to Yakutsk

At first mainly from Ilimsk Uyezd and later mostly from Baikalia provisions (chiefly flour and groats) were floated down the Lena River to Yakutsk from the "upper Lena places." This passage was faster and cheaper than land transport over the Yakutsk Track linking Irkutsk and Yakutsk along the Lena, which, moreover, was not completed until 1773. Frozen or unfrozen, the Lena, one of the world's great rivers, was an adequate waterway. Around 1755 Governor Myatlev asserted that "to Yakutsk the Lena River is suitable and quickly navigated. . . ."[1] Usually ample in depth and width and free of rapids, waterfalls, and zigzags, the 2,500-mile Lena was navigable as far upstream as Kachuga, about 113 miles from its source in the high mountains abutting the western shore of Lake Baikal. The Lena was not rapid, save briefly during spring breakup, yet its current was strong enough to nullify the effect of headwinds on riverboats. Its level was low for only a short time between spring breakup and summer rains. Navigation began in early May and ended in late October, the upper course above Yakutsk freezing in late October and melting in early April.[2] In 1784 an official topographer reported that "at low water its current is gentle; its bottom is sandy; there are no rapids whatsoever; in places the banks are rocky and mountainous. . . ."[3] Peter Dobell, an American in the service of the Russian Government, called the Lena "one of the safest navigable rivers of its size in the world. . . ."[4] And another admirer, the exiled Decembrist and writer Bestuzhev (who wrote as Marlinsky), in 1828 declared it "a navigable road in summer and the sole route in winter; it is the Volga of Eastern Siberia."[5]

All goods sent from Russia to Yakutsk, Okhotsk, and Kamchatka passed through Irkutsk; goods from Baikalia were prepared for shipment at Irkutsk during the winter by the government and by private merchants,* as well as by the Russian-American Company. Flour, groats, tobacco, liquor, gunpowder, and manufactures were packed in bags, boxes, and flasks, which in turn were encased in rawhide in order to keep the contents dry during river passages and rainy spells.[6] In the early 1800's there was a special group of artisans in Irkutsk called *shiryalshchiks* (wrappers), who "wrap in hide goods sent to Okhotsk and Yakutsk. . . ."[7] The contents of each container were adjusted to weigh no more than ninety pounds so as to facilitate their later conveyance by pack horses on the Yakutsk–Okhotsk Track.[8]

Sometime in May, depending upon the date of the spring breakup, these goods were carted northward from Irkutsk 145 to 160 miles over the Yakutsk Track across the Bratsky Steppe to the head of navigation on the Lena at Kachuga Landing. As described by one Ivan Miller in 1814: "The settlement of Kachuga has about fifty households with a wooden church. The inhabitants are engaged in stock keeping and grain cultivation. At the beginning of the month of May many merchants gather here, coming with goods from Irkutsk and farther provinces in order to go on barges at high water to Yakutsk and beyond. At the same time many necessities are sent from here to Okhotsk and Kamchatka by the state, as well as necessities for the North-American settlements by the [Russian-American] Company."[9] In the early 1830's goods worth almost a million rubles arrived annually at Kachuga from Irkutsk.[10] The

---

* Some Irkutsk merchants became wealthy from provisionment contracts with the government (James Holman, *Travels through Russia, Siberia, Poland, Austria, Saxony, Prussia, Hanover* . . . [London: George B. Whittaker, 1825], 2 : 104–105). Such a merchant was Sibiryakov, onetime mayor of Irkutsk, who in 1786 received a contract from Governor-General Jacobi to provision the Billings Expedition; Sibiryakov undertook to deliver to Verkhne-Kolymsk an eighteen-month supply of provisions for 100 men and to Okhotsk a three-year supply of provisions for 250 men (Martin Sauer, *An Account of a Geographical and Astronomical Expedition to the Northern Parts of Russia* . . . [London: T. Cadell, Jr. and W. Davies, 1802], p. 25). The Ushakov brothers of Irkutsk also prospered from the provisionment of northeastern Siberia around 1700 (O. I. Kashik, "Torgovlya v Vostochnoy Sibiri v XVII-nachale XVIII vv." ["Trade in Eastern Siberia in the XVIIth-To the Beginning of the XVIIIth Centuries"], in *Voprosy istorii Sibiri i Dalnevo Vostoka,* ed. Akademiya nauk SSSR, Sibirskoye otdelenie [Novosibirsk: Izdatelstvo Sibirskovo otdeleniya AN SSSR, 1961], p. 191).

freight was loaded onto river vessels, which were floated 1,500 to 1,700 miles "down along the great river Lena" to Yakutsk. Freight from Ilimsk Uyezd was sent downriver from various river ports, like Zhigalovo and Ust-Kut, 100 miles and 300 miles, respectively, below Kachuga. Provisions were carted to these landings in winter from villages throughout the uyezd.

Several kinds of bargelike river vessels were used to transport provisions downstream. From the 1640's until the second quarter of the eighteenth century probably six to seven hundred river transports were built at the landings of Ilimsk Uyezd.[11] *Doshcheniks* (from *doska*, meaning "board" or "plank") were the mainstay of Lena traffic. They were flat-bottomed, single-decked, one-masted cargo vessels of timber, with a single square sail, a deck stove, and a stern rudder. Pointed in bow and in stern, doshcheniks were rowed and steered with up to ten sweeps (long oars), each sweep operated by two men. In the second quarter of the nineteenth century they measured 70 to 105 feet in length, 14 to 28 feet in width, and 4⅔ to 7 feet in height; they carried as few as 126 and as many as 271 tons but usually 144 to 180 tons of cargo. In 1657 alone eighty-eight doshcheniks were launched in Ilimsk Uyezd, including fifty at Ust-Kut.[12]

Barkas were essentially huge, square boxes, being flat-bottomed, straight-sided, four-cornered, deckless, unmasted cargo vessels, crudely made from stout hewn timber, with four to ten oars, a stern rudder, a deck stove, and a huge bin covered with a pitched roof and containing two compartments for holding flour, groats, salt, and the like. They measured 35 to 63 feet in length, 28 to 42 feet in width, and 6 to 7 feet in height and carried 108 to 180 tons of freight. Often these "floating granaries" carried only flour. Each barka was accompanied by one pilot and five hands, as well as by several Cossack overseers.[13]

Pavozkas (or *pauzkas* or *pavukas*), which transported cargo or passengers, were keelless and undecked vessels with a pointed bow and a pointed stern, sails, four oars, and a rudder. They measured up to 56 feet in length, up to 14 feet in width, and up to 3½ feet in height and carried 21 to 27 tons of cargo. Each pavozka required some eight men. There were actually two kinds of pavozkas: "passing" pavozkas, which went directly to Yakutsk with goods for Yakutsk, Okhotsk, and elsewhere, and "trading" pavozkas, which stopped at each settlement along the river to trade.[14]

Kayuks (cargo vessels with a gable roof and a pointed bow), *kochas* (single-decked vessels with sails and oars), and *lodkas* (wherries) also hauled freight down the Lena. Each lodka carried 18 to 36 tons of freight. Peasants living along the Lena between Yakutsk and Ilimsk Uyezd sometimes shipped foodstuffs to Yakutsk in large bins on simple rafts (*plots*) made from pine or larch, each raft handled by two to three men. Rafts plying from Ilimsk Uyezd to Yakutsk were managed by one pilot and four hands, plus several Cossack supervisors, and carried 25 to 32½ tons of freight. The first steamboat, incidentally, did not appear on the Lena until 1856.[15]

Flour, groats, salt and the like were loaded on barkas in bulk and covered with boards, while other goods were loaded on pavozkas and lodkas in bags, sacks, boxes, and baskets.[16]

From 1655 or 1656 these river vessels were built by certain state servitors called "boat carpenters," and from 1725 they were built by peasants. After 1772, when the peasants of Ilimsk Uyezd were freed from the obligation of building vessels and shipping grain to Yakutsk, peasant and merchant contractors transported grain downriver. Each vessel had a pilot and several hands, hired at the upper Lena landings. A pilot was necessary because the Lena's channel shifted every spring; the hands were needed to remove the vessel from shoals and to row it through channels.* The grain merchants (*busovshchiks*—probably derived from *bus,* meaning "flour dust") who plied vessels to Yakutsk went from village to village in Ilimsk Uyezd buying or bartering for flour and then selling it along the Lena. The riverboats—built during the winter—left the upper Lena landings "at floodwater," that is, at high water, in May and June[17] (Table 4). In late May of 1830 one observer found forty pavozkas and barkas at Kachuga awaiting the peak of the spring runoff.[18] They proceeded in strings of two to four vessels. It took them fourteen to forty days to go from Kachuga to Yakutsk, depending upon the depth of the water, the rapidity of the current, and the speed of the vessels, as well as the skill of the handlers. By contrast, the return trip upstream (loaded) took two months by means of arduous "tracking" (cordelling) with men and horses.[19]

In the middle of the seventeenth century fifteen to eighteen doshcheniks and eight kochas annually descended the Lena to Yakutsk

---

* Around 1830 each pavozka pilot was paid 70 to 100 rubles and each hand 30 to 50 rubles for the trip from Kachuga to Yakutsk (N. Shch. [Shchukin], *Poyezdka v Yakutsk* [*Journey to Yakutsk*] [St. Petersburg: Tipografiya Konrada Vingebera, 1833], pp. 27, 63–64, 112).

TABLE 4

Riverboats Departing from Ust-Kut Landing for Various Years between 1767 and 1781

Year	Start of Navigation	April	May	June	July	August	September	October	Total
1767	May 15		59	4	3	3	3	2	74
1774	May 11		70	4	0	0	0	0	74
1776	May 12		65	43	6	8	13	1	136
1778	May 10		35	3	4	6	6	0	54
1779	April 25	10	16	12	2	7	10	2	59
1780	May 8		26	6	2	4	10	7	55
1781	May 4	___	28	11	7	9	8	0	63
Total		10	299	83	24	37	50	12	515

SOURCE: Sherstoboyev, *Ilimskaya pashnya*, 2 : 488.

from the upper Lena landings with grain, salt, and timber. In 1682 alone nine doshcheniks, five lodkas, two barkas, and one kocha hauled grain from Ilimsk Uyezd to Yakutsk. From 1682 through 1697 a total of 134 grain vessels (112 doshcheniks and kayuks and 22 barkas) went from the Ilimsk landings to Yakutsk. During the middle of the second half of the eighteenth century about seventy-four vessels transported roughly 1,687 tons of freight a year downriver to Yakutsk[20] (Table 5). At the

TABLE 5

Number of Vessels and Amount of Freight Sent down the Lena River to Yakutsk for Various Years between 1767 and 1781

Year	Number of Vessels	Amount of Freight
1767	74	2,843 tons, 200 lbs.
1774	74	unknown
1776	136	2,764 1,240
1778	54	1,405 1,600
1779	59	1,224
1780	55	988 400
1781	63	896 920

SOURCE: Sherstoboyev, *Ilimskaya pashnya*, 2 : 487–489.

end of the century it was reported that in June, when the fair at Yakutsk began, forty to fifty barkas and several pavozkas with grain, and three to four doshcheniks with Russian and Chinese goods arrived there from upriver.[21] Around 1815 barkas and pavozkas hauled nine to fifty-four tons of freight downriver to Yakutsk annually. In 1830 forty barkas and pavozkas arrived at Yakutsk with 1,800 tons of flour alone, which was reckoned insufficient.[22]

Most of the freight shipped downriver to Yakutsk was wheat, rye, and oat flour, barley and buckwheat groats, rye malt, whole oats, and rusks. The remainder included various commodities like honey, hops, soap, salt, cedar nuts, coarse cloth, hemp, and so forth. In the mid-seventeenth century Yakutsk, on the average, annually received 450 to 540 tons of grain via the Lena and annually dispatched 1,080 tons of grain and salt on twenty-eight doshcheniks to ostrogs and zimvoyes on the north and east.[23] In the late 1740's the government ordered that Yakutsk be supplied annually with 1,208 tons, 959 pounds of grain; and, in 1757, 1,286 tons, 200 pounds of grain were shipped downriver to Yakutsk on fifty rafts.[24] In some years at the beginning of the nineteenth century Yakutsk imported up to 1,800 tons of flour alone. Altogether, Yakutsk annually received 72 to 450 tons of grain during the 1600's, 360 to 540 tons during the 1700's (up to 1,800 tons during the late 1700's), and 1,800 to 5,400 and more tons during the 1800's.[25] The sources of supply, according to an astronomer's account of 1769, were Irkutsk and Ilimsk uyezds and peasants living along the Lena.[26]

Yakutsk in 1737 stood on the left bank of the "big bend" of the Lena and had 249 houses, 99 *yurtas* (native dwellings), 60 shops (stalls), and 28 warehouses. By 1784 it had grown to include 69 storehouses for provisions alone, plus 332 houses, 25 yurtas, 100 shops, a bazaar, 9 saloons, 3 churches, 3 smithies, 2 almshouses, a hospital, a school, a post office, and a police station.[27] In the early 1830's Termin commented that "here are unloaded goods shipped from Kachuga Landing, such as: grain, salt, wine, tea, and various other Russian goods, imported for the provisionment of both the inhabitants of Yakutsk Oblast [Yakutia] itself and the inhabitants of Okhotsk Town and Uyezd, and part is shipped to Kamchatka."[28] In 1769, 150,000 rubles worth of freight was brought down the Lena to Yakutsk, half of which was forwarded to Okhotsk and Kamchatka.[29]

Upon unloading, state goods were stored in "magazines" (government warehouses), while private goods were put in warehouses and shops. The storehouses at Yakutsk for cargo bound for Okhotsk and Kamchatka were situated at the landing on the riverbank. The goods remaining at Yakutsk were sold and bartered at the summer fair, when all merchants were allowed to lease public shops for selling their wares;

before and after the fair, however, such vending was monopolized by half a dozen burghers at high prices.[30] Grain and rusks were the chief items of Yakutsk Oblast's trade as observed in 1830;[31] in 1784 it was officially reported that "of the Yakutskians [Yakutsk traders] the poorer sell victuals and the richer go to Okhotsk Port, driving cattle there and conveying sugar, groats, ham, cow's butter, and fat. . . ."[32] In addition, of course, the state (and from 1799 the Russian-American Company) transported provisions to Okhotsk from Yakutsk.

Westbound goods (chiefly furs) unloaded at Yakutsk were reloaded on doshcheniks, lodkas, and sometimes pavozkas for rowing and towing upstream. At Ust-Kut furs destined for the state and the fairs of Western Siberia were discharged for transshipment over the Ilimsk Portage to the Yenisey system; at Kachuga furs destined for the Chinese market were unloaded for transshipment to Kyakhta via Irkutsk. Around 1815 such upstream traffic totaled over five tons annually. In the early 1830's up to 3,000,000 rubles worth of furs for transshipment were sent annually from Yakutsk upriver: to Ust-Kut 200,000 to 300,000 rubles worth and to Kachuga 2,500,000 rubles worth. Doshcheniks and lodkas (and sometimes pavozkas) were returned upstream from Yakutsk; barkas (and sometimes pavozkas) were dismantled at Yakutsk and sold for firewood or construction wood.[33]*

From Yakutsk to the Okhotsk Seaboard

Goods brought down the Lena to Yakutsk, apart from those intended for Yakutsk and vicinity, were dispatched thence to the ostrog of Udsk, the port of Okhotsk, the commissariats (tax-collecting points) of Verkhne-Vilyuisk, Zashiversk, and Sredne-Kolymsk, and the Yakut settlements.[34] From Yakutsk to the Okhotsk Seaboard provisions were conveyed via five routes. Three of these linked Yakutsk and Okhotsk: a spring-and-summer land route, a spring-and-summer water route, and a winter land route.

By far the most important of these three routes, and indeed of all

---

* In the early 1830's along the upper Lena a doshchenik cost 400 to 700 rubles, a barka 300 to 500 rubles, and a pavozka 150 to 300 rubles (Major Termin, "Kratkoye obozrenie reki Leny i sudokhodstva po onoy" ["Brief Survey of the Lena River and of Navigation on It"], *Zhurnal putey soobshcheniya*, no. 32 [1835], p. 83).

five, was the spring-and-summer land route, commonly called the Ya-kutsk–Okhotsk Track or simply the Okhotsk Track or Aldan Track (Map 7). This route was probably never a single, well-defined trail, except in certain places, chiefly between Yakutsk and the Aldan River; as late as the end of the eighteenth century, at least, it was irregular and ill-defined.[35] The trail varied from time to time in accordance with the vagaries of the weather and the memories of the Yakut guides and lead horses. Lyudmila Rikord, the wife of the new Commandant of Kam-chatka, remarked at Yakutsk in 1817 that "here there were not what we call roads: the horses wander at will, choosing paths in various direc-tions. By such an unsuitable route were supplied and provisioned two oblasts, Kamchatka and Okhotsk."[36] Horse bones and horse hairs (hung on branches by the pagan Yakuts to propitiate the forest spirits) not only recalled the hardships of the horses and the superstitions of the Yakuts but also marked the trail, for there were no guideposts.[37] In general, the Yakutsk–Okhotsk Track, trending northwest–southeast, de-scribed a more or less direct path between the two places, as shown on Map 7. It measured 600 to 750 miles in length. Travelers were invaria-bly impressed by the variegated landscape. Between Yakutsk and the Aldan River the track crossed undulating, grassy lowland, which con-trasted sharply with the rugged, forested mountains between the Aldan River and Yudoma Cross and the dissected, wooded plateau between Yudoma Cross and the Okhota River.

It is uncertain when the Yakutsk–Okhotsk Track was first uti-lized. At first the spring-summer passage was accomplished primarily via the river route. Toward the end of the seventeenth century, however, the land route had become the main link between the Lena River and the Okhotsk Sea. The land passage became even more important with the discovery of the sea route to Kamchatka from Okhotsk in 1716–17; thereupon the Yakutsk–Okhotsk–Kamchatka route replaced the old Yakutsk–Verkhoyansk–Nizhne-Kolymsk–Anadyrsk–Kamchatka link. At first the land route was simply a pathway used by Cossacks, who traveled light. The need for a more substantial route did not arise until the regular sending of large numbers of personnel and large amounts of supplies. This need first occurred in 1718 in connection with the Great Kamchatka Detail (1716–19), an abortive expedition to explore and to pacify the Okhotsk Seaboard, Kamchatka, and Chukota, which failed largely because of difficulties with supply. In 1715 a horse trail had been initiated between Yakutsk and Okhotsk. In 1718 the Great Kamchatka

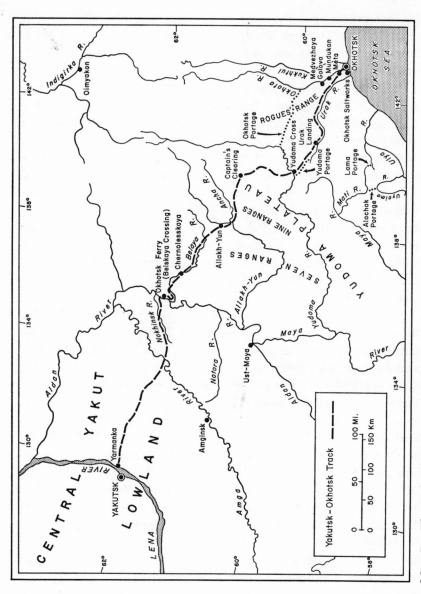

MAP 7. The Yakutsk–Okhotsk Track.

Detail began construction of a road from the Notora River to Okhotsk and founded several way stations along the route; for example, Captain Abyshtov established ten cabins, six warehouses, and two smithies at one spot, which was thereafter called Captain's Clearing.[38]

The Yakutsk–Okhotsk Track developed further at the time of Bering's two expeditions, which utilized both the land and river passages between Yakutsk and Okhotsk. In 1732 the land passage was reconnoitered and measured by the surveyor Shatilov. That fall the pilot Birev with thirty-two men was ordered to clear a track twenty-one feet wide from Yakutsk to Yudoma Cross for unrestricted horseback travel and to build a corduroy road for vehicles thirty-five feet wide from Yudoma Cross to the Urak River and twenty-one feet wide from the Urak River to Okhotsk, with corduroy over quagmires and ferries or bridges at river crossings. Birev's party managed to clear a road only from Yudoma Cross to Okhotsk. Receiving neither reinforcements nor provisions, the men starved in 1733 and 1734; some members deserted to Yakutsk, and eight of them died en route.[39]

Then, in the spring of 1733, Bering was commanded to establish permanent bimonthly post communication between Yakutsk, Okhotsk, and Kamchatka. Accordingly, in 1734 the sailor Belyayev with thirty men widened the track from Yakutsk eastward for a distance of 113 miles, building bridges over streams and marshes. Two years later a trail was cleared between Yudoma Cross and Urak Landing. The entire track was surveyed that year by Baskakov for the Second Kamchatka Expedition, and Bering himself established way stations with Yakuts and horses along it—although they were soon deserted. From 1736 the land route from Yakutsk to Okhotsk was preferred to the river route because the latter went largely upstream and encountered many rapids, so that numerous hands were required. By 1741 everyone used the land passage in spring and summer, although its condition deteriorated following the Second Kamchatka Expedition.[40]

Thus, the importance of the Yakutsk–Okhotsk Track dates largely from the Second Kamchatka Expedition. Thereafter the track was by far the foremost route between Yakutsk and the Okhotsk Seaboard. Its pre-eminence continued until the middle of the nineteenth century, when it was neglected as a result of the transfer of the Russian-American Company's factory from Okhotsk to Ayan in 1844 and the removal by the government of the port facilities of Okhotsk to Ayan and Petropavlovsk in 1850–51. Even then, at least for a while, goods bound from Yakutsk to Ayan continued to be freighted over the Yakutsk–Okhotsk Track, since on the upstream river route from Yakutsk to Ayan the Aldan and especially the Maya River were lined with trees, boulders, and bogs that severely hampered tracking.[41]

The river passage between Yakutsk and Okhotsk was at first, at least, also an important spring-and-summer route, often being used in the seventeenth century[42] (Figures 6 and 7). Originally there were three river passages: the Lena–Aldan–Maya–Lama Portage–Ulya or Urak route, the Lena–Aldan–Maya–Yudoma Portage–Urak route, and the Lena–Aldan–Maya–Yudoma–Okhota Portage–Okhota route. As early as 1646 the Cossack Kolobov, a member of Moskvitin's expedition, recommended use of the Lena–Aldan–Maya–Lama Portage–Ulya river route, declaring that the trip could be accomplished in doshcheniks in about nine weeks.[43] The first and second routes were evidently the two main passages followed by Cossacks and promyshlenniks in the seventeenth century, the first being dominant in the middle of the century and the second in the last half of the century. In 1715 Maksimov and Antipin surveyed the Lena–Aldan–Maya–Yudoma–Urak–Okhota route, measuring distances between places and lengths of portages, determining the names of rivers followed by the route, and deciding which trees could be used in shipbuilding and what boats could be portaged. Further development of the river passage was generated by the opening in 1716–17 of the sea route to Kamchatka;[44] for example, the river route was preferred by the Great Kamchatka Detail, undoubtedly because of the "great difficulty" that it experienced on the land route. In early 1727 the Privy Council itself recommended that freight be sent from Yakutsk to Okhotsk via the river route: "down the Lena, up the Aldan, Maya, and Yudoma rivers to Yudoma Portage, and across Yudoma Portage to the Urak River by horses, and via the Urak to the sea. . . ."[45]

About this time variations developed at both ends of the river passage. Instead of freight being shipped 133 miles down the Lena to the Aldan and 667 miles up the Aldan to the Maya, it was sometimes conveyed faster and cheaper 200 to 220 miles overland from Yakutsk to the Aldan via the Yakutsk–Okhotsk Track to Okhotsk Ferry or, more commonly, 200 miles overland southeastward via Amginsk to Ust-Maya for transshipment upstream. And at the eastern end of the river route goods unloaded at Yudoma Cross were sometimes hauled 48 to 60 miles overland to Urak Landing on the upper Urak and thence boated 100 to 130 miles downstream to the Okhotsk Sea and 15 miles along the seacoast to Okhotsk or conveyed 144 to 220 miles overland via the last leg of the Yakutsk–Okhotsk Track from Yudoma Cross to Okhotsk.[46]

The river passage from Yakutsk to Okhotsk reached the peak of its importance during the time of Bering's two expeditions. Most of the expeditions' supplies, especially the heavy items, were shipped via the river route, mainly via the Yakutsk–Ust-Maya and Yudoma Cross–Urak Landing variation. Along this route Bering constructed way stations, storehouses, landing places (e.g., Ust-Maya), and vessels. In 1731 the new commandant of Okhotsk, Skornyakov-Pisarev, who had not yet arrived, was ordered to send provisions "from Yakutsk by water to [Yudoma] Cross. . . ."[47] And in 1740 Steller advised Gmelin, a fellow member of the Second Kamchatka Expedition, to travel from Yakutsk to Okhotsk via the river route from Ust-Maya to Yudoma Cross (while sending empty horses ahead) in order to avoid the "injury and expense" of the land passage.[48]

Following the Second Kamchatka Expedition, very little is heard of the river route, so overshadowed was it by the Yakutsk–Okhotsk Track. The faster and cheaper land route forced the virtual abandonment of the river route.[49] Since most of the traffic between Yakutsk and Okhotsk went from west to east, river transport was mostly upstream, involving laborious rowing and tracking by men and horses.* Also, the river route was indirect, being more than half again as long as the Yakutsk–Okhotsk Track. Moreover, the rivers were torrents in the spring and trickles in the summer, so that navigation was difficult in both seasons. The Urak, for instance, was too shallow to navigate in summer; one source even claims that it flowed only in spring and during rainstorms. Frequently boats were wrecked and loads were lost on the Urak,

---

* In 1737 Krasheninnikov boated down the Yudoma from Yudoma Cross to the Maya in three days, whereas boats took five to six weeks to perform the same trip upstream (Krasheninnikov, *Opisanie zemli Kamchatki,* p. 531). De Lesseps in 1788 took four days to raft down the same stretch. At the Maya he met nine boats belonging to the Billings Expedition under the command of Vitus Bering's grandson, who expected that tracking the reverse journey would take six weeks (M. De Lesseps, *Travels in Kamtschatka, during the Years 1787 and 1788* [London: J. Johnson, 1790], 2 : 295). On the other hand, rafts floated down the Urak from Urak Landing to the Okhotsk Sea in seventeen hours with ease and without oars (G. P. [*sic:* G. F.] Muller, *Voyages et découvertes faites par les Russes* . . . , trans. C. G. F. Dumas [Amsterdam: Marc Michel Rey, 1766], 1 : 209; S. [*sic:* G. F.] Muller, *Voyages from Asia to America* . . . [London: T. Jeffereys, 1761], p. 25; Waxell, *Russian Expedition to America,* p. 56).

while the passage from its mouth up the coast to Okhotsk was safely navigable only in spring, when the ice was offshore and the intermediate strip of open water was calm.[50] In 1743 river transport between Yakutsk and Okhotsk was discontinued by the Yakutsk governors because rates had risen to 2 rubles, 50 to 70 kopeks per pud.[51] Captain Chirikov recommended in vain in 1746 that provisions be sent to Okhotsk via the river route (which would have entailed the use of six boats on the Yakutsk–Yudoma Cross section, twenty-five men and fifty reindeer on the Yudoma Cross–Urak Landing portage, and twenty rafts on the Urak Landing–Okhotsk stretch).[52] Provisions, which formed the bulk of the freight conveyed from Yakutsk to Okhotsk, could be divided into smaller and lighter packages quite easily for transport by land, and they ran less risk of damage from soakage or deterioration than during a prolonged trip by water. It was still cheaper, however, as Bering noted, to send heavy freight (like anchors and cannon) to Okhotsk via the river route than overland.[53] This fact probably explains Governor Soimonov's calculation that the state lost more than 500,000 rubles from 1743 through 1759 by not using the river route.[54]

The river route was not completely abandoned, however. In 1760 Governor Soimonov recommenced river transport, and during the early 1760's up to 1,080 tons of freight were shipped annually from Yakutsk to Okhotsk by river at a cost of sixty to seventy kopeks per pud.[55] This temporary turnabout was probably caused by the inability and refusal of Yakut outfitters to provide horses for land transport. Although the "secret expedition" (1764–70) of Krenitsyn and Levashev found the land route to be preferable to the river route, the Billings Expedition (1785–94) utilized the river passage, even succeeding for the first time in transporting freight from Irkutsk to Okhotsk by water in one season.[56] But in 1802 the naval officer Davydov found that the Yakutsk–Okhotsk river route, "attended besides with difficulties and protraction, has been completely abandoned by reason of the usually large loss."[57] In 1784 it was officially reported that it was better to go from Yakutsk to Okhotsk by land than by water because the river route was too long and so uninhabited that in emergencies horses and hands could not be procured en route.[58] Even the furs received at Okhotsk were not shipped to Yakutsk via the rapid downstream river route,* apparently because of the risk of soakage.

* De Lesseps, for example, rafted down the Yudoma in 1788 at the rate of six to nine m.p.h. (De Lesseps, *Travels in Kamtschatka,* 2 : 294).

Yakutsk and Okhotsk were also linked by a winter route, which at first was identical with the spring-and-summer route; but sometime during the eighteenth century the Yakutsk–Oimyakon–Okhotsk route, measuring 793 miles, became the winter communication. The first half of this track approximated the present Yakutsk–Oimyakon Road, while the last half ran southward from Oimyakon to the upper reaches of the Okhota River, which it followed to Okhotsk. Then in the early nineteenth century the winter passage was rerouted along the spring-and-summer track, which was only half as long as the Yakutsk–Oimyakon–Okhotsk route and less subject to blizzards. In any case, the winter route was used only by the post; apparently no provisions were transported over it.[59]

Yakutsk was also linked with the Okhotsk Seaboard at Udsk on the left bank of the Uda River, forty-seven to sixty miles upstream. The Yakutsk–Udsk route, which was open from late April until October, measured 698 to 933 miles via Amginsk, Kompaneisk, and Uchur Crossing[60] (Map 8). This link was an indefinite route without way stations and post horses, and along it, the geographer-historian Shchukin noted, "in summer mud and marsh and in winter frost and deep snow stop the traveler at every step."[61] The principal items sent to Udsk were flour, rusks, and butter.[62]

The fifth route connecting the middle Lena and the Okhotsk Seaboard was the Yakutsk–Ayan route, the successor to the Yakutsk–Okhotsk Track. The Yakutsk–Ayan route did not materialize until 1844, when, as we have said, the Russian-American Company transferred its Okhotsk factory to Ayan (which was officially renamed Ayan Port two years later) and the government followed suit by transferring its port facilities partly to Ayan. Although the Yakutsk–Ayan route, which measured 775 to 925 miles, was longer than the Yakutsk–Okhotsk Track, in the middle 1840's Russian-American Company goods were transported from Ayan to Yakutsk in sixteen days but from Okhotsk to Yakutsk in no less than twenty-four days. The Yakutsk–Ayan route comprised three sections: the vehicular road from Yakutsk to Ust-Maya, 235 to 255 miles; the river passage from Ust-Maya to Nelkan, about 400 miles; and the horse trail from Nelkan to Ayan, some 150 miles across the rugged range of the Dzhugdzhur (meaning "big bulge" in Tungus) (Map 8). In 1867 the route was closed, and most of its settlers were transferred to Amuria.[63]

Of the five routes linking Yakutsk and the Okhotsk Seaboard,

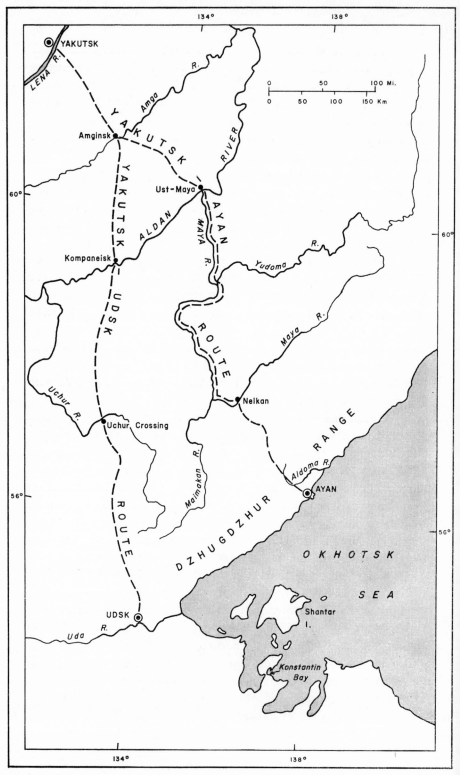

MAP 8.   The Yakutsk–Udsk and Yakutsk–Ayan Routes.

then, the Yakutsk–Okhotsk Track was by far the most important. It was this route that handled the bulk of the foodstuffs transported to the Okhotsk Seaboard and the Kamchatka Peninsula under overland-oversea provisionment.[64] It was reported in 1822 that by far the majority of goods shipped eastward from Yakutsk went to Okhotsk.[65] And grain was the foremost item sent from Yakutsk to Okhotsk and beyond by the state, and perhaps by merchants as well.[66]

Freight was dispatched from Yakutsk to Okhotsk via the warm-season land route twice during the year—in mid-spring and in early summer. The first dispatch left Yakutsk in late April or early May and reached Okhotsk between mid-June and early August. This transport, which left Yakutsk long before the arrival of the river vessels from the upper Lena, was called the *plastovoy* or spring transport or route, the name being derived from *plast,* which in Siberia designated a hard crust of snow capable of supporting horses.* The shipment left Yakutsk early in order to cross the broad rivers (especially the Aldan) and marshes between Yakutsk and the Seven Ranges before the spring thaw. The plastovoy transport accounted for most of the freight conveyed from Yakutsk to Okhotsk.[67]

The second shipment of goods from Yakutsk was termed the *yarmarochny* or summer transport or route. It comprised goods just brought down the Lena on riverboats to Yakutsk, where they were checked and sorted and then lightered four and a half to six miles directly across the Lena to the landmark of Yarmanka (or Yarmonka or Yarmonga) at the mouth of the Suola River on the right bank—hence the name yarmarochny transport.** The local produce of Yakutsk, butter and candles, was lightered first, followed by the goods brought

---

* Dal, the foremost lexicographer of nineteenth-century Russia, states that the spring route from Yakutsk to Okhotsk was called the *lastovy* route after *last,* a measurement of the capacity of some merchant vessels equaling 120 puds (4,320 pounds) (Vladimir Dal, *Tolkovy slovar zhivovo velikorusskovo yazyka* [*Explanatory Dictionary of the Living Great Russian Language*] [Moscow: Gosudarstvennoye izdatelstvo inostrannykh i natsionalnykh slovarey, 1955], 2 : 239). Perhaps Dal is referring to the river route or to the second transport, which awaited the arrival of the riverboats at Yakutsk.

** Every station on the Yakutsk-Okhotsk Track where horses and lodging could be obtained was also called a *yarmanka* (Protoiyerey Prokopy Gromov, "Put ot Irkutska v Kamchatku" ["The Route from Irkutsk to Kamchatka"], *Pribavleniya k Irkutskim yeparkhialnym vedomostyam,* 7, no. 5 [1869] : 56).

down the Lena. This was the time of the Yakutsk fair (from mid-June until August), when the government maintained a ferry service across the river. This ferry service, which was founded in 1772, was operated for five months by eleven exiles, with each of the four-oared lighters carrying up to 2,880 pounds. Yarmanka (from *yarmarka,* meaning "fair") was the general rendezvous of all merchants and cargoes bound for the eastern and northeastern extremities of the empire, especially Okhotsk. Here were several hundred tethering posts and spacious meadows with ample grass for the herds of pack horses and the droves of cattle. The yarmarochny transport left Yakutsk in mid-June and arrived at Okhotsk in mid-August.[68]

Being more hazardous and more expensive, the yarmarochny transport handled less freight than the plastovoy transport. Thus, most provisions reaching Yakutsk were wintered there because they arrived too late for the safer and cheaper plastovoy transport. At first most of the pack trains left Yakutsk in early April, hurried to reach Okhotsk in May, and returned in mid-September in order to cross the quagmires when they were frozen; but by the end of the eighteenth century the convoys had to go back and forth all summer because of the increased amount of traffic. Eventually, however, summer traffic was diminished by anthrax, which claimed thousands of horses. Of the 6,000 to 10,000 horses annually packing state freight to Okhotsk in the late 1810's, 3,000 to 4,000 used the yarmarochny route; in 1820–21 only 500 to 1,000 horses; and from 1822 through 1825, only 100 of the 6,600 pack horses used the yarmarochny route. Goods urgently needed at Okhotsk were dispatched via the earlier plastovoy route; otherwise they were sent via the yarmarochny route.[69]

The carriers on the plastovoy and yarmarochny routes were Yakut pack horses, conducted by Yakut guides.* Cattle were driven

---

* Horses, reindeer, and dogs were used on the winter route (I. Bulychev, *Puteshestvie po Vostochnoy Sibiri* [*Journey through Eastern Siberia*] [St. Petersburg: n.p., 1856], pt. 1, pp. 53, 70; G. I. Davydov, *Dvukratnoye puteshestvie v Ameriku morskikh ofitserov Khvostova i Davydova* [*Double Voyage to America of the Naval Officers Khvostov and Davydov*] [St. Petersburg: Morskaya tipografiya, 1810], 1 : 98; Erman, *Travels in Siberia,* 2 : 303; M. Gedenstrom, *Otryvki o Sibiri* [*Excerpts on Siberia*] [St. Petersburg: Ministerstvo vnutrennikh del, 1830], pp. 102–103). Rafts and horses were used on the summer river route, which was not, of course, an all-water route. Early in the eighteenth century camels were used experimentally on the spring-summer land route, but their arrival at Yakutsk coincided with an outbreak of smallpox there, which the superstitious

overland by Yakut drovers in June for slaughtering at Okhotsk. Occasionally groups of convicts, sentenced to hard labor at the Okhotsk saltworks, were also driven overland, shackled and tied in pairs to a thick rope and escorted by eleven Cossacks.[70] The construction of a wagon road from Yakutsk to Okhotsk was precluded by the inimical nature of the terrain, with its extensive quagmires, rugged mountains, dense forests, and torrential rivers.[71] The horses and conductors were hired by the government and merchants, as well as by the Russian-American Company. The Yakutsk authorities usually notified the Yakuts in advance of the number of horses required by the government; the Yakuts then apportioned this responsibility among themselves, every two or three or five to eight male Yakuts having to furnish a horse. The Yakut contractors were then assembled in Yakutsk in early spring to make contracts, for they allegedly could not be trusted otherwise. Contracted horses were called "assigned" or "posted" horses; horses requisitioned by decree in emergencies were termed "collected" horses. Merchants did their hiring from November until March, and their chief outfitter was usually a rich Yakut or a well-known *toion* (chieftain), who provided half the required number of horses or obtained the entire number from other Yakuts. Eighty horses were commonly provided by five to six such outfitters.[72]

The transport of state goods eastward from Yakutsk became an obligation of the Yakuts of the Yakutsk and Vilyuisk *uluses* (tribal districts) in 1736. From 1753 the transport of state provisions only was contracted to Russians; that of other state goods remained an obligation of the Yakuts. From 1763 the Yakuts bemoaned the increasing amount of freight and their growing shortage of horses for transport on the Yakutsk–Okhotsk Track. Their complaints, plus the very slow movement of goods, prompted the state in 1774 to contract Okhotsk deliveries to the Irkutsk merchants Sibiryakov and Kiselev for 1 ruble, 25 kopeks per pud, but such contracting soon proved disadvantageous. In 1782 transport to Okhotsk was re-entrusted to the Yakuts (although it was contracted to Shelekhov from 1792 through 1795), and in 1800

Yakuts blamed on the bactrians; one of the camels was packed and dispatched to Okhotsk, but it died en route near a river subsequently called *Verblyuzhaya Reka,* i.e., Camel River (Johann Georg Gmelin, *Voyage en Siberie* . . . [Paris: Desaint, 1767], 1 : 419, 421). This incident was also commemorated in the name of a gulch, *Verblyuzhaya Pad,* located thirty-seven miles east of Allakh-Yun on the Yakutsk-Okhotsk Track (Davydov, *Dvukratnoye puteshestvie v Ameriku,* 1 : 104).

this transport became their obligation. This duty became particularly burdensome with the establishment of the Kamchatka Regiment in 1798,* whose needs greatly increased the volume of freight on the Yakutsk–Okhotsk Track.[73]

From 1810 through 1825 four-year contracts for the transport of state goods to Okhotsk were concluded by the Yakutsk authorities with the representatives of the Yakut uluses, each ulus furnishing a certain number of horses. One horse was required from every four Yakuts in 1773 and from every six Yakuts in 1774. The contracts usually stipulated (1) the destination of the freight; (2) the number of horses; (3) the transport charges, including the price per horse and the period of payment; and (4) the responsibility for the freight, including the manner of receiving and depositing goods.[74] The nature of the contracts is exemplified by one signed in 1808 at Irkutsk, whose conditions were as follows: the entire matter of transporting goods and persons was assumed by the local ulus communes, which were obligated to have ready no fewer than 10,000 horses for all transport, mainly to Okhotsk; since the cost of hiring and of buying horses fluctuated, new charges were to be concluded with the government every three years; the number of transports and their destinations were to be allotted to the uluses and *naslegs* (villages) in accordance with the number of census souls in each; all contracted horses were to be considered the property of one commune, so that in case of a loss of horses in one convoy, its conductor could use the spare horses from another convoy that was not depleted (like a returning convoy without freight or with little freight, such as empty containers and fur tribute); in dire emergencies the government could demand horses from the nearest uluses and naslegs; packing of freight was to be done by members of the Yakut ulus; the transports were to be accompanied to their destinations by Yakuts from the uluses and naslegs, and government inspectors with Cossacks were to check the transports; deductions of five rubles per horse were to be made for undelivered freight; if fewer than 10,000 horses were needed, then the

* The Kamchatka or Somov Regiment comprised companies of no less than sixty men each at Nizhne-Kamchatsk (headquarters), Petropavlovsk, Bolsheretsk, Okhotsk, and Udsk (A. Sgibnev, "Okhotsky port s 1649 po 1852 g." ["Okhotsk Port from 1649 to 1852"], *Morskoy sbornik*, 105, no. 11 [November, 1869] : 76–77). Formed in response to the Napoleonic threat, it was disbanded in 1812, probably in order to release troops for the European front.

government was to deduct from the agreed payment two rubles for each horse, and if the government needed more than 10,000 horses, then it was to add to the agreed payment two rubles for each extra horse.[75]

The Yakuts began receiving payment from the state for transport to Okhotsk in 1763, for transport to Kolymsk in 1773, and for transport to all points in 1784. Transport of state goods from Yakutsk to all points cost the government 168,017 rubles in 1811, 166,400 rubles in 1815, 200,000 rubles in 1820, 261,000 rubles in 1825, and 270,000 rubles in 1830. The Yakuts, who were expert packers, furnished horses and conductors at specified rates per pud, per versta (two-thirds of a mile), or (usually) per horse, plus charges for conductors, containers, and rations. Charges varied from time to time and from route to route. To Okhotsk the Yakuts charged sixty-three kopeks per pud in 1763, two to three rubles or more per pud around 1780, no less than six rubles per pud in 1794, up to nine and more rubles per pud around 1800, and fourteen rubles per pud in the late 1820's.[76] In 1822 it was reported that the cost of transport per pack horse "is increasing gradually from time to time"[77] (Table 6). It was normally cheaper to hire pack horses for the plastovoy than for the yarmarochny transport, since in spring the horses were weak from insufficient feed, while in summer "contagion" (anthrax) reduced the number of available horses. Speransky reported in 1820 that the government paid the Yakuts thirty-five rubles per pack horse for plastovoy transport to Okhotsk and fifty rubles for yarmarochny transport;[78] the same differential prevailed in 1822. It was also cheaper to hire horses in winter than in summer, when the road was in worse condition. In the early 1830's, for example, the state paid eighty rubles per horse for summer transport and forty for winter transport. Moreover, transport to Okhotsk was more expensive than transport elsewhere. Although at first the costs of pack horse transport from Yakutsk to Okhotsk, from Yakutsk to Udsk, and from Yakutsk to Kolymsk were roughly equal, by the early 1830's pack horse transport in summer to Okhotsk cost twice as much as to Kolymsk and four times as much as to Udsk, despite the fact that the Yakutsk–Okhotsk Track was the shortest of the three routes. "Light" (fast) pack horses, used for express travel to Okhotsk, were more expensive than ordinary pack horses; and so-called "free" (noncontracted) pack horses were dearer than contracted ones. In 1822, for example, the Yakuts charged 55 to 60 rubles in spring and 100 to 130 rubles in summer for each noncon-

TABLE 6

Cost of Contracted Pack Horse Transport in Spring from Yakutsk to Okhotsk for Various Years between 1773 and 1833

Year	Cost per Horse	
1773	3 rubles, 15 kopeks	
1774–81	6	25
1782–84	5½–6	
1785	10	
1786–88	6	75
ca. 1790	7	
1792–97	14	
1798–1803	13–14	
1805	35–45	
1807	30	
1809	34	
1811	34	
1820	35	
1822	35	
1830–33	48	48

SOURCES: G. P. Basharin, *Istoriya agrarnykh otnosheny v Yakutii (60-ye gody XVIII-seredina XIX v.)* [*History of Agrarian Relations in Yakutia (1860's to the Middle of the XIXth Century)*] (Moscow: Izdatelstvo Akademii nauk SSSR, 1956), pp. 232–234, 236; D. M. Pavlinov, N. A. Vitashevsky, and L. G. Levental, *Materialy po obychnomu pravu i po obshchestvennomu bytu Yakutov* [*Materials on the Customary Law and on the Social Life of the Yakuts*], "Trudy Komissii po izucheniyu Yakutskoy Avtonomoy Sovetskoy Sotsialisticheskoy Respubliki," vol. 4 (Leningrad: Izdatelstvo Akademii nauk SSSR, 1929), pp. 309, 311–312, 314–317; Fyodor Shemelin, *Zhurnal pervavo puteshestviya rossiyan vokrug zemnavo shara . . .* [*Journal of the First Voyage of a Russian around the Globe . . .*] (St. Petersburg: Meditsinskaya tipografiya, 1818), pt. 2, p. 204; V. Vagin, *Istoricheskiya svedeniya o deyatelnosti grafa M. M. Speranskavo v Sibiri s 1819 po 1822 god* [*Historical Information about the Activities of Count M. M. Speransky in Siberia from 1819 to 1822*] (St. Petersburg: Tipografiya Vtoravo otdeleniya Sobstvennoy Ye. I. V. Kantselyarii, 1872), vol. 2, p. 3, suppl., pp. 407, 409, 412–413, 448; G. H. Von Langsdorff, *Voyages and Travels in Various Parts of the World . . .* (London: Henry Colburn, 1814), pt. 2, p. 334.

tracted pack horse and 35 rubles in spring and 50 rubles in summer for each contracted pack horse. Usually transport by "free" horses cost at least ten rubles more per horse than transport by contracted horses.[79]

For transport from Okhotsk to Yakutsk the Yakuts rented pack horses very cheaply in order to avoid returning unloaded. In 1798 merchants paid twelve to twenty rubles per horse for transport from Yakutsk to Okhotsk and only six to fifteen rubles per horse for the reverse journey; the amount of the differential depended upon the quantity of freight from Kamchatka and Alaska awaiting shipment to Yakutsk at Okhotsk.[80]

The Yakuts provided spare horses in case of exhaustion, sickness, or injury. For the Billings Expedition the ratio was one spare horse for every three loaded horses, but evidently the normal ratio was one to twenty-five.[81] The Yakuts received "travel expenses" for victuals. According to a Senate decree of June 1, 1763, this allowance was not to exceed fifty rubles. In 1798 a Yakut conductor took as victuals up to 180 pounds of sour cream and up to 108 pounds of rye flour (a six-month supply) on the plastovoy route and up to 108 pounds of sour cream and up to 90 pounds of rye flour (a four-month supply) on the faster yarmarochny route; at the cost of fifty kopeks per pud his travel expenses were more than adequate.[82]

The various charges for pack horse transport are shown by the 1822 contract, under which the Yakuts received the following payments for one string of twelve pack horses sent to Okhotsk in summer: twenty-five rubles for each of ten loaded horses, twenty-five rubles for the one spare horse, twenty-five rubles for the conductor's mount, sixty rubles for the conductor himself, a hundred rubles for provisions to Okhotsk and back, sixty rubles for the two horses that were expected to perish, and tolls for ferrying the Aldan (fifteen kopeks per packed or ridden horse), Yudoma (five kopeks per packed or ridden horse), and Kukhtui (five kopeks per packed or ridden horse). These charges totaled no less than sixty rubles per horse. At the end of the eighteenth century Yakut earnings from freighting to Okhotsk alone totaled 200,000 to 250,000 rubles yearly. For the transport of state goods alone to Okhotsk from Yakutsk the Yakuts received more than 200,000 rubles per year in the early 1830's and 203,000, 185,000, and 160,000 rubles, respectively, in 1841, 1842, and 1843.[83] The decrease reflected the decline of the Yakutsk–Okhotsk Track with the rise of Ayan. Such income supported many Yakuts. The exile Bestuzhev noted in 1828 that "the transport of provisions to Okhotsk provides them their sole means of paying taxes, for hunting is a haphazard business."[84]

The Yakut horses, reared in immense numbers in the Central Yakut Lowland, were whitish to grayish in color, moderate in size (14 hands, i.e., 4 feet, 8 inches, high at the withers), and stocky in build, with strong bones and hoofs (unshod), powerful muscles, large and rough heads, short and thick necks, long and broad bodies, shaggy coats, and long manes. They were strong, hardy, docile,* and intelligent and were distinguished by their endurance on difficult routes, their ability to subsist on little feed, their late maturation (five to six years), and their longevity.[85] The merchant Kiselev remarked that "Yakutsk horses are so sturdy and so used to enduring hunger that from the outset each passenger is astonished."[86] According to another observer, they were usually serviceable for thirty years.[87] The writer Goncharov noted in 1854 that "Yakutsk horses are small, but strong, sturdy, and step measuredly and surely."[88] Earlier, Dobell had found them to be "certainly the strongest and hardiest beasts in the world."[89] They were considered the best horses in Siberia. They were generally well treated by their Yakut masters, who preferred scolding to beating them. During the Russian conquest of Eastern Siberia, where travel was not facilitated by rivers as much as in Western Siberia, Yakut horses became very important as both passenger and cargo vehicles for Cossacks, promyshlenniks, traders, and postmen. During the early 1840's they cost 100 to 150 rubles each.[90]

At Yakutsk or, more commonly, at Yarmanka the pack horses were loaded with provisions and other goods, which were sealed in wooden boxes and rawhide bags. Melted Yakut butter was conveyed in satchels made of birch bark. The wooden boxes or cases (*yashchiks*) were made of thin boards and were covered with rawhide. The rawhide bags, called *sumas,* were made by the Yakuts from untanned horsehide or oxhide. The outer side of the hide, stripped of its hair, became the outer side of the suma, whose smooth, whitish exterior resembled parchment. The best sumas were cylindrical in shape, three to four inches in depth and eighteen inches in diameter, with a small opening in the side. Ordinary sumas, however, were simply crude saddle bags. Both fancy and plain sumas were used primarily for transporting flour, which was packed tightly while the sumas were damp to form a half-inch protective crust of caked flour. They were purchased from the Yakuts for two and a half rubles apiece in 1813.[91]

The sumas and yashchiks, called "pieces" of freight, were filled with 72 to 108 pounds of goods and rarely more. Usually two such

---

* One observer, however, states that the half-wild Yakut horses were unruly pack animals (Al. Markov, *Russkie na Vostochnom okeane* [*Russians on the Eastern Ocean*], 2d ed. [St. Petersburg: Tipografiya A. Dmitriyeva, 1856], p. 19).

pieces of equal weight were placed on each horse to form what was termed a *vyuk* (pack or pack load). Sometimes atop light vyuks were placed small packages, called *prikladkas* ("trimmings" or "levelers"), of nine to eighteen pounds. Altogether, vyuks ordinarily weighed 210 pounds and sometimes 228, but never more than 246 pounds. Normally no more than 228 pounds could be packed on the Yakutsk–Okhotsk Track; it was too boggy, narrow, and mountainous for the horses to haul heavier loads. Pack horses carried 228 pounds on the plastovoy route and 210 pounds on the yarmarochny route. Returning from Okhotsk to Yakutsk no more than 144 pounds were packed, probably owing to the smaller amount of westbound freight and to the weakness of the horses occasioned by the paucity of forage at Okhotsk.[92]

The two pieces of freight were hung from the ends of two sticks fastened crosswise on the saddle. The so-called saddle, which was underlain by a horse "blanket" of matted grass or hair, was merely two small, perforated boards attached at an angle by thongs. For light transports single pieces of freight were tied squarely on the backs of the horses. All goods weighing more than 126 and less than 432 or 540 pounds, as well as some tenderfeet, were conveyed in a kind of covered litter made of canvas. This litter was hung from the crosspieces of two poles whose ends were fastened by thongs to the necks of two horses walking tandem or to the backs of two horses walking abreast. A special Yakut led this procession. To transport in this manner was "to conduct by swing," and such litters were called *kachkas*. They were seldom utilized because of their inconvenience. Most heavy goods were dismantled at Yakutsk and packed piecemeal in regular fashion to Okhotsk, where they were reassembled. Anchors, for example, were taken apart and rope was unwound and cut into lengths of forty-nine to fifty-six feet.[93]

Following loading, the pack horses were dispatched in "caravans" or "convoys" of 100 to 150 horses (including 5 to 8 spares), grouped in "strings" or "bunches," each of which included 5 (or less) to 13 but usually 10 or 12 horses, with a Yakut conductor astride the lead horse.* During the second half of the eighteenth century 1,200 to 1,600 Yakut conductors were employed annually on the Yakutsk–Okhotsk Track. Each string usually consisted of six loaded horses, one or two

---

* Similarly, Yakut conductors rode the lead bulls in the cattle drives to Okhotsk (Sir George Simpson, *Narrative of a Journey Round the World* . . . [London: Henry Colburn, 1847], 2 : 266).

spares, and one or two riding horses bearing the Yakut guides, who conducted the horses in single file, owing to the narrowness of the track. The horses were "strung" (connected) from tail to head with a horse-hair cord. Strings hauling heavier goods like anchors, cannon, and rigging involved more conductors and more spare horses. Effort was made to limit the number of pack horses leaving Yakutsk for Okhotsk to no more than 200 a day, since there was not enough forage en route for more.[94]

On an open track the pack horses generally marched at the rate of four to five m.p.h. for ten to twelve hours at a stretch, but because of various obstacles they averaged only about thirteen miles a day. At sundown the convoys halted for the night at spots with enough water and grass for the horses; here the horses were unloaded and turned loose to graze, and next morning they were collected by hallooing. Sometimes the horses were rested for several days after crossing quicksandy bogs, steep mountains, or large rivers. It normally took the convoys one or two months to reach Okhotsk, depending upon the stamina of the horses, the competence of the conductors, and the condition of the trail. Provisions dispatched from Yakutsk too late to reach Okhotsk before snowfall were stored in magazines at Yudoma Cross and Urak Landing, where some Cossacks were stationed.[95]

At Okhotsk the unpacked goods belonging to the state and to the Russian-American Company were first weighed and then stored in magazines for local consumption or loaded onto vessels for transshipment to Kamchatka and Alaska. There were twenty-eight magazines (ten for provisions, six for coal, five for gunpowder, four for salt, two for weapons, and one for furs) at Okhotsk around 1795.[96] Private goods arriving at Okhotsk were marketed at the local fair. This "plastovoy fair" began as early as June 26 and ended as late as October 12. It attracted merchants from Russia and Siberia with all kinds of wares and provisions brought from Germany, Russia, and China, as well as merchants from Kamchatka and Alaska with furs. Here people who did not receive grain salaries, or whose grain salaries were insufficient, could buy provisions. In 1839 the Okhotsk fair received 548,388 rubles worth of goods.[97]

The unloaded pack horses were rested and grazed for periods ranging from a few days to two or three weeks at pasture on the seacoast near Okhotsk and then were returned to Yakutsk either empty or laden with furs, up to seventy-two pounds of which were packed in one suma or yashchik. The return trip sometimes took only eight days. Horses were returned to Yakutsk even without loads because of the dearth of pasture and hay at Okhotsk;[98] Captain Chirikov opined that only two hundred to three hundred horses could be supported at Okhotsk.[99] There was some pasture along the Okhota River about seventeen miles above Okhotsk, but it could support only about thirty horses.[100]

Cochrane asserted in 1821 that "formerly, when the horses were more numerous, from eighty to one hundred thousand were annually employed between Okhotsk and Yakutsk by the merchants, the American Company, and the government. . . ."[101] Like Cochrane's other estimates, this figure is undoubtedly exaggerated, but traffic on the Yakutsk–Okhotsk Track was undeniably heavy. En route from Okhotsk to Yakutsk in July of 1842, Governor Simpson of the Hudson's Bay Company found the road "absolutely alive with caravans and travellers, all proceeding to Ochotsk with goods, provisions, and cattle; and of flour alone not fewer than five thousand loads had passed us before the close of this our fifth day [out of Okhotsk]."[102] The number of pack horses in use undoubtedly fluctuated in accordance with the number of horses available and the quantity of goods required, but it seems that generally 10,000 to 12,000 and sometimes 15,000 or perhaps even 30,000 horses were utilized yearly on the Yakutsk–Okhotsk Track in the early nineteenth century to transport state and private (including Russian-American Company) freight[103] (Table 7).* At an average of, say, 180 pounds of goods per pack horse, 900 to 1,080 and sometimes 1,350 or perhaps even 2,700 tons of freight, mostly provisions, were hauled by pack horses each year from Yakutsk to Okhotsk in the early 1800's.**

Most of these pack horses hauled state freight. Sometime during the early nineteenth century the proportional usage of pack horses

---

* The versatile Russian scholar Berg, however, states that a modest average of "more than 4000 horses had to be maintained" (L. S. Berg, *Ocherki po istorii russkikh geograficheskikh otkryty* [*Sketches on the History of Russian Geographical Discoveries*], 2d ed. [Moscow and Leningrad: Izdatelstvo Akademii nauk SSSR, 1949], p. 130).

** By comparison, albeit roughly, over the entire Great Siberian (or Moscow) Track, constructed in 1735–72 between Moscow and Nerchinsk, up to 36,000 tons of freight were transported yearly by 50,000 horses (cartage) around the middle of the nineteenth century (Akademiya nauk SSSR, Institut geografii, *Vostochnaya Sibir: ekonomiko-geograficheskaya kharakteristika* [*Eastern Siberia: Economico-Geographical Character*] [Moscow: Gosudarstvennoye izdatelstvo geograficheskoy literatury, 1963], p. 137).

TABLE 7

Number of Horses Packing Freight from Yakutsk to Okhotsk for Various Years between 1740 and 1840

Year	Annual Number of Horses
1740–60	4,000–5,000
1750–1800	6,000–10,000
late 1760's	6,000
1780–1800	20,000–30,000
ca. 1800	15,000
1800–1820	12,000
1805	14,000–15,000
ca. 1807	6,000–8,000
1809–18	7,000–12,000
1813	10,000
1816–30	9,000–10,500
ca. 1820	18,000
1821	up to 30,000
1828	over 20,000
1840	10,000

SOURCES: Akademiya nauk SSSR, Institut geografii, *Vostochnaya Sibir: ekonomiko-geograficheskaya kharakteristika* [*Eastern Siberia: Economico-Geographical Character*] (Moscow: Gosudarstvennoye izdatelstvo geograficheskoy literatury, 1963), p. 138; Akademiya nauk SSSR, Institut yazyka, literatury i istorii Yakutskovo filiala AN SSSR, *Istoriya Yakutskoy ASSR* [*History of the Yakut ASSR*] (Moscow: Izdatelstvo Akademii nauk SSSR, 1957), 2 : 89, 148; Cochrane, *Narrative of a Pedestrian Journey*, p. 305; Charles Herbert Cottrell, *Recollections of Siberia* . . . (London: John W. Parker, 1842), p. 328; Dobell, *Travels in Kamtchatka and Siberia*, 1 : 300; Mauritius Augustus Count De Benyowsky, *Memoirs and Travels* . . . (Dublin: P. Wogan, L. White, P. Byrne et al., 1790), 1 : 252; E. [E. I. Stogov], "Ssylno-katorzhnie v Okhotskom sole-varennom zavode" ["Hard-Labor Exiles at the Okhotsk Saltworks"], *Russkaya starina*, 22 (August, 1878) : 626–627; A. Marlinsky, *Polnoye sobranie sochineny* [*Complete Collection of Works*] (St. Petersburg: Tipografiya N. Grecha, 1832), 1 : 218; Rear-Admiral Minitsky, "Opisanie Yakutskoy oblasti" ["Description of Yakutsk Oblast"], *Zhurnal Ministerstva vnutrennikh del*, bk. 6 (1830), p. 170; Pavlinov, Vitashevsky, and Levental, *Materialy po obychnomu pravu*, pp. 36, 308–309, 317–318; A. Sgibnev, "Amurskaya ekspeditsiya 1854 goda" ["The Amur Expedition of 1854"], *Drevnyaya i novaya Rossiya*, 4, no. 11 (November, 1878) : 216; Shemelin, *Zhurnal pervavo puteshestviya rossiyan*, pt. 2, pp. 203–204; S. A. Tokarev, *Ocherk istorii yakutskovo naroda* [*Sketch of the History of the Yakut People*] (Moscow: Gosudarstvennoye sotsialno-ekonomicheskoye izdatelstvo, 1940), p. 126; Von Langsdorff, *Voyages and Travels*, pt. 2, p. 334.

between Yakutsk and Okhotsk for one year was 9,000 by the state, 1,500 by the Russian-American Company, 1,200 by large merchants, and 300 by petty merchants. In 1805 the Yakuts provided up to 10,000 horses for state freight, 2,000 to 3,000 for Russian-American Company freight, and 1,500 for merchant freight. From 1816 through 1830, 6,000 to 6,500 horses annually packed state goods from Yakutsk, principally to Okhotsk, while 3,000 to 4,000 horses annually packed goods to Okhotsk for the Russian-American Company and for merchants. Thus, the proportional usage of pack horses between Yakutsk and Okhotsk during the first quarter of the nineteenth century was 65 to 75 percent by the state, 12.5 to 22.5 percent by the Russian-American Company, and 10 to 17.5 percent by merchants.[104] Table 8 shows by decades from

TABLE 8

Number of Horses and Conductors Transporting State Freight Eastward from Yakutsk, 1736–85 and 1796–1830[a]

| Years | Number of Conductors | Number of Horses | | | | |
		Packed	Spares	Ridden	Total	Annual Average
1736–46	1,435	7,784	778	1,435	9,997	909
1747–56	2,749	13,801	1,269	2,529	17,599	1,760
1757–66	8,052	43,468	2,421	4,844	50,733	5,073
1767–76	5,388	26,965	2,586	5,371	34,922	3,492
1777–85	1,700	8,547	854	1,700	11,101	1,222
Total and Average	19,324	100,565	7,908	15,879	124,352	2,487
1796–1806	. . .	. . .	. . .	. . .	68,577	6,234
1807–16	. . .	. . .	. . .	. . .	90,459	9,046
1817–26	. . .	. . .	. . .	. . .	63,144	6,314[b]
1827–30	. . .	. . .	. . .	. . .	27,273	6,818
Total and Average					249,453	7,259
Grand Total and Average					373,805	4,563

[a] Data for 1786–95 are unavailable.

[b] According to another source, during the early 1820's 10,000 pack horses were required annually at Yakutsk for transporting state goods, mainly to Okhotsk (Vagin, *Istoricheskiya svedeniya*, vol. 2, suppl., p. 406.)

SOURCE: Basharin, *Istoriya agrarnykh otnosheny*, p. 235.

1736 through 1830 (excepting 1786–95, for which data are unavailable) the number of horses and conductors used to transport state goods, mostly provisions, eastwards from Yakutsk, primarily to Okhotsk.

Okhotsk was by far the chief destination. According to some sources, the annual number of horses packing state freight from Yakutsk to Okhotsk averaged 3,000 to 4,000 in the late eighteenth century, 6,000 to 10,000 around 1820 (including 3,000 to 4,000 in summer), and 6,600 from 1822 through 1825.[105] Other sources give slightly higher eighteenth-century and rather lower nineteenth-century figures, but Okhotsk's pre-eminence is maintained (Table 9).

TABLE 9

Amount of Freight and Number of Horses Sent by the State from Yakutsk to Okhotsk, Udsk, and Kolymsk, for Various Years between 1773 and 1833

Year	Amount of Freight (in tons)[a]	Number of Horses[b]
1773	396[c]	(4,400)[d]
1774–81	914–915	(10,162)
1782–84	(20–21)[e]	5,636[f]
1785	723–724[g]	(8,040)[h]
1786–87[i]	792	8,000
1788[j]	(390–392)[k]	4,677[l]
1789	(415–416)	4,200
1790	(345–346)	3,487
1791	(354–355)	3,584
1800–1803	1,550–1,911[m]	(15,661–21,228)[n]
1805	(225–249)	10,509
1809	(989–1,089)	10,996
1811	(542–598)	6,031
1812	(660–727)	7,343[o]
1814	(604–665)	6,720[p]
1815	(539–576)	5,992
1816	(558–614)	6,200
1817	(585–644)	6,500
1818	(615–678)	6,841
1819	(572–630)	6,360
1820	(513–565)	5,700
1824	(561–618)	6,235
1825	(587–646)	6,525
1826	(574–632)	6,383
1828	(595–655)	6,612
1829	(599–655)	6,661
1830	(630–693)	7,000
1831	(630–693)	7,000
1832	(630–693)	7,000
1833	(630–693)	7,000

[a] Figures in parentheses denote estimates calculated by me on the basis of 180 to 198 pounds per horse.

[b] Figures in parentheses denote estimates calculated by me on the basis of 180 to 198 pounds per horse. These figures do not include spare horses and horses ridden by conductors. In the nineteenth century for every string of eight horses hauling provisions

The state freight hauled by these horses consisted largely of grain. For example, up to 6,000 horses were used to transport state flour alone to Okhotsk in the early 1830's, when, according to Table 9, 7,000 horses altogether hauled state freight of all kinds from Yakutsk not only to Okhotsk but to Udsk and Kolymsk as well. Traffic through Okhotsk was long dominated by provisions. Around 1820 grain traffic comprised by value two-thirds of the entire commerce (imports and exports) of Okhotsk Port, exclusive of the trade of the Russian-American Company. This proportion is all the more meaningful in view of the fact that foodstuffs were by weight much less valuable than furs.[106]

When the river route between Yakutsk and Okhotsk began to be used, doshcheniks, each carrying 27 to 125 tons of freight and each requiring twenty to thirty hands, went from Yakutsk down the Lena to the Aldan and then tracked up the Aldan to the Maya. There their loads were transferred to smaller boats (each requiring up to twenty men) for the further 200 miles of tracking to Yudoma Cross; in that stretch rapids at two spots prevented the passage of larger boats. From 1734 doshcheniks were replaced by barkas, each carrying seven to twenty-seven tons of cargo—or four barkas to a doshchenik.[107] The Second Kamchatka Expedition recommended that boats holding no more than 3,600 pounds and requiring five men be used on the Maya–Yudoma stretch;[108]

---

there was one conductor's horse and one spare horse, while strings hauling heavier goods were accompanied by more conductors and by more spares (Pavlinov, Vitashevsky, and Leventhal, *Materialy po obychnomu pravu*, pp. 305–306n).

c 360 tons to Okhotsk, 36 to Kolymsk.

d 4,000 horses to Okhotsk, 400 to Kolymsk.

e (16–17) tons to Okhotsk, (3–4) to Udsk.

f 4,650 horses to Okhotsk, 986 to Udsk.

g 612 tons to Okhotsk, 111–112 to Kolymsk.

h (6,800) horses to Okhotsk, (1,240) to Kolymsk.

i One source asserts that in 1786 alone horses packed 720 tons of state and private freight just to Okhotsk (Pavlinov, Vitashevsky, and Leventhal, *Materialy po obychnomu pravu*, p. 312).

j In addition, in 1788 the Yakuts furnished the Billings Expedition with 4,300 horses (Basharin, *Istoriya agrarnykh otnosheny*, p. 233).

k 360 tons to Okhotsk, 4–5 to Udsk, (26–27) to Kolymsk.

l 3,637 horses to Okhotsk, (45) to Udsk, 272 to Kolymsk.

m 1,440–1,800 tons to Okhotsk, 110–111 to Kolymsk.

n (14,545–20,000) horses to Okhotsk, (1,116–1,228) to Kolymsk.

o Part to Okhotsk, part to Kolymsk.

p Part to Okhotsk, part to Kolymsk.

SOURCES: Basharin, *Istoriya agrarnykh otnosheny*, pp. 232–234, 236; Pavlinov, Vitashevsky, and Leventhal, *Materialy po obychnomu pravu*, pp. 309, 311–312, 314–317; Vagin, *Istoricheskiya svedeniya*, 2 : 8.

the Billings Expedition in 1788 used boats carrying up to 2,520 pounds and drawing three feet of water, each towed by seven men.[109] Small vessels, each carrying up to 7,200 pounds, plied the Urak to Okhotsk, whence they were not returned to Urak Landing.[110]

From Okhotsk to Kamchatka and Gizhiga

From Okhotsk Port provisions were shipped annually on government vessels to other points on the Okhotsk Seaboard, primarily Gizhiga, and to Kamchatka. Besides the goods brought from Yakutsk, salt from the works just south of Okhotsk was also shipped on state vessels to the rest of the Okhotsk Seaboard and to Kamchatka, where it was needed in great amounts for curing fish; in 1773, for example, 7,200 pounds of salt were shipped from Okhotsk to Bolsheretsk and Verkhne-Kamchatsk. Even cloudberries and cowberries were shipped to Bolsheretsk. Cattle were shipped both live and butchered (salted). In addition, supplies were dispatched from Okhotsk to Alaska by the Russian-American Company on its own ships.[111] These operations were tersely described by Commandant Minitsky in 1812:

> At the port there are now seven state transport vessels, well finished and outfitted as brigs. State and private goods are sent on them to Kamchatka's roadsteads, namely, to Petropavlovsk Harbor, to the Kamchatka River [Nizhne-Kamchatsk], to Bolsheretsk, Tigilsk, and Gizhiga Fortress. These vessels, returning to Okhotsk Port, bring furs from the Kamchatka Peninsula and from Gizhiga, belonging mostly to private merchants. In the same way ships of the Russian-American Company leave this port with freight bound for the Northwest Coast of America, where the Company has its colonies and hunting.[112]

Most of the government transports were constructed at Okhotsk; a few were built at Nizhne-Kamchatsk. Along the Kukhtui (especially) and Okhota rivers and along the middle Kamchatka River grew stands of larch, sometimes called fir by the Russians, a "fairly strong but extremely brittle" wood suitable for shipbuilding, since it resisted rot. This timber was floated down the Kukhtui and Okhota without difficulty to the shipyard at Okhotsk. Timber growing on stony, sandy, or dry ground was found to be hard, strong, tall, and thick and thus suitable for shipbuilding, while timber growing in low-lying places and along the coast was moist and weak, short and thin, and hence was used for building houses, making charcoal, or for firewood.* The best stands were soon depleted;[113] in 1786 Sarychev found few trees near Okhotsk large enough for building ships for the Billings Expedition.[114]**

The ships built at Okhotsk, especially at first, were small, heavy, clumsy craft, too short for their width, resembling early Dutch ships.[115]† They were improved somewhat during the last half of the eighteenth century, however. Most of the state cargo vessels were outfitted as brigs (two-masted, square-rigged ships carrying 150 to 300 tons) and galiots (two-masted, oblique-rigged ships carrying up to 100 tons). The government usually maintained three or four cargo vessels, as well as a couple of packet boats, at Okhotsk. In 1775 there were four state transports at Okhotsk "for transporting men and provisions, as well as merchants' goods, to Kamchatka and to Izhiga Fortress. . . ."[116] Five state transports were stationed at Okhotsk in 1786. During the existence of the Kamchatka Regiment eight were needed.[117] In 1801 the Admiralty College ordered the construction of four brigs (each up to sixty feet long) and five galiots (each up to fifty feet long) at Okhotsk, the brigs for transport (once yearly) of supplies to Petropavlovsk and Nizhne-Kamchatsk and the galiots for transport (twice yearly) of supplies to Tauisk, Yamsk, Gizhiga, Tigilsk, and Bolsheretsk.[118] The Okhotsk Flotilla comprised eight brigs and galiots and two packet boats in 1804 and three galiots, two brigs, and two cutters in 1806 (all save one built of larch at Okhotsk),[119] "which go annually to Kamchatkan harbors: Gizhiginsk, Bolsheretsk, Tigil, Petropavlovsk, and Nizhnyaya Kamchatka."[120] There were seven state transports at Okhotsk in 1809 and in 1811, four around 1815 (each with a capacity of 135 to 160 tons), and three in 1816 and in 1819. Each of the state transports built at Okhotsk

---

* Around 1800 in Russia ships were built primarily from larch and oak; pine and birch were the main trees used for firewood (William Tooke, *View of the Russian Empire, During the Reign of Catherine the Second, and to the Close of the Eighteenth Century*, 2d ed. [London: T. N. Longman and O. Rees, 1800], 3 : 253–255).

** Sarychev found suitable trees only at Chyornolesye and at Mundukan on the Okhota River fourteen and fifty miles, respectively, upriver from Okhotsk (G. A. Sarychev, *Puteshestvie po severo-vostochnoy chasti Sibiri, Ledovitomu moryu i Vostochnomu okeanu* [*Journey through the Northeastern Part of Siberia, the Arctic Sea and the Eastern Ocean*] [Moscow: Gosudarstvennoye izdatelstvo geograficheskoy literatury, 1952], p. 54).

† The Russian shipbuilders of Pomorye, some of whom worked at Okhotsk, were strongly influenced by Dutch models.

in 1817 weighed 200 to 350 tons and accommodated up to 215 tons; two to three such vessels could have handled the state freight then arriving from Yakutsk. It seems that at least half of the state provisions arriving at Okhotsk proceeded to Kamchatka, for 195½ of 390¾ tons of provisions dispensed in 1774 by Okhotsk's state magazines went to Kamchatka.[121]

Every summer in August or September, when westerly winds prevailed and after the last convoys had arrived from Yakutsk, the government transports, laden with state and private goods (chiefly provisions), left Okhotsk for Gizhiga (650 miles), Tigilsk (440 miles), Bolsheretsk (660–725 miles), Petropavlovsk (1,040 miles), and Nizhne-Kamchatsk, where they arrived in September or October. During the 1730's the voyage from Okhotsk to Bolsheretsk sometimes took four to five days but usually ten to fourteen—unless the winds were contrary. In the middle of the nineteenth century state transports took no less than twelve days and usually a month to reach Petropavlovsk. Following unloading of their cargoes (mainly for local consumption but also for final transshipment to outlying posts), the ships wintered there and returned to Okhotsk in June or July of the next year, when easterly winds prevailed, with state and private furs from Chukotka and Kamchatka, passengers, and ballast. The navigation season lasted from June through October.[122] In 1775 Captain Timofey Shmalev, Commandant of Okhotsk, reported that supply ships plied annually from Okhotsk to Gizhiga, Tigilsk, and Bolsheretsk,[123] with the Gizhiga transport also supplying Tauisk and Yamsk. However, because of the risky "harbors" at Tigilsk and Bolsheretsk, the Senate decreed in 1813 that the government transports were to sail only to Gizhiga, Petropavlovsk, and Nizhne-Kamchatsk.[124]

6

PERFORMANCE

"The fact is that bread and salt are unquestionably items that the lowest beggar in Europe does not lack. The inhabitants of Kamchatka are poorer than this. Often they have neither bread nor salt."

I. F. Kruzenshtern, *Puteshestvie vokrug sveta*, p. 226.

Amounts of Shipment

Despite the incompleteness of statistical data, enough figures are available to indicate that large amounts of provisions were transported overland-oversea from Eastern Siberia to the Okhotsk Seaboard and the Kamchatka Peninsula, and that the shipments gradually increased in amount. Irkutsk Province supplied the Second Kamchatka Expedition (1733–42) with 900 to 1,080 tons of grain,[1] or 90 to 108 tons per year. By 1753 it was reported that up to 270 tons of state provisions were sent annually to the seaboard and the peninsula.[2] Probably in response to an Imperial order that provisions be sent to Okhotsk "every year without delay . . . ," 286½ tons of state flour were shipped to Okhotsk in 1754; and half this amount was shipped in 1755 and again in 1756.[3] In 1758 the Yakuts delivered up to 360 tons of provisions to Okhotsk.[4] Tables 10 and 11 illustrate the monthly amounts of state foodstuffs received and dispensed at Okhotsk in 1774–75 and at Gizhiga in 1784.

Overland-oversea provisionment sharply increased with the formation of the Kamchatka Regiment in 1798. In that year alone 1,107 tons of flour and 90 tons of groats were shipped from Irkutsk to the seaboard and the peninsula just for the regiment.[5] Around 1805 each of the region's 1,600 Cossacks, soldiers, and sailors received annually 671 pounds of flour for a total of 536 tons, plus 78 tons of groats for the sailors, making a grand total of 613 tons of flour and groats, which, in addition to many other goods ranging from canvas to bar iron, were imported.[6]

The government was not always able to satisfy the huge food

TABLE 10

Monthly Inlay and Outlay of State Provisions at Okhotsk, 1774–75

Month	Incoming		Outgoing	
1774				
January	0 tons,	82 lbs.	13 tons,	224 lbs.
February	0	0	14	297
March	0	103	14	302
April	0	195	16	1,243
May	0	1,420	13	172
June	0	508	0	653
July	195	1,181ª	229	934ᵇ
August	156	61	15	1,689
September	1	35	20	1,463
October	1	1,668	26	122
November	0	66	13	1,119
December	0	731	13	1,335
Total	356	50ᶜ	390	1,553ᵇ
1775				
January	0	0	13	905
February	0	0	13	1,334
March	0	32	20	1,283
April	0	192	9	1,253
May	0	74	13	591
June	0	0	2	937
Total	0	298ᵈ	73	303

ª All for Kamchatka.
ᵇ Including 195 tons, 1,181 lbs. sent to Kamchatka.
ᶜ Plus 107 tons, 1,357 lbs. left from 1773.
ᵈ Plus 77 tons, 1,851 lbs. left from 1774.

Source: Timofey Shmalev, "Vedomost o nakhodyashchemsya proviante v Okhot-skom porte" ["List of Provisions Found at Okhotsk Port"], TsGADA, f. 199, port. 528, pt. 1, d. 13, fol. 1.

requirements of Kamchatka during the existence of the Kamchatka Regiment. In 1802 or 1803, for example, the regiment requested 209 tons, 572 pounds of provisions from Okhotsk but received only half this amount. A severe shortage of provisions resulted, with the soldiers receiving only half their grain ration, the other half being given in money, fish flour, and dried fish; but no more than 2 tons, 752 pounds of porsa were prepared and all the yukola save 1 ton, 1,600 pounds spoiled.[7] In 1809–10 six shiploads of flour sent to Kamchatka from Okhotsk proved insufficient.[8] Consequently, the peninsula's lower ranks received grain rations only three months instead of twelve months of the

TABLE 11

Monthly Inlay and Outlay of State Provisions at Gizhiga, 1784

Month	Incoming		Outgoing	
January	34 tons,	920 lbs.	7 tons,	360 lbs.
February	0	1,006	0	36
March	0	0	3	1,546
April	0	0	3	1,474
May	0	43	7	902
June	0	0	0	144
July	0	0	2	1,724
August	0	0	3	120
September	0	0	2	1,688
October	0	0	2	1,904
November	0	0	0	72
Total	34 tons, 1,969 lbs. (costing 3,206 rubles, 91 kopeks)		33 tons, 1,970 lbs. (costing 3,129 rubles, 77 kopeks)	

SOURCE: Anonymous, "Delo o zapiske v prikhod kazyonnovo provianta 1784 goda" ["File Noting the Arrival of State Provisions of 1784"], TsGADA, f. 1,096, op. 1, d. 47, fol. 19.

year; Vasily Golovnin, in noting this situation, remarked that it would be difficult to find a hungrier, lonelier, and duller country than Kamchatka.[9] Indeed, the difficulty of meeting the food demands of the Kamchatka Regiment played a decisive role in its disbandment. Following its dissolution in 1812, the size of state food shipments to the peninsula dropped steeply: for instance, from 720 tons in 1802 to only 165 in 1820.[10]

Progressively larger amounts of state provisions were also transported overland-oversea to Gizhiga. In 1784 it received 35 tons of state provisions. During the fish famine of the last half of the 1810's Gizhiga required more grain; an average of 93 tons, 300 pounds of state grain was sent there annually from 1816 through 1819. In 1819 an official inspector found that state provisionment of Gizhiga totaled 63 to 108 tons of grain yearly, plus some private grain imported and sold by merchants.[11]

The decrease in overland-oversea shipments of provisions to the Okhotsk Seaboard and the Kamchatka Peninsula following the disbandment of the Kamchatka Regiment was but a temporary lull. Around 1820 at least 540 tons of state goods, primarily foodstuffs, were sent yearly to Okhotsk from Yakutsk.[12] Probably in 1821 the seaboard and the peninsula imported up to 630 tons of state grain,[13] and it was reported in 1822 that 720 to 900 tons of state goods were shipped annually to Okhotsk and Kamchatka via Yakutsk, including 540 tons of flour.[14] This resurgence was also short-lived, for during the 1840's overland-oversea shipments of provisions to Okhotsk again decreased with the decline of the Yakutsk–Okhotsk Track. Thus, in 1841, 1842, and 1843, respectively, 486 tons, 450 tons, and 414 tons of state goods (roughly half the 1822 total), mainly provisions, were transported overland from Yakutsk to Okhotsk. By about 1850 only up to 324 tons of state provisions and private goods were shipped yearly from Okhotsk to Gizhiga and Kamchatka.[15]

Even when the traffic in provisions was at its heaviest from Yakutsk to Okhotsk and beyond, particularly on behalf of the state, it sometimes failed to solve the food supply problem of the Okhotsk Seaboard and the Kamchatka Peninsula. This failure occurred especially during the existence of the Kamchatka Regiment (1798–1812); and even afterward supply sometimes failed to satisfy demand. In 1822, for example, it was estimated that the region required 591¼ tons of flour but received only 540 tons of state flour[16]—although the deficiency may have been overcome by private shipments. Observers invariably noted the dearth of provisions on the seaboard and the peninsula, especially among the poor, who simply could not afford scarce and expensive foodstuffs.

Costs of Shipment

Not surprisingly, the costs of provisionment by the long and difficult overland-oversea route were staggering. It cost the government 100,000 to 120,000 rubles to deliver to Okhotsk the 900 to 1,080 tons of grain supplied by Irkutsk Province for the Second Kamchatka Expedition; this expense alone accounted for up to 8 percent of the expedition's cost of 1,500,000 rubles.[17] In 1788 the government spent 140,304 rubles on provisionment via Irkutsk–Yakutsk–Okhotsk,[18] and it was reported in 1802 that it cost the government up to 400,000 rubles annually to supply Okhotsk and Kamchatka via Yakutsk.[19] This latter figure represented almost 0.5 percent of total state expenses of 91,400,000 rubles in 1803.[20] In the early 1830's the state spent 320,000 rubles yearly on overland transport of grain to Okhotsk. This expenditure decreased with the decline of the Yakutsk–Okhotsk Track during the 1840's, and from 1838 through 1847 the government spent only 66,000 rubles annually on provisionment via this route.[21]

A striking example of the expensiveness of overland-oversea provisionment is afforded by the transport of the 1,107 tons of flour and the 90 tons of groats from Irkutsk in 1798 to the seaboard and the peninsula for the Kamchatka Regiment. It cost the government 23,295 rubles to buy the flour and groats at Irkutsk and to ship them to Yakutsk, and 63,224½ rubles to pack them from Yakutsk to Okhotsk (8,888 rubles for 6,464 flour sumas, 1,708½ rubles for 670 groat sumas, and 39,928 rubles for 2,852 pack horses at 14 rubles per horse) and to Udsk (1,582 rubles for 1,152 flour sumas, 306 rubles for 120 groat sumas, and 10,812 rubles for 636 pack horses at 17 rubles per horse). A total expense of 86,519½ rubles was incurred as far as Okhotsk and Udsk.[22] From 1799 through 1808 it cost the government 1,791,566 rubles to supply the Kamchatka Regiment with provisions and ammunition.[23]

The expensiveness of overland-oversea supply naturally made prices of goods high on the Okhotsk Seaboard and the Kamchatka Peninsula, and sheer scarcity inflated them further. The expensiveness of transport from Yakutsk to Okhotsk was cited about 1780 by Soimonov, former Governor of Siberia and now Secretary of State to Catherine the Great, as the foremost handicap of entrepreneurs in northeastern Siberia.[24] Academician Redovsky during a visit to Okhotsk in 1806 attributed the very high cost of living there principally to "roadlessness" (i.e., transport difficulties) between Yakutsk and Okhotsk.[25] Around 1755 some goods costing ten kopeks at Irkutsk and Yakutsk cost one ruble at Okhotsk. In 1801 at Okhotsk such items as sailcloth, rope, iron, tin, anchors, and nails cost twice as much as at Irkutsk and thrice as much as at St. Petersburg; and in 1804 rye flour at Okhotsk cost the Russian-American Company six times as much as at Irkutsk. Transport raised the price of a pud of grain in 1805 from between 1 ruble and 1 ruble, 20 kopeks at Yakutsk to 8 to 10 rubles at Okhotsk. In the early 1840's rye flour and groats, which cost, respectively, one and a half rubles and two and a half rubles per pud at Yakutsk, cost eight to ten and ten to twelve rubles per pud at Okhotsk, since transport over the Yakutsk–Okhotsk Track then cost thirty to forty rubles per pack horse, each of which carried five puds.[26] Goods from Yakutsk commanded such high prices at Okhotsk, especially in winter, that postmen, whose eight or nine sleighs carried very little mail (two or three items), profited handsomely by taking additional articles to Okhotsk for sale (like calico, costing twenty-five to twenty-six kopeks per yard at Yakutsk and bringing seventy-seven to ninety kopeks per yard at Okhotsk) and returning to Yakutsk with balyk (costing five kopeks each at Okhotsk and bringing twenty-five to fifty kopeks each at Yakutsk).[27] One postman recalled that "no track brought as much profit as the Okhotsk and the Petropav-lovsk."[28]

Transport from Okhotsk to Gizhiga was also costly and was largely responsible for making sustenance at Gizhiga twice as expensive as at Okhotsk.[29] As for transport from Okhotsk to Kamchatka, a Senate edict of 1731 decreed that "whoever wants to go to Kamchatka with goods is to be given a place on the ships by paying one ruble per person and four grivnas [forty kopeks] per pud of freight. . . ."[30] Later this freightage fee increased to 50 kopeks per pud, and it reached 1 ruble, 50 kopeks by 1773, when the sea voyage from Okhotsk accounted for one-third to one-half the cost of rye flour at Bolsheretsk. In 1787 transport across the Okhotsk Sea raised the price of "corn brandy" (vodka) from eighteen rubles per *vedro* (three and one-quarter gallons) at Okhotsk to almost forty-two rubles per vedro at Bolsheretsk.[31] Over-land transport from Kamchatka's ports to its interior was costly, too. In the early 1740's it cost no less than four rubles per pud to transport goods overland from Bolsheretsk to Nizhne-Kamchatsk, so that the cost of transporting a pud of butter from Bolsheretsk to Nizhne-Kamchatsk equaled half to three-quarters of its price at Bolsheretsk, where it sold for six to eight rubles.[32] Steller declared that at Bolsheretsk "the Cossacks earn not a little transporting goods on boats to the other ostrogs."[33] In 1773 flour and groats cost twice as much at Nizhne-Kamchatsk as at Bolsheretsk, mainly because of the expense of transport between the two places: one and a half rubles per pud, although this transport cost had decreased by two-thirds since the early 1740's. In 1818 it cost three to four rubles per pud to transport grain overland from Tigilsk and Petro-pavlovsk to Bolsheretsk and Verkhne-Kamchatsk.[34]

Transport as far as the coast of Kamchatka also inflated the prices of imports in the peninsula. Commandant Shmalev noted in 1773 "the great expensiveness of provisions and goods" at Verkhne-Kam-chatsk because of the long haul from Irkutsk.[35] Around 1740 Krashenin-nikov found that rye flour, bought for 25 kopeks per pud, probably along the upper Lena, and cow's butter, bought at 1 ruble, 20 kopeks per pud at Yakutsk, sold in Kamchatka for 4 to 8 rubles and 6 to 8 rubles per pud, respectively:[36] a sixteen-fold to thirty-two–fold differential in the case of flour and a fivefold to sevenfold differential in the case of butter.

The exorbitant prices of foodstuffs in Kamchatka, however, were due in part, at least, to graft—made all the easier by the scarcity of goods. Governor Simpson of the Hudson's Bay Company noted in 1842 that "the freight from Ochotsk to Kamchatka as fixed at head-quarters, is not to be more than half a rouble a pood, while, as exacted on the spot, it amounts to fifteen roubles."[37] Large profits were made. In 1755 provisions costing less than one ruble per pud at Yakutsk were transported to Kamchatka for three and sold there for ten rubles per pud,[38] so that profits sometimes amounted to at least 150 percent.

Basis of Transport Charges

The charges for transport differed in accordance with the difficulty more than with the distance of transport. In 1813 a pud of flour cost fifty to sixty kopeks at Irkutsk, one to one and a half rubles at Yakutsk, nearly ten rubles at Okhotsk, and eleven and a half to twelve and a half rubles in Kamchatka; approximately the same differential prevailed in the late 1820's.[39] Behind these prices lay the costs of transport, which in 1813 amounted to forty kopeks to one ruble per pud from Irkutsk to Yakutsk (ca. 1,650 miles), eight and a half to nine rubles from Yakutsk to Okhotsk (600 to 750 miles), and one and a half to two and a half rubles from Okhotsk to Kamchatka (660 to 725 miles to Bolsheretsk). The Yakutsk–Okhotsk Track, the most difficult of these three sections of the supply route, was by far the costliest. Around 1820, when it cost the government thirteen rubles per pud to ship grain from Irkutsk to Kamchatka, ten rubles of that amount went for transport from Yakutsk to Okhotsk. Of the fourteen rubles per pud it cost the state in 1822 to transport flour from Irkutsk to Kamchatka, exactly half was ascribed to the Yakutsk–Okhotsk Track. Rankholding officials traveling between Yakutsk and Okhotsk were allowed travel expenses double those between Irkutsk and Yakutsk.[40]

The transport of provisions, then, was costliest over the shortest section and cheapest over the longest section of the supply line. The cheapest stretch—from Irkutsk to Yakutsk—was over twice as long as each of the other two stretches. In 1801 transport from Irkutsk to Okhotsk cost 6 rubles, 55 kopeks per pud (1 ruble, 10 kopeks per pud from Irkutsk to Yakutsk and 5 rubles, 45 kopeks per pud from Yakutsk to Okhotsk), while transport from St. Petersburg to Irkutsk, for example, which was more than twice the distance from Irkutsk to Okhotsk, cost the same price (6 to 8 rubles per pud).[41]

It is also evident that water transport was much cheaper than land transport. In 1813 transport from Okhotsk to Bolsheretsk cost only a fourth to a fifth as much as that from Yakutsk to Okhotsk, both legs being about equal in length. The same differential prevailed in 1755, when the costs of transporting provisions on these two stretches were fifty kopeks per pud and two and a half rubles per pud, respectively.[42]

Moreover, downriver transport was cheaper than that by sea. In 1813 transport from Irkutsk to Yakutsk cost but half to a third of that from Okhotsk to Bolsheretsk because of the downstream direction of traffic and the simple nature of vessels on the river route.

The cost of overland-oversea provisionment was so high that around 1750 Siberia's Governor Kinderman proposed "to provision the troops of northeastern Siberia with mashed birch bark in order to avoid losses to Her Imperial Highness' Treasury."[43]

7

TRANSPORT PROBLEMS

> "It can be said that, for our sins, on the Okhotsk Road we suffered
> the ten tortures, similar to the Egyptian [tortures]. Rabid horses;
> quagmires, where the land turned into water for us; nocturnal dark-
> ness, often catching us en route among the thick woods; branches
> threatening to blind us; hunger; cold; mosquitoes; gadflies—these are
> truly *biting flies;* dangerous fords across rivers; and sores [anthrax]
> on the horses—the tenth punishment!"
>
> Protoiyerey Prokopy Gromov, "Put ot Irkutska," p. 217.

From Irkutsk to Yakutsk

A plethora of difficulties plagued overland-overseas provisionment. Downstream transport on the Lena River was faced with fewer
obstacles than transport on the Yakutsk–Okhotsk Track and on the sea
lanes from Okhotsk. In some places between the river's headwaters and
Yakutsk navigation was hampered by swift shoals; in June and July it
was sometimes almost halted by low water.[1] The Governor of Yakutsk
reported to Moscow in 1675 that low water and insufficient workers
delayed the "Yakutsk delivery": "25 men were sent to Ilimsk Ostrog for
grain, and these men bring grain supplies to Yakutsk with great need;
and they navigate from Ilimsk Uyezd from the mouth of the Kuta River
to Yakutsk with grain supplies on kochas, doshchaniks, barkas, and rafts
at two and three men per vessel on account of the shortage of men, and,
because of the scarcity of men, they founder on shoals and they sail to
Yakutsk in five weeks and more; and 60 state servitors are needed for
sending for grain supplies."[2]

Lorenz Lang, a high official of Ilimsk Uyezd, reported in 1740
that shipping down the Lena to Yakutsk from the upper Lena landings
encountered "great difficulty" every year because of shallow water. For
example, five of the thirty-two loaded rafts sent downriver to Yakutsk in
1740 with freight for the Second Kamchatka Expedition were stopped
by shallow water.[3] The problem was described by two peasant pilots in

mid-June of 1758: "because at present the Lena River is shallow . . . it is by any means impossible and hopeless to send not only loaded but even empty rafts, for in many places in the Lena River there are great shoals across the entire river, so that already there is no more than three-quarters of an arshin [twenty-one inches] of water, and in some places half an arshin [fourteen inches]. And a loaded raft needs more than an arshin [twenty-eight inches] of water. . . ."[4] In 1830 an observer reported that barkas, the chief grain vessels, were "sometimes" and "not infrequently" wrecked.[5] At Yakutsk the resultant "lack of the first item of provisionment was very long [until the middle of the eighteenth century] a sore point and one of the most difficult matters of the local administration."[6]

From Yakutsk to Okhotsk

The difficulties of the Irkutsk–Yakutsk stretch, however, were minor compared with those of the Yakutsk–Okhotsk section of the supply line, especially the land version. No other Siberian route sapped the Russian Treasury of so much money as did the Yakutsk–Okhotsk Track. Generally proceeding at the rate of four to five m.p.h. for ten to twelve hours a day, the Yakut pack horses should have reached Okhotsk (600–750 miles) in ten days at the least or in nineteen days at the most; instead, they often took twelve to fifteen days just to travel the 144 to 220 miles from Yudoma Cross to Okhotsk, while it usually took them six weeks and sometimes even two to three months to cover the entire route from Yakutsk to Okhotsk[7] (Map 7). This discrepancy stemmed from many natural and human difficulties, difficulties that loomed large in the harrowing experiences of the First and Second Kamchatka Expeditions. Almost half of the second expedition's ten years were spent transporting supplies, mostly provisions, from Yakutsk to Okhotsk. In the summer of 1770 a party of exiles took 95 days to go from Yakutsk to Okhotsk with eighty horses, of which sixty-three died en route.[8] This was not an uncommon occurrence on the Okhotsk Track. Around 1750 an anonymous observer declared that "this route is so difficult, that there is hardly one like it in all of the Russian state."[9] Peter Dobell asserted that the tracks between Yakutsk and Okhotsk were "the worst and most dangerous roads I ever travelled";[10] and the Decembrist Zavalishin, who journeyed from Okhotsk to Yakutsk in 1824, contended that the route was "one of the hardest and worst roads in the world. . . ."[11] The explorer Gedenstrom found the Yakutsk–Okhotsk Track in the late 1820's to be "almost impassable and the most difficult in the entire Empire"; he added that "the road is a riding one, but in its difficulties, unique in Russia."[12] Baron Von Wrangel, on his way to become Governor of Russian America, remarked in 1830 that the difficulties of the track were embodied in an almost proverbial phrase: "in Siberia the Okhotsk Road means the most fatiguing and the most dangerous journey."[13] And Governor-General Muravyov, the first Siberian governor to travel the Yakutsk–Okhotsk Track, called it "one of the most difficult of all journeys" in a letter to his brother but refrained from describing it further because it was so "interesting and unusual" that to describe it would have taken more than a letter.[14]

The meandering, unmarked trail might have passed for an obstacle course with its numerous torrents, extensive bogs, thick brush and dense woods, stony ground, steep slopes, snowy and icy passes, bears and wolves, clouds of midges and mosquitoes, emaciated horses, unreliable conductors, and thieving, murderous marauders. Naval Lieutenant Khvostov, reporting in 1804 on his activities under Count Rezanov's diplomatic mission to Japan, declared that the track was in "very bad condition" because: (1) it was periodically obliterated by streams; (2) in many places it was overlain with rotting corduroy, whose holes and chinks tripped the horses; (3) small trees, bent by heavy snow in winter, became entangled, blocking the trail; and (4) pack horses, always following the same trail in strings, beat a path pocked with water-filled potholes.[15]

Running across the dense drainage network of the Aldan Basin, the Yakutsk–Okhotsk Track encountered a host of large and small watercourses, ranging from the slow, wide Aldan to the swift, narrow Belaya. Most of them had to be forded (like the Belaya), although a few had ferries (such as the Aldan, the Allakh-Yun, and the Yudoma) and some had bridges—which were usually washed out by spring thaws and summer rains. Especially on the Aldan–Okhotsk section the track followed the natural passages carved by mountain torrents, but the winding courses and varying banks of these streams necessitated numerous crossings. Captain Minitsky, successively Commandant of Okhotsk and Yakutsk, told the so-called "pedestrian" traveler Cochrane in 1822 that the total number of stream crossings on the Yakutsk–Okhotsk Track was no less than 1,000,[16] or one crossing every two-thirds of a mile. Cochrane himself, riding from Okhotsk to Yakutsk, crossed the Urak River nine times within forty miles. The Belaya had to be crossed no fewer than thirty times.[17] In July of 1834 Father Gromov's party had to cross one river eight times one day and another river twelve times another day.[18] According to the surveyor Termin, the Aldan–Okhotsk section of the track crossed up to 1,200 streams, although this figure does not jibe with Minitsky's overall estimate.[19] Between the Lena and the Aldan (inclusive) the track crossed only eleven to twelve rivers.[20] Many of these watercourses, however, were dry in summer, rains permitting.

Ordinarily these streams were fordable, but during spring breakup and summer downpours they became impassable torrents, like the Allakh-Yun, which means "swift river" in Yakut. Sometimes in fording the Kukhtui River to reach the new site of Okhotsk after 1815 pack horses were drowned and loads were drenched.[21] In 1842 Sir George Simpson learned that once three hundred laden horses had drowned in the swollen Luktur River, a tributary of the middle Urak.[22] The heavy summer rains in particular often caused widespread flooding; caravans might be marooned on high ground for days or weeks (even a month) waiting for the rains to cease and the freshets to subside. Sometimes flash floods caught the caravans on low ground; the conductors had hastily to construct makeshift platforms (called *labazas*) from branches in the treetops, where they secured themselves and the freight, leaving the horses or cattle at the mercy of the floodwaters.[23] Needless to say, many horses and cattle were drowned and much freight was lost or damaged during fording and flooding. The merchant Shelekhov reported in 1794 that "very often, on account of rain, goods are abandoned on the road and undergo damage and loss. . . ."[24] After floodwaters had subsided, soggy ground retarded travel; it took six to eight weeks to reach Okhotsk when the Yakutsk–Okhotsk Track was muddy.[25] And even in dry weather transport eastward across first the Seven Ranges and then the Nine Ranges between the Aldan and Yudoma rivers was an arduous ordeal. Their steep and rugged slopes, whose summits here and there reached elevations around 3,000 feet, exhausted the heavily laden pack horses.

The Lena–Aldan stretch of the route, known locally as the "Siberian Caucasus" (apparently because of its physiographic resemblance to the northern foreland of the Caucasus), was generally the best section of the whole track, while the Aldan–Okhotsk stretch was the most difficult leg.[26] "In general," wrote Krasheninnikov, "it is possible to say of this road that from Yakutsk to Belskaya Crossing [Okhotsk Ferry] it is very tolerable, but thence to Okhotsk it is so rough that it is impossible to imagine a more difficult thoroughfare, for it runs either along river banks or wooded mountains."[27] In 1834 a cleric observed that "the Okhotsk Road consists of *badarans* ('quagmires'), sometimes of dry lowland, but mostly of openings between dense forests. . . ."[28] Although the Lena–Aldan stretch was devoid of the dense forest and the rugged relief that hampered transport east of the Aldan, it did traverse treacherous bogs, which were also found in spots east of the Aldan. It was especially boggy between the Amga and the Aldan rivers, where pack horses could walk all day without once stepping on firm ground. The worst bogs occurred along the stretch between Nokhinsk and the lower Belaya River. Although the conductors scrutinized the path up to seventy feet in advance of the convoys, mishaps were common, the horses sinking to their knees, bellies, or even necks in the muck. If they could not be extricated, which apparently was usually the case, their packs were removed and put on spare horses, leaving the mired animals to be swallowed by the quicksandy bogs. Many horses, not to mention cattle, were lost in this way.[29] The bogs were particularly dangerous during spring thaw and summer rains, when they became almost impassable. It was the object of the early plastovoy transport to cross these bogs and the rivers while they were still frozen. Permafrost, besides promoting bogs, obstructed drainage of the thawed surface of the track elsewhere, producing still more muck.

Corduroy roads (*gats*), called "bridges" by locals and "logways" or "wooden causeways" by visitors, were constructed over some of the bogs, apparently around the beginning of the nineteenth century and especially during the late 1810's and early 1820's.* There were 50 to 100 miles of corduroy between the Amga and the Aldan rivers. Corduroy sections were especially common along the Aldan River between Okhotsk Ferry and the mouth of the Belaya River; fully two-thirds of the first thirty miles of track east of the Aldan were corduroy in 1842.[30]

---

* Corduroy roads were not uncommon in Russia. As late as the 1820's much of the road between St. Petersburg and Moscow was corduroy (Capt. John Dundas Cochrane, *Narrative of a Pedestrian Journey through Russia and Siberian Tartary* . . . [Philadelphia: H. C. Carey, I. Lea, and A. Small, 1824], p. 53; Erman, *Travels in Siberia,* 1 : 70). Cochrane found in 1820 that the road between Moscow and Novgorod was almost entirely corduroy. Such roads were colloquially termed "spine crushers" (Erman, *Travels in Siberia,* 1 : 234).

The mode of construction was to drive three rows of piles into the ground, place three parallel lines of logs atop the piles, and peg un-barked poles transversely on the logs.* Some corduroy sections were two miles and even three and a half to four and a half miles long.[31] The corduroy roads themselves, however, were treacherous enough, for the horses often fell on the slick, uneven surface. Also, damage from spring breakup and summer rains, and eventual decay, created gaps in the corduroy that frequently ensnared and felled pack horses.[32]

Rivers and bogs were the principal obstacles to transport on the Yakutsk–Okhotsk Track. When thaws and rains temporarily made the rivers uncrossable and the bogs impassable, seventy and even eighty days might be spent in going from Yakutsk to Okhotsk.[33] But there were additional impediments. On the plastovoy route the underfed horses, after the long winter and before the spring grass, were very weak. And forage was meager along the track. De Lesseps describes one such horse that he obtained at Okhotsk in early April of 1788: "At sight of the horse I was to mount, I drew back with horror and compassion. I had never seen so wretched an animal. His sides were lank and hollow, his buttocks narrow and peaked, so that you might count every bone they contained, his neck unsupported, his head between his legs, his haunches nerveless and weak. Such is the exact description of my steed. You may judge of the figure of the other horses, among which mine passed for one of the least despicable."[34] In such condition the pack horses quickly tired under their heavy loads and often succumbed to exhaustion. The small wooden saddles were light; but the large saddle "blankets," which were never dry, were heavy as well as galling burdens, giving the horses sores. In addition, the horses mangled their unshod hoofs on sharp stones, broke their legs in chinks in the logways or in holes in the ground, and gashed their bodies on snags in the bogs or on trees, stumps, bushes, and rocks along the trail. Large, sharp rocks were especially hazardous. The shortage of time and grass and the presence of bears precluded resting the injured horses until they recovered.[35] According to Krasheninnikov, no horses reached Okhotsk from Yakutsk with intact hoofs.[36] Trees, upright and fallen alike, were formidable obstacles. Bering reported to the Siberian Office in 1738 that "the road is not cleared and at present not a few horses are lost en route, for there are trees lying on the road

* Sometimes the logs were placed across rather than along the trail (Alexander Rowand, *Notes of a Journey in Russian America and Siberia* . . . [Edinburgh? : n.p., n.d.], p. 34).

which are blown down and piled up on the road by the wind, and besides many horses prick themselves on the branches of the trees standing near the road and die . . . ."[37] Termin found in the early 1830's that even the Yakutsk–Aldan stretch was overgrown with trees.[38]

Predators were another hazard. Brown bears and timber wolves, which were very numerous along the track, frequently attacked the convoys of horses and the droves of cattle.* In 1828 an exile noted the "incredible number of bears" along the track, and added, "rare is the night when they do not pluck one caravan or another."[39] Sir George Simpson observed in 1842 that "the bears are both fierce and numerous on this road. . . ."[40] Because the beasts were particularly ravenous and aggressive between their winter hibernations and the fish runs of late spring and early summer, both the plastovoy transport and the yarmarochny transport were troubled by them. The bears were attracted by the abundance of cadavers along the track, and they acquired a taste for horseflesh.** Bear traps were set along both banks of the Ancha River.[41] Even dogs attacked the horses. As Sauer, a member of the Billings Expedition, noted in 1786, at Okhotsk in spring "the dogs then become so ravenous, that it is not uncommon for them to destroy one another; and the first horses that arrive are generally torn to pieces."[42] Swarms of mosquitoes and midges completed the torment. In 1807 the whitish horses of the Yankee traveler D'Wolf became pinkish from blood drawn by countless mosquitoes along the trail.[43] This experience was not unusual.

Furthermore, after arriving in Okhotsk the Yakut conductors had to wait a long time until goods were ready for transport to Yakutsk, for which more horses than necessary were always retained. During the 1822–25 contract period, however, the Yakuts were permitted to leave no more than two hundred horses at Okhotsk, and then only until September 1. Horses returning to Yakutsk later in the season not infrequently floundered in heavy snow, scarcely one of every hundred surviving.[44] Men as well as horses were frozen; at Yakutsk at the end of

* Bears also attacked the post (Rowand, *Notes of a Journey*, p. 27). Captain Vasilyev's journal of his round-the-world expedition of 1819–22 was badly damaged by a marauding bear on the Yakutsk-Okhotsk Track (Cochrane, *Narrative of a Pedestrian Journey*, p. 324).

** The Yakuts, too, were fond of horsemeat; perhaps the bears and the wolves did not scavenge all the carcasses. Indeed, the Yakuts were suspected of butchering ailing horses prematurely (Gmelin, *Voyage en Siberie*, 1 : 417–418).

the eighteenth century men with crippled or wooden legs, the results of gangrene, were not uncommon. Even in the middle of summer the Yakutsk–Okhotsk Track traversed ice for half a day (two and one-half to three miles) at Captain's Clearing, the site of a perennial icefield produced by permafrost.[45]

Yet another equine hazard was disease. Von Langsdorff noted in 1807 that many Yakut pack horses were dying from murrain, which first occurred in 1804 and recurred in 1806 and 1807.[46] "Siberian sores" or "contagion" (anthrax) was a commoner ailment. Stricken horses, weary and emaciated, easily succumbed, especially in the heat of summer, and died within three days. Anthrax especially impeded freighting from 1816 through 1819, just when the Okhotsk Seaboard was also enduring a shortage of fish. During the winter of 1820–21, 1,874 horses perished on the Yakutsk–Okhotsk Track, including 1,646 from anthrax and 28 from fatigue. In 1829 up to 2,500 horses died from anthrax on the track; the government indemnified the Yakut owners at the rate of twelve rubles per horse.[47] It was reported in 1830 that 5,000 to 6,000 horses perished annually from the disease on the track.[48] In one year alone anthrax killed over 10,000 horses on the Yakutsk–Okhotsk Track, and some 5,000 horses succumbed to it in Okhotsk Kray in 1834.[49] All in all, in the words of one observer, "it is difficult to express the torment to horse and rider on this track. . . ."[50]

Every convoy that arrived at Okhotsk was missing many horses.[51] Vasily Shmalev, Timofey's brother, estimated that up to 1776 no less than 100,000 horses had died carrying state freight alone on the Yakutsk–Okhotsk Track.[52] Assuming that he was reckoning from 1736, when such transport became an obligation of the Yakuts, this estimate entails an average annual loss of 2,500 horses. In 1775 at least 1,000 horses perished.[53] In 1776 Timofey Shmalev warned Governor-General Bril of Irkutsk Province that every year many horses died on the track;[54] and Shelekhov cautioned Bril in 1794 that "often the Yakuts lose many of their horses" on the track.[55] De Lesseps estimated in 1788 that 4,000 to 5,000 horses were lost yearly on the track.[56] Here the Yakuts lost over 10,000 horses in 1808 and up to 10,000 horses in 1818.[57] Around 1820 it was estimated that a "substantial part" of the at least 6,000 horses used annually to transport state goods from Yakutsk to Okhotsk perished en route, even when the trail was dry; during one six-year period over 10,000 horses died.[58] The Yakut outfitters figured in 1822 that two horses out of every string of twelve packed to Okhotsk would perish,[59] although a Russian observer contended at the beginning of the century that it was usual for the Yakuts to lose over half the horses that they furnished for transport to Okhotsk.[60] For example, the fatality rate among the horses used by the Second Kamchatka Expedition between Yudoma Cross and Okhotsk exceeded 50 percent.[61] An exile stated in 1828 that "horses perished by the thousands on the Okhotsk Road. . . ."[62] During the late 1830's, when anthrax was absent, the Yakuts lost 5,000 to 7,000 horses each summer on the Yakutsk–Okhotsk Track.[63]

The losses were so considerable that at times there was a shortage of horses for transport between Yakutsk and Okhotsk. In 1820 only 3,000 were available for state transport to Okhotsk, while 4,869 were needed. Especially during the 1810's the Yakuts were impoverished by the increased traffic on the Yakutsk–Okhotsk Track, for whenever the required number of horses exceeded 8,000, they had to use not only stallions but also mares and colts, which, not being strong enough for packing, soon died en route.[64] Consequently, the value of a Yakut horse soared from seven to nine rubles in 1772 to twenty to twenty-five rubles in 1798 to a hundred rubles in 1805. Thus, the indemnity of twelve rubles per horse paid the Yakuts by the government in 1829 was quite inadequate, to say the least. Although the caravans included spare horses, so many loaded horses died that their packs had to be cached en route until they could be retrieved by fresh horses. Many Yakuts, impoverished by the losses, were reluctant to lease horses. In 1822 the Yakuts were so affected that 12,706 of 40,430 taxable Yakuts were unable to pay taxes.[65]

No Siberian route rivaled the Yakutsk–Okhotsk Track in loss of horses, although many died in packing on the Yakutsk–Kolymsk and Yakutsk–Udsk routes and in tracking up the Lena River.* In 1750, for example, all pack horses on the Yakutsk–Udsk Track perished in deep snow. This disaster, coupled with the shortage of fish in the Uda River, resulted in the starvation of many Cossacks and peasants at Udsk; normally the pack horses were left at Udsk as food for the inhabitants

---

* Many pack horses also perished on the Yakutsk–Anadyrsk route. In 1754, for instance, a party of Cossacks under Major Ivan Shmalev, Timofey's and Vasily's father, traveled from Yakutsk to Anadyrsk with 652½ tons of provisions, which required 14,500 sumas and 7,250 horses. Up to half of these horses did not return, including "several thousand" that died (Russia, Pravitelstvuyushchy senat, *Senatsky arkhiv* [*Senate Archive*] [St. Petersburg: Tipografiya Pravitelstvuyushchavo senata, 1892–1901], 9 : 367–368).

and the dogs, the Yakut transporters returning to Yakutsk from late March on foot or on skis. Again, in the spring of 1788 the Yakutsk–Udsk Track was flooded, and on one occasion that May more than three hundred pack horses going to Udsk were drowned by the high waters of the spring breakup.[66] Cochrane estimated in 1820–21 that altogether the Yakuts lost at least 50,000 horses annually, including 15,000 to 20,000 on the Yakutsk–Okhotsk Track.[67] (His figures, as usual, are probably inflated.) This track was harder on horses than the Yakutsk–Udsk Track because, although drier, it was hillier and rockier, crossed more rivers, and offered less pasture.[68] Thousands of horses died on it every year from drowning, miring, freezing, predation, disease, exhaustion, and so on.

The Yakutsk–Okhotsk Track was littered with the carcasses and skeletons of pack horses. De Lesseps, en route from Okhotsk to Yakutsk in 1788, exclaimed that "every ten steps we see skeletons of these horses, and from Okhotsk to the cross of Yudoma, I imagine that I passed more than two thousand."[69] The heads of mired horses could be seen protruding from quagmires along the track.[70] Minitsky, Commandant of Yakutsk, reported to Irkutsk in 1819 that it was necessary every year to send Yakuts over the Yakutsk–Okhotsk Track to dispose of the horse cadavers, which in summertime were found in abundance along the track and caused contagion. During one summer 869 dead horses and 39 dead cattle were thus removed.[71] One boggy spot halfway along the trail was named Chikhonoye Plachishche ("Chikhonoy's weeping place") after a Yakut who lost there all his horses, the stench of which attracted numerous bears.[72] Sir George Simpson commented on the toll of horses taken by the Yakutsk–Okhotsk Track: "When compared with this corner of the world, England, which is sometimes said to be the hell of horses, must be contented with the secondary honour of being their purgatory. The unfortunate brutes here lie down to die, in great numbers, through famine and fatigue; and this road is more thickly strewed with their bones than any part of the plains on the Saskatchewan with those of the buffalo."[73]

Around 1820 Governor Speransky, shocked by the great loss of horses, recommended that Okhotsk and Kamchatka be provisioned by sea from Kronstadt instead of by land from Irkutsk and that the Russian-American Company use the oversea route instead of the Yakutsk–Okhotsk Track.[74] His recommendation was not heeded.

Transport over the Yakutsk–Okhotsk Track was plagued by human as well as by physical difficulties. The trail was sparsely settled, so that little relief was available en route for stricken convoys. In 1782 there were only eleven stations (one every twenty miles) with thirty-seven persons and 107 horses on the Lena–Aldan stretch, which crossed the most settled part of the country between Yakutsk and Okhotsk. Sometimes the convoys were plundered by *brodyagas* (runaway convicts) who had escaped from forced-labor operations near Okhotsk.[75] Speransky reported in 1822 that convicts often escaped from the Okhotsk saltworks and "first they go along the track from Okhotsk to Yakutsk, rob merchant transports, attack small settlements. . . ."[76] And in 1827 Commandant Golenishchev of Kamchatka reported that the convicts at the Okhotsk saltworks, "making their escape, cause great disorder and destruction to the traders going from Yakutsk to Okhotsk with goods."[77] A chain of hills between the Okhota and the Urak rivers was called Rogues' Range "because they are the common place of resort of the criminals that escape every year from Ochotsk."[78]

The Yakuts themselves, though unexcelled handlers of horses, were not always trustworthy, sometimes absconding with contracted freight.[79] Sometimes, too, they abandoned it en route. Speransky reported in 1819 that "the Yakuts, not being able to accomplish the agreed transport, despite high payment, discard its [Russian-American Company's] goods in the forests and swamps."[80] The amount of provisions that reached Okhotsk was not infrequently less than what left Yakutsk.

Russian officials and merchants were also at fault. The receipt and the dispatch of supplies at Okhotsk and elsewhere were marred by much corruption, particularly by embezzlement. In 1732 Zhadovsky, Commandant of Yakutsk, embezzled 21 tons, 120 pounds of breadstuffs and ironware intended for Okhotsk.[81] Officials also cheated the Yakuts, frequently retaining money intended for them. Around 1813, when the Yakuts were supposed to be paid eighty to eighty-five rubles for the transport of every loaded pack horse from Yakutsk to Okhotsk, they received little more than half that sum, the rest going into the numerous and commodious pockets of government officials.[82] In the late 1810's the Yakuts complained in a petition to the Tsar that they had to furnish up to 10,000 horses annually for transport over the Yakutsk–Okhotsk Track; they leased each horse at thirty to sixty rubles but received only ten rubles, while most of their horses perished on the road. Much of the money was embezzled by Yakut chieftains and by Russian officials.[83] Even when the Yakuts did receive full payment, it was still often exceeded by their expenditures on transport. This debit among the Yakuts of the Namsky Ulus, for instance, totaled 35,590 rubles, 90 kopeks (7 rubles, 85 kopeks each) in 1799; 50,381 rubles, 58 kopeks (11 rubles, 12 kopeks each) in 1800; and 69,506 rubles, 6 kopeks (15 rubles, 3 kopeks each) in 1801.[84] The Yakuts were also exploited by merchant contractors. In the last half of the 1770's the contractors Sibiryakov, Kiselev, Shubin, and Sitnikov received eleven to twelve rubles from the government for each pack horse they dispatched from Yakutsk but paid their Yakut outfitters only five and a half rubles per horse.[85] In 1786–87 the Yakuts even sent an envoy to Catherine II at St. Petersburg with a "Plan about the Yakuts," which embodied their complaints of abuses in contracting.[86] The procurement of sumas was also marred by graft.[87] Little wonder, then, that, in the words of one distraught official, "Yakuts never provide the full number of horses. . . ."[88] At times, as in 1762, they even refused to transport freight to Okhotsk.[89]

The dreadful condition of the Yakutsk–Okhotsk Track was a result partly of the elements and partly of the incompetence and indifference of the builders and the repairers. Peter Dobell observed that in general "the method of making and repairing roads there [Siberia] is very little understood . . ." and "the management of the business is for the most part given to spravniks [police chiefs], or other officers of the civil list, many of whom are drunkards, or men unworthy of such a trust: so that time, labour, and money are oftentimes expended without producing any advantage or improvement."[90] Termin found in the early 1830's that, although Yakuts were dispatched every year to repair the Yakutsk–Aldan stretch, it was always in bad condition because of negligence and unskillfulness on the part of the repairers.[91] Some of the labor was performed perfunctorily by convicts, whose hearts were undoubtedly not in their work. Shoddy construction and seasonal washouts made the upkeep of the Yakutsk–Okhotsk Track a Sisyphean task. Moreover, realization of the unsuitability of Okhotsk Port and the quest for a better site discouraged upkeep of the track.[92]

The river route was not much better than the land route between Yakutsk and Okhotsk. Most importantly, it was longer in both distance and (upstream at least) time, so that it was seldom used.* Westward (largely downstream) movement was rapid, but eastward (largely upstream) traffic was slow. For example, it took less than three days to boat down the Yudoma River from Yudoma Cross to the Maya River, whereas boating up the same stretch took five to six weeks. There were no ready-made carriers or experienced conductors like the Yakut horses and men on the Yakutsk–Okhotsk Track; wooden rafts had to be constructed and Russian raftsmen recruited. Since the river route was uninhabited, hands could not be hired on the way. Upriver passage against the swift currents of the Maya and the Yudoma rivers necessitated laborious tracking by men and animals, while freight was continually threatened with dunking. While the Maya River section was free of rapids, on the Yudoma River traffic was hampered by several rapids and cataracts. One of these, some fifty miles below Yudoma Cross, was partially bypassed by a crude canal, which, however, was dry at low water.** Yudoma Cross was seldom reached from Yakutsk by river in one summer. In the summer of 1788 it took Sarychev's flotilla of seventeen boats six weeks to track from Ust-Maya to Yudoma Cross; and near its junction with the Maya the Yudoma was so swift that thirty men could barely tow one loaded boat upstream. Passage on the Urak River was particularly arduous, dangerous, and prolonged,† for the river was swift and shallow and full of rocks and bars, such as the rapids forty miles and fifty-four miles upstream.[93] Timofey Shmalev asserted in 1775 that the swiftness and the rapids of the Yudoma and the Urak rivers rendered them "very dangerous" and the whole river route "very

* For example, it took Krasheninnikov thirty-four days (excluding stops) in 1737 to go from Yakutsk to Okhotsk via the land route and eighteen days (excluding stops) in 1741 to go from Okhotsk to Yakutsk by the river route (including seven days by land from Okhotsk to Yudoma Cross and five days by land from Ust-Maya to Yakutsk) (Krasheninnikov, *Opisanie zemli Kamchatki,* pp. 529, 531).

** Instead of portaging around the cataracts on the Yudoma, the Russians sometimes first unloaded their boats and then ran the cataracts (De Lesseps, *Travels in Kamtschatka,* 2 : 290).

† However, Captain Walton of the Second Kamchatka Expedition boated down the Urak River from Urak Landing to the Okhotsk Sea, a distance of 100 miles, in seventeen hours, despite many stops (Krasheninnikov, *Opisanie zemli Kamchatki,* p. 159). Waxell, another member of the expedition, covered the same distance several times in no more than seventeen hours also, without oars or sails (Waxell, *Russian Expedition to America,* p. 56).

useless,"[94] an opinion which Lieutenant Khvostov shared in 1804 when he deemed the river route useless because of the swiftness of the waters.[95]

Also, the Urak was deep enough for rafting only in spring and during rains. During flash floods it was easy for rafts on the overflowing river to drift off course and become stranded high and dry away from the river after the floodwater had subsided. Often rafts and goods, and sometimes men, were lost; for example, in June of 1738 four of forty vessels plying the river under Captain Walton to supply the Second Kamchatka Expedition were sunk by the swift current and the ice with a loss of 10 tons, 1,319 pounds of provisions.[96] And sometimes boats bound for Okhotsk had to wait a week at the mouth of the Urak for a calm sea. The stretch between the river's mouth and Okhotsk was safe only in spring, when the surf was minimized by offshore ice.[97]

All in all, the Yakutsk–Okhotsk river route was a most unsuitable passage, except perhaps for downstream shipment, and it was little used after the Second Kamchatka Expedition. When the river route was utilized, two long stretches of it—Yakutsk to Ust-Maya and Yudoma Cross to Okhotsk—were usually supplanted by land passages. It was best to go from Yakutsk to Okhotsk by land in mid-summer, in order to avoid the muck of early summer and the snow of late summer, and to return by land as far as Yudoma Cross, thence by river as far as Ust-Maya, and thence by land to Yakutsk;[98]* but horses packed to Okhotsk could not be rafted back.

From Okhotsk to Gizhiga and Kamchatka

The difficulties of overland-oversea provisionment were by no means confined to the overland section. The entrepôt of Okhotsk, which connected the overland and the oversea sections of the supply line, was a poor port. The town itself, before its transfer by Minitsky in 1815–16 to Tungus Spit at the mouth of the Kukhtui River, was situated on an exposed, soggy tongue of land (fourteen to twenty-five feet above sea level, one to two and one-half miles long, and 10 and 200 paces wide at,

---

* However, Krasheninnikov declared that the period between spring breakup and midsummer was the best time of the year for travel between Yakutsk and Okhotsk (Krasheninnikov, *Opisanie zemli Kamchatki*, p. 529).

respectively, its narrowest and broadest points) called Askew Spit or Okhotsk Spit, where oozing precluded the use of cellars[99] (Figures 8 and 9). In some years as much as a quarter of the town was destroyed by the ice-choked waters of the Okhota River during spring breakup. Okhotsk was severely damaged by flooding in twenty different years from 1723 through 1813 (1723, 1725, 1733, 1736, 1755, 1759, 1768, 1769, 1770, 1771, 1774, 1775, 1777, 1782, 1783, 1786, 1801, 1810, 1812, and 1813). Usually several houses were destroyed and several persons drowned each time. The flash flood of July 27, 1736, for example, inundated the ostrog, destroying many buildings, drowning numerous animals, and damaging and destroying Cossack supplies, as well as sinking a boat with six men and cutting a new mouth through the spit.[100] Captain Timofey Shmalev complained in a report of October 12, 1774, to Governor-General Bril at Irkutsk that every year at Okhotsk the beach was shrunk and several houses were destroyed by flooding;[101] another report stated that houses at Okhotsk were "not infrequently" destroyed by flooding.[102] A flood alarm bell was finally installed in 1775. Many vessels, as well as several streets, were destroyed by unusually high surf in 1749, 1759, 1768, 1782, and 1786; and the spit was severely eroded by flooding in 1733, 1742, 1755, 1777, and 1783. In 1810 the Okhota, its mouth jammed by ice, cut a new channel through the neck of the spit, thereby isolating the townsite.[103]

The overall harbor of Okhotsk, formed by the confluent mouths of the Okhota and the Kukhtui rivers, was spacious enough (10 miles long and 3 miles wide); but the navigable channel within the harbor was narrow and shallow: 210 to 280 feet wide and 4 to 6 feet deep at ebbtide, and 7 to 17 feet deep at floodtide. Merchant ships, which displaced ten to twelve feet of water, had to await floodtide before entering.[104] Between high and low tides the harbor admitted ships drawing no more than eight feet of water. It was ice-free only six months of the year (from late May until late November). The navigation season normally lasted only three to four months (from early June until late September), although often ships could not leave Okhotsk until July.[105] At any rate, shallowness was more of a problem than ice. Three-quarters of the harbor was dry at low water. The main channel of the Okhota, which ranged in depth from six to eight feet at high water to one-half to two and one-half feet at low water, was navigable only up to five miles by small, empty vessels. It was really too shallow for harborage. Wintering vessels ran the risk of bilging by ice during spring breakup. The passage between the harbor and the sea, which was impeded by a bar, was also narrow and shallow, being but 1,500 feet wide and 12 feet deep at high tide and 180 feet wide and 5 feet deep at low tide.* Moreover, this channel was shifted every year—and sometimes two or three times during the year—by river ice from the Okhota, so that it had to be reconnoitered periodically.[106] Navigation of the channel was further endangered by contrary winds and by very strong tides, which ebbed as fast as seven m.p.h. and flooded as fast as six m.p.h., while normally flowing three to four m.p.h.[107]

Owing to these obstacles, ships spent considerable time entering and leaving this so-called harbor. Departure was possible only with the turning of the tide, and sometimes ships had to wait three weeks or longer for a fair wind.[108] Shelekhov complained in 1794 that virtually half the duration of a ship's voyage from Okhotsk to Alaska was spent leaving the port.[109] In 1840 the brig *Okhotsk,* laden with provisions for Gizhiga, was detained for forty days by contrary winds and did not reach Gizhiga until October 15, where it barely escaped being wrecked by ice.[110] Adverse winds sometimes also forced ships to wait a month before entering the port.[111]

Waxell described the difficulties of Okhotsk Port in the late 1730's.

> The harbour there is not one that I can particularly praise, though we were forced to use it for want of a better. The current runs terribly strongly both at the ebb and flow, so that we had the greatest difficulty in keeping our ships at their berths. At low water they were one and all lying on dry land. Indeed, it is quite useless hoping to keep vessels with a draught greater than ten or, at the most, twelve feet, unharmed in the harbour. There is, besides, danger in the spring that the ice may wreak destruction. To put it briefly, this is an emergency harbour and not one that you can use with any confidence.[112]

Over a century later a Russian observer (1851) summarized Okhotsk's handicaps as a port.

> The coming and going of vessels is extremely difficult here: arriving vessels must stop at anchor at a completely open roadstead or stand under sail to await without fail a fair wind and the incoming tide; departing vessels must ready themselves so that, having a fair

* This shallowness continued far offshore. Eight miles off Okhotsk the depth was only ten fathoms and the bottom was loose stones, not compact enough to hold an anchor against even a moderate breeze (Sauer, *Account of an Expedition,* p. 42).

wind, they can proceed with the commencement of the outgoing tide; the swiftness of the current, the narrowness of the passage, the limited depth, and continual changes in the direction of the channel itself hamper these operations greatly, especially departures, and despite every care hardly one vessel of the Okhotsk Flotilla has not suffered some mishap; many have been wrecked. In the river itself the mooring of vessels, on account of the swift current and the crowded accommodations, is not safe enough; and in winter the vessels usually have to be dragged ashore.[113]

Another visitor, Father Gromov, exclaimed that "at Okhotsk there is neither land nor water."[114] "The name 'Okhotsk Port' is pure mockery," commented still another;[115] and Lieutenant Khvostov termed the site "one of the most unfortunate in the world."[116]

Not a few vessels and cargoes (including provisions) were delayed, damaged, or destroyed in leaving or entering Okhotsk Port.* Upkeep of the port was costly, amounting in 1806 to 182,355 rubles (excluding expenses for the purchase and delivery of supplies), compared with only 4,449 rubles in revenue.[117] Yet despite its drawbacks Okhotsk was long considered the best harbor on the Okhotsk Seaboard. "There is, in fact, no better place on this coast," said Bering.[118] This opinion was verified by various surveys of the coast undertaken by the Russian Government and by the Russian-American Company in the late eighteenth and early nineteenth centuries. Okhotsk's only advantages were the presence of abundant fish and the proximity of suitable ship-building timber (larch), although by 1774 such timber was found no closer than thirteen miles up the Okhota and most fish were caught from ten to seventeen miles (and even as far as sixty-six miles) up the Okhota, while in wintertime fresh water had to be obtained 3 and more miles away.[119] Nevertheless, these advantages were sufficient to enable Okhotsk to remain the chief port of the Okhotsk Seaboard until the mid-nineteenth century, when it was replaced by Ayan.**

From Okhotsk provisions were shipped on government transports to Gizhiga and the ports of Kamchatka—Tigilsk, Bolsheretsk,

---

* For example, in July of 1789 it took almost three weeks to get one of Billings' ships, the *Slava Rossii,* from Okhotsk harbor out to sea, while the other ship, the *Dobroye Namerenie,* was wrecked on the sandbanks at the entrance to the mouth of the Okhota (Sarychev, *Puteshestvie,* pp. 110–112; Sauer, *Account of an Expedition,* pp. 140–141).

** Magadan on Nagayev Bay, nowadays by far the dominant port of the Okhotsk Seaboard, did not materialize until the Soviet period in connection with the accelerated mining of gold in the upper reaches of the Kolyma River.

Petropavlovsk, and Nizhne-Kamchatsk. With the notable exception of Petropavlovsk, these ports were no better than Okhotsk. The "harbors" of Gizhiga, Tigilsk, Bolsheretsk, and Nizhne-Kamchatsk were nothing more than estuarial anchorages, exposed and shallow, which did not even qualify as roadsteads. All these anchorages, save Nizhne-Kamchatsk, were really primitive outposts, like Ust-Tigil and Ust-Bolsheretsk, located downstream from their parent settlements at the heads of navigation. Bolsheretsk was located on the right bank of the Bolshaya River twenty to twenty-two miles from its mouth, and Nizhne-Kamchatsk was situated on the left bank of the Kamchatka River twenty miles from its mouth.[120] The shallow entrances to the Gizhiga, Tigil, Bolshaya, and Kamchatka rivers were further marred by shifting sandbanks and strong tides, which caused many shipwrecks. At Bolsheretsk "neither on the river nor on the coast was found a suitable harbor for sea-going vessels. . . ."[121] Steller found in the early 1740's that along Kamchatka's west coast "there is not one calm bay or sheltered cove for ships" and that this coast was "extremely dangerous for sailors" because "these shores are not only very steep and rocky but framed with many visible and submarine rocks and reefs stretching far asea. . . ."[122] The mouth of the Kamchatka River, which was navigable well above Nizhne-Kamchatsk, was only eight to nine feet deep at high tide.[123]

Petropavlovsk, on the other hand, was a splendid port (Figure 10). Avacha Bay, large, deep, and protected, is one of the world's finest harbors. Sauer pronounced it "probably the safest and most extensive in the world."[124] while Sarychev believed that "along all the shores belonging to Russia, of the seas here [North Pacific], there is not a more suitable and safer place than this for the docking of ships."[125] The bay measured 26 miles in circumference, with an entrance 2¼ miles wide; the Harbor of St. Peter and St. Paul itself, one of four around the bay, was over a mile in circumference and 56 feet in depth, with an entrance 280 feet wide and 49 to 56 feet deep.[126] Waxell considered it "the best harbor I have seen in all my days."[127] So sheltered was the harbor by the ambient mountain rim that ships could lie there unanchored. However, this volcanic rampart was also responsible for the bay's two disadvantages. The entrance to the bay was so confined and so hidden by abrupt mountain walls that it was difficult to find;[128] ships often spent days seeking it. Also, the steep mountain walls impeded access to the interior of the peninsula; transshipment of goods to, say, Verkhne-Kamchatsk was slow and costly.

Indeed, the transshipment of freight from all Kamchatkan ports to the interior was another irksome problem of provisionment. Both horses and roads were scarce in Kamchatka; transport was largely confined to dogsled in winter, while summer travel on horseback or foot was hampered by innumerable lakes, streams, and marshes. The trouble with dogsled transport was the necessity of carrying food (fish) for the dogs; in addition, eight to ten times as many dogs as horses were required to draw the same amount of freight (1,440 pounds).[129] Thus, the transshipment of goods (including provisions) from the coast to the interior of the peninsula was an expensive matter.

Until the second quarter of the nineteenth century the provisionment of the Okhotsk Seaboard and the Kamchatka Peninsula from Okhotsk was also plagued by a shortage of sound ships and able sailors. In 1804 Lieutenant Khvostov listed the following necessary conditions for improving Russian navigation in the far North Pacific: better ships, proper equipment, experienced officers, and diligent sailors.[130] The quality of ships built at Okhotsk was not high. Shipwrights were few and gear was scarce at this remote outpost. The compass was unknown on the Okhotsk Seaboard until 1714, when its use was ordered by the Tsar; and special shipwrights (including foreigners) had to be sent to Okhotsk in order to build and man a seaworthy vessel for opening the sea route to Kamchatka in 1716–17. Thereafter, bonfires were used in place of lighthouses until the 1790's.[131] At first the seagoing craft were incredibly crude and flimsy. They were single-decked and single-masted, short (usually thirty-five to fifty feet, and rarely over eighty feet in length) and broad (up to fourteen feet in width), with flat-bottomed hulls, anchors of wood, and sails of reindeer skin. The roughly hewn and poorly fitted sideboards, unseasoned and four to six inches wide, were attached to the timbers by osiers or thongs for want of nails and pegs and chinked with moss for want of caulking, the seams being covered with laths about two inches wide to prevent dissolution of the moss. Because the planks were "sewn" together, these vessels were called *shitiks* (from *shit,* "to sew"), meaning "sewn ones." The largest were manned by seventy and the smallest by forty men, the crews generally comprising about an equal number of Russians and Kamchadals.[132] Carrying up to eighteen tons, these rickety vessels plied from Okhotsk to Kamchatka and even to the Kuriles and the Aleutians.

Shipbuilding at Okhotsk improved somewhat during the last half of the eighteenth century. Many expert shipwrights were recruited from

Pomorye, and a few master smithies were established at Okhotsk and in Kamchatka; Kamchadals were employed as carpenters and caulkers.[133]* Stronger and larger vessels, mainly galiots and brigs, were built. Nevertheless, around 1803 the Admiralty College admitted that "transport vessels sailing the local seas [Okhotsk and Bering Seas] are subject to disasters, owing to the incompetence of their handlers and to the unsuitable construction of the vessels, on which are made sides rising four feet above the deck, so that the ship is engulfed with agitation and the water is unable to flow into the scuppers and is kept on deck and enters the hatches; moreover, there are many goods, badly fastened, which with the agitation are loosened and thrown to all sides, so that they have to be cast overboard. . . ."[134] In 1802 Midshipman Davydov complained that he "truly could not imagine that . . . there could exist anywhere such bad ships as at Okhotsk."[135] He found that "ships at this time are built at Okhotsk in the worst way; for they are made either by one of the promyshlenniks, who has no idea of the building of sea vessels, or by some shipbuilding apprentice, who also knows absolutely nothing."[136] Moreover, it took a long time to construct even such bad ships: three years for the government transports, but only one year for the Russian-American Company ships.[137] The state vessels were also very costly. It was reported in 1802 that ships built at Okhotsk cost twice as much as the same ships, fully equipped and copper-bottomed, bought at Hamburg or as ships built in Russian America (Novo-Arkhangelsk).[138] Von Langsdorff found in 1807 that "a small ship of two hundred tons, which would cost at Cronstadt or Archangel, from fifteen to twenty thousand rubles, built of excellent wood, with excellent rigging, at Ochotsk would cost not less than seventy or eighty thousand rubles, and be built of indifferent wood, with very indifferent rigging."[139] Incidentally, there were no dry docks at Okhotsk; in winter the ships were simply hauled onto the beach or sometimes even left in the ice.

During the first half of the nineteenth century the quality of

---

* Iron, hemp, canvas, tar, and other materials were imported at great expense from Russia via Okhotsk. Some tar was procured locally; and in Kamchatka some rope was made from nettles, but the product was much weaker than hemp. Anchors were forged at Okhotsk and in Kamchatka from imported iron, but they proved light (V. A. Divin, "Vtoraya Sibirsko-tikhookeanskaya ekspeditsiya i voprosy khozyaistvennavo osvoyeniya Dalnevo Vostoka" ["The Second Siberia-Pacific Ocean Expedition and Questions of the Economic Development of the Far East"], *Letopis Severa,* 2 [1957] : 167).

government transports plying between Okhotsk and Kamchatka again improved, partly as a result of the appointment of naval officers as commandants of Okhotsk (like Minitsky) and Kamchatka (like Rikord) and partly as a result of the sending of vessels from Kronstadt to Okhotsk for the Siberian Flotilla based there.

The imperfection of the Russian ships was matched by the incompetence of the Russian seamen. At Okhotsk navigators were as scarce as shipwrights in the eighteenth century. During his first expedition (1725–29) Bering found only four navigators in Kamchatka and at Okhotsk, and commissaries employed state servitors in lieu of sailors for boating between Okhotsk and Kamchatka.[140] *Zemleprokhodetses* (landsmen) with some experience in rafting on the rivers of Siberia, as well as Kamchadals, whose naval experience was limited to riverine and coastal excursions in baidarkas and baidaras, were used as *morekhods* (seafarers). These "sailors," some of whom had never before seen an ocean or a ship, were usually ignorant of navigation and relied wholly on landmarks, becoming lost once out of sight of land. Voyaging was thus restricted largely to skirting along coasts and skipping between islands. No wonder, for example, that Billings and Sarychev were unable to recruit experienced sailors at Okhotsk for their expedition to the Bering Sea. Of the crew of Billings' *Slava Rossii* on its voyage in 1791, "not one of the common sailors had ever seen a ship before; which, indeed, was the case with all the petty officers, except three."[141] Sarychev himself complained that "most of the men found with us had never been to sea before. . . ."[142] For sailors the expedition recruited Cossacks from various Siberian towns who had never before seen a ship or been to sea; some sailors were also recruited at Okhotsk, but they "were not much more skilful than the Cossacks."[143] In 1802 Davydov found that at Okhotsk skippers were chosen from "old voyagers," that is, from veteran promyshlenniks who had made several trips to the Aleutians, their naval skill consisting of an acquaintance with the compass and the course, which skipped from one beach or headland to another.[144] Von Langsdorff, a passenger on the Okhotsk–Petropavlovsk run in 1805, described the ship's crew as "composed of adventurers, drunkards, bankrupt traders, and mechanics, or branded criminals in search of fortune . . . most of them, though they had made the voyage from Ochotsk to Kamschatka the preceding year, had, notwithstanding, to learn anew even the names of the sails and ropes: they were always standing in each other's way, and in case of a change of wind, fifteen men could scarcely perform the services which would have been amply performed by ten ordinary sailors. . . ."[145]

Such were the crews of government transports plying the Okhotsk Sea. Corrective measures, public and private alike, were long in coming and short in succeeding. Bering, upon returning from his first expedition, recommended to the Admiralty College in 1730 that navigational schools be established in Siberia to train Cossack children in seamanship; this recommendation was approved by the College, which in 1731 ordered the Commandant of Okhotsk, Skornyakov-Pisarev, to establish a school of navigation there.[146] In 1732 the Admiralty College assigned six sailors and three navigators to Okhotsk with orders to train the children of the Okhotsk Cossacks in seamanship, but it was not until 1740 that thirty children were selected for instruction in reading, writing, drawing, and arithmetic. The school's fortunes fluctuated widely; sometimes there were no teachers, no pupils, no finances, no books, or no instruments. It contained twenty-one students in 1741, twenty students in 1756, four students in 1764, and sixty-seven students in 1818.[147] Mainly for lack of teachers, it soon declined.*

Bering's arrival at Yakutsk was accompanied by the opening of a school of navigation there in 1736 by Larionov for 110 Cossack children. However, this too did not prosper; by 1766 it had but forty students, and in 1792 it was closed.[148] The schools of navigation at Irkutsk and Nerchinsk, founded in 1753–54, fared better, but their output of graduates remained small and sporadic. Graduates of the Irkutsk School of Navigation and Geodesy were assigned to state and private ships plying from Okhotsk, whose naval command in 1801 totaled 145 men.[149]

The plight of shipping off the Okhotsk Seaboard and the Kamchatka Peninsula, thus handicapped by defective ships and by deficient seamen, was aggravated by the adverse oceanographic and climatic conditions of the far North Pacific. Coastal waters were shallow and uncharted, tides ample and powerful, and currents strong and changeable; high winds alternated with dead calms, and fogs were thick and frequent.** The fogs and currents of the Kurile Straits were especially

---

* It was not until 1830 that Okhotsk had a naval library. At its transfer to Petropavlovsk in 1850 it comprised 2,150 volumes (Sgibnev, "Okhotsky port," 105, no. 12 : 34).

** Muller, however, described the Okhotsk Sea itself as "very safe" (G. F. Muller, "Geografiya ili nyneshnoye sostoyanie zemli Kamchatki 1737 goda" ["The Geography or the Present Condition of the Land of Kamchatka of 1737"], TsGADA, f. 199, port. 527, d. 3, fol. 26).

hazardous. Here the merging currents of the Okhotsk Sea and the Pacific proper produced very rough seas that menaced shipping.[150] Around the first of the Kurile Islands "an extremely strong and very dangerous" breaker, called *sulo* by the Cossacks, occurred at ebbtide, with waves allegedly reaching 140 to 210 and more feet in height even in calm weather![151] The Russian Admiralty eventually ordered the Okhotsk transports not to use the first Kurile strait (Lopatka Channel) because of the high incidence of shipwrecks there.[152] On the east coast of Kamchatka ships sometimes had to wait three weeks before entering Avacha Bay because of fog.[153] Stormy weather imperiled shipping in the fall. Russians with forty years of seafaring experience vowed that the winds and storms that raged over the Bering Sea between Kamchatka and Alaska in autumn were fiercer than any they had ever seen. In November, December, and January on the Okhotsk Sea east and southeast winds sometimes blew so strongly that for two or three days running one could not stay upright.[154] In the middle 1750's Governor Myatlev ordered the Okhotsk authorities to dispatch state vessels from Okhotsk only in June, July, August, and, in emergencies, early September.[155] By 1787 the Russian Government had prohibited the plying of state transports between Okhotsk and Kamchatka later than September 26,[156] for the best time for sailing these waters was the period from May through August.

Such inimical oceanographic and climatic conditions, plus the low quality of both shipbuilding and seamanship, resulted not surprisingly in frequent groundings and founderings of both state and private vessels. Krasheninnikov vividly described his perilous voyage from Okhotsk to Bolsheretsk in the fall of 1737.

> We left the mouth of the Okhota River safely at two o'clock in the afternoon [of October 4/15], and toward evening we were out of sight of the shore. At eleven o'clock such a leak was found in our vessel that the men in the hold were up to their knees in water. Although we bailed water with two pumps, kettles, and whatever was handy, nevertheless it did not subside. Our vessel was so loaded that water poured through the scuppers. There was no escape other than lightening by ejecting goods, for there was then a dead calm at sea (which greatly facilitated our escape), and it was not possible to return to Okhotsk. Everything lying on the deck and hanging on the ship was thrown overboard, but, since this resulted in no advantage, up to four hundred puds were then jettisoned at random from the hold. Unfortunate were they whose casks were on top. Finally the water began to diminish after everybody bailed, but it was not possible to leave the pumps, for the water rose two inches in half a

minute of the watch-glass. Everybody on board, except the sick, had to take turns pumping one hundred times.

We proceeded in this manner until October 14 [25], suffering from the discomfort of hard frost and daily sleet, and about 9 o'clock in the morning on the aforementioned day we arrived at Bolsheretsk mouth and entered it. But our entry was unhappier than our voyage. The morekhods did not know whether the tide was going out or coming in, mistook the ebbtide for the floodtide, and had barely run into the white breakers, which occur at the mouth at the commencement of ebbtide and floodtide even in the calmest weather and which were now much increased by a strong north wind, when they despaired, for the waves went over the ship. The frail vessel creaked everywhere; and no hope whatsoever remained of entering the mouth, partly because of the lateral wind and partly because of the strong ebbtide. Many advised going out to sea and waiting for the floodtide, and if we had done so, then our vessel would have been completely destroyed, for the fierce north wind continued for more than a week, which would have taken us to the open sea, and at such a time our vessel could not have been saved from foundering; however, others showed that it was safer to run the ship onto the shore, which was done, and our ship was beached 100 sazhens [700 feet] south of the mouth of the Bolshaya River, where it remained on dry land for an hour, for the ebbtide was continuing.

Toward evening, following floodtide, we removed the mast, and the next day we found only a few fragments of our vessel, the rest having been carried out to sea, and then we could see how untrustworthy was the *Fortune,* for all the planks were black and rotten and could be broken by hand without difficulty.

We lived by the sea until the 21st of the month [November 1], waiting in balagans and barabaras [native huts] for a boat from the ostrog [Bolsheretsk], and during that time an earthquake occurred almost incessantly. . . .

We left the sea on October 21 and arrived at Bolsheretsk the next day toward evening.[157]

Krasheninnikov's harrowing experience was not unusual. It was reported in 1794 that the Okhotsk transports were "not infrequently" wrecked, so that the military personnel in Kamchatka "suffered much," being "repeatedly subjected to extreme inanition" from lack of food.[158] Ships were rarely retired; most were wrecked. Of the eighty-one vessels (mostly brigs and galiots) built and bought by the Okhotsk Flotilla from 1715 through 1853, almost every one was wrecked; their life span averaged approximately eight years, including wrecked vessels that were repaired and refloated.[159] Thirty of the fifty ships built at Okhotsk from 1715 through 1796 were wrecked. From 1715 through 1774, twenty-three state and seven private vessels were built at Okhotsk (twenty-three from larch along the Okhota River and seven from larch along the

Kukhtui River); by the end of 1774, seventeen of them had been wrecked and four retired, while nine were still in service; twelve of the fifteen state vessels built at Okhotsk in 1715–60 were wrecked, while the remaining three were retired. From 1753 through 1755 alone five vessels from Okhotsk were wrecked on the coast of Kamchatka with a loss of over forty men; only one vessel was rescued.[160] Government transports were often wrecked at Okhotsk itself. Sir George Simpson's companion, Rowand, learned at Okhotsk in 1842 that "out of 80 or 90 vessels that have been built here, scarcely one has escaped shipwreck, and this occurrence has generally happened on the neighbouring sand bars."[161]

Around 1810 there were so many derelict vessels at Okhotsk that Commandant Minitsky was able to convert many of them into magazines, thereby forming "a complete *museum* of vessels, presenting curious specimens of antique ship building, from the commencement of the enterprises of the first Russian traders to the north-west coast of America, down to modern times."[162] The residents of Okhotsk told an English visitor of 1849 that one-third of all voyages between Okhotsk and Kamchatka had ended in shipwreck.[163] Sir George Simpson asserted that one of the three Okhotsk transports serving Kamchatka was lost every two to three years.[164] The American Dobell, who spent most of the 1810's and 1820's on the Okhotsk Seaboard and the Kamchatka Peninsula in the employ of the Tsar, trenchantly described the frequent mishaps aboard government ships, blaming them on badly proportioned and poorly outfitted ships and inexperienced officers.[165] Shipwrecks of state transports were so frequent that the resultant flotsam and jetsam were utilized in the building and equipping of private vessels engaged in the maritime fur trade. In the early 1790's the Billings Expedition discovered that "the materials of the very frequently wrecked transport vessels, though lost to government, are found the chief means of fitting out such an enterprise, and greatly lessen the expence."[166] But private vessels fared little better than state transports. At the end of the eighteenth century Captain Kruzenstern, commander of the first Russian circumnavigation, declared that "up to this time the ignorance and inexperience of the masters of the [private] ships were the reasons why one of three ships was usually lost every year."[167]

Vessels for transporting supplies from Okhotsk, then, were often scarce. In 1750 at Okhotsk there were only two seagoing ships, plus a couple of dilapidated boats remaining from the Second Kamchatka Expedition, as well as two pilots and a few sailors.[168] During the late

1810's three ships transported supplies from Okhotsk to Gizhiga, Tigilsk, and Petropavlovsk, whereas, according to Speransky, at least six ships were needed; consequently, Gizhiga received no grain in 1815 and Kamchatka received none in 1818 or in 1819.[169] In 1819, 100 tons, 616 pounds of flour destined for Kamchatka had to be left at Okhotsk for want of state transports.[170] From 1824 through 1828, when fish were scarce in Kamchatka, three state transports from Okhotsk were lost in the Okhotsk Sea; Commandant Golenishchev reported that this misfortune, which he blamed on faulty shipbuilding and inadequate knowledge of the Kamchatka coast, "was greatly felt in Kamchatka."[171] A two-year supply of grain was supposed to be kept on hand in the peninsula, but Golenishchev asserted in 1828 that never more than one year's supply of provisions, and sometimes less, was shipped from Okhotsk.[172] Sometimes, too, there were enough cargo ships but not enough cargo space. Around 1803 Major-General Koshelev, Commandant of Kamchatka, complained that the Okhotsk transports hauled mostly Russian-American Company goods at the expense of state provisions.[173] The shortage of government transports at Okhotsk sometimes necessitated the use of private ships. In 1787 and 1789, because of shipwrecks, there were no state transports at all at Okhotsk, so that Shelekhov voluntarily freighted state supplies (including provisions) to Kamchatka on one of his company's ships in order to prevent starvation in the peninsula. Dobell's *Sylph* was used in 1813 and 1818 to convey state freight between Okhotsk and Petropavlovsk.[174]

The numerous groundings and founderings of state and private vessels contributed, of course, to the loss, spoilage, and delay of supplies, especially provisions, which were more prone to spoilage than other goods. The time taken to convey provisions from Irkutsk to Okhotsk and Kamchatka was alone enough to cause some deterioration. Grain prepared for shipment at Irkutsk during the winter and barged down the Lena River in spring often reached Yakutsk a year after its harvest. On account of the difficulty of transporting heavy freight thence to Okhotsk by the yarmarochny route, it was instead conveyed the following year by pack horses via the plastovoy route, arriving two years after its harvest. At Okhotsk it was usually stored for a year and then loaded onto state transports in July and August for delivery to Gizhiga and Kamchatka, where it arrived in September, three years after its harvest in Baikalia and two years after its preparation in Irkutsk. It was not used until the grain already on hand was consumed. Thus the grain eaten in Gizhiga and Kamchatka was not uncommonly four to six years old, had become stale, and had lost some of its nutritiousness.[175]

This condition was aggravated by spoilage en route. The spoilage of flour on the route from Irkutsk to Kamchatka has been described well by Dobell:

> There is also much to be altered in the manner of transporting the flour on the Lena and to Ochotsk. Flour is generally sent down the Lena in large square flat-bottomed vessels called barques, in bulk; and, as it is often badly dried, it heats, becomes bitter, and loses much of its nutritious quality. When it arrives at Yakutsk it is thrown into magazines, also in *bulk,* where it becomes further heated, and is more or less spoiled.* If it were sent in bags from Irkutsk it would be much better preserved, and the additional cost would be trifling, as the bags would serve many years in succession. At Yakutsk the flour is packed into leathern bags, called sumas, made of ox-hides untanned, but dressed white, and the hair taken off. To pack the flour into them tightly, so that each suma shall contain two poods and thirty-five pounds, it is necessary to wet them; the flour that adheres to the wet suma dries and becomes as hard as a stone, and is thus rendered impenetrable to all sorts of weather; so that if the suma be good there cannot be a safer mode of conveying the article; but unfortunately the sumas that are now contracted for at about two roubles and a half a-piece, are so thin and bad, that the flour often spoils, and the sumas only serve for a season or two, instead of lasting four or five years, as was formerly the case. It would be cheaper to pay five roubles for a good strong suma, that would last several years, than to buy such trash because it is cheap. However, it would of course prove less profitable to the parties concerned, if the sumas were good and the contracts fewer. During five years residence in Kamchatka, I paid from eleven and a half to twelve roubles and sixty kopecs a pood for the rye-flour I consumed; and I never saw a suma that was not either bitter-flavoured, tasting of the leather, or having sand mixed with it. One additional cause, however, of the spoiling of the sumas must be mentioned, because it proceeds from neglect. That there are rats in the magazines at Ochotsk and Kamtchatka arises from their not having been properly built. The floors and ceilings should be either composed of solid square birch logs, laid close together, or else lined with sheet-iron. Either of these methods would effectually keep out the rats. . . . Their getting into the transports is owing to the neglect of the commanders, who do not take the necessary precautions to prevent them; or if they get in, surely a good smoking would destroy them in a few hours. If there were not a great deal of improper management and bad conduct, surely the flour might be carried cheaper, and be sold for much less than twelve roubles and sixty kopecs at Kamtchatka.[176]

> * Dobell added the following note at this point: "As I have been three times at Yakutsk, and lived there once for ten months, the reader will perceive that I speak of those matters from my own experience."

Especially on the Yakutsk–Okhotsk Track sumas were soaked during downpours and wadings, so that groats, flour, and biscuit became hard and moldy; in addition, they acquired a bitter and horsey flavor.[177] At Okhotsk stored provisions were sometimes spoiled by flooding. For instance, in June of 1723 all supplies stored there for the Great Kamchatka Detail (1716–19) were destroyed by flooding; in December, 1742 flooding damaged Okhotsk's stored provisions; and in January, 1768, 330 sumas of rye flour (each containing 180 pounds), as well as 990 empty sumas and 130 reams of writing paper, stored in the state magazine, plus 2,400 of the 10,900 full sumas of rye flour in the emergency magazine, were damaged by flooding sea water.[178] Vasily Shmalev reported in 1775 that most of the state buildings at Okhotsk were "unfit" because of "dilapidation," with the roofs of the provision magazines needing repairs.[179] The spoilage of provisions in transit and in storage was well summarized by Captain Kruzenstern, who found that only one-third of the provisions awaiting his expedition at Petropavlovsk in 1804–5 were usable.[180] Sometimes grain even arrived green in Kamchatka.[181]

Provisions were also depleted through embezzlement. Dobell claimed that two-legged "rats" pilfered 3,240 pounds of flour annually in Kamchatka in the early 1810's.[182] He also blamed those real rodents, mice, which abounded on Siberia's Pacific Coast, for raiding grain stores. In 1846 the Russian Admiralty ordered cats sent to Petropavlovsk in response to Commandant Mashin's report that mice were responsible for the annual shortages of provisions in the state magazines.[183]

8

REACTIONS

"It is very necessary to find a way of transporting provisions and all kinds of supplies to Okhotsk without such labor as formerly. . . ."
Vitus Bering, 1733, in A. Pokrovsky, ed., *Ekspeditsiya Beringa*, p. 135.

Difficulties such as we have glimpsed prompted officials and merchants to seek various remedies, primarily alternate routes between Yakutsk and the Okhotsk Seaboard and alternate sites for Okhotsk Port. The sea route could be little altered; only the ships and the sailors could be improved, and there improvement was slow in coming. Thus, attention was focused on the Yakutsk–Okhotsk Track and its eastern terminus of Okhotsk, both of which became the subjects of periodic remodeling and eventual relocation.

As early as 1719, less than three years after the opening of the sea route to Kamchatka from Okhotsk, the Russian Government, dissatisfied with the Yakutsk–Okhotsk river route, ordered the Kamchatka commissar (tax collector) Kharitonov to find a shorter route by land to Okhotsk—but he failed to find one.[1] The next two decades saw the development of both the land and the river routes between Yakutsk and Okhotsk by Bering's two expeditions. As a result of Bering's resolve to make unnecessary "such labor as formerly," i.e., during the First Kamchatka Expedition, one of the tasks of the Second Kamchatka Expedition was to explore the coast of the Okhotsk Sea "for the finding of a shorter route to the Kamchatka [Okhotsk] Sea, not going through Yakutsk . . ." but via the Uda River;[2] the Uda was considered navigable and as having "sufficient timber and rich land."[3] Accordingly, two surveyors, Skobeltsyn and Shatilov, tried three times (1735, 1736, and 1737) to find such a route but failed.[4] They concluded that the Zeya River–Uda River route was unsuitable, being uninhabited and beset with "impassable places, rocky mountains, and swampy bogs."[5] Moreover, it was on the Chinese frontier, which the Russian Government was reluctant to disturb lest China retaliate by halting the lucrative **Kyakhta** trade. In 1738 another member of the Second Kamchatka Expedition, Captain Spanberg, suggested that Okhotsk itself be moved fifteen miles southward to the mouth of the Luktur River on the middle Urak;[6] and in 1741 Commandant Devier suggested moving it to the mouth of the Malchikan River twenty miles up the Okhota.[7] Neither of these proposals was approved.

By the middle of the century the land passage was the main route between Yakutsk and Okhotsk. But since it was far from satisfactory, periodic attempts were made to rebuild or reroute the Yakutsk–Okhotsk Track. In the middle 1750's the track was reconstructed by convicts, but by 1758 the Yakuts were petitioning the Governor of Siberia about its atrocious condition. Governor Soimonov then ordered Lieutenant Sindt to inspect the route between Yakutsk and Udsk, which he found to be worse than the Yakutsk–Okhotsk Track. In 1762 the Yakuts refused to transport supplies to Okhotsk because of the state of the track, but on May 21/June 1, 1763, the Senate ordered the Yakuts to take turns transporting supplies to Okhotsk regardless, for which, however, they were to receive travel allowances.[8]

In 1764 Plenisner (Plenstner), the new Commandant of Okhotsk, was ordered by a Senate decree "to find another more suitable track" between Yakutsk and Okhotsk negotiable by carts in summer and by sledges in winter, and "to find another more suitable and less dangerous place" for Okhotsk Port, while a reward of up to 1,000 rubles was offered for finding a better route from Yakutsk to Okhotsk.[9] The next year a Yakutsk Cossack, Ivan Baishev, reported finding "a shorter track to Okhotsk for transporting provisions and goods more conveniently . . . ,"[10] evidently via the Notora River and the Allakh-Yun. Plenisner sent the pilot Dolzhantovykh over this route, and Dolzhantovykh compiled a description of it and founded stations on it. Irkutsk received Plenisner's report on Baishev's route in early 1767, and in early 1768, in accordance with a Senate decree, Governor-General Bril sent the surveyors Voinov of Irkutsk and Chemyasov and Danilov of Yakutsk to examine the new route. They found that it was shorter than the old track and had fewer quagmires and more grass. In early 1770 Bril ordered the sending of provisions and goods to Okhotsk via Baishev's route and the founding of magazines and barracks on it, including a Yakut town on the Aldan River. However, the Yakut transporters objected because the new route was uncleared and unsettled, while the funds for settlement were insufficient. Irkutsk then ordered Commandant Benzing, Plenisner's successor, and Reinikin (Reineke), Commandant of Kamchatka, to examine Baishev's route. They reported it suitable even for carriage traffic, but this report brought no action because of Benzing's suggestion that Okhotsk Port be moved to the mouth of the Ulya River. By 1779 the new town on the Aldan River had proven unsuitable, so that it was moved to Ust-Maya, while the other stations on Baishev's route were moved to the old track.[11]

Meanwhile, the Shmalev brothers, Timofey and Vasily, were seeking a better route between Yakutsk and Okhotsk and a better site for Okhotsk Port, Vasily beginning in 1767 and Timofey trying from June of 1771 until September of 1774. In 1772, after questioning Yakuts and Tunguses at Okhotsk about possible routes, Vasily Shmalev reconnoitered by horse and by boat the Okhotsk–Ulya River–Uyaima River–Naptaringa River–Alachak Portage–Mati River–Maya River–Ust-Maya–Yakutsk route; and in 1772–73 his subordinate, Bakhborodin, retraced this route by sledge and by horse. Bakhborodin found this route to be better than the Yakutsk–Okhotsk Track. In late 1773 Shmalev reported his findings to Governor-General Bril at Irkutsk, asserting that the new track was shorter and grassier than the usual trail. He recommended that Okhotsk be moved to the mouth of the Ulya River and that from Yakutsk provisions be transported by land on sledges in winter and on carts in summer to Ust-Maya and thence by water on boats carrying five to nine tons via the Maya River, Mati River, Alachak Portage, Naptaringa River, Uyaima River, and Ulya River. While all these rivers but the Maya were shallow, Shmalev felt that this river route was better than the usual one because the Yudoma and Urak rivers contained both shallows and rapids.[12] In 1774 Timofey Shmalev also recommended to Governor-General Bril that Okhotsk be moved to the mouth of the Ulya River, where, he held, the harbor was better, fish and fresh water were more abundant and less distant, and grass for livestock and timber for shipbuilding were available.[13] However, the recommendations of the Shmalev brothers were not implemented, although in the summer of 1776 the surveyor Fyodor Nesoizvolenol investigated the mouth of the Ulya River as a possible new site for Okhotsk. Then another new route, lying along the Otamga River, was suggested by Shelekhov for transporting freight from Yakutsk to Okhotsk, but it was found to be unsuitable in 1780 by the Yakutsk surveyor Fyodorov.[14]

Attention was then temporarily focused on improving rather than on replacing the Yakutsk–Okhotsk Track. On March 6/17, 1783, the Senate, upon seeing the 1777 report of Commandant Zubov of Okhotsk on the necessity of establishing post stations between Yakutsk and Okhotsk, ordered the settlement of five to ten families of peasant exiles every thirteen to eighteen miles along the track. Orders were given to found post stations manned by Yakuts, to build a magazine between every few stations, to establish ferries on rivers like the Amga, Aldan, and Allakh-Yun, and to clear a road with bridges and corduroy between Yakutsk and Ust-Maya; in addition, it was ordered to provide ten men for each boat tracked on the river route, to send light freight via the land route and heavy freight via the river route, and to transport goods to Okhotsk in winter if not enough goods were delivered in summer. The Yakutsk administration estimated that such development would require 1,175 settlers and 716,815 rubles, while Governor-General Jacobi reported to the Senate that it would be sufficient to settle 175 families at a cost of 100,000 rubles at twenty-one places selected on the track by one Voznitsyn.[15] His plan was not approved by the Senate, however, owing to its excessive cost; instead only a few post stations were established on the track at intervals of 134 miles and more.[16]

Now the government decided to abandon the Yakutsk–Okhotsk Track and to find a new route to the Okhotsk Seaboard from Yakutsk, for which the Aldan–Maya–Aldoma and the Aldan–Uchur–Uda river systems seemed most promising. However, Shelekhov's suggestion of 1788, which was seconded by a Commission on Commerce, that Okhotsk Port be transferred to the Uda River was rejected by the Russian Government because of the closeness of the Uda to the sensitive Chinese frontier. In 1794 Shelekhov again suggested that Okhotsk Port be moved to the Uda River or elsewhere and that a new route be sought between the Lena River and the Okhotsk Sea.[17] Meanwhile, during the late 1780's Rear Admiral Fomin explored the Yakutsk–Udsk route, the harbor of Udsk, and the southern half of the coast of the Okhotsk Sea. Sarychev assisted Fomin by reconnoitering the seacoast between Okhotsk and Ayan Bay, Ayan Bay itself, the Aldoma River, and the route from Ayan Bay to the Maya River, finding that the Yakutsk–Ayan Bay route was better than either the Yakutsk–Okhotsk route or the Yakutsk–Udsk route. Fomin concluded that the mouth of the Uda River was too shallow to admit ships and that the mouth of the Aldoma River (Ayan Bay) was the only suitable site for a port because it was sheltered from winds except from the south. The port of Okhotsk should be moved to Ayan Bay, and the Yakutsk–Okhotsk Track should be replaced by the Aldan–Maya–Aldoma river route, allowing five years for completion of the new port and three years for completion of the new route, with the help of the Russian-American Company.[18] This plan was approved by the government. A decree of March 4/16, 1800, ordered the construction of wagon roads between Yakutsk and Ust-Maya and between Nelkan Landing and Ust-Aldoma (Ayan) "for the avoidance of the difficult horseback transport [on the Yakutsk–Okhotsk Track], attended by exhaustion of the Yakut horses."[19] This project was begun in 1801. The wagon roads were almost completed when another route was chosen in 1804 and yet another in 1807. After the expenditure of 67,042 rubles on road construction, the project was abandoned because of the Russian-American Company's decision not to build the new port on account of excessive cost.[20]

Meanwhile, in 1803 Lieutenant Khvostov had examined the mouth of the Ulya River, and, having concluded that it was a better site for a port than Okhotsk, had recommended that Okhotsk Port be moved there.[21] In 1805 Commandant Bukharin vainly tried first to find a better site for Okhotsk on the coast to the south and then to relocate Okhotsk at Bulgin, a low spot on the mainland across the Okhota River from Okhotsk Spit. And in 1809 Commandant Minitsky explored the coast as far south as the mouth of the Ulya River in an unsuccessful attempt to find a better site for Okhotsk.[22]

The Yakutsk–Okhotsk Track escaped abandonment but not notice. Lieutenant Khvostov, upon his return to Irkutsk from Okhotsk in 1807, reported to Governor-General Pestel that "that road is utterly neglected. Rivers and streams from the mountains have washed it away in many places. Across the entire road lie rotten trees, which obstruct the passage of horses, and there are deep potholes filled with water, and in the boggy places, owing to the lack of corduroy, the horses sink up to their necks."[23] Following Khvostov's report, Pestel ordered the Yakutsk authorities to repair the track, but they replied that improvement was impossible until the track was settled; they suggested settling 128 Yakuts on it at a cost of 32,309 rubles.[24] On October 19, 1811 the Russian Government ratified a plan of the Ministry of Internal Affairs to settle 128 Russian and Yakut males, or 64 families, and 75 exiles at Chernolesskaya, Allakh-Yun, Mundukan, Meta, and Medvezhaya Golova (Map 7) at a cost of 15,232 rubles; the settlers there were to be exempted from all taxes for ten years.[25] Settlement of the track continued until 1813, largely at the expense of merchants trading to Okhotsk and Kamchatka. By 1816, for example, Allakh-Yun included 65 males, 16 magazines and sheds, 9 yurtas, 9 cattle barns, 60 cattle, and 56 horses.[26]

Then it was ordered to convert the track into a carriage road within two years. Trees were felled, bogs were corduroyed, grades were reduced, streams were bridged, and ferries were established—but still the track remained very difficult and passable only on horseback in summer. While one section was being reconstructed, another section was being obliterated by freshets.[27] Minitsky, Commandant of Yakutsk (1817–21), reported to Irkutsk on October 21/November 2, 1819, that throughout that summer damaged bridges had been repaired and six new bridges had been built, about one and a half miles had been corduroyed, about one and a quarter miles had been cleared, post stations had been repaired, and so forth. He explained that such work was necessary every year not because of slipshod workmanship but because of overflowing rivers, which seasonally swept away bridges and corduroy.[28] It was finally decided to halt reconstruction and to entrust repairing to the new settlers. But they failed to prosper; the rivers contained few fish and the woods harbored few fur bearers, while pasture was neither abundant nor nutritious. Their cattle became emaciated, especially in winter, and gave very little milk, with most of the calves dying. Consequently, most of the settlers soon left.[29]*

Thus, over a decade of official effort failed to improve the Yakutsk–Okhotsk Track. It remained in abominable condition and the Yakuts continued to balk. Matters were worsened by the long-awaited transfer of Okhotsk Port from the Okhota to the Kukhtui side of the Okhota–Kukhtui mouth in 1815–16.** This move was finally under-

---

* The track was periodically resettled, however—in 1845, for instance, with eighteen families of Yakuts and eleven families of Russians (Sgibnev, "Okhotsky port," 105, no. 12 : 46).

** This move, which had been contemplated by Commandant Plenisner as early as 1769, was ordered by St. Petersburg in 1815 (Russia, *Polnoye sobranie zakonov rossiiskoy imperii* [*Complete Collection of Laws of the Russian Empire*], 1st. ser. [1649–1825] [St. Petersburg: Kantselyariya Yevo Imperatorskavo Velichestva, 1830], vol. 33, doc. 25,793, pp. 33–34; Timofey Shmalev, "Primechanie uchinyonnoye Kapitanom Timofeiyem Shmalevym k ne sposobnomu vpred bytyu Okhotskavo Porta . . ." ["Comment Made by Captain Timofey Shmalev Concerning the Insupportable Existence of Okhotsk Port in the Future . . ."], TsGADA, f. 199, port. 539, pt. 1, d. 9, fol. 5).

taken at the urging of Minitsky following severe flooding in 1810, 1812, and 1813. The transport of goods from Yakutsk to Okhotsk now became even more difficult. Thirty miles before Okhotsk it was necessary to ferry goods across the Okhota River to its left bank and proceed along it through "impassable" places. Also, the convoys now stopped at Bulgin, that point of land separating the joint mouths of the Okhota and Kukhtui rivers, where the goods were unloaded from the pack horses onto barges for the crossing to the new port site. Because of the shallowness of the water, the barges could not get within two-thirds of a mile of the shore, so the Yakuts had to wade ashore with the goods. Speransky reported this difficulty to the Senate, which on June 30/July 12, 1822, ordered the Commandant of Okhotsk to examine the route along the Kukhtui River, clearing it if necessary, and to establish ferry service on the upper Okhota and upper Kukhtui rivers.[30] The Senate decree said in part that "although the Yakuts by contract must deliver the provisions to the landmark of Bulgin, their condition cannot be guaranteed because of, one, the lack of magazines at Bulgin and, two, the difficulty of ferrying provisions across the two mouths of the river."[31] When the route along the Kukhtui proved impracticable because of swampiness, the Commandant of Okhotsk suggested the establishment of magazines at Bulgin, at an estimated cost of 20,000 rubles, and the yearly assignment of 7,485 rubles for the transport of provisions to Okhotsk by the winter route. His suggestion was not implemented, and the Yakuts continued to deliver provisions in the former manner.[32] It was estimated in the early 1830's that the transport of goods by cart or by sledge from Yakutsk to Okhotsk would save the state at least 100,000 rubles annually, so that reconstruction of the Yakutsk–Okhotsk Track for vehicles, which would cost 500,000 rubles, would be repaid in five years.[33] However, no action was taken in this direction.

Meanwhile, the new (1815–16) site of Okhotsk Port proved unsatisfactory. There was no fresh water at the new site, the residents having to fetch it some two and a half miles away beyond the Kukhtui River. More importantly, the new site was subject to progressive erosion by the sea; the distance between the Russian-American Company's factory and the sea decreased from 280 feet in 1827 to 63 feet in 1839 and 28 feet in 1844. The sea had encroached upon the old (1736) site of Okhotsk, too; for example, several houses and magazines built 70 feet from the sea in the 1730's were found at the water's edge by 1775, and a ravine located 350 feet from the Okhota River in the 1730's was found to be only 140 feet from it by 1775.[34] This shrinkage left less and less space for habitation. In 1803 Lieutenant Khvostov had found that "the town is now so cramped that 15 persons are quartered in a room of one square sazhen [49 square feet], and there were instances of people, for want of shelter, having to live in the churches."[35] Okhotsk's relocation afforded only temporary relief from such conditions. In 1832 Commandant Balk vainly explored the coast between Okhotsk and Gizhiga, hoping to find a better site for a port on Tauisk Bay.[36]

Not only the government but also the Russian-American Company tried to improve the Yakutsk–Okhotsk supply line. At first the Company turned its attention to the Yakutsk–Udsk route, with the intention of constructing a port near the mouth of the Uda River.[37] In 1829 the Company informed Minister of Finance Kankrin that it was investigating the Yakutsk–Udsk Track as a possible supplementary or even alternative route to the Yakutsk–Okhotsk Track because the "extreme difficulties" of transport on the latter were impeding the supply of Russian America.[38] It sent Serebrennikov, Kolesov, and Basin in 1828 and Kozmin in 1829 to find a harbor on the Okhotsk Seaboard south of Okhotsk, hopefully around the mouth of the Uda. Their instructions said in part:

> The road to Udsk is as difficult for travel as the Okhotsk Road, but the latter can by no means be made suitable for travel by cart; in contrast, the road to Udsk, on account of its levelness and many other circumstances, needs only repairing; moreover, nothing prevents making it passable and suitable for transporting goods by cart; at least another more suitable route from Yakutsk to the Okhotsk Sea, as far as is known, does not exist.[39]

The instructions added that

> although it is known that the mouth of the Uda is very shallow, perhaps ocean-going vessels can enter the river at floodtide and find a suitable place for mooring. At Okhotsk ships can enter the river only at floodtide, and then with much danger, and at ebbtide they lie on their sides; but, despite this inconvenience, a port has long existed there, and hence, if Udsk Port has the same inconvenience and is no more suitable for landing ships than Okhotsk, at least as regards inconvenience it is quite equal to the latter, and in such a case it will be possible to select the mouth of the Uda River for the establishment there of a port.[40]

The investigators found that the mouth of the Uda was the best place for a port.[41] However, Kozmin held that it would be possible to build a wagon road only as far as the Aldan River from Yakutsk and that "in summertime no freight whatsoever can be safely transported along the Udsk Road: it can truthfully be said that a quarter of it is irrevocably ruinous."[42] Nothing more came of this project.

When Captain-Lieutenant Zavoiko was appointed head of the Russian-American Company's factory at Okhotsk in the early 1840's, the transfer of the factory to a better site became his main concern. Zavoiko and Orlov examined the coast of the Okhotsk Sea south of Okhotsk, concluding that the best site for a port was Ayan Bay, located some two hundred miles southwest of Okhotsk. Ayan's advantages were already known from Fomin's report of 1790 and had been verified by Shilov in 1831. Now Beryozin was sent to inspect the route from Ayan to Yakutsk, while Orlov spent the winter at Ayan to ascertain when the bay became free of ice, and Gavrilov was sent on the Company vessel *Promysel* to make a marine survey of Ayan Bay and sixty miles around. Beryozin demonstrated the superiority of the Yakutsk–Ayan route over the Yakutsk–Okhotsk route, and the Yakut contractors were willing to transport goods from Yakutsk to Ayan at half their charges from Yakutsk to Okhotsk. Orlov found that Ayan Bay became ice-free somewhat earlier than Okhotsk.[43] Meanwhile, at a meeting in St. Petersburg on April 21, 1842, the Company's shareholders decided to transfer the Company's factory from Okhotsk to Ayan if Ayan "proves to be a good harbor and suitable for the establishment of a port, and the transport of freight from Ayan to Yakutsk will not be slower or costlier. . . ."[44] It was found that, although timber for shipbuilding, and fish, were scarce at Ayan (which means "bay" in Tungus), its harbor was deeper and its climate was better, while "black earth" (*chernozem*)* and pasture were present. Ayan's chief advantage over Okhotsk was the fact that ships could enter Ayan Bay regardless of wind. In 1844 Zavoiko ordered Orlov to examine the Maya and the Aldan rivers, which proved navigable for vessels drawing no more than three feet of water. That year the transport of Company goods by Yakuts proved to be one-third cheaper from Yakutsk to Ayan than from Yakutsk to Okhotsk, and in the summer of 1845 the Company transported goods from Yakutsk to Ayan faster than to Okhotsk by eight days. Consequently, in 1845 the Russian-American Company, following Zavoiko's advice, moved its Okhotsk factory to Ayan, a move that had been recommended in 1832 by

---

* The soil at Ayan was not true chernozem, which is confined to the temperate grasslands; rather, it was probably dark alluvium. Russians tended to call any dark soil chernozem.

Lenzhe, then the head of the Okhotsk factory. Also in 1845, the Company established logways, boats, ferries, stations, and settlers (eighteen Yakut families and eleven Russian families) on the Yakutsk–Ayan route, and from 1846 Company goods were shipped from Yakutsk via Ayan rather than via Okhotsk. In 1852 the Yakutsk–Ayan Track was rebuilt, with the government spending over 20,000 rubles and settling 211 persons on it.[45]

Although possessing some advantages over Okhotsk, Ayan was nevertheless not a good port. Ships drawing more than six to seven feet of water could not winter there, and the bay was ice-bound from December until June. Also, there were no suitable timber stands or fishing grounds nearby. Finally, river transport was suitable only for freight bound from Ayan to Yakutsk, owing to the directional flow of the Maya and Aldan rivers; generally it took thirteen to twenty-three days to go from Ayan to Yakutsk but thirty to forty days to go from Yakutsk to Ayan.[46]

Nevertheless, the government soon followed the Russian-American Company's lead. In 1845 Bishop Innokenty found that the Yakutsk–Ayan route was "much better" than the Yakutsk–Okhotsk Track and wished that "the Crown had paid attention to Ayan and to the Ayan Road and had transferred to it the stations from the Okhotsk Road."[47] He recommended that the Yakutsk–Okhotsk Track be replaced by the Yakutsk–Ayan Track and that Okhotsk Port be transferred to Petropavlovsk.[48] In 1847 Captain-Lieutenant Vonlyarlyarsky, Commander of the Okhotsk Flotilla, suggested that Okhotsk Port be moved to Konstantin Bay (just southeast of Udsk Bay) and that a carriage road, to be settled by peasants, be built thither along the southern flank of the Yablonovoy Range from the grain-growing districts of Transbaikalia.[49] This ambitious proposal was rejected by Muravyov, Governor-General of Eastern Siberia, who planned to regain the Amur River and to concentrate Russia's Far Eastern power there. It was in 1849 that Muravyov became the first Siberian governor to travel to Okhotsk via the Yakutsk–Okhotsk Track. The deplorable condition of the track and the unsuitable site of Okhotsk Port so appalled him that he decided to abandon both without delay, choosing the Yakutsk–Ayan route and Ayan as replacements. He recommended the abolition of Okhotsk Port and the transfer of its facilities to Petropavlovsk; the construction of storehouses at Ayan; the division of the Okhotsk Maritime Administration into Okhotsk Okrug (under Yakutsk Oblast) and Kamchatka-Gi-

zhiga Military Province; the transfer of the seat of the American episco-
pate from Novo-Arkhangelsk to Petropavlovsk; the establishment of
steamer communication between Kamchatka and the Okhotsk Seaboard,
using coal found at Tigilsk and near Ayan; increased whaling in the
Okhotsk Sea; the fortification of Petropavlovsk; and the sending of
3,000 families of Russian peasants to Kamchatka. With these measures
Muravyov initially hoped to concentrate Russia's Far Eastern strength in
Kamchatka, although he was shortly to decide to make the Amur Valley
the focus of the Russian Far East.[50]

At any rate, Muravyov was determined to abandon Okhotsk. He
wrote Count Perovsky that "all our activities here will only serve to
convince distant skeptics that Okhotsk should not have existed a
hundred years ago."[51] An Imperial edict of December 14, 1849, decreed
that "Okhotsk Port, on account of its unsuitability, as well as the local
Maritime Administration, is abolished. . . ."[52] From 1850 through 1852
the Siberian (Okhotsk) Flotilla was engaged exclusively in transferring
all state property from Okhotsk to Ayan and Petropavlovsk. Simultaneously, Okhotsk Kray was demoted in administrative rank to an okrug of
Yakutsk Oblast.* The resultant loss of importance by Okhotsk was
reflected in the decline of its population from 1,660 in 1839 to 884 in
1846, 207 in 1855, and 100 in 1865. In 1854 Okhotsk comprised only
thirty-three dwellings, twelve shops, four churches, four chapels, two
storehouses, a bazaar, a powder magazine, a wine cellar, and a guard-
house; in 1865 there remained only thirty private houses, two government houses, and four magazines, all dilapidated. By then the Okhotsk
Seaboard and the Kamchatka Peninsula were being provisioned overland-oversea from Baikalia via the Amur River route, which replaced
the Yakutsk–Ayan route, itself a recent successor to the old Yakutsk–
Okhotsk Track. Okhotsk itself first received goods by sea from Nikolay-
evsk in 1870, although such transport had been considered in 1865.[53]
Acquisition of the Amur River route (Prince Kropotkin's "Mississippi
of the East") in the middle 1850's, when China's Manchu Dynasty was
disintegrating, fulfilled an old Russian dream that had long envisaged
easy supply of the Okhotsk Seaboard and the Kamchatka Peninsula and
easy delivery of their furs to Kyakhta, both by way of the Amur River
Valley, which the Russians regarded as a potential granary. However, by

---

* In 1856 Okhotsk Okrug became part of the new oblast of Primorsk,
which comprised Russia's possessions along the Pacific Coast of Siberia,
including the newly-won Amur Valley.

then the fur base had been depleted and the fur market had been satiated, so that the seaboard and the peninsula, together with their problem of provisionment, were no longer very important. Russia was now preoccupied with Amuria, which has remained the center of attention in the Russian Far East up to the present.

PART III

❊ *Local Agriculture*

9

INTRODUCTION

> "The overland transport of provisions from Yakutsk to Okhotsk, by its difficulty, immediately showed the government, first, the difficulty and the hopelessness of this delivery, second, the need for extraordinary expenses, and, third, the burdening and the ruining of the Yakuts. . . . These circumstances were the grounds for the proposal to establish grain cultivation in Kamchatka."
>
> Pervy sibirsky komitet, "O predpolozheniyakh Nachalnika Kamchatki," fol. 19^v.

Agricultural Settlement of Siberia

The many difficulties impeding overland-oversea provisionment of the Okhotsk Seaboard and the Kamchatka Peninsula prompted the Russian Government in the second quarter of the eighteenth century to undertake the agricultural development of the region, particularly of Kamchatka. As early as the beginning of the century the Cossacks of the seaboard and the peninsula became discontented and rebellious because of frequent deficiencies in their grain salary.[1] Similarly, the difficulties of overland provisionment of Siberia under the system of "Siberian deliveries" had earlier induced Moscow to develop agriculture east of the Urals. The farther Russian promyshlenniks and state servitors had advanced eastward in Siberia, the more difficult had become the delivery of the "Tsar's grain supplies," so that the agricultural development of Siberia had become imperative. Already in 1592 Siberian officials had been instructed "to seek the best lands for cultivation."[2] Siberia's agricultural settlement, initiated mainly during the second quarter of the seventeenth century with peasants from Pomorye, was implemented "by decree" and "by instrumentation." Settlement "by decree" involved the compulsory resettlement of "Treasury" (Crown) peasants from European Russia (mostly from Pomorye) in Siberia by special order of Moscow; settlement "by instrumentation" involved the voluntary migration of free peasants to Siberia from European Russia with state assistance. Thus, "by decree" Crown peasants from Pomorye, instead of delivering provisions to Siberia, were forcibly resettled there in order to produce provisions on the spot. Some "local people," i.e., Siberian natives, were also forcibly settled in agricultural villages and required to pay taxes in grain instead of in furs.[3]

However, the reserve of Crown peasants was small, and many of them "went their separate ways," that is, deserted, while the Siberian natives, forced into serfdom and unaccustomed to the arduous agricultural routine, perished.[4] Consequently, the government ordered its Siberian officials "to grant plowland near strongholds to be cultivated for the state by all kinds of people,"[5] thereby leaving the agricultural colonization of Siberia largely to migration "by instrumentation" of "black peasants" (free peasants) and runaway serfs attracted by the abundance of free land, the absence of landlords (save the state and the Church), the lack of conscription (until 1761), and the availability of state assistance (tax exemptions, money loans, and free seed, livestock, and implements) in Siberia. Voluntary migration was further encouraged by increasing serfdom, natural calamities (like the famine of 1601–3), and political disturbances (such as the Time of Troubles of 1598–1613) in European Russia. By the end of the sixteenth century the Russian Government had already ordered its Siberian governors to "give lands to all who would henceforth be any kind of grain cultivators, and do not transport grain."[6] Voluntary colonists with governmental assistance were settled in large communal villages called *slobodas,* located and prepared by the state.[7] Voluntary migrants without governmental assistance colonized the *dikaya zemlya* ("wild land") in *zaimkas* (homesteads), some of which eventually became agricultural villages called *derevnyas* (peasant villages without a church) and *selos* (peasant villages with a church). All voluntary colonists, who were eventually classified as "state peasants," had to render either barshchina (corvée) or obrok (quitrent) to the state. Some voluntary migrants were obligated to cultivate "Treasury plowland" ("Tsar's plowland"), usually two desyatinas (about 5½ acres), as well as their own (*sobinnaya*) plowland, commonly at a ratio of one to five; other voluntary migrants were obligated to relinquish to the state a certain proportion of their harvests, usually three puds (108 pounds) of grain from each desyatina (2.7 acres) of sobinnaya plowland.[8]* It seems that some involuntary migrants (Crown peasants), however, worked solely for the state.

* The obligation to cultivate "Treasury plowland" was eventually replaced by payments in money or in kind with the increase in the number

FIGURE 1. Petropavlovsk in 1741 (from [Stepan P. Krasheninnikov], *The History of Kamtschatka, and the Kurilski Islands, with the Countries Adjacent*, trans. James Grieve [London: T. Jefferys, 1764], facing p. 14).

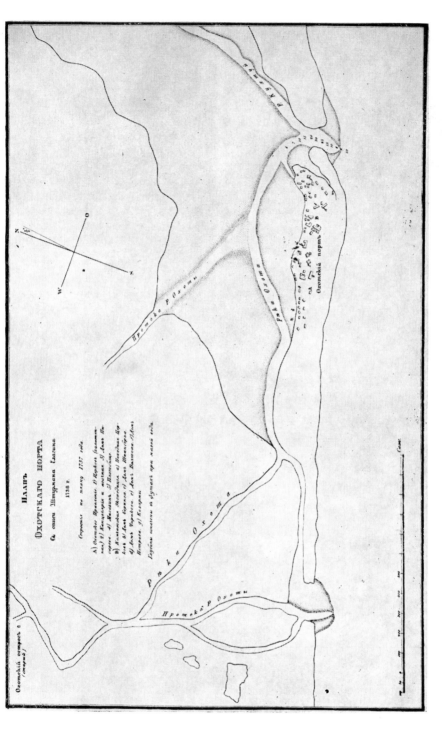

FIGURE 2. Plan of Okhotsk in 1738 (from Savin, "Okhotsk," *Zapiski Gidrografi-cheskavo departamenta Morskavo ministerstva*, pt. 9 [1851], facing p. 149).

FIGURE 3. Nizhne-Kamchatsk in 1741 (from [Krasheninnikov], *History of Kamtschatka*, facing p. 70).

FIGURE 4. Okhotsk in 1741 (from [Krasheninnikov], *History of Kamtschatka*, facing p. 14).

FIGURE 5. Okhotsk in 1786 (from Martin Sauer, *An Account of a Geographical and Astronomical Expedition to the Northern Parts of Russia* . . . [London: T. Cadell, Jr., and W. Davies, 1802], facing p. 40).

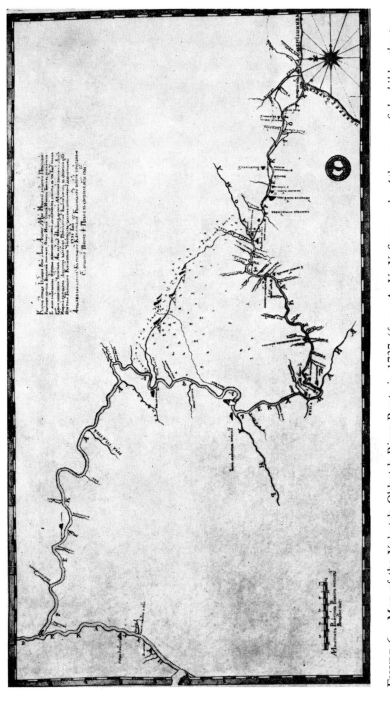

FIGURE 6. Map of the Yakutsk–Okhotsk River Route in 1737 (from A. V. Yefimov, ed., *Atlas geograficheskikh okryty v Sibiri i v Severo-Zapadnoy Amerike XVII–XVIII vv.* [*Atlas of Geographical Discoveries in Siberia and Northwestern America of the XVIIth–XVIIIth Centuries*] [Moscow: Izdatelstvo "Nauka," 1964], plate 92).

FIGURE 7. Map of the Yakutsk–Okhotsk River Route in 1788 (from G. A. Sarychev, *Puteshestvie flota kapitana Sarycheva . . . [Voyage of Fleet Captain Sarychev . . .]* [St. Petersburg: Tipografiya Shnora, 1802], atlas volume).

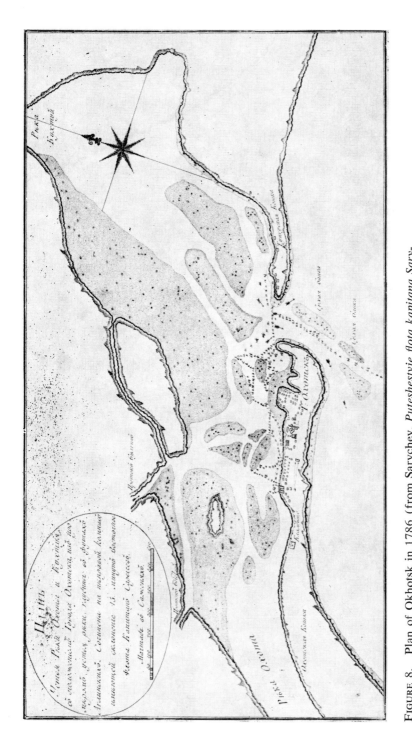

FIGURE 8. Plan of Okhotsk in 1786 (from Sarychev, *Puteshestvie flota kapitana Sary-cheva*, atlas volume).

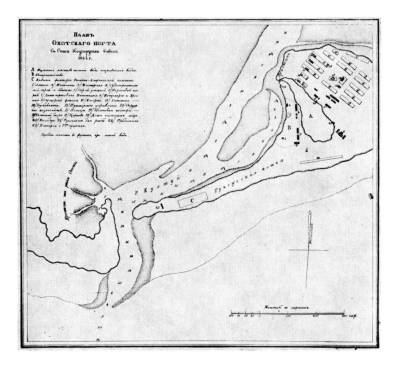

FIGURE 9. Plan of Okhotsk in 1844 (from Savin, "Okhotsk," facing p. 149).

FIGURE 10. Petropavlovsk in 1807 (from G. H. Von Langsdorff, *Bemerkungen auf einer Reise um die Welt in den Jahren 1803 bis 1807* [*Notes of a Voyage Around the World in the Years 1803 to 1807*] [Frankfurt am Mayn: F. Williams, 1812], vol. 2, plate 14).

Criminal and political exiles also became agriculturalists in Siberia. From the middle of the seventeenth century malefactors with their wives and children were banished to Siberia "for cultivation," although many of them died en route, the mortality rate reaching as high as 75 percent.⁹* In addition, state servitors, "suburbanites" (*posadskie lyudi*— artisans, traders, and farmers inhabiting the outskirts of towns), and monasteries also engaged in agriculture in Siberia. State servitors could receive plowland instead of grain salary. Obrok was rendered by state servitors and by suburbanites with plowland.

The organization of agriculture was entrusted to the governors, who were responsible for finding "good arable places," for establishing slobodas, for recruiting peasants, for allotting "sought-after lands" and assistance in money and in kind to the peasants, and for appointing stewards, who supervised the "state economy" in the slobodas so that the peasants would "not steal" grain, would plant at a "pleasing time," would "supply the land with sufficient manure," and so forth.¹⁰

By 1662 the Russian male population of Siberia totaled 70,000, half of whom were peasants (31,500 state peasants and 3,000 Crown peasants) and one-tenth of whom were exiles.¹¹ Agricultural colonization, while found mostly in Western Siberia, comprised four separate districts along the main route from the Urals to the Pacific between Verkhoturye and Amginsk: Tobolsk, Tomsk–Kuznetsk, Yeniseisk–Krasnoyarsk, and Angara–Ilim–Lena, in decreasing order of importance¹² (Map 9). On the basis of these four agricultural regions Siberia was supplying itself with grain before the end of the seventeenth century, so that in 1685 the Siberian deliveries were discontinued. This was no mean accomplishment, since the technological level of the Siberian peasantry was not high and since the climatic and pedologic conditions of the four regions were not very favorable for agriculture.

---

and in the productivity of sobinnaya plowlands. This process happened especially in the eighteenth century with the advance of Russian settlement southward into the fertile wooded steppe and steppe of Siberia, although the development of "Treasury plowland" was intensified in Eastern Siberia in the 1700's (*Sibirskaya sovetskaya entsiklopediya* [*Siberian Soviet Encyclopedia*] [Novosibirsk: Zapadno-Sibirskoye otdelenie Ogiz, 1929–32], 1 : 728).

* The route of deportation to Siberia, called the *Vladimirka*, linked Moscow and Nerchinsk via Vladimir, Nizhny-Novgorod, Perm, Tyumen, Tobolsk, and Tomsk; most of it was river passage, which reduced expense and simplified surveillance (*Sibirskaya sovetskaya entsiklopediya*, 1 : 502).

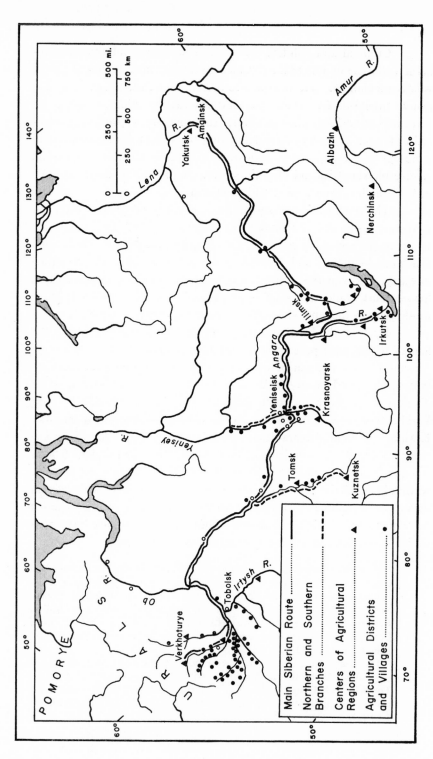

MAP 9. The Main Agricultural Regions of Siberia in the Seventeenth Century.

Thus, the inauguration of Russian agriculture on the Okhotsk Seaboard and the Kamchatka Peninsula in the second quarter of the eighteenth century was not an isolated development; rather, it was simply the next step in the eastward advance of Russian agriculture across Siberia, just as overland-oversea provisionment of the region had been the next step in the system of Siberian deliveries. Also, what might be called the Okhotsk-Kamchatka agricultural region was in a sense the successor to the planned fifth agricultural region of Nerchinsk-Albazin, or Preamuria, whose agricultural development was arrested in 1689 by the Treaty of Nerchinsk. If Russia had not lost the Amur Valley in 1689, probably the nascent agricultural region of Nerchinsk-Albazin, which then comprised at least 277 peasant households,[13] would have become the supplier of provisions for the Russian Far East, thereby obviating the protracted, costly, and laborious efforts to establish agriculture on the Okhotsk Seaboard and the Kamchatka Peninsula; in fact, when Russia re-acquired Amuria in the middle 1850's, the upper Amur Valley did become a source of foodstuffs for the seaboard and the peninsula, where agriculture had proven unsuccessful.

10

AGRICULTURAL SETTLEMENT

"And *it is possible to cultivate grain* in the Kamchatkan and Kurilian lands, because the places are *warm* and *the lands are black and soft,* but there are no cattle on them, and the natives, who know nothing about sowing, do not cultivate them."

Vladimir Atlasov, 1697, in N. Ogloblin, "Dve 'skaski' Vl. Atlasova," p. 17.

The introduction of agriculture on the Okhotsk Seaboard and the Kamchatka Peninsula, then, was prompted by the extraordinary difficulties of overland-oversea provisionment. The "Kamchatka delivery" was more problematical than the "Okhotsk delivery," although the quantity and the variety of fish were greater in the peninsula than on the seaboard.[1] According to Devier, Commandant of Okhotsk, in 1740 grain cost 4 to 5 rubles per pud in Kamchatka and 3 rubles per pud at Okhotsk.[2] In the early 1740's rye flour and cow's butter, bought at Irkutsk and Yakutsk, respectively, for 25 kopeks and for 1 ruble, 20 kopeks per pud, cost 4 to 8 rubles and 6 to 8 rubles per pud in Kamchatka, where at the same time imported grain cost twice as much as at Okhotsk.[3] Muller noted in 1737 that "provisions are rarely imported for sale in Kamchatka."[4] Bread, the Russian staff of life, was then so scarce in Kamchatka that it was eaten only on holidays—although there were not a few holidays on the Russian religious calendar. And there was no fresh meat in the peninsula, except tame reindeer and wild game, while many Yakut cattle were driven to Okhotsk annually.[5] Agriculture thus was more necessary in Kamchatka than at Okhotsk. It is not surprising that agricultural experiments were concentrated in the peninsula, whose interior, moreover, was physically more suitable for agriculture than the Okhotsk Seaboard.

Monastic Settlement

Probably the first attempts at agriculture in the region were made in the early eighteenth century along the lower Kamchatka River by the lay brothers of Uspenskaya Hermitage, which was founded in 1717–19[6] by the monk Ignaty Kozyrevsky "on a site suitable for the cultivation of vegetables and for the sowing of grain. . . ."[7]* Established under the auspices of Yakutsk's Spassky Monastery (1663), one of the most active centers of agriculture in the basin of the middle Lena River, Uspenskaya Hermitage was located on the right bank of the lower Kamchatka River at the mouth of the Klyuchevka, less than a mile and a half below old Nizhne-Kamchatsk. In 1718 grain and vegetable seeds were sent from Yakutsk to Kamchatka at the request of Ignaty, who had reported from the peninsula that land was sufficient and that grain would grow.[8] Krasheninnikov recorded that "monastic servitors came there at the time for the plowing of the land under barley and other garden vegetables. For at that place barley grows passably and turnips prolifically."[9] In 1724 the hermitage planted a dozen bushels of rye, which yielded well.[10] Three years later Bering found that "barley, hemp, radish grow at the hermitage of Yakutsk Monastery which is a versta from the Kamchatka church: and turnips are grown by many 'serving men' at all three ostrogs [Bolsheretsk, Verkhne-Kamchatsk, and Nizhne-Kamchatsk]. . . ."[11] Allegedly nine-pound turnips were grown.[12] Bering also observed that the plowland at the hermitage, for want of livestock, was "without manure" and was plowed "with men";[13] in other words, natives were hitched to plows. Bering's party planted rye and oats at the hermitage, "but whether or not they ripened is unknown. . . ."[14] In 1728 Brother Iakov successfully grew oats, barley, and vegetables.[15]

Uspenskaya Hermitage was destroyed in 1731 along with old Nizhne-Kamchatsk during the "great rebellion" of the Kamchadals, but it was soon rebuilt. In 1737 Muller reported that at the hermitage "they boast about their arable land above everything else . . . ," that "they plow with horses, oxen, and local serfs . . . ," that "a little rye is grown from year to year . . . ," and that garden vegetables grow "passably," with turnips reaching the size of a man's head.[16] Around 1740 Krasheninnikov observed that "the servitors of Yakutsk-Spassky Monastery, who have lived on the Kamchatka [River] for many years, sow 7 to 8 puds [5¼ to 6 bushels] of barley, and from that they have so much benefit that they not only supply themselves with groats and flour but

---

* However, another source contends that the hermitage was founded in 1715 (Anonymous, "Materialy dlya istorii Kamchatskavo kraya" ["Materials for the History of Kamchatka Kray"], *Severnaya pchela,* no. 252 [November 4/16, 1844], p. 1008).

furnish others in case of need; and they plow the land with men."[17] Steller in 1743 noted that "some time ago the inhabitants of Nizhne Ostrog [Nizhne-Kamchatsk] annually sowed 8–10 puds [6 to 7½ bushels] of barley and for that reason plowed the land with Kamchadal girls and obtained so much benefit from this that the local monastery annually had abundant stocks of groats and flour for all kinds of bakes."[18] Apparently the lay brothers farmed not only at the hermitage but also at two zaimkas, one on the lower Yelovka River and one near the mouth of the Kamchatka River.[19]*

State Settlement

Thus private experiments in agriculture had already been successfully made by the time the Russian Government decided in 1727 to establish "Treasury plowland" in Kamchatka. That January the Privy Council recommended that Russians be settled at Ust-Maya, Yudoma Portage, Okhotsk, Udsk, and Kamchatka "for the cultivation of grain, because in those places it is possible to grow grain, and there are sufficient haylands and all kinds of arable lands. . . ."[20] On March 13/24 it gave the order "to establish grain cultivation in those places of Kamchatka where the climate is favorable, having settled Russian peasants there."[21] The implementation of this decree, however, was delayed by the return of Bering from his first expedition with his optimistic observations on agriculture in Kamchatka. In April of 1730 Bering presented to the Senate his "Proposals" for another expedition, including observations and suggestions on the economic development of the seaboard and the peninsula. In his fourth and fifth proposals he discussed agriculture, noting that "it is possible there [Kamchatka] to plow the land and to sow all kinds of grain: because during my stay I made tests with all kinds of garden vegetables, and I also sowed rye; and before us were sown barley, turnips and hemp, which thrived; but they plow with men."[22] Bering also asserted that there was enough grass but no cattle in

---

* According to Slovtsov, the second zaimka was located between Lake Nerpichye and the mouth of the Kamchatka River ([P. A. Slovtsov], *Istoricheskoye obozrenie Sibiri* [*Historical Survey of Siberia*] [St. Petersburg: Tipografiya I. N. Skorokhodova, 1886], 2 : 205), but Krasheninnikov located it on an island in the Kamchatka River near its mouth (Krasheninnikov, *Opisanie zemli Kamchatki*, p. 102).

Kamchatka, at Okhotsk, and along the Urak River and that the state servitors of Kamchatka wanted to import cattle on state vessels. He suggested that three or four families of Yakuts be settled at Okhotsk to tend cattle and horses in order to supply travelers between Yakutsk and Kamchatka with meat and pack animals; that cows and pigs be sent from Yakutsk to Okhotsk and thence to Kamchatka by land or by sea; and that one or two families of Yakuts be settled at each ostrog in Kamchatka to tend cattle, since the Kamchadals were unaccustomed to cattle raising.[23]

Much of Bering's advice was promptly implemented by the government. The decree of May 10/21, 1731, that appointed Skorn-yakov-Pisarev Commandant of Okhotsk ordered him to establish agriculture there with exiles (debtors), as well as a shipyard and a wharf.[24] These instructions were reiterated on July 22/August 2.[25] Yet another edict of July 30/August 10 commanded Skornyakov-Pisarev to recruit up to fifty families of Russian peasants ". . . from Ilimsk Uyezd, or other places . . ." and thirty Tunguses for settlement "for life" at Yudoma Cross, at Okhotsk, along the Uda River, and at the ostrogs of Kamchatka, giving each family ten rubles and a two-year supply of grain.[26] One thousand rubles were assigned to him by the Tobolsk authorities for the purchase of cattle and horses for the settlers, and all kinds of grain seed from Yakutsk were to be distributed to them free of charge.[27] By a Senate decree of May 2/13, 1732, it was ordered "to transfer for life up to 50 families of volunteer peasants from Ilimsk Uyezd, or from other places, and three dozen Tunguses, and to settle as many as are required according to inspection near Okhotsk, on the route to the landmark called Cross between the Yudoma and the Urak Rivers, and on the Uda, as well as at the Kamchatkan ostrogs, providing them with ten rubles per family and grain for two years for enthusiasm [incentive] and for the first case [trial], as well as to give them tax and cartage privileges [exemptions] for four years. . . ."[28] The decree also ordered "to settle near Okhotsk four and more families of Yakuts, who could have cattle and horses . . ." and "to place near every ostrog one or two families of Yakuts for cattle grazing. . . ."[29] In addition, horses, cattle, and pigs were ordered sent from Yakutsk to Okhotsk and Kamchatka.[30] Finally, on October 7/18, 1732, the Senate instructed the Irkutsk authorities to increase the cultivation of grain in Kamchatka.[31] Under this program of agricultural development the Russian Government envisioned a time "when grain and cattle are raised at Okhotsk and at other localities and provisions from Yakutsk will not be needed. . . ."[32]

This program, however, was not fully implemented. The transfer of both settlers and livestock to the seaboard and the peninsula was marked by delays and losses. In January of 1738 Bering reported to the Siberian Office that the Russian peasants and Tunguses and the cattle and horses stipulated by the decrees of 1731 had not yet been settled at Okhotsk or in Kamchatka.[33] Of all cattle and horses purchased for 1,000 rubles at Yakutsk for shipment to the seaboard and the peninsula (probably 400 to 500 head), only thirty-three horses reached the peninsula. Most of the animals died en route for want of forage, while others were appropriated at Okhotsk by Bering for naval provisions.[34] In 1733 Major Pavlutsky established a pair of cattle at Bolsheretsk; these animals are the first cattle known to have reached Kamchatka, although some two hundred head may have arrived in 1732. In 1734 a pair of cattle and a pair of horses were sent to Kamchatka on the ship *Gabriel*. Bering dispatched the Cossack Lvov to Anadyrsk to procure cattle and horses from the Kolyma River, but the shortage of livestock there nullified this effort. By 1740 no horses had yet reached Kamchatka,[35] and Commandant Devier of Okhotsk reported that all cattle sent to Kamchatka had died on the way for want of feed.[36] In 1741 twenty-nine cattle and three horses were sent to Kamchatka by land and by sea,[37] but it is not known whether all of them arrived. Thus few dairy cattle and draft horses reached the Okhotsk Seaboard and the Kamchatka Peninsula (especially), and some of the few that did arrive subsequently perished from hunger.

The movement of settlers was not much more successful than that of livestock. From 1722 through 1744, 128 families left Ilimsk Uyezd for Okhotsk and Kamchatka, but many of them never arrived. Apparently the first settlers, thirty families, were dispatched in 1732 from the upper Lena River; in 1733 some of them were assigned plowland at Okhotsk, while the rest were forwarded to Kamchatka, where they were established first at Bolsheretsk but moved later (around 1738) to Klyuchi. In 1733–34 thirty Yakut families were sent to Okhotsk, but they were halted by flooding rivers; in 1734 forty-three families of Russian peasants from the upper Lena River reached Okhotsk, where they were detained as workers by the Second Kamchatka Expedition.[38] Although these colonists were selected (by lot) on the basis of their being "young, healthy and self-supporting" and able to "get to the decreed place without want," were given state assistance in money and in kind, and were escorted by Ilimsk and Yakutsk state servitors, many of them were killed, sickened, detained, or disqualified en route.[39] For example, fifty families of Russian peasants were dispatched from Yakutsk and Ilimsk Uyezd in 1733, "but they did not soon reach Okhotsk . . .";[40] on the way two families died, one family fell ill, and seven families that proved unfit were returned to Yakutsk.[41] The problem of replacing them remained unresolved as late as 1740, when eleven peasant families were selected in Ilimsk Uyezd and three peasant families were chosen at Yakutsk and sent to Okhotsk and Kamchatka for settlement; all but four of these families deserted en route.[42]

Other migrants complained that they were unfairly selected and deprived of assistance and consequently were not accepted by the authorities of Okhotsk and Kamchatka; such rejections sometimes engendered fruitless correspondence and infinite delays. Still others escaped "from the road," since they were involuntary migrants with no desire to go to godforsaken Kamchatka. One list from the 1740's of transmigrants from Bratsk (Prebaikalia) records sixteen families that deserted en route.[43]

Many colonists were impressed at Yakutsk and Okhotsk by the Second Kamchatka Expedition, which continually retained six hundred Russian peasants and five hundred to seven hundred Yakuts with horses for transport duty between Yakutsk and Okhotsk. For instance, the forty families (twenty-eight from Yakutsk and twelve from Ilimsk Uyezd) remaining from the fifty dispatched in 1733, together with their 53 tons, 560 pounds of seed and 93 tons, 566 pounds of provisions, were detained at Yakutsk by Bering for expeditionary work (transport) until 1739, when ten were sent to Udsk. Six families were settled at Amginsk, 120 miles east of Yakutsk, and in 1740 the remaining twenty-four, plus ten other families, reached Okhotsk, whence ten were sent to Insk (Map 10), 65 miles north of Okhotsk. In 1741, following completion of their freightage and depletion of their livestock by Bering, the remaining twenty-four families were sent to Kamchatka on Bering's ships as hands for want of regular crewmen; only one cow was sent with each family. Simultaneously, ten additional families of peasants with three cows and three horses were dispatched from Okhotsk to Kamchatka by land around Penzhina Bay; their fate is unknown. Of the twenty-four families who accompanied Bering to Kamchatka, five were settled at Trapeznikovsk, a zaimka near the confluence of the Bistraya

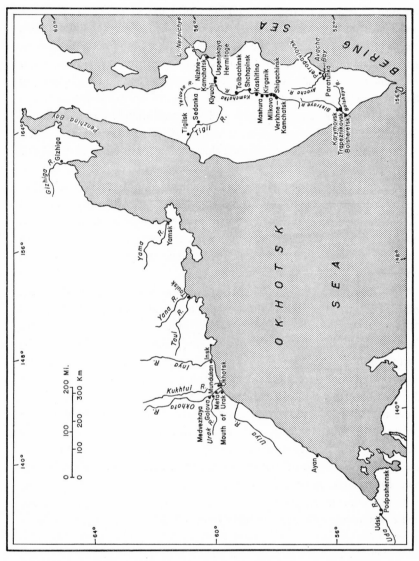

Map 10. The Main Agricultural Settlements on the Okhotsk Seaboard and the Kamchatka Peninsula.

and Bolshaya rivers; two at Karymovsk, a zaimka ten miles up the Bistraya; two outside Bolsheretsk itself; and the remaining fifteen were forwarded to Verkhne-Kamchatsk, whence two were settled eight miles downriver at Shigachinsk, three were settled eight to nine miles downriver at Milkovo, and ten at Klyuchi on the site of old Nizhne-Kamchatsk Ostrog (Map 10).* In 1746 the nine families in the vicinity of Bolsheretsk were resettled along the Apachinsk Banks of the lower Bistraya River twenty-nine to thirty miles from Bolsheretsk on the trail linking Bolsheretsk and Verkhne-Kamchatsk.[44]

Thus during the 1730's and early 1740's the transfer of Russian peasants and Yakut stockmen to the seaboard and the peninsula resulted in the placement of only a few dozen families. Nevertheless, the rudiments of state agriculture were established. Around 1740 Krasheninnikov noted with satisfaction the progress being made in "the establishment of plowland, which by the wisdom of Her Imperial Highness and Gracious Majesty [Empress Anne] has long since already begun to be implemented, as well as the conveyance hither of some families of peasants with a sufficient number of horses, horned cattle, and all implements necessary for cultivation."[45]

Apparently influenced by the favorable rather than the unfavorable points in the reports of Krasheninnikov and other members of the Second Kamchatka Expedition, just as it had been encouraged by Bering's earlier reports, the Russian Government transferred more peasants from the upper Lena River to the seaboard and the peninsula, chiefly to the Kamchatka River Valley. In 1744 and 1745 several families of peasants with a sizable number of draft animals arrived in Kamchatka, and others probably were added on the Okhotsk Seaboard.[46] Occasionally thereafter more peasants, as well as more livestock, seed, and equipment, were sent to the region; nevertheless, the pre-1750 arrivals formed the basic stock of peasantry from which sprang most of the subsequent agricultural operations.

By the mid-eighteenth century then, the agricultural settlement of the Okhotsk Seaboard and Kamchatka had more or less been com-

---

* Another source states that twenty peasant families were settled in 1743 in Kamchatka—nine near Bolsheretsk, six at Nizhne-Kamchatsk, and five at Verkhne-Kamchatsk, with four families later moving from Bolsheretsk to the Kamchatka River Valley (I. Bulychev, "Ob opytakh zemledeliya v Kamchatke" ["Concerning Agricultural Experiments in Kamchatka"], *Vestnik Imperatorskavo russkavo geograficheskavo obshchestva,* pt. 8 [1853], p. 78).

pleted, and henceforth agriculture was one of the main concerns of the commandants of the region. By 1750 there were probably up to a hundred families of Russian and Yakut agriculturalists dotting the seaboard and peninsula. It is known that in 1749 there were up to thirty families of peasant cultivators in Kamchatka and at Okhotsk, and around 1750 there were 209 peasants in Kamchatka and at Udsk.[47] At this time perhaps fifty families lived in the Kamchatka River Valley, chiefly in the villages of Milkovo, founded in 1743 on the upper Kamchatka River eight to nine miles below Verkhne-Kamchatsk, and of Klyuchi on the lower Kamchatka River fifty-four to fifty-six miles above new Nizhne-Kamchatsk. Milkovo was formed from the zaimka of Zaporotskovsk, and Klyuchi may have been based on the farmland of Uspenskaya Hermitage.[48] Outside the central valley there were a few families of agriculturalists at Bolsheretsk. Subsequently, agriculture was established elsewhere in the peninsula, as at Tigilsk and at Paratunka near Petropavlovsk.

Along the Okhotsk Seaboard agricultural settlement was largely confined to the lower courses of the Uda, Okhota, and Inya rivers. At Udsk, situated on the left bank of the Uda River forty-six to fifty miles upstream, ten or twelve families of Russian peasants with "sufficient" cattle, seed, and implements were settled in 1735 or 1736[49] "on account of the goodness of the land and the warmth of the climate. . . ."[50] Ten more families were added in 1739. Another agricultural settlement, Podpashennsk, arose near Udsk. At Okhotsk there were thirty-seven families of cultivators and five families of herders around 1750. Along the lower reaches of the Okhota River were several agricultural settlements, such as Meta, Mundukan, and Medvezhaya Golova, mostly occupied by Yakuts, who tended cattle rather than crops. Fifteen peasants were living at Medvezhaya Golova around 1760. The first Yakut cattlemen arrived at Okhotsk in 1735, and later others were settled along the lower Urak River, at Tauisk by the mouth of the Yana River, and at Yamsk by the mouth of the Yama River. Insk, a "level place" (lowland) just over four miles upstream from the mouth of the Inya River, comprised several families of Russian peasants settled there in 1735. Ten more families were added in 1740. In 1750 there were eight families of Russian peasants at Insk; the village in 1806 contained eight izbas, three balagans, one chapel, one bathhouse, and fifty-eight souls.[51] All in all, then, agricultural settlement was sparse and spotty.

Organization and Type of Agriculture

The agriculture was communal in organization and mixed or general in type. The Crown peasants lived in communal villages. Their agricultural operations were supervised by stewards, usually sergeants (assisted by *starostas* [village elders]), who distributed seed to the peasants "for sowings in proportion to the family [size] with lists and notes," i.e., with instructions.[52] In Kamchatka the post of agricultural supervisor or steward was inaugurated in 1742, the first stewards being Pyotr Rakhvalov and Pyotr Kholmovsky.[53] The stewards were supposed to oversee planting and harvesting by the peasants so that "all the distributed seed was sown up to the last kernel without any retention and theft . . ." and so that the crops were "reaped from the fields and piled in layers, and then threshed and safely stored in the magazines for state sealing without any pilfering."[54] The peasants were supposed "to sow grain on the very best and most suitable lands . . ." and "to manure sufficiently with dung, without idleness. . . ."[55] Further, "no grain at all was to be given to peasants with worthless sowings."[56] In 1743 the Udsk authorities were ordered to supervise strictly the planting of grain and "to beat unmercifully with cudgels" those peasants who did not sow all their grain, as well as "all those, who pursue agriculture carelessly."[57] The stewards also compelled the peasants with state livestock "to tend and guard [them] strictly, so that not a single animal can be lost for nothing . . . ,"[58] "and if any of the peasantry kills one of them for food on account of old age, then for each cow is to be exacted from them 50 rubles for the Treasury."[59] The peasants were also supposed "to prepare sufficient hay. . . ."[60]

All land, livestock, seed, and implements, as well as the entire harvest, were owned by the state. However, in Kamchatka at least, in 1765 state livestock, seed, and implements were given all at once to the peasants, who thereafter were entitled to part of the harvest. Some state servitors also farmed; those not wishing to sow could give their seed to the peasants for cultivation in return for half the harvest.[61]

Since arable land was not abundant, except perhaps in the Kamchatka River Valley, probably the traditional three-field system of tillage in strips was practiced—the communal plowland being divided into three fields, with each rotated in winter grain, spring grain, and fallow. The agriculture was mixed, the peasants cultivating spring and winter grains (chiefly barley, rye, and oats) and vegetables (mainly turnips and radishes) and keeping cattle (especially) and horses. At least in Kamchatka by the early 1740's there were no pigs, sheep, goats, or poultry. Grain cultivation predominated.[62]

11

PRODUCTION

". . . in Kamchatka (in places and at times) it is possible to grow grain. . . ."

P. K., "O vozmozhnosti uluchsheniya," p. 288.

Introduction

Members of the Second Kamchatka Expedition, such as Chirikov, Steller, and Krasheninnikov, were instructed to investigate the agricultural potential of Okhotsk-Kamchatka Kray and to conduct agricultural experiments there. In 1738 Krasheninnikov established an experimental garden at Bolsheretsk; he made trial plantings there of grain and vegetables with Major Pavlutsky and Lieutenant Krasilnikov, as well as later with Captain Chirikov at Petropavlovsk. In 1740 experimental sowings of grain were made at Bolsheretsk, Milkovo, and Klyuchi.[1] Krasheninnikov and Steller concluded that the most suitable forms and the most favorable locales for agriculture in Kamchatka were the raising of spring grains, tuberous vegetables, and cattle in the valleys of the Kamchatka and Bistraya rivers.[2] Steller felt that spring grains (barley and oats) could, in addition, be grown between Verkhne-Kamchatsk and Petropavlovsk, where there were "sufficiently extensive and suitable places for agriculture . . . ," but that there was little hope for grain cultivation, especially for winter grains, on Kamchatka's west coast because of the infertile soil and the prolonged snow cover; it was not possible to cut winter grains there until the end of June, when the weather was usually damp, so that the grain formed high stalks but barren ears.[3] As Krasheninnikov put it: "There is also little hope near the Penzhinsk [Okhotsk] Sea, because the land there is mostly damp and hummocky," while "in other places near the Eastern [Bering] Sea, both north and south of the Kamchatka [River], there are no lands suitable for the establishment of plowland: because the coastal places are sandy, stony, or boggy."[4]

Krasheninnikov was not hopeful either about the agricultural prospects of Okhotsk and Udsk: "almost the chief lack of this place [Okhotsk] is that there are no good cattle pastures nearby, on account of which the local inhabitants cannot as yet introduce cattle."[5] About Udsk he wrote: "it is said that there are no hopes that grain will be grown in those places because the land there is unsuitable for cultivation."[6]

Krasheninnikov and Steller were highly sanguine, however, about the prospects of cultivation in the Kamchatka River Valley. Krasheninnikov asserted that "as regards spring grain, many experiments have been made at both Verkhne- and old Nizhne-Kamchatsk Ostrogs, and barley and oats grow there so passably that better cannot be desired."[7] He claimed that around Verkhne-Kamchatsk "larger and better arable places are nowhere to be found."[8] He concluded that "although the land of Kamchatka is not everywhere suitable for [agricultural] production, the places along the Kamchatka River, however, as well as about the headwaters of the Bistraya, will from surplus supply with grain not only the local inhabitants but those of Okhotsk."[9] Steller agreed: "in the presence of such an abundance of localities suitable for agriculture in the country, here could be grown not only the amount of grain necessary for the local population but, in the course of time, as much as would be needed for supplying Okhotsk Kray and other enterprises."[10]

Steller did note that succulent varieties of vegetables, such as cabbage, lettuce, and peas, developed numerous and large leaves and stalks but small heads and kernels, while nonsucculent varieties, like radishes and rutabagas, which needed much moisture, developed large tubers.[11] Waxell drew from this situation the conclusion: "The soil of the country is black and obviously good, yet plants that must ripen above ground will neither grow nor thrive there, though the attempt has been made many times. . . . On the other hand, plants that ripen below ground can be grown most successfully, for example, turnips, radishes and several other roots."[12]

Captain Chirikov reported to the Admiralty College in 1742 that the experimental sowings of grain and vegetables made at Petropavlovsk by the Second Kamchatka Expedition had failed on account of late and early frosts: "rye, wheat, peas, buckwheat, and others, except barley, and perhaps *yaritsa* [spring grains in general and spring rye in particular], grow very improbably here, because the low places here are snow-covered right up to the first [middle] of June, and the snow never leaves the high mountains; in summer fog and, in parts, rain occur here, and in September cold, hard frost again occurs and sometimes snow falls. For such a short time, grain cannot ripen."[13]

Both Krasheninnikov and Steller were confident that livestock would thrive in Kamchatka. "Concerning the rapid increase of horned cattle," wrote Krasheninnikov, "on account of the convenience and sufficiency of feed of the localities, there is no doubt whatsoever. . . ."[14] He added that "the grasses throughout Kamchatka are without exception so high and succulent that it is difficult to find their likes in all the Russian Empire"; "on account of this it is not possible to wish for a more favorable place for the keeping of cattle."[15] Steller again concurred: "concerning meadow grasses . . . it can definitely be said that Kamchatka is supplied with them in abundance and that similar high and succulent grasses are nowhere to be found in all of the Russian Empire."[16] He added that "near rivers and lakes, and in the interior of the country in forests and clearings, grass reaches a height of over two sazhens [fourteen feet]. Besides this there are many broad meadows in the country."[17] "Because of the height and the thickness of the grass, here it is possible to gather much hay. . . ."[18] Surprised by the "incredible growth and good build" of livestock in Kamchatka, Steller affirmed that the cattle and horses sent to the peninsula from Yakutsk improved so much in size and quality that after one year it was impossible to recognize them as Yakut breeds. Yakut heifers calved a whole year earlier in Kamchatka.[19] He felt that "it would be possible to raise pigs there without any difficulty: because they reproduce rapidly and there is more feed for them in Kamchatka than elsewhere in Siberia."[20] Sheep, Krasheninnikov believed, could not be raised in Kamchatka because the climate was too cold and damp and the grass too succulent and watery.[21]

Chirikov had at best qualified hopes for stockbreeding: "there are found a few dry places, on which sufficient grass grows, with which it is possible to support livestock here, although not in such freedom as back home, because in the short and rainy summer it is necessary to prepare grass for livestock for at least seven and a half months."[22]

Thus expectations were mixed for agriculture in Kamchatka. The Russian Government chose to act as if it believed in the high hopes, envisioning the Kamchatka River Valley in particular as a granary and a stockyard for the peninsula and the seaboard. These hopes, however, were to be dashed.

Grain Production

Except for the occasional bumper year, grain yields proved low, while livestock multiplied slowly. Only vegetables regularly yielded well. The harvest of grain was sometimes bountiful but usually meager, seldom returning the seed, let alone enough for subsistence or export, since grain stemmed and eared but seldom ripened.

Yields of rye, barley, and yaritsa were negligible from the very beginning of state agriculture in Kamchatka. At Milkovo, the peninsula's chief agricultural settlement, up to 1,800 pounds of rye, barley, and yaritsa were sown from 1743 through 1756, but no grain ripened. From 1758 through 1763 at Milkovo only barley yielded over twofold, with 71.1 bushels producing 164.5 bushels, including 72.8 unripe bushels in 1761, while 28.9 bushels of rye produced only 39.2 bushels and yaritsa produced nothing at all.[23] Agriculture was generally less successful at Klyuchi, the peninsula's second most important agricultural settlement, than at Milkovo. From 1758 through 1760 at Klyuchi only 39 bushels of barley were harvested, and all of it was green, so that it was used for feed instead of seed. In 1764–65, 386.2 bushels of grain (mostly barley), almost one-third of it unripe, and 202.5 pounds of ripe hemp seed* were harvested at Klyuchi.[24] Throughout Kamchatka, in 1765, 75 bushels of barley were planted and 202.5 bushels were harvested, but in 1766 all barley (75.75 bushels) was killed by frost in July.[25]

As Table 12 indicates, oats yielded best and wheat worst in a group of five neighboring settlements; nevertheless, all yields here were variable and low, averaging less than onefold (.83). By contrast, the average yield of grain in European Russia during the first half of the nineteenth century was three and one-halffold.[26]

When the peasants of Kamchatka were allowed to farm for themselves as well as for the state from 1765, grain yields from their own plowland were no better than those from the Crown plowland. In 1770, for example, the peasants of Milkovo, Klyuchi, Kashitino (Kasitinsk), and Shigachinsk planted 2,286 pounds of grain and 45 pounds of

---

* Hemp was grown in Kamchatka, especially at Bolsheretsk, to meet the great demand for fish nets (Yu. A. Gagemeister, "Khozyaistvenno-statistichesky obzor Kamchatki" ["Economico-statistical Survey of Kamchatka"], *Zhurnal Ministerstva vnutrennikh del,* pt. 42 [1853], p. 252; Timofey Shmalev, "Kratkoye opisanie o Kamchatke . . ." ["Brief Description of Kamchatka . . ."], *Opyt trudov Volnavo rossiiskavo sobraniya pri Imperatorskom moskovskom universitete,* pt. 1 [1774], p. 211).

TABLE 12

Acreages and Yields of Grain at Kirganik, Mashura, Milkovo, Shigachinsk, and Verkhny, 1763–66

Year	Acres	Bushels Planted	Bushels Reaped
Barley			
1763	4.7	14.3	18.1
1764	5.4	20.1	32.0
1765	6.8	30.4	12.7
1766	8.1	34.1	13.8
Oats			
1763	0.3	1.1	3.9
1764	1.4	9.0	14.2
1765	4.1	30.0	36.6
1766	2.7	21.9	8.6
Rye			
1763	5.4	7.2	4.1
1764	8.1	13.6	8.9
1765	8.1	13.5	9.4
1766	0.0	0.0	0.0
Wheat			
1763	0.9	0.6	0.7
1764	0.3	0.4	0.0
1765	4.1	0.1	0.0
1766	0.0	0.0	0.0

SOURCE: I. Bulychev, "Ob opytakh zemledeliya v Kamchatke" ["Concerning Agricultural Experiments in Kamchatka"], *Vestnik Imperatorskavo russkavo geograficheskavo obshchestva*, pt. 8 (1853), p. 82.

hemp for the state and 4,572 pounds of grain for themselves, but only hemp yielded.[27]*

The 1770's were nevertheless the most productive years of grain cultivation in Kamchatka. In 1771 barley yielded threefold at Milkovo, barley and oats two- to threefold at Klyuchi, and barley and rye fourfold

* However, the Billings Expedition found in the early 1790's that the peasants of Milkovo neglected the Crown plowland but obtained abundant harvests of rye and buckwheat from their own plowland (Sauer, *Account of an Expedition,* p. 291).

at Kashitino. During the administration of Major Bem (1773–79) rye yielded eleven- to fourteenfold and barley five- to sixfold, so that the peasants of Milkovo and especially of Klyuchi annually sold 3,600 to 10,800 pounds of surplus barley and wheat.[28] In his petition to St. Petersburg asking to be relieved of his duties Bem stated that "in 1775 the harvest was good for rye, barley, oats, yaritsa, wheat, and hemp; from a small amount of sown seed were received up to 778 puds [28,008 pounds]."[29] When Bem left Kamchatka in March, 1779 there were up to 36,000 pounds of stored grain and 1,800 pounds of planted rye. During his six-year tenure the peninsula experienced only one crop failure.[30]

Following Bem's departure Kamchatka's production of grain became more erratic, with the poor years outnumbering the good ones. From 1785 through 1790 over eighteen tons of grain were harvested at Verkhne-Kamchatsk alone, but only part of it could be sold.[31] In 1794 it was reported that "recently" grain had yielded only one-quarter-fold at worst.[32] In 1807 Von Langsdorff found that the village elder of Milkovo had obtained grain yields of fivefold to eightfold for nine successive years and that a peasant at Vorovskaya (on the west coast about a hundred miles north of Bolsheretsk) had obtained buckwheat yields of fourfold to sevenfold for five successive years.[33] At Milkovo in 1822 barley yielded sevenfold, and in 1831 some 41,500 pounds of grain were harvested at Milkovo and Klyuchi together. Such successes, however, were noticeably rare; failures were more frequent, as in 1832, when nineteen peasants at Milkovo planted 4,159 pounds of grain, all of which was killed by frost.[34]

And so grain production went in Kamchatka—many bad years interspersed with some fair years and several good years. Consequently, many peasants abandoned farming for fishing and trapping, which in Kamchatka were more reliable and less laborious livelihoods than agriculture. Like the natives, they acquired dogs for traveling, spent the summer catching and drying fish, which replaced bread in their diet, and in winter trapped furs, which they exchanged for all necessities.[35] It was reported in 1794 that Kamchatka's peasantry engaged mostly in stock raising and that they cultivated little grain because of the lack of supervision, their own laziness, the abundance of fish, and the dearth of seed.[36] In 1800, 160 peasant families in Kamchatka had completely renounced agriculture for fishing and trapping. By then the peninsula's Crown plowland had deteriorated. In 1812 state agriculture was abandoned in Kamchatka; private agriculture continued, but with little success. After 1825 grain cultivation declined markedly, and in 1828 Kamchatka's entire grain harvest amounted to but 279 bushels of barley —although then it reportedly yielded eightfold and sometimes more. In 1831, 855 bushels of barley were harvested by the peasant settlements along the Kamchatka River.[37] The Commandant of Kamchatka reported in 1840 that the condition of grain cultivation in the peninsula was "weak and insignificant."[38]

Grain growing on the Okhotsk Seaboard was even less productive than in Kamchatka. Although state servitors had been sent from Yakutsk as early as 1718 to open plowland and plant grain at Udsk, by 1740 grain still had not been sown. Then for several years running the Udsk peasants farmed both sides of the river near the ostrog; but no sooner did they harvest a surplus than it was appropriated for seed by the authorities, who were under strict orders from Okhotsk to store grain and to propagate agriculture.[39] In 1749 Okhotsk ordered that all harvested grain be delivered to the state magazines for seed, that henceforth diligent peasants be rewarded with half the harvest, and that farming soldiers be freed from military duty during plowing and harvesting.[40] But grain yields remained low. Udsk's eight families of peasants reported to the authorities in 1744 that on 13½ acres of grainland 1,512 pounds yielded merely 720 pounds in 1742 and 1,260 pounds yielded only 1,440 pounds in 1743.[41] Available grain yields at Udsk are shown in Table 13: barley averaged just over twofold and rye just over threefold, whereas it was estimated in the late nineteenth century that an average yield of fourfold was necessary for the stabilization of grain cultivation on the Okhotsk Seaboard.[42]

Such negligible harvests of grain at Udsk necessitated the importation of grain seed from Yakutsk. In 1762 and 1763, respectively, 504 pounds and 972 pounds of seed grain (barley, oats, and rye), plus 1,080 pounds of iron for making implements, were sent to Udsk. In 1773 grain cultivation was even abandoned for several years,[43] and in 1775 Udsk reported that for several years running no grain had been planted.[44] Consequently, sometime between 1774 and 1782 Yakutsk decided to provision Udsk by overland supply, although local agricultural efforts continued. Grain was sown annually from 1783 through 1789, but the poor results precipitated an inspection of Udsk's agriculture in 1790.[45] In 1799 Udsk reported that there were only nine peasants farming less than five and a half acres of plowland and less than forty-two acres of pasture, that grain grew in some years but not in others, that grain was not planted for want of seed, and that vegetables were not grown.[46] A Cossack at Udsk in 1814, despite an extremely severe summer, planted sixteen pounds of barley and harvested seventy-two pounds. But by 1844 grain cultivation was limited to two low-lying and poorly drained plots, each comprising 980 square feet; barley yielded threefold on the communal plot and fivefold on the private plot. Even these meager remnants ceased in 1851–53, although the priests continued to plant potatoes. In 1852 there was no grain cultivation but some vegetable

TABLE 13

Grain Yields (in Bushels) at Udsk for Various Years between 1742 and 1789

	Barley		Rye	
Year	Sowing	Harvest	Sowing	Harvest
1742	unknown	unknown	5.1	17.4
1743[a]	19.5	35.3	3.5	1.9
1749	6.0	24.0	4.2	18.0
1751	30.0	51.8	unknown	unknown
1752	unknown	27.8	unknown	unknown
1753	12.0	36.0	unknown	unknown
1761	3.4	5.6	unknown	unknown
1762	6.0	15.0	unknown	unknown
1781	1.7	3.3	1.0	8.5
1783	3.4	7.6	1.7	3.5
1784	unknown	10.9	unknown	9.0
1785	unknown	unknown	3.7	unknown
1786	1.5	unknown	3.2	unknown
1787	unknown	unknown	1.1	unknown
1788	1.3	unknown	unknown	unknown
1789	1.3	unknown	0.8	unknown

[a] In addition, 4.5 bushels of oats were sown, and 6.8 bushels harvested.

SOURCES: A. Middendorf, *Puteshestvie na severe i vostoke Sibiri* [*Journey in the North and the East of Siberia*] (St. Petersburg: Tipografiya Imperatorskoy akademii nauk, 1867), pt. 1, suppl. 3, pp. xii–xiv; F. G. Safronov, *Okhotsko-Kamchatsky kray* (*Puti soobshcheniya, naselenie, snabzhenie i zemledelie do revolyutsii*) [*Okhotsk-Kamchatka Kray* (*Routes of Communication, Population, Supply and Agriculture before the Revolution*)] (Yakutsk: Yakutskoye knizhnoye izdatelstvo, 1958), p. 73; F. G. Safronov, "Popytki prodvizheniya granitsy sibirskovo zemledeliya do beregov Tikhovo okeana v XVIII v." ["Attempts at the Extension of the Boundary of Siberian Agriculture up to the Shores of the Pacific Ocean in the XVIIIth Century"], *Izvestiya Vsesoyuznovo geograficheskovo obshchestva*, 86, no. 6 (1954) : 523; P. P. Semyonov, ed., *Zhivopisnaya Rossiya* [*Picturesque Russia*] (St. Petersburg and Moscow: Izdanie Tovarishchestva M. O. Volf, 1895), vol. 12, pt. 2, p. 164.

gardening at Udsk; the inhabitants were preoccupied with fishing in summer and with trapping in winter. No grain was cultivated in Udsk Okrug in 1865, although some inhabitants maintained small vegetable gardens (potatoes, cabbages, turnips, and radishes) and several head of livestock.[47]

At Okhotsk, where grain (rye, barley, and oats) was first planted in 1732 or 1733 by the pilot Birev, it failed the first three years. Evidently this grainland was soon abandoned, for there was no grain cultivation in 1769—and by 1775 there were no peasants. In 1781 experimental sowings of grain (imported from Irkutsk) were made at Okhotsk with little success.[48]

Grain yields were also meager along the lower courses of the Inya and the Urak rivers. In 1745, 19.9 bushels of winter rye and in 1746, 10.8 bushels of spring barley were planted here; the grain strawed and eared but did not kernel. During Minitsky's administration at Okhotsk (1809–16) no grain was cultivated in Okhotsk Kray.[49]

At Gizhiga grain cultivation was nonexistent in 1819; and in 1865 there was no grain cultivation in Gizhiga Kray, although some inhabitants had small vegetable gardens (turnips and potatoes) and a few head of cattle.[50]

Vegetable Production

While grain production on the Okhotsk Seaboard and the Kamchatka Peninsula was negligible, vegetables yielded well, especially tuberous ones like turnips, radishes, and potatoes. Turnips in particular did well;[51] the nine-pound ones of Uspenskaya Hermitage will be recalled. Krasheninnikov found turnips measuring up to three inches in diameter along the Bolshaya River and four to five times larger along the Kamchatka River, while Waxell ate tasty Kamchatka turnips weighing two to three pounds each.[52] In 1822 cabbages, turnips, and radishes weighing six pounds apiece, and one-pound potatoes and carrots, were grown at Petropavlovsk.[53]

While root vegetables thrived, succulent vegetables like lettuce and peas failed, just as Krasheninnikov and Steller had warned. Lettuce seldom headed and peas rarely pulsed; even cabbage sometimes failed to head. For example, from 1765 through 1767 in Kamchatka plantings of forty-three pounds of peas yielded nothing.[54]

Vegetable growing did not become widespread in the peninsula until the administration of Bem. When he arrived in 1773, only turnips were being grown—with good results—at all ostrogs; other vegetables (cabbages, radishes, carrots, beets, and cucumbers) were raised only at Verkhne-Kamchatsk. Bem promptly established vegetable gardens at all settlements, and later he introduced potatoes.* Thereafter Russians and Kamchadals alike raised turnips, rutabagas, carrots, radishes, beets, potatoes, cucumbers, and cabbages with excellent results.[55] Commandant Rikord noted during his tour of Kamchatka in 1822 that the Kamchadals were voluntarily growing vegetables,[56] and in the early 1830's Commandant Golenishchev observed that all of the peninsula's inhabitants, except those in the far north, grew vegetables.[57] By the 1850's every native settlement had a garden containing turnips, radishes, and potatoes.[58] Vegetables grew larger in the drier and sunnier interior than on the coasts,[59] and at Klyuchi they were "raised with greater facility than in any other part of the Peninsula."[60]

The potato was an important innovation, since it did fairly well on the west coast as far north as Tigilsk, where vegetables could not be planted until late June and where only potatoes (especially) and turnips grew well. In 1831 there were 159,152 square feet (over 3½ acres) of gardens at Tigilsk, probably mostly in potatoes. In 1782 potatoes yielded thirty-twofold at Bolsheretsk and twenty-fivefold at Verkhne-Kamchatsk; in 1822 they rendered fiftyfold at Petropavlovsk and forty-eightfold at Milkovo.[61] The Russian circumnavigator Von Kotzebue observed in 1824 that in Kamchatka "potatoes generally yield a triple crop [three crops a year]. . . ."[62] During the early 1830's the average yield of potatoes at Tigilsk was thirteenfold. In 1832, 29,916 pounds of potatoes were harvested at Milkovo alone. At thirty-seven settlements, in 1840, 29,340 pounds yielded 249,012 pounds of potatoes, including 86,400 pounds at Klyuchi; in 1844 throughout the peninsula 57,456 pounds yielded 720,540 pounds of potatoes; and in 1845, 648 gardens produced 648,000 pounds of potatoes. When fish were scarce in the peninsula in 1845–46, potatoes constituted a lifesaving substitute.[63]

* A Senate decree of 1765 ordered the propagation of "ground apples" in Russia, and in 1767 seed potatoes were sent from Irkutsk to Okhotsk and Kamchatka (V. N. Sherstoboyev, "Zemledelie severnovo Predbaikalya v XVII–XVIII vv." ["Agriculture of Northern Prebaikalia in the XVIIth–XVIIIth Centuries"], in *Materialy po istorii zemledeliya SSSR,* ed. B. D. Grekov [Moscow and Leningrad: Izdatelstvo Akademii nauk SSSR, 1952], collection 1, p. 291).

They were reported to have yielded seventyfold to a hundredfold in 1847;[64] by comparison the Siberian yield of potatoes at this time averaged sevenfold to tenfold. A sixfold crop of potatoes totaling over 606,000 pounds was harvested in Kamchatka in one year of the early 1850's.[65] By 1857 the American entrepreneur Collins found that potatoes, as well as turnips, radishes, cucumbers, and cabbages, were grown in Kamchatka "with great ease and in abundance. . . ."[66]

On the Okhotsk Seaboard vegetables were grown more successfully than grain but less successfully than in Kamchatka. It was not until 1781 that experimental vegetable gardens were established at Okhotsk. Large and tasty turnips and radishes were produced, lettuce and cabbage yielded well (although the heads of the lettuce were not firm and the taste of the cabbage was unpleasant); but carrots, parsley, and parsnips did not yield at all.[67] Sarychev noted in 1786 that along the lower Okhota River potatoes, radishes, and carrots were grown successfully but not abundantly, while cabbage managed to leaf but failed to head.[68] In 1806 at Okhotsk itself Academician Redovsky counted about twenty small gardens, which contained cabbage, turnips, and potatoes; their yield did not meet the settlement's needs. Turnips grew best, as large as a saucer in circumference, while potatoes yielded poorly and did not ripen every year. At Insk Redovsky also found gardens, where only radishes, cabbage, and turnips ripened.[69] Commandant Minitsky reported in 1815 that at Okhotsk "garden vegetables, especially turnips and radishes, grow well, [whereas] cabbage does not curl into tendrils but grows mostly to leaf."[70] Later he summarized vegetable growing on the seaboard: "potatoes, cabbages, turnips ripen in the best years, but cabbages fail to come to a head."[71] By 1823 potatoes were grown only at Okhotsk and Insk; at Okhotsk the yield averaged sevenfold. At Udsk the local authorities were ordered in 1813 to supervise the propagation of potatoes, which yielded tenfold in 1844. In 1852 vegetable gardens were kept only by the Udsk clergy.[72]

Livestock Production

Livestock, chiefly cattle, were essential to the success of agriculture on the Okhotsk Seaboard and the Kamchatka Peninsula, for they provided draft-power and manure, as well as meat, milk, butter, and cheese. Thus, livestock were included in the earliest attempts at agriculture in the region.

Kamchatka's cattle and horses were of the Yakut breed. The cattle were strong and hardy, with thick hair; the horses developed into the Kamchatka strain, also distinguished by its strength and hardiness.[73] However, despite their sturdiness and despite the optimism of Krasheninnikov and Steller, the peninsula's livestock multiplied very slowly. Table 14 shows that in over a century cattle increased less than ninefold, while horses multiplied even more slowly.

Such were the disappointing results of more than a hundred years of stockbreeding in Kamchatka. The Russian circumnavigator Kruzenstern was appalled by "the great scarcity of horned cattle in Kamchatka" in 1804–5.[74] The few cattle were scattered, in 1822, among more than fifty settlements in the peninsula. In 1831 there were 138 cattle at Tigilsk. By 1850 cattle and horses were found at almost all settlements, but the total number (ca. 1,600 head) was small. The principal horsebreeding center was Milkovo, which possessed up to eighty horses in 1787 but only twenty-two in 1807.[75]

Although cows were not numerous, they allegedly produced ample milk. Around 1740 Krasheninnikov found that Kamchatka's cows gave abundant milk year round,[76] and almost a century later the German traveler Erman found them yielding "plenty of milk both in summer and winter."[77]*

Information on livestock production on the Okhotsk Seaboard is scanty, but it is sufficient to indicate that stockbreeding there was no more productive than in Kamchatka. At Udsk in 1744 there were only seven cattle and nine horses among eight peasant families. In 1747 more cattle and horses were sent to Udsk, but for eighty-five years the number of cattle there did not exceed twenty-three head.[78] Table 15 shows that the number in 1744 and in 1844 was identical—only seven.

In the 1730's several abortive attempts at cattle raising were made along the lower Taui River. At Insk in 1794 the ten families of Russian peasants had only four cows and three horses;[79] a visitor noted in 1806 that cattle were reared with fair success and horses with little success.[80] Along the lower Okhota and the lower Urak rivers cattle were kept successfully by Yakut and Russian settlers, but they were few in number and low in milk production (no more than three-quarters of a

---

* However, another source states that generally Kamchatka's cows gave little milk (M. G. Levin and L. P. Potapov, eds., *Narody Sibiri* [*Peoples of Siberia*] [Moscow and Leningrad: Izdatelstvo Akademii nauk SSSR, 1956], p. 984).

TABLE 14

Number of Livestock in Kamchatka for Various Years between 1743 and 1852

Year	Number of Cattle	Number of Horses
1743	up to 200	unknown
ca. 1750	up to 200	unknown
Late 1750's	up to 100	unknown
1771	63 (state)	4 (state)
1772	200–570	unknown
1773	587	unknown
1781	272	138
1794	50 (state)	69 (state)
1804–5	ca. 600	unknown
1818	250	51
1821	968	109
1822	718	91
Early 1840's	1,564	289
1848	1,498	309
1852	1,700	400

SOURCES: D. K. Chernykh, "Kratkoye istoricheskoye obozrenie zemledeliya v Kamchatke" ["Brief Historical Review of Agriculture in Kamchatka"], *Zemledelchesky zhurnal . . . ,* no. 1 (1833), p. 106; Cochrane, *Narrative of a Pedestrian Journey,* p. 294; Yu. A. Gagemeister, "Khozyaistvenno-statistichesky obzor Kamchatki" ["Economico-statistical Survey of Kamchatka"], *Zhurnal Ministerstva vnutrennikh del,* pt. 42 (1853), p. 250; [Kapitan Mashin], "Vypiska iz pisma Nachalnika Kamchatki, Mashina, k Nepremennomu sekretaryu V. e. obshchestva" ["Extracts from a Letter of the Commandant of Kamchatka, Mashin, to the Permanent Secretary of the F. E. Society"], *Trudy Imperatorskavo volnavo ekonomicheskavo obshchestva,* no. 6, pt. 2 (1848), sec. 3, pp. 109–111; P. Pallas, "Izvestiya o vvedennom skotovodstve i zemlepashestve v Kamchatke i okolo Okhotska, pri Udskom ostroge lezhashchem podle Okhotskavo morya" ["Information about Stockbreeding and Cultivation Introduced into Kamchatka and around Okhotsk, Lying alongside the Okhotsk Sea near Udsk Ostrog"], *Prodolzhenie trudov Volnavo ekonomicheskavo obshchestva . . . ,* pt. 3 (1783), pp. 36–38; N. P. Rezanov, "Zapiska gorodnichevo Nizhne-Kamchatska Voyevodskovo o sostoyanii Kamchatki i vygodnosti yeyo ekspluatatsii dlya kazny" ["Note of Mayor Voyevodsky of Nizhne-Kamchatsk on the Condition of Kamchatka and the Advantages of Its Exploitation for the State"], TsGADA, f. 796, op. 1, d. 285, fol. 2; Flot Kapitan Rikord, "O sostoyanii poluostrova Kamchatki i o blagotvoritelnykh zavedeniyakh v onoy uchrezhdayemykh" ["Concerning the Condition of the Peninsula of Kamchatka and the Charitable Institutions Founded in It"], *Zhurnal Imperatorskavo chelovekolyubivavo obshchestva,* 8 (April, 1819) : 9; Sgibnev, "Istorichesky ocherk," 102 (May, 1869) : 81*n;* 103 (July, 1869) : 6, 24; 103 (August, 1869) : 67, 102; Shmalev, "Kratkoye o Kamchatke obyasnenie," fol. 4; Shmalev, "Kratkoye opisanie o Kamchatke . . ." ["Brief Description of Kamchatka . . ."], *Opyt trudov Volnavo rossiiskavo sobraniya pri Imperatorskom moskovskom universitete,* pt. 1 (1774), p. 209; Shmalev, "Statisticheskiya i Geograficheskiya Primechaniya," fol. 22ᵛ ; Otto Von Kotzebue, *A New Voyage Round the World, in the Years 1823, 24, 25, and 26* (London: Henry Colburn and Richard Bentley, 1830), 2 : 20–21; Captain A. J. Von Krusenstern, *Voyage Round the World in the Years 1803, 1804, 1805, & 1806,* trans. Richard Belgrave Hoppner (London: John Murray, 1813), 2 : 238.

quart each per day), so that the annual summer drives from Yakutsk continued. In 1854 there were 640 cattle and 152 horses in Okhotsk Okrug, including 21 cattle and 9 horses at Okhotsk. Gizhiga Kray in 1865 had 72 cattle and 7 horses.[81]

TABLE 15

Number of Cattle at Udsk for Various Years between 1744 and 1856

Year	Number of Cattle
1744	7
1786	23
1790	21–23
1799	22
1830	41
1844	7
1848	10
1856	25

SOURCES: Middendorf, *Puteshestvie na Sibiri*, pt. 1, suppl. 3, p. xvi; Safronov, *Okhotsko-Kamchatsky kray*, p. 101; Semyonov, *Zhivopisnaya Rossiya*, vol. 12, pt. 2, p. 165; Shchukin, "Udskoye selenie," *Russky invalid*, 35, no. 115 : 460; Shchukin, "Udskoye selenie," *Zhurnal Ministerstva vnutrennikh del*, p. 181.

12

AGRICULTURAL PROBLEMS

"The monks in the monastery [Uspenskaya Hermitage] at Nishnij [Nizhne-Kamchatsk] have made various experiments and succeeded in getting barley to ripen. That, however, is not possible every year, but only in a dry summer, and when there are not too many mists off the sea, and such favourable weather will scarcely come once in ten years."

Sven Waxell, *Russian Expedition to America*, p. 140.

Physical Problems

Most of the numerous obstacles which limited agricultural production on the Okhotsk Seaboard and the Kamchatka Peninsula stemmed from the region's harsh physical environment. The foremost impediment was the inimical climate, specifically the short growing season, caused by the prolonged snow cover and by the late and early frosts. In that short growing season, as we have seen, crops usually blossomed but seldom ripened: grain eared, legumes podded, and salads leafed, but they rarely kerneled, pulsed, or headed. Only roots and tubers like radishes and potatoes escaped the killing frosts. In Kamchatka the snow cover lasted eight to nine months, almost until the end of May.[1] In the words of an official report, "snow falls very early and leaves very late, so that grain does not have time to ripen."[2] Plowing was not begun until June, and vegetables were not planted until late June. In places along the lower Okhota River the snow cover lasted until late June. It was impossible to plant grain at Udsk in 1754 because of deep snow, and in June of 1764 falling snow killed the sown grain.[3]

Frosts occurred late and early—in fact, almost continuously. Upon returning from his first expedition, Bering warned of early frosts along the lower Kamchatka River;[4] and Krasheninnikov's experimental sowings of barley at Bolsheretsk were thwarted "because of the early frosts, which almost without fail commence at the beginning [middle] of August. . . ."[5] Along the lower Bistraya River grain was killed by frost every year from 1746 through 1757, and thereafter the peasants "lived idly."⁶ Major Bem concluded that the frosts of late spring constituted the chief handicap of agriculture in the peninsula.⁷ Late frosts even occurred during the second week of July; in 1767, for instance, grain was killed by frost on July 16. The late frosts, which forced the peasants to plant late, were promptly followed by early frosts in early August or even late July that prevented crops from ripening.* For example, at Milkovo in 1820 hoar frosts on July 27, 28, and 29 killed all grain and vegetables. Usually hoar frost began in late August and no later than the first days of September.⁸

Late and early frosts, then, sharply curtailed Kamchatka's growing season, which around 1800 normally lasted from the middle of June until the beginning of September, or two and a half months.** By contrast, the growing season for spring grains in European Russia then lasted three to three and a half months. At Petropavlovsk, where the first early frosts struck in August, potatoes could not be planted until the middle of June and cabbage until the beginning of July, so that they usually did not have time to ripen. In the Kamchatka River Valley winter grains, mainly rye, planted in mid-August and harvested in late September of the next year, were more susceptible to frost damage than

---

* The peasants had one defense against early frosts that they utilized especially during the administrations of Bem and Koshelev. Whenever hoar frost threatened in August, they shook the cold dew from the grain by yanking on cords strung among the stalks; however, this method was feasible only with limited grainland (Gagemeister, "Khozyaistvenno-statistichesky obzor Kamchatki," p. 251; P. P. Semyonov, ed., *Zhivopisnaya Rossiya* [*Picturesque Russia*] [St. Petersburg and Moscow: Izdanie Tovarishchestva M. O. Volf, 1895], vol. 12, pt. 2, p. 39).

** The climate of Kamchatka and the Okhotsk Seaboard, like that of Alaska, may have slightly ameliorated from the middle of the nineteenth century. Nowadays on the average Petropavlovsk experiences no frost in June, July, or August, Klyuchi has only one day of frost in June and none in July or August, and Bolsheretsk has only three days of frost in June, none in July, and but one in August (P. I. Koloskov, "Klimatichesky ocherk poluostrova Kamchatki" ["Climatic Survey of the Kamchatka Peninsula"], *Izvestiya Dalnevostochnovo geofizicheskovo instituta,* no. 2 [1932], p. 133). Captain Lebedev, Commandant of Kamchatka, contended around 1750 that the climate of the peninsula had become more severe after 1743 (Bulychev, "Ob opytakh zemledeliya," p. 78; A. Sgibnev, "Istorichesky ocherk glavneishikh sobyty v Kamchatke" ["Historical Sketch of the Main Events in Kamchatka"], *Morskoy sbornik,* 102 [May, 1869] : 81). Although both monthly averages and personal impressions are deceptive, even a slight climatic change would be critical for marginal agriculture.

were spring grains, mainly barley, which were sown in late May and reaped in mid-September of the same year.* If nipped by frost before kerneling, grain was fit only for straw; if nipped after kerneling, it was suitable for flour but not for seed. Consequently, it was frequently necessary to ship seed grain to Kamchatka. During 1770–74, for example, 383 bushels of seed grain (barley, oats, and rye) were sent annually from Irkutsk to Kamchatka.[9] With good reason, then, the peninsula's authorities attributed the failure of cultivation to the fact that "the hoar frost falls early and the grain is not allowed to ripen."[10] The agronomist Chernykh underlined the problem when he wrote that "the weather, often in a few minutes, reduces to nothing the labors of an entire year."[11] Another investigator, Lyubarsky, who spent five years in Kamchatka around 1820, concluded that the cold, not the peasants, was responsible for the failure of agriculture in the peninsula, which "cannot manage without imported grain."[12]

Growing conditions were no better on the Okhotsk Seaboard. Late frosts delayed the planting of spring crops until late May or early June, while cool summer weather prevented their ripening before the onset of early frosts in late or even mid-summer. Commandant Minitsky reported in 1812 that crops could not ripen at Okhotsk because of the occurrence from late August of cold, salty dew.[13] At Okhotsk and Insk from 1839 through 1843 grain sown on orders from Commandant Golovnin failed every year because of the short season, so that he reported grain growing in Okhotsk Kray to be impossible.[14] At the same time, however, good vegetables were being grown at Okhotsk; they were nursed in hothouses in spring and then transplanted outdoors after the melting of the snow cover. At Udsk, where traditionally spring grains were sown on May 24 and winter grains on July 29, crops were regularly killed by early frosts, which occurred in July and August. Here har-

---

* However, in 1794 Mayor Voyevodsky of Nizhne-Kamchatsk reported that it was better to plant winter grains because, while they sprouted in the cold season, they did not ear until after the disappearance of snow and frost by mid-June (N. P. Rezanov, "Zapiska gorodnichevo Nizhne-Kamchatska Voyevodskovo o sostoyanii Kamchatki i vygodnosti ekspluatatsii dyla kazny" ["Note of Mayor Voyevodsky of Nizhne-Kamchatsk on the Condition of Kamchatka and the Advantages of Its Exploitation for the State"], TsGADA, f. 796, op. 1, d. 285, fol. 1). Winter grains succeeded only where there was enough snowfall to insulate them against severe frost (Yu. A. Gagemeister, *Statisticheskoye obozrenie Sibiri* [*Statistical Survey of Siberia*] [Tipografiya II otdeleniya Sobstvennoy Yevo Imperatorskavo Velichestva Kantselyarii, 1854], pt. 1, p. 188).

vested grain repeatedly proved fit for flour but not for seed, so that seed grain frequently had to be imported.[15]

On both the peninsula and the seaboard the shortness of the growing season was aggravated by the dearth of sunlight in summer. Only in the Kamchatka River Valley were the summers generally clear; elsewhere they were foggy, cloudy, and rainy, so that crop growth, already abbreviated by snow and frosts, was further retarded by insufficient sunshine.[16] At Okhotsk, as Sir George Simpson noted, "summer consists of three months of damp and chilly weather. . . ."[17] The average temperatures of the vegetative period* are 53.2° F. at Milkovo and Klyuchi, 51.3° at Petropavlovsk, 49.5° at Bolsheretsk, 46.4° at Okhotsk and Ayan, and 53.6° at Udsk; all of these averages fall closer to the minimum growth temperatures (32°–41° F.) than to the optimum growth temperatures (77°–87.8° F.) for northern cereals.[18] Steller was appalled by the frequency of fogs in Kamchatka: "I do not think that it is possible to meet more of them anywhere else on the globe. . . ."[19] Waxell noted the "continual dampness and thick mists coming off the sea, so that the sun is unable to exert its influence on the land, with the result that nothing ripens, but just dries up and is destroyed."[20] He added that barely once every decade were summers ever dry enough in the lower Kamchatka River Valley to permit barley to ripen.[21] In 1810–11 the circumnavigator Vasily Golovnin estimated that Kamchatka might render only one harvest every twenty or twenty-five years because of its severe climatic conditions.[22] The Billings Expedition found the air at Okhotsk "unwholesome in the extreme, as fogs, mists, and chilling winds, constantly prevail, which so much affect the products of the earth, that nothing grows within five verstas [ca. 3½ miles] of the sea."[23] This opinion was reiterated in 1865 by an anonymous observer, who stated that "the air at Okhotsk is damp, unhealthy, scorbutic, and fatal for animal and vegetable organisms, so that nothing grows or thrives closer than 4 verstas [ca. 2½ miles] [from the coast]. . . ."[24] At Udsk in 1791 grain did not even sprout because of the pouring rain and the damp, cold air.[25]

Furthermore, even in clear weather parts of Kamchatka were in the shadow of high mountains much of the day. At Petropavlovsk lofty mountains blocked the summer sun until 10 A.M. and after 2 P.M., thereby offsetting the benefit of long hours of daylight.[26] The same effect

---

* The vegetative period (growing season) is that time of year when the average daily temperature exceeds 41° F.

was necessarily felt in parts of the Kamchatka River Valley, abruptly bounded as it was by high ranges. Thus, high mountains combined with murky skies to restrict the long (but weak) sun of summer, which might otherwise have partially compensated for the shortness of the frost-free period. The sunless weather hampered the ripening of grain and the drying of hay. Lyubarsky in 1820 found grain being threshed green at Milkovo, for example.[27] Green or damp grain sometimes spoiled or burned in storage.[28]

The scarcity of cultivable land was a major problem on the Okhotsk Seaboard. It was reported in 1775 that there were only 27 acres of "excellent" arable land at Udsk.[29] In 1779 an anonymous investigator found only 112 acres of plowland at Udsk and only 30 acres of plowland at nearby Podpashennsk.[30] In 1786, 152 parcels of cropland at Udsk comprised 666¼ acres of suitable plowland and 64⅘ acres of unsuitable plowland, and there were but 263¼ acres of obrok (quitrent) plowland at Udsk in 1790, including 226 acres suitable for cultivation. Along the Okhota River agricultural land was also limited. Around 1760 at Medvezhaya Golova, for instance, there were only 94½ acres of land fit for cultivation and only 135 acres of land fit for haymaking.[31]

Soil infertility was a minor problem. The "black earth" of the Kamchatka River Valley was a fertile mixture of sand, clay, and volcanic ash, seven inches in depth, atop a gravel subsoil. Elsewhere in Kamchatka and along the Okhotsk Seaboard agriculture was conducted on the alluvial soil of the lower courses of small river valleys. This soil was suitable for agriculture, although at Udsk it was "sandy and firry" and required manure for cropping, while Siberian peasants were unaccustomed to dunging.[32]* Seasonal flooding replenished the soil with silt, but it also either drowned the crops or delayed their planting, leaving insufficient time for ripening. In 1805 the commander of the company of the Kamchatka Regiment at Udsk reported to Governor-General Selifontov that Udsk was not suited to agriculture "on account of the sandy ground and the frequent flooding."[33] One such flood occurred in 1806.[34]

Agriculture in Kamchatka was probably little affected by volcanic eruptions and earthquakes, since they were generally mild and infrequent. However, Krasheninnikov was told by the peninsula's inhab-

---

* Count Benyovsky, the Polish exile who fomented a revolt at Bolsheretsk in 1771 and escaped from Kamchatka, asserted that in the peninsula grain succeeded only on manured ground (Mauritius Augustus Count De Benyowsky, *Memoirs and Travels* . . . [Dublin: P. Wogan, L. White, P. Byrne, et al., 1790], 1 : 145).

itants in 1737 that Mount Klyuchevskaya erupted two or three times a year, covering the ground for two hundred miles around with hot ashes to a depth of one and three-quarters inches.[35] Major eruptions of this volcano occurred in 1729, 1737, 1762, 1790, 1796, 1829, and 1853. Mount Kamchatskaya, whose eruptions usually lasted a week or less, was active continuously from 1721 through 1730, especially from 1727. Such strewings may have injured crops and livestock. Tremors also may have wreaked agricultural havoc. On October 17, 1737, Kamchatka was racked by a strong earthquake, whose aftershocks continued until the following spring, killing many natives, wrecking numerous dwellings, and flooding several fields and meadows.[36]

Plowland would have benefited from manure, but dung was scarce, since livestock were not numerous; consequently, at Okhotsk, for example, gardens were fertilized with rotten fish.[37] Stockbreeding was plagued by several problems. Pasture was generally ample or even abundant, especially in Kamchatka, where in places, particularly along rivers and around lakes, succulent grass grew so tall and so fast that it exceeded the height of a man and could be cut two to three times a year. A small plot could produce a great deal of hay. Along the lower Okhota River, too, grass grew tall and dense. Yet at Okhotsk itself forage was scarce; there was some good pasture, but at times it was under water.[38] Commandant Timofey Shmalev reported in 1775 that it was "quite impossible" to keep cattle at Okhotsk for want of suitable grass.[39] At Udsk grass (especially couch grass) was plentiful,[40] and Academician Middendorf calculated in 1844 that the 270 acres of pasture could feed 200 cattle.[41] Up to two and one-third tons of hay could be secured from each acre.[42] In 1779 an anonymous investigator found 283 acres of pasture within twenty miles of Udsk (including 98 acres within two to three miles), but the peasants mowed no more than 42 acres of hay-land.[43] In the 1830's an employee of the Russian-American Company found 351 acres of pasture (mostly) and plowland along both banks of the Uda River within fifty-three to fifty-four miles of Udsk.[44] Hayland at Insk was scarce.[45]

However, while grazing was generally easy, haying was often difficult, and much hay was needed to last the long winters and to provide extra body heat for the livestock in the region's chilly climate. In Kamchatka hay was made late (August and September) in deference to summer fishing; by then the grass had lost much of its nutritiousness from overripeness, and it lost more when drying was impeded by the rains of late summer and early fall. Shipbuilding also competed with haying.[46] Fodder was so scarce that the cattle were usually at pasture even in winter, when they were fed the bark of birch and aspen, willow twigs, and fresh fish (late winter–early spring), as well as a little hay. Kamchatka's horses pastured at large all year, browsing the meager forage of the "blowns" (open spots blown free of snow) and the fallen needles of the evergreen forests. When the snow was crusted, the horses ate alder bark and willow twigs, and only rarely were they fed hay, which was usually reserved for cows. As a result of being at large year round, the horses became so wild that they were caught with difficulty; in fact, herds of feral horses eventually formed in the Kamchatka River Valley and around Gizhiga.[47] At Udsk the haymaking season (from late August until October) coincided with clear weather but also with fishing time.[48] The peasants complained in 1748 that the local authorities compelled them to fish at planting time and at mowing time.[49] Around Okhotsk, on account of the dearth of hay and grain, cattle, pigs, and poultry ate mainly fish meal in winter and in spring, supplemented by twigs.[50] In 1786 a member of the Billings Expedition was told by the Commandant of Okhotsk that cattle there had been fed nothing but fish offal from mid-April until the beginning of July.[51] Beef and milk tasted fishy. Pigs, allegedly because of their fishy diet, became skinny, hungry, and sterile, with tainted, fatless meat. Thus livestock on the seaboard and the peninsula fed well only in summer, and were undernourished for three seasons of the year, so that cattle probably produced little milk or meat most of the year. Certainly not a few animals starved. At Udsk cattle were so underfed that in the middle 1840's cows dressed scarcely 252 pounds and bulls dressed only 360 pounds. Animals in this poor condition succumbed easily to diseases, such as anthrax. In 1820 twenty of the forty-one cattle at Udsk died from disease and hunger.[52]

Livestock suffered in other ways. Shelter was inadequate for the severe winter. In Kamchatka cattle were "housed" in unwalled or roof-less sheds; consequently, cows suffered from frostbitten udders, and many calves perished from the bitter cold. The poor shelter increased the need for feed from the meager store. Livestock were inadequately supervised, too. Since cattle were not tended by herders, cows remained unmilked for several days running, were poisoned by toxic plants (like poison hemlock and aconite), caught in quagmires, and killed by predators (such as bears and wolves).[53] Krasheninnikov noted that "bears and wolves are especially numerous in Kamchatka . . . ,"[54] and Steller agreed that "wolves . . . are found in Kamchatka in abundance" and that "black bears . . . are found throughout Kamchatka in indescribable abundance; it is possible to see entire herds of them strolling through fields. . . ."[55] Around 1815 an anonymous observer noted that many cattle left unattended by the Kamchadals were killed by bears.[56] In 1816–17, emboldened by hunger caused by a scarcity of fish, bears rampaged throughout the peninsula, devouring cattle, dogs, and fish stocks and attacking people and even one another. The inhabitants dared not leave their homes unarmed during that winter; marauding bears killed eighty cattle and three persons (and injured nine others), while up to 5,000 bears were killed by natives throughout the peninsula and 197 were slain by Russians at Petropavlovsk alone. Bears were particularly prone to attack livestock in places where fishing was difficult for them, as at Klyuchi and Verkhne-Kamchatsk.[57] Sled dogs, which were turned loose at the end of winter to fend for themselves until late fall, also attacked the unattended livestock, not only calves and colts but cows, bulls, mares, and stallions, as well as poultry. The presence of dogs by itself discouraged the keeping of small stock like pigs, sheep, and goats, and fowl in Kamchatka.[58] Siberian tigers sometimes appeared at Udsk, where they may have ravaged livestock.[59] An example of losses by predation is the experience of one Krechetov, a Russian peasant of Kamchatka, who lost at least fourteen cattle to predators in 1768–70, which left him with only seventeen head.[60] In addition, pests also ravaged crops; at Udsk, for instance, barley was eaten by hares and vegetables by mice.[61]

Because of the continual losses of livestock in Kamchatka—and the need to butcher breeding stock for food when fish were scarce, as happened in 1845–46—fresh stock had to be imported regularly from Yakutsk. Most of these animals perished en route, however. In 1805, for example, 219 cattle and 194 horses were sent to Kamchatka via Gizhiga, but only 73 cattle and 36 horses arrived. Thus there was a chronic shortage of livestock on the peninsula (especially) and the seaboard, with its concomitant dearth of dung for manuring and scarcity of oxen for plowing. At first plows were drawn by men in Kamchatka; later cultivation was done by hand with such tools as wooden mattocks.[62]

Cultural Problems

The scarcity of draft animals was particularly serious in light of the shortage of labor, a chronic impediment to economic development of the Okhotsk Seaboard and the Kamchatka Peninsula. Count Rezanov reported to the Tsar in 1804 that the "insufficient quantity of cattle and horses, and small population do not let farming develop as it should [in Kamchatka]."[63] This remote and primitive region attracted few Russians, including peasants, most of whom, moreover, were immobilized by the bonds of serfdom. The peasants of the seaboard and the peninsula were Crown serfs, sent there involuntarily in small numbers—since the reserve of Crown serfs was always small—and replenished only occasionally by new transmigrants, also few in number, so that the peasant population remained negligible. In 1765–66 there were only eighteen families of Crown peasants (fifty-seven persons) in Kamchatka, located at four derevnyas (churchless villages) along the Kamchatka River between Verkhne-Kamchatsk and Nizhne-Kamchatsk.[64] Peasant labor was so scarce that during his administration Major Bem had to assign ten men from the Verkhne-Kamchatsk garrison to Milkovo to assist the peasants there in cultivation.[65] De Lesseps, while visiting Milkovo in 1787, became "convinced that greater advantages might be derived from this source [agriculture], if the cultivators were more numerous."[66] In 1783 there were only 160 tax-paying peasants in Kamchatka. In 1792 the peninsula contained 255 peasants, who in 1794 were confined to three villages: Klyuchi, Milkovo, and Mashura; and there were only eighty peasants at Milkovo in 1807. By 1818 Kamchatka contained 398 Russian peasants, settled at six villages, the largest of which were Klyuchi (202 Russians) and Milkovo (113 Russians); all the male peasants of Klyuchi were descendants of eighteenth-century colonists. In the early 1820's Klyuchi and Milkovo, the peninsula's largest agricultural settlements, contained sixty and twenty-five cultivators, respectively. The number of Russian peasants in Kamchatka fell to 391 in 1820, rose to 407 in 1823, fell again to 354 in 1829 (172 at Klyuchi, 110 at Milkovo, 31 at Verkhne-Kamchatsk, 25 at Nizhne-Kamchatsk, and 16 at Bolsheretsk), and rose to 431 in 1831. The peasant population probably never exceeded 500 souls.[67]

Because of the shortage of farmers members of the Kamchatka Regiment, upon its disbandment in 1812, were encouraged to remain as peasants by such lures as free livestock, seed, and implements and exemption from taxes for three years and from conscription for twenty.[68] In 1829 the agronomists Lazarev and Chernykh ascribed the failure of agriculture in Kamchatka to the dearth of both peasants and seed.[69] Very few Kamchadals adopted agriculture, except for some herding and

TABLE 16

Agricultural Population of Okhotsk, Insk, and Udsk, for Various Years between 1735 and 1856

Year	Persons[a]
Okhotsk	
1750	(37)
1809	42
Insk	
1740	(10)
1750	(8)
1776	39
1783	39 (10)
1806	58
1817	32
Udsk	
1735–36	(10–12)
1738	(10)
1744	(8)
1748	(8)
1761–62	15
1782	(2)
1790	11 (males)
Late 1790's	5
1796	13
1799	9
1848	7 (5)
1849	32
1852	(5)
1856	(5)

[a] Figures in parentheses indicate families or households.

SOURCES: A. I. Alekseyev, *Okhotsk—kolybel russkovo Tikhookeanskovo flota* [*Okhotsk —Cradle of the Russian Pacific Fleet*] (Khabarovsk: Khabarovskoye knizhnoye izdatel-stvo, 1958), p. 67; Anonymous, "Opisanie Irkutskoy gubernii," fol. 46ᵛ; Anonymous, "Opisanie Udskavo ostroga" ["Description of Udsk Ostrog"], *Moskovsky telegraf*, pt. 1 (1825), pp. 321–322; Ivan Borisov, "Vedomost sochineniya v Yakutskoy voyevod-skoy kantselyarii po trebovaniyu Akademii Nauk professora Gerarda Fridrikha Gospodina Millera o sostoyanii goroda Yakutska i Yakutskovo vedomstva . . ." ["List of Works in the Yakutsk Gubernatorial Office Relating to the Request of Professor of the Academy of Sciences Mr. Gerhard Friedrich Muller about the Condition of the Town of Yakutsk and Yakutsk Province . . ."], TsGADA, f. 199, port. 528, pt. 7, d. 481, fol. 335; V. A. Divin, "Vtoraya Sibirsko-tikhookeanskaya ekspeditsiya i voprosy khozyaistvennavo osvoyeniya Dalnevo Vostoka" ["The Second Siberia-Pacific Ocean Expedition and Questions of the Economic Development of the Far East"], *Letopis Severa*, 2 (1957) : 163; Middendorf, *Puteshestvie na Sibiri*, pt. 1, suppl. 3, pp. xii–xiii, xv

some gardening. By 1810 the Kamchadals kept some cattle and grew some vegetables but planted no grain.[70] Commandant Golenishchev argued in 1833 that the Kamchadals should not and could not become farmers because they caught valuable furs, and because farming and fishing conflicted temporally.[71] For trapping a Kamchadal needed at least six dogs; these beasts required 3,600 dried fish, which took one man at least two and a half months to catch. For himself and for his dogs a Kamchadal usually had to catch up to 20,000 fish, most of which were caught during the growing season. Nevertheless, by the middle of the century the natives dominated stockbreeding: in 1848 they owned 934 of the peninsula's 1,498 cattle and 201 of the 309 horses.[72]

There were even fewer Russian peasants on the Okhotsk Seaboard, as indicated by Table 16. The number of peasant households in Okhotsk Okrug fell from 104 in 1783 and in 1800 to 34 in 1856.[73]

Very few, if any, Lamuts adopted agriculture; but some Yakuts, transferred from Yakutsk, engaged in stockbreeding. It was reported in 1789 that "some" Yakuts reared cattle and caught fish near the mouths of the Urak River and the Luktur River, which entered the Urak on its left bank forty to fifty-four miles upstream.[74] In 1809 there were ninety-two Yakuts in six settlements along the lower Okhota River within forty-seven miles of Okhotsk and in one settlement at the mouth of the Urak River sixteen miles south of Okhotsk. Around 1817 there were ninety-seven Yakut stockmen along the lower Okhota and lower Urak rivers (mainly) and at Tauisk and Yamsk.[75]

The number of peasants remained especially small at Udsk. In 1848 Udsk Kray contained only ten families of Russian peasants,[76] exactly the number that had originally been sent to Udsk more than a century earlier.

Minitsky, "Nekotoria izvestiya," p. 90; Minitsky, "Opisanie Okhotskavo porta," 5 : 216; Rezanov, "Zapiska gorodnichevo Nizhne-Kamchatska Voyevodskovo," fol. 3; Safronov, *Okhotsko-Kamchatsky kray*, pp. 73, 101; Safronov, "Popytki prodvizheniya," p. 523; Semyonov, *Zhivopisnaya Rossiya*, vol. 12, pt. 2, pp. 164, 166; Sgibnev, "Okhotsky port," 105, no. 11 : 53; I. P. Shaskolsky, ed., *Geograficheskoye izuchenie Sibiri XVII–XIX v.v.* [*Geographical Study of Siberia of the XVIIth–XIXth Centuries*], "Materialy Otdeleniya istorii geograficheskikh znany Geograficheskovo obshchestva Soyuza SSR," no. 1 (Leningrad: Geograficheskoye obshchestvo SSSR, 1962), p. 28; Shchukin, "Udskoye selenie," *Russky invalid*, 35, no. 114 : 456; Shchukin, "Udskoye selenie," *Zhurnal Ministerstva vnutrennikh del*, p. 177; Shmalev, "Statisticheskiya i Geograficheskiya Primechaniya," fols. 6, 21ᵛ; N. Sverbeyev, "Sibirskiya pisma" ["Siberian Letters"], *Vestnik Imperatorskavo russkavo geograficheskavo obshchestva*, vol. 8, pt. 7 (1853), p. 106.

Disease was partly responsible for the slow growth of the agricultural population. In 1768 and 1769 smallpox from Okhotsk ravaged Kamchatka, killing two-thirds to three-fourths of its inhabitants; in 1768 alone 5,368 persons succumbed.[77]* De Lesseps learned in 1787 that smallpox had reduced the peasant population of Klyuchi by more than half.[78] Yellow fever killed two-thirds of the peninsula's inhabitants in 1799.[79] In 1821 Cochrane observed that the majority of the inhabitants of many settlements in Kamchatka were incapacitated by disease, mainly smallpox and syphilis.[80]

The agricultural population of Kamchatka and the Okhotsk Seaboard was also depleted by the forsaking of farming for trapping and fishing. With plowing, planting, reaping, and threshing severely handicapped by the elements, as well as loosely supervised by agriculturally ignorant Cossack sergeants in accordance with the conflicting and mercurial policies of inexperienced commandants,** and with most of the meager, hard-won harvest going not to the peasants but to the state magazines, many Russian peasants neglected or abandoned agriculture for the more reliable and more profitable returns of trapping and fishing. This disinterest was especially marked in Kamchatka, where fish were superabundant and where the pelts of sables and foxes excelled all others in Siberia in quantity and in thickness and sheen, save those of

* Another source, however, asserts that some 20,000 Kamchadals alone were killed by smallpox in 1768 (I. V. Shcheglov, *Kronologichesky perechen vazhneishikh dannykh iz istorii Sibiri 1032–1882 gg.* [*Chronological List of the Major Facts from the History of Siberia 1032–1882*] [Irkutsk: Tipografiya Shtaba Vostochnavo Sibirskavo voyennavo okruga, 1883], p. 288).

** In this connection the short tenure of Kamchatka's commandants was deprecated by Cochrane: "Kamchatka neither can nor will thrive so long as its chiefs are sent for five years only: such a short period scarcely allows them the time of doing good, however well disposed they may be. The general mode of occupying the allotted term may be thus described. The first year is employed in looking about and forming plans for the improvement of the country, the amelioration of the condition of the aborigines, etc.: the second year is passed in making reports, stating opinions, etc.: the third year brings the reply of the government, directing or authorizing the mode of administration: the fourth is employed in preparing, or at most acting upon such orders: while the fifth, and last year is generally employed in preparing to return to Europe, and levying a party contribution: —and thus the whole five years are, more or less, taken up in trading and accumulating as much money as possible" (Cochrane, *Narrative of a Pedestrian Journey*, p. 310).

the foxes of Anadyrsk.* Hence the "indolence" of the peasants commonly remarked by observers. Fish were stored for food, and furs were traded for other wants. Fishing especially interfered with farming, since the fishing season (from late spring until late summer) coincided with the agricultural season; the conflict of fishing and haying has already been mentioned.[81] In 1810 Vasily Golovnin found that fishing was the chief livelihood of the peasants of Milkovo.[82] During the administration of Commandant Minitsky at Okhotsk (1809–16), the Russian and the Yakut peasants of Okhotsk Oblast obtained their sustenance chiefly from fishing rather than from farming.[83] The inclination of Udsk's peasants for fishing, as well as their stupidity and laziness, was cited in a 1775 report as one of the reasons for the decline of agriculture among them.[84]

Although trapping and farming conflicted little temporally, they did clash spatially. In Siberia "where there are Russian settlements," wrote Krasheninnikov, "there is no sable hunting whatsoever: because sables are not found near habitations, but far away in desolate forests and on high mountains."[85] He warned that clearing for agriculture along the Kamchatka and Bistraya rivers must be done carefully lest the burning disturb the sables: burning of the forest along the upper Lena River had displaced the sables there; and Khudoy Shantar (Little Shantar Island, in the southwestern corner of the Okhotsk Sea), which once abounded in sables, had been stripped of all fur bearers when fires set by Gilyak natives destroyed the tree cover.[86]** Steller felt that forest clearing for agriculture in Kamchatka would not oust fur bearers as long as the forests were not fired, for such burning, he asserted, had dislodged sables and foxes along the Lena River.[87] The government's concern over encroachment on the sable's habitat by felling and burning led it in 1683 to prohibit, under penalty of death, the cutting or firing of trees in "sable places" throughout Siberia.[88]

Usually agriculture was neglected rather than completely abandoned in favor of more profitable pursuits, for the Russian peasants were, after all, used to, and fond of, bread. This neglect was noted by many observers. Kruzenstern remarked in 1804–5 that "the husband-

* However, the blacker sables of the Vitim and Olyokma basins were worth over four times as much as Kamchatkan sables around 1740 (Krasheninnikov, *Opisanie zemli Kamchatki*, pp. 255–256).
** Appropriately, *khudoy* means "emaciated."

men who were conveyed from the banks of the Lena to Kamtschatka only grow as much [grain] as is sufficient for their own use, devoting the rest of their time to the catching of sables, and other business, where they are certain of a greater profit."[89] De Lesseps noted in 1787 that Kamchatka's authorities had forbidden the peasants to trap;[90] this measure proved to no avail, for in the early 1790's the Billings Expedition reported that the peasants of Klyuchi and Milkovo "find it easier to accumulate wealth, by acting as retailers for the merchants of Kamtshatka, and going themselves on the chase for sables, etc. than in pursuing the more toilsome labour of cultivating the earth, which they neglect."[91] In 1812 Dobell observed that "at Klutchee there were about eighty or ninety peasants who formerly cultivated the ground . . . but at this actual time there are not more than three or four amongst them who sow a little barley; the chase being more attractive and more profitable."[92] An anonymous observer around 1815 noted that at Milkovo and Klyuchi with the death of the elderly peasants the rest had adopted the way of life of the Kamchadals and had even lost their taste for bread.[93] And around 1820 Lyubarsky affirmed that the peasants of Milkovo caught fish in summer and trapped furs in winter, scarcely farming at all except to grow hemp for nets.[94]

In turning to trapping and fishing the Russian peasants became more or less indistinguishable from the Kamchadals,* as Dobell noted in 1812 at Klyuchi, where "every thing has been neglected for fishing and the chase; and these people [Russian peasants] are actually no better off than the Kamtchatdales" and "instead of drawing the natives to their mode of living and industry, neglect everything like civilization, and are themselves now quite as wild and uncouth as the Kamtchatdales; besides being infinitely more vicious."[95]**

On the Okhotsk Seaboard Russian peasants also became disenchanted with agriculture. By 1776, for instance, all of the thirty-nine Russian peasants of Insk had forsaken agriculture for trapping and

---

* It was probably because of such assimilation that the term "Kamchadal" came to include both the Itelmen natives and the Russian "old settlers" of the peninsula.

** This process was not confined to Kamchatka. At Amginsk, another marginal agricultural settlement southeast of Yakutsk, Krasheninnikov found in 1737 that the Russian peasants had abandoned not only their precarious agriculture but also their native tongue and had adopted the way of life of their Yakut neighbors, being distinguishable from them only in religion (Krasheninnikov, *Opisanie zemli Kamchatki,* p. 524).

fishing.[96] And in 1829–30 Kozmin found that the peasants of Udsk "do not sow now; only the parish priest has a garden. . . ."[97] Here, too, livestock could not compete with fish; according to Academician Middendorf, the abundance of fish was the chief obstacle to stock raising at Udsk.[98]

This occupational conflict was closely connected with the problem of too few Russian settlers; there were simply not enough people to perform the various necessary duties entailed by Russian occupation and exploitation. This dilemma was pinpointed by Dobell:

> How is it possible for 2500 souls, who are principally hunters, dispersed over that immense tract of country [Kamchatka], to become farmers, mechanics, labourers, etc. etc. at one and the same time? I am persuaded the Kamtchatdales, nay, even the Russians born in Kamtchatka, can never be weaned from their fondness for hunting and an uncivilized life, until the country shall become well peopled, and the fish and game much scarcer than at present.[99]

Dobell reiterated and elaborated this point:

> The cultivation of the ground will never be attended to until the country becomes peopled, and the chase less advantageous. A people who are content to eat dried fish instead of bread, and can catch in a few days as many as will serve them for the winter, cannot be easily weaned from that mode of life. In the winter, if they have good luck, they catch as many sables and foxes as will procure them watky [vodka], tobacco, and tea; and they are perfectly indifferent to every other luxury.[100]

Dobell failed to realize, however, that once the fur trade became unprofitable, Kamchatka would attract even fewer Russians, since the fur trade was the raison d'être of the Russian occupation.

Thus, marginal, onerous farming could not compete with more profitable, reliable, carefree, and exciting pursuits like fishing and trapping, at least as long as the copious runs of fish continued and the lucrative market for furs prevailed. The high value of pelts enabled the settlers to pay the high cost of imported necessities, including grain, which could be heavily supplemented and even partially supplanted by fish products. Indeed, it seems that some officials discouraged agriculture for their own reasons. Dobell again wrote: "the people who are sent to govern the eastern parts of Siberia are generally so fond of sables and foxes that they regret to see any attempts at agriculture and improvement, for fear of being deprived of their favourite furs, which not only serve to line their garments, but also, and that exceedingly well, their pockets."[101] Moreover, some officials opposed agricultural development lest it interfere with the grain trade, from which they also profited handsomely. In 1813 Dobell noted that "unfortunately the Governor of Yakutsk [Ivan Khartachevsky] acts on the opinion, that agriculture would interfere with his contracts for flour, transportation, etc. and would decrease the number of hunters."[102] This attitude may well have occurred on Kamchatka and the Okhotsk Seaboard. Until the arrival of Commandant Devier at Okhotsk in 1740, the introduction of agriculture into Kamchatka was stymied by conflict between the Okhotsk authorities and the leaders of the Second Kamchatka Expedition, conflict which, Steller wrote, caused "the ruination of many persons"; by selfishness and indifference on the part of the Cossacks, who "demanded only hay, vodka, and tobacco . . ."; and by drunkenness, avarice, and pilfering on the part of the officials of Kamchatka, who "care only about their own benefits and not about the interests and well-being of the kray, making good soldiers but bad administrators and economists."[103]

Agriculture on the seaboard and the peninsula might not have been outdone by competing occupations had it been properly supervised by stewards and elders. Obviously farming was laxly supervised by local overseers, or the peasants would not have been able to turn to trapping and fishing so readily. Undoubtedly such lax supervision was partly deliberate on the part of authorities, who feared that agriculture would lessen their profits from the fur and grain trades. Sauer, noting the success with which the peasants of Klyuchi grew grain and vegetables, declared that "had they a proper inspector to superintend their business, they might with ease grow corn enough of every kind to supply not only the peninsula, but all the neighbouring country, Ochotsk, etc."[104] However, while supervision might have improved output somewhat, it is doubtful, in view of the climatic restrictions, that even with the best supervision Kamchatka's plowland could have produced much surplus grain.

Peasant neglect and lax supervision facilitated the concentration of agricultural property into the hands of a few peasants, and this further limited agricultural efforts. For example, in 1771, fifty-five of Kamchatka's sixty-three state cattle were kept by three peasants, and at Udsk an investigation in 1790 revealed that most of the plowland was owned not by the peasants but by the merchant Struchkov and by the clerics.[105] Some peasants, then, lacked land for cultivating and livestock for breeding.

Even when the peasants did have plowland, their efforts were hampered by the open-field system, which was probably followed. Each household's plowland comprised several long, narrow strips scattered throughout the village fields. The strips might be far from one's home; they were too narrow to permit cross plowing; and field boundaries and access routes occupied considerable space. Also, under communal cultivation everybody did the same chores at the same times, so that individual initiative and technical innovation were stifled.[106]

Under such conditions the government erred in imposing obrok on the uncertain rudiments of agriculture on the peninsula and the seaboard. The Udsk archives, according to Semyonov, showed that the untimely exaction of obrok impeded agricultural settlement there in 1786, 1788, and 1796.[107] The change of policy in 1764 that gave state livestock, seed, and implements to the peasants and allowed them to farm for themselves as well as for the state was but a halfway measure; agriculture here needed the encouragement of *all* the fruits of one's labor —and perhaps more.

13

REACTIONS

"There is not much hope of progress in grain cultivation [in Kam-chatka]."

Timofey Shmalev, "Kratkoye opisanie," p. 209.

"The land [of Kamchatka] is extremely fertile and very suitable for cultivation."

Major Von Bem, "O Kamchatskom zemledelii," p. 41.

Russian reactions to the disappointing performance of agriculture on the Okhotsk Seaboard and the Kamchatka Peninsula are well documented for the peninsula, which was the focus of the region's agricultural activity. Kamchatka's agricultural successes, though infrequent, were nevertheless sufficient to persuade the Russian Government to pursue stubbornly its goal of agricultural autarky for the peninsula; in the face of conflicting opinions from its administrators there it continued to try to improve its agricultural policy in various ways.

In 1749 Khotuntsevsky, Archimandrite of Kamchatka, suggested to the Holy Synod that a large agricultural-manufactural monastery be established on the former site of Uspenskaya Hermitage, employing the peasants of Kamchatka and Okhotsk, who "live idly, [and] keep only state cattle, which are few in number. . . ."[1] With such an establishment Khotuntsevsky hoped that "grain pursuits will soon appear in Kam-chatka, as before, when the monastery [Uspenskaya Hermitage] stood intact."[2] His suggestion was not implemented.

At this time the Siberian authorities at Tobolsk, recalling their agrarian intentions in Kamchatka (embodied in the decrees of the late 1720's and the early 1730's), inquired about the state of agriculture there. Commandant Lebedev replied that agriculture had well-nigh ceased because the peasants were improperly supervised. He asserted that it would succeed if the peasants were put under strict supervision and if they were moved to Nizhne-Kamchatsk and Verkhne-Kamchatsk, where, in his opinion, the climate was milder.[3]

Henceforth the Siberian authorities paid more attention to Kamchatka's agriculture, and, although the peasants were not moved, Pyotr Kholmovsky, the peninsula's second steward, was appointed expressly to supervise grain cultivation. After repeated experiments, he concluded that grain could not be grown there.[4] Kholmovsky was succeeded by Lieutenant Nedozrelov, who was sent to the peninsula in 1761 "for the propagation of grain cultivation. . . ."[5] He reported that the peasants neglected agriculture because it was unproductive and because haymaking interfered with the catching of fish, their main sustenance.[6] Nedozrelov's recommendation that for four years no planting be made without his personal supervision was approved and implemented; however, his experiments also failed, early frost killing the standing grain.[7] In 1762 one Rozinov was sent to Kamchatka under orders "to supervise constantly, so that they [the peasants] sow all the grain given them up to the last kernel without any concealment or theft," "to observe strictly how much is cut, threshed, and collected into the magazines," and "for sowing to select the very best lands . . . which are to be fertilized with manure without laziness, using for this all possible labor."[8] Rozinov was given 1,000 rubles for the purchase of sixty implements and 1,512 pounds of seed "for the propagation of grain cultivation in Kamchatka. . . ."[9] The results of his endeavors are unknown, but his successor, Timofey Shmalev, who found that hemp was Kamchatka's most successful crop, concluded that "there is not much hope of progress in grain cultivation."[10]

Nevertheless, the state continued to promote agriculture in the peninsula. In 1760 Fyodor Cheredov, who had served as a sergeant in Kamchatka during the administration of his father, presented to the Senate a project for the large-scale development of agriculture in Okhotsk Kray, which then included Kamchatka.[11] This project was approved by the Senate, which in February, 1761 ordered Cheredov, "on account of the shortage of provisions for the upkeep of the military command, . . . to establish grain cultivation in such places found to be suitable for the growing of grain. . . ."[12] The Senate hoped that "from this it will be possible to supply with grain not only the Kamchatka military command but also the commands found at Okhotsk Port and at Anadyrsk Ostrog. . . ."[13] Cheredov was appointed Governor of Yakutsk, assigned 1,000 rubles for "the procurement of materials and other needs pertaining to grain cultivation, as well as seed grain . . . ,"[14] and permitted to transfer peasants with cattle from Irkutsk Province to Kamchatka, while his father, Vasily Cheredov, was sent to Kamchatka to supervise agriculture with permission "to utilize local Cossacks and soldiers with extreme care . . ." (i.e., without antagonizing them) as agriculturalists if the peasants proved insufficient.[15] Upon arriving at Yakutsk, Fyodor Cheredov dispatched his father to Kamchatka with instructions to grow grain at Verkhne-Kamchatsk and at Nizhne-Kamchatsk "with all-zealous diligence" and to seek arable lands at Bolsheretsk and Tigilsk and on the Kurile Islands.[16] These plans, however, were thwarted first by the younger Cheredov's illness and then by the dismissal in 1763 of both Cheredovs for graft and murder. In 1765 the assigned money was withdrawn.[17]

Little seed grain and few agricultural implements were received by Kamchatka and the Okhotsk Seaboard. In 1762 only 16½ bushels of barley seed, 13 bushels of rye seed, and 720 pounds of seed for wheat, oats, hemp, and peas from Irkutsk and only 20 plowshares, 20 sickles, and 20 axes from Yakutsk were sent to Kamchatka. Some of the seed (3¾ bushels of barley and 18 pounds of hemp) and some of the implements (6 plowshares and 6 sickles) were supposed to be kept at Okhotsk for experimental sowings there, but the Okhotsk authorities forwarded them to Kamchatka because of the acute shortage of seed grain and agricultural implements in the peninsula. In 1763 Yakutsk dispatched to Kamchatka only 26¼ bushels of barley seed, 22½ bushels each of oat seed and of rye seed, and 360 pounds of hemp seed and only 30 sickles, 20 chisels, 10 plowshares, and 5 augers. To Udsk in 1762–63 Yakutsk sent only 15¾ bushels of barley seed, 13½ bushels of oat seed, 8½ bushels of rye seed, and 144 pounds of hemp seed and only 20 axes, 10 plowshares, 10 sickles, and 10 scythes. The necessity of such shipments attests the degree of failure of agriculture on the seaboard and the peninsula, which often could not even yield enough for seed, let alone for consumption. In 1764 Empress Catherine II sent seed, cattle, and implements from her own estate to Kamchatka in a vain attempt to stimulate agriculture there.[18]

In 1763 Governor Soimonov submitted to the Senate a plan for the rejuvenation of agriculture throughout Siberia. To encourage the peasants to cultivate beyond what they must for obrok, Soimonov proposed that anyone be allowed to farm and that the state buy surplus grain production.[19] The Senate ratified the plan on November 11/22, and at the beginning of 1764 the authorities of Yakutsk, Okhotsk, and Kamchatka were ordered to implement it "without delay and omission." The peninsular authorities were also commanded "to resume grain cultivation and to maintain it in a proper manner," and the peasants of Bolsheretsk were moved to Verkhne-Kamchatsk and to Nizhne-Kamchatsk.[20] However, Kamchatka's agriculture continued to lag.

Thus, radical measures were needed to halt the disintegration of the peninsula's agriculture. Plenisner, Commandant of Okhotsk, had been ordered in 1761 by the Senate to "heed" grain cultivation in Kamchatka and by Governor Soimonov to investigate agriculture in the peninsula. From his tour of inspection in late 1764 he concluded that agriculture was failing because of unsuitable siting of the farmlands and lack of interest on the part of the Crown peasants in toiling solely for the benefit of the state. To encourage the peasants Plenisner gave them some state livestock and all spoiled state grain (suitable for feeding or milling but not for seeding) as a reward for their past efforts. Also, following his inspection he recommended that they be allowed to retain some of the output of their agricultural labor, such as all grain harvested on state plowland every three years. This recommendation was approved by Governor Chicherin.[21] It was about this time, and without knowing Plenisner's efforts, that the Tsar issued a decree that went even farther than Plenisner's recommendations. By this Imperial decree of September 30/October 11 of 1764 state livestock, seed grain, and agricultural implements in the peninsula were given all at once to those who desired to farm, and the Crown peasants were permitted to farm for themselves as well as for the state.[22]

Now it was decided to establish separate farms to be cultivated exclusively for the state. The first state farm was developed at Kashitino, a site selected by Plenisner's inspector, Timofey Shmalev, who settled two families of peasants there in 1766. The site was an admirable one, comprising a fertile plain over seven miles wide astride the Kamchatka River at its confluence with the Kashitino River. Both rivers abounded in fish, and mixed timber and fine pasture grew along their banks. It was planned to construct flour mills along the two rivers and to ship the harvest by water. The navigable Kamchatka River afforded easy access downstream to Nizhne-Kamchatsk (265 miles), where the fur traders were concentrated, and upstream to Milkovo (36 miles) and Verkhne-Kamchatsk (41 miles), both of which could be reached in a day. In 1767 Sergeant Roznin, who was experienced in agriculture, succeeded Shmalev, arriving with seed and implements to demonstrate to the peasants the proper way of growing grain and to supervise their agricultural activities.[23]

However, despite the innovations and donations of the government and the inspections and suggestions of Plenisner, Shmalev, and Roznin, both state and private agriculture continued to languish, chiefly on account of the harsh climate. The output of Kashitino's state plowland for its first four years did not, on the average, return the seed, as shown by Table 17. Wheat was killed by frost in three of the four years.[24]

TABLE 17

Total Crop Yields on State Plowland at Kashitino, 1765–68

Crop	Bushels Planted	Bushels Reaped
Barley	98.8	76.5
Oats	62.0	63.2
Rye	34.3	22.4
Wheat	1.1	0.7
Peas	0.7	0.0
Hemp	401.4	426.0

SOURCE: H. Beaumont, "Essais d'agriculture dans le Kamtchatka" ["Attempts at Agriculture in Kamchatka"], *Mémoires de la Société de Géographie de Geneve*, **1** (1860) : 123.

Then, in the middle 1760's, an audacious fraud named Ivan Ryshkov arrived in Kamchatka. After vainly seeking wealth, successively in trapping, teaching, and clerking, he tried farming, selecting for his agricultural experiments first Yelan and then Mashura, both on the Kamchatka River. Ryshkov attracted attention with his claim that in the fifth year of his experiments at Yelan there was no cold dew or hoar frost, so that his yaritsa, rye, and wheat had fully ripened. In early 1768 he submitted to the Senate a project for the organization of various agricultural undertakings in Kamchatka, requesting at the same time tenth-class rank (Titular Councillor), financial assistance, and certain privileges. While the Senate was considering his project, Ryshkov obtained a loan of 1,500 rubles for growing grain from Nilov, Commandant of Kamchatka,* who was trying desperately to solve the peninsula's problem of food supply posed by a shortage of fish. With the loan Ryshkov planted yaritsa, rye, and barley at Mashura in 1771, claimed a good harvest, and requested another loan from Nilov. Then it was discovered that all of Ryshkov's grain had been frost-killed and that he

* This was the Nilov who was subsequently duped and slain during the insurrection at Bolsheretsk.

had developed no new plowland. The Irkutsk authorities demanded the return of the money loaned him, but he was unable to repay; he was arrested and escorted to Irkutsk.[25]

Following Benyovsky's insurrection at Bolsheretsk in 1771, Kamchatka was removed from Okhotsk Kray in 1772 and made a separate administrative unit. Major Bem was appointed Commandant of the new kray and was given wide powers. He paid particular attention to agriculture, having been instructed as follows in 1772: "Upon arriving in Kamchatka you will gather detailed information: what and where the harvest was in each year, and from that consider where grain cultivation should be expanded and requisition settlers for it. Appoint trustworthy people for supervision of the grain cultivators and try to bring it [grain cultivation] up to [the point] where the necessity of importing grain from the Lena River is not encountered."[26] Bem strove sincerely and energetically to improve agriculture in Kamchatka. Figuring that livestock were essential for the expansion of grain cultivation, he established a state stock farm at great expense at Verkhne-Kamchatsk with cattle and horses from Yakutsk Oblast. At Shigachinsk he founded Kamchatka's third state farm, where at first rye yielded thirteen- to fourteenfold and barley five- to sixfold. At every settlement in the peninsula he established state and private vegetable gardens. His other agricultural measures included acquainting the Kamchadals with potatoes, building two threshing barns, placing state livestock under special supervision, and appointing an elder (peasant bailiff) for Milkovo. Despite these efforts, agriculture did not thrive, although grain sometimes yielded well during his administration. But Bem refused to believe that agriculture was impossible in Kamchatka, attributing its lag to carelessness and mistakes on the part of local managers rather than to the inimical climate. He felt that the peninsula would be able to supply itself with grain if his successes continued.[27] After returning to Russia he wrote that "the land [of Kamchatka] is extremely fertile and very suitable for cultivation. Meadows, haylands, and pastures are everywhere in great abundance. The climate is very temperate; for there is neither severe frost in winter nor unbearable heat in summer. . . ."[28]*

Bem was succeeded in 1780 by Franz Reinikin, who, upon his appointment in 1779, was instructed to pay special attention to grain

---

* However, another source states Bem reported to Irkutsk that grain cultivation was impossible in Kamchatka because of late frosts that in some years occurred in mid-July (Sgibnev, "Istorichesky ocherk," 103 [July, 1869] : 13).

cultivation. Arriving with four peasant families from the upper Lena River, Reinikin energetically devoted himself to grain growing, truck farming, and stock raising. Before his departure in 1784, despite shortages of both laborers and horses, he founded state farms at Mashura and Sedanka in 1782, established flour mills (including one on the Milkovaya River that existed until 1830) and hand millstones, and supported with strict measures the state and the private gardens founded by Bem, informing all villages how to grow potatoes and other vegetables. Reinikin put stockbreeding in good condition by importing fresh livestock and by personally overseeing stock raising.[29] He reported to Irkutsk that grass grew higher than a man along Kamchatka's rivers and lakes, and that hay could be made twice a year.[30] He also personally supervised grain cultivation, always planting carefully on well-prepared virgin soil. However, while truck farming flourished, grain growing failed to prosper, the grain seldom returning the seed. Consequently, the new state farm at Sedanka was abandoned.[31]

From 1785, as a result of the reorganization of Kamchatka's administration, including the transfer of its capital from Bolsheretsk to Nizhne-Kamchatsk, the peninsular authorities neglected agriculture. The state farms decayed, and the Russian peasants and the Cossacks were increasingly "Kamchadalized," becoming more and more content with dried fish in place of bread.[32] Nevertheless, the Russian Government continued its agricultural efforts, perhaps in response to optimistic opinions that it hoped to hear. For example, Baron Steingel, Reinikin's successor (1784–88), who lived many years in Kamchatka (and whose son became a prominent Decembrist), submitted to the government a plan for the improvement of the peninsula in which he asserted that "from a long course of observations made during my residence in Kamschatka, I am convinced that both the climate and soil are such as that agriculture might be carried on with the most complete success."[33] And Sarychev, a member of the Billings Expedition, reported that "it is impossible to wish for a better place for stock raising than Kamchatka. . . ."[34] Despite such pronouncements, however, agriculture continued to flounder. Pallas recommended in 1783 that crop varieties more suited to Kamchatka's climate be grown there, such as Tartarian (Polish) wheat (which grew fast and ripened early), Tartarian buckwheat (which also ripened early), and the common nettle or, better yet, the Siberian hemp nettle (for cordage).[35] It is unknown whether Pallas' advice was heeded.

The problem of provisioning the Kamchatka Regiment, formed

in 1798, again turned the government's attention to agriculture in the peninsula. The Mayor of Nizhne-Kamchatsk, Voyevodsky, was ordered to report on the matter. He replied that above all it was necessary to increase the peasant population; he proposed bringing 104 families of Russian peasants from the Okhotsk Seaboard, and converting Kamchatka's Cossacks and soldiers into farmers. He also suggested that supervision of agriculture be tightened, that state grain seed be kept on hand for lending to the peasants in emergencies, and that more state funds be assigned to the military posts for buying the rye flour and the barley groats produced by the peasants.[36] This project was reviewed and approved by Major-General Somov, Commander of the Kamchatka Regiment, who in 1800 reported to Governor-General Lezzano at Irkutsk, suggesting that the prospective colonists be augmented by fifty more peasant families from Irkutsk. Some of these would be settled at Kamchadal villages in order to acquaint the natives with grain cultivation, the rest along the Kamchatka River to cultivate grain and raise livestock. In addition, Somov recommended that three hundred Cossacks be settled for agriculture and that 27,000 rubles worth of livestock, implements, and other needs be purchased.[37] This ambitious project, however, was not ratified.

Governor-General Lezzano, having collected and studied the information on Kamchatka's agriculture, issued the following statement on August 13/25, 1801:

> On the one hand, because of the great expenses to the Treasury for supplying the Somov Regiment with provisions and ammunition, because of the exhaustion of the Yakuts, and because of the irregular and often disastrous conveyance of provisions across the [Okhotsk] sea on transport vessels, and on the other hand, because of the suitability of Kamchatka's climate to the expansion of grain cultivation and stock raising, it would be extremely helpful for the garrisoned Somov Regiment to follow the example of the former battalion of land militia [i.e., engage in agriculture]; afterward from that all the expenses of the Treasury would be recompensed, and not only would the local troops of the kray partake of the grain from their agriculture but all the well-off inhabitants would be able to supply themselves with it.[38]

This pronouncement was followed by another on September 19/October 1:

> The places considered suitable for agriculture are: near Nizhne-Kamchatsk, comprising two companies of 219 men; near Petropavlovsk Harbor, 101 men, and at Udsk Ostrog, 144 men, and I dare

say a company of 93 men at Bolsheretsk to be transferred—because of the unsuitability of the land there for cultivation—to Petropavlovsk, my finding it proper to have two companies at that place, for only it is liable to attempts by enemies. The Okhotsk company can supply itself with provisions from Kamchatka.[39]

Lezzano emphasized in his report to the Tsar that "on account of the difficulty of transporting provisions for the Kamchatka Regiment, accompanied by great expense and by burdening of the Yakuts . . . ," the soldiers of the regiment should engage in agriculture in order to provision not only themselves but the other residents of Kamchatka and even of Okhotsk.[40] Lezzano suggested that two-thirds of the soldiers undertake agriculture, while the rest stay on military duty.[41]

On September 30, 1801, or January 1, 1802, the government ratified Lezzano's proposals. The soldiers began farming in 1802, mainly with one company near Klyuchi and one company near Mashura. However, the seed grain on hand proved unfit for planting, having spoiled from long storage in damp magazines, so that it was milled into flour. In 1803–4 only three cabins were built for the soldiers-cum-farmers, and no grain cultivation was initiated. At Udsk twenty-two soldiers were settled for agriculture. In January, 1803, 33,333 rubles, 21 kopeks were assigned to Somov for the purchase and delivery of seed grain, agricultural implements, and cattle; but the 198 boxes (six tons) of seed purchased with this money were not sent from Irkutsk until 1807, and only 8 boxes reached Kamchatka that year. The rest took until 1810 on account of "roadlessness" (transport difficulties). In 1805, 11,145 pounds of seed grain were sent to the regimental company at Udsk, but most of it spoiled.[42]

A "considerable number" of cattle for the regiment were sent from Yakutsk to Kamchatka by land in 1801 or 1802, but most of them died at Yamsk for want of hay and others were killed for food; only a few reached Tigilsk after "several" years. Later, some cattle were sent to Kamchatka from Sredne-Kolymsk, but most of these, too, perished on the way; only a few made Gizhiga in 1807. In 1803 forty-five horses and twenty-eight cattle were sent from Yakutsk to Udsk's regimental company, but in the following two years thirty-six of the horses and fourteen of the cattle died. Meanwhile, Somov's demands for farriers, curriers, millers, and the like were incessant. The soldiers soon neglected agriculture, since they continued to receive adequate salaries in money and in kind regardless of their agricultural performance. The failure of

Lezzano's scheme was attributed to the damp climate as well as to the unwillingness and the laziness of the soldiers. The attempt, upon dissolution of the regiment in 1812, to persuade the lower ranks to remain in the peninsula as farmers seems to have won few converts.[43]

While the Kamchatka Regiment was vainly trying to provision itself, Kamchatka's commandants were striving to improve agriculture. Commandant Koshelev, who began his administration in 1802, actively devoted himself to agriculture,* but the results were negligible, owing to fatal frosts.[44] He expressed amazement to the Governor of Siberia for believing that agriculture could be established in the peninsula in spite of its cold climate.[45] But in 1804 an inspector reported to the Tsar that "farming [in Kamchatka] is possible."[46] Koshelev was succeeded in 1808 by Petrovsky, who tried in vain to grow grain on a large scale. Apparently this failure was decisive, for in 1812 state agriculture was finally abandoned in Kamchatka. Commandant Rudakov, who replaced Petrovsky in 1813, was ordered to give state cattle and seed to those members of the disbanded Kamchatka Regiment who wished to remain in the peninsula as farmers, and to sell the rest.[47]

Meanwhile, in 1811 a special committee (consisting of Sarychev, Kruzenstern, Von Langsdorff, and the savant Gagemeister and headed by Governor-General Pestel) had been formed to investigate affairs in Kamchatka and Okhotsk krays. The ninety findings of this committee, which deliberated three weeks, were ratified by the government on April 9/21, 1812.[48] Article 34 of the committee's report declared that "according to past procedures, foodstuffs and other needs for the provisionment and supply of the military command of Kamchatka and Gizhiga were delivered from Okhotsk. At present this delivery will continue on the former basis, until cultivation in Kamchatka has reached the intended degree or until other ways of supplying all the necessary wants of this remote land have been devised."[49]

But agriculture did not reach the "intended degree." With the abandonment of state farming in 1812, private farming continued, but it failed to prosper in spite of such inducements as free seed grain and rewards for the best harvests. Commandant Rikord (1817–22) re-

---

* However, an inspector reported in 1805 that Koshelev neglected agriculture and that "everything is going to ruin here [Kamchatka]" (Alaska History Research Project, *Documents Relative to the History of Alaska* [College: University of Alaska, 1936–38], 3 : 196).

garded agricultural development as his prime duty, but his efforts, as well as those of his assistant, Captain-Lieutenant Golenishchev, were fruitless.[50]

Golenishchev, nevertheless, persisted. In 1827 he proposed to Governor-General Lovinsky that Russian peasants (nonexiles) from Siberia be resettled in the Kamchatka River Valley (where they would replace 534 Kamchadals, who would be moved to the peninsula's east coast) in those places suitable for grain cultivation; that Yakuts also be resettled there in those places unsuitable for cultivation but suitable for stockbreeding; and that Kamchatka's forty-six *meshchanins* (lower middle-class townspeople) be converted into agriculturalists; all transmigrants would be freed from taxes. Golenishchev counseled that the Russian peasants should be "capable and healthy," that they should come "voluntarily" at the rate of twenty families (sixty persons) per year from the peasants living along the Lena River (one to two families from each village), that each family should be given fifty kopeks per day and thirty-six pounds of flour per month by the state until they arrived in Kamchatka, that after reaching Kamchatka each should be given by the state one cow, one horse, one cultivator, one ax, one adze, one sickle, one scythe, one spade, thirty-six pounds of yarn for fish nets, and clothing and shoes, and that each male peasant should be given by the state seventy-five rubles for buying household needs, as well as exemption from taxes for ten years. Golenishchev also advised that Yakuts should be sent from Yakutsk Oblast at the rate of five families (fifteen persons) per year, that they should be "healthy and not older than 40 years . . . ," that the first and second transfers should be accompanied by livestock (mainly horses), and that each Yakut should be given by the state fifty kopeks per day and thirty-six pounds of flour per month en route, as well as tax exemption for ten years.[51] This plan, however, was not implemented.

In 1828, when Golenishchev became the first Kamchatka-born commandant of the peninsula, the horticulturalist Johann Rider and two student assistants (Lazarev and Chernykh) from the Moscow Agricultural School were sent to Kamchatka at Golenishchev's request to instruct the natives in growing grain and vegetables and to build hothouses for the transplantation of vegetable seeds, since imported seeds often proved worthless. At the same time fifty horses were sent to Kamchatka from Yakutsk via Gizhiga at a cost of 7,500 rubles in order to facilitate the agricultural operations. Rider, who was paid 3,000 rubles in money and 1,404 pounds in grain annually, arrived in 1828 under orders also to establish a state garden and to collect botanical specimens for the St. Petersburg Imperial Botanical Garden. His experiments with grain, vegetables, and fruit were less successful in 1831 and in 1832 than in 1830 because of the coldest and rainiest summers that the inhabitants could remember. His efforts were also hampered by chronic illness, and he died in July, 1833. Chernykh replaced him.[52] In late 1829 Chernykh and Lazarev had concluded that agriculture was possible around Petropavlovsk because there were no night frosts in summer and no snow from the middle of May until the end of October. They found no sizable amount of arable land at Petropavlovsk itself, but nearby (two and one-half miles northwest) were about 216 acres of suitable sandy-clayey land. Lazarev improved grain cultivation near Bolsheretsk and vegetable gardening along the west coast, doctored livestock, and taught the Kurile natives to grow potatoes. His principal success was in propagating the growing of vegetables, especially potatoes.[53] The Commandant of Kamchatka reported in 1840 that, thanks to Lazarev, "most of the Kamchadals and peasants are accustomed to the usefulness of establishing and propagating agriculture and of experimentation. . . ."[54] In the early 1840's, however, Lazarev became a drunkard.

Meanwhile, in 1830 Golenishchev formed the shareholding Kamchatka Agricultural Company with thirty-seven shares and twenty-eight members, including the Russian Government and the Imperial Agricultural Society of Moscow. The aim of the Company was at most to increase the amount of grain cultivation in the peninsula or at least to decrease the amount of grain imported via Okhotsk at great expense. Approved by the government in 1831, the Company was authorized to settle fifteen families of grain cultivators in Kamchatka at state expense and to occupy suitable uninhabited lands for twenty years; thereafter they could be disposed of to anybody. The Imperial Agricultural Society of Moscow, despite its report from Rikord that agriculture was impossible in Kamchatka on account of the inimical climate, assigned 1,000 rubles a year to the undertaking. Three directors were chosen: Rider, Chernykh, and one Paderin. The Company began its experiments in 1831 along the Avacha River about eighteen miles from Petropavlovsk on an allotment of 77,376⅗ acres. In 1832 another company farm was founded at Varlatonka between Verkhne-Kamchatsk and Milkovo, and in 1833 the Company established yet another farm near Klyuchi. Rikord was soon vindicated by the company's repeated crop failures, caused by frost and mice. At the Avacha farm grain was killed by frost in September, 1831, and in August, 1832, although 300 stacks of hay were made in 1831, 500 stacks in 1832, and 800 stacks in 1833, enough to feed the farm's twenty-five cattle and two horses.[55] Also, labor was insufficient. Chernykh complained that there were not enough hands for the Company's work in 1832; for example, there were only enough to farm twenty-seven acres.[56] For work at its Avacha farm the Company had but two to six workers in 1831 and only two to five workers in 1832, hardly enough to manage the farm's 77,376⅗ acres.[57] In 1835 Commandant Shakov reported to the Governor-General of Eastern Siberia that, except for what its unsuccessful experiments demonstrated, the Company brought no benefit to the peninsula.[58] Although the Free Economic Society of St. Petersburg, hoping to encourage agriculture in Kamchatka, awarded a gold medal to the Company's director and silver medals to three other Company employees in 1837, the stockholders decided to dissolve the enterprise. It was abolished by government order on November 12/24, 1840, and the remaining capital was assigned to the establishment of an agricultural school in the peninsula.[59]

At the request of Commandant Shakov two agricultural students, Sorokin and Rychagov, had been sent to Kamchatka in 1836 to supervise grain cultivation. Most of Sorokin's ten years in the peninsula were spent clerking for the Commandant, while Rychagov mostly drank. In 1840 the Ministry of State Domains sent the Prussian agronomist Kegel to Kamchatka to collect data on its climate and soil as a basis for determining what kind of economy would be possible and beneficial for the peninsula. Kegel was given a salary of 857 rubles, 1,296 pounds of flour, and 108 pounds of groats per year. He was instructed to observe grain growing in Yakutsk Oblast and Okhotsk Kray en route to Kamchatka. On the peninsula he was supposed to compile a botanical description, make meteorological observations, investigate the fertility and the depth of the soil, make experimental sowings of spring and winter grains, vegetables, and fruits, and at the end of two years report his findings to the Ministry of State Domains. Kegel left Okhotsk for Kamchatka on September 20/October 2, 1841, on the brig *Kamchatka*. The wreck of that vessel near Bolsheretsk spoiled all of his seed, so that new seed had to be sent in 1843. In the spring of 1842 Kegel and Sorokin toured Kamchatka.[60] Afterward Kegel reported to the Minister of State Domains, Kiselev, that "the Great Kamchatka Valley, protected

on the north and the east by high mountains, is suitable for the settlement of up to 100,000 peasants and for the development of grain
cultivation, if only assistance is rendered in the clearing of woods and in
the supply of cattle. The old farms are located on bad sites and are
neglected."[61] Kegel also recommended that the Kamchadals of the west
coast be moved to the east coast and there raise chickens, for which it
would be necessary to destroy all dogs on the east coast.[62] Commandant
Strannolyubsky and the "old settlers" of Kamchatka advised Kegel not
to compromise himself with such a report; but Kegel disregarded their
advice and even stated in his report that Strannolyubsky, with whom he
had quarreled, opposed him in everything.[63] The authorities then decided that Kegel was not benefiting the peninsula and removed him to
Okhotsk in 1846. His accomplishments were limited to the planting of
grain at Shchapinsk and Tolbachinsk, whereas Russian and German
newspapers erroneously credited him with having introduced the potato
into Kamchatka.[64]

The administration of Commandant Zavoiko (1850–55) saw
the last serious attempt to develop agriculture in Kamchatka before
1856. Zavoiko, former head of the Russian-American Company's factory at Okhotsk, tried hard to expand agriculture. Along the Avacha
River he founded an agricultural settlement, which was named after him
and which was intended to become a model farm. He also founded mills
and smithies and introduced the first sheep, which were soon annihilated
by dogs.[65] In 1850 he suggested sending eighty farmers to Kamchatka to
cultivate grain with the Kamchadals;[66] as a result, in 1853 twenty-five
families of Russian peasants (139 persons) were sent to the peninsula.[67]
Zavoiko tried to introduce grain growing among the Kamchadals, but
their first sowings yielded only threefold, as did those of the Russian
peasants. The latter, seeing the futility of farming, planted at first on
pain of punishment but soon stopped sowing altogether and adopted the
hunting-and-fishing way of life of the natives. Truck farming did flourish
under Zavoiko, all the Russian peasants and Kamchadals having gardens, in which mainly potatoes but also turnips, carrots, cabbage, and
other vegetables were grown. With Zavoiko's departure from Kamchatka agriculture quickly declined, especially after Russia's seizure of
the Amur Valley. Governor-General Muravyov had planned to rejuve-
nate Kamchatka Kray economically, partly by sending 3,000 families of
Russian peasants there, but the opening of the Amur Valley drew
Russian attention away from Kamchatka, which declined in importance.[68]

PART IV

❋ *Retrospect*

14

SUMMARY AND CONCLUSION

> "The further development of the Siberian lands was, throughout the eighteenth and nineteenth centuries, limited by three factors: the lack of adequate communications, the bitter climate, and the difficulty of acquiring sufficient provisions."
>
> Barbara Jelavich, *Century of Russian Foreign Policy,* p. 163.

The Problem of Provisionment

The Russians came to the Okhotsk Seaboard and the Kamchatka Peninsula in search of furs, just as they had originally entered Siberia for sables and ultimately reached Alaska for sea otters. They first reached the Pacific in 1639, but for the next half century there was little settlement. Then the Treaty of Nerchinsk of 1689 turned Russia from the Amur Basin to northeastern Siberia; the opening of the sea route between the seaboard and the peninsula in 1716–17 obviated the long and difficult land route between Yakutsk and Kamchatka; and the First and Second Kamchatka Expeditions of 1725–29 and 1733–42 revealed the presence of sea otters. All of these events stimulated settlement.

Apart from the depletion of fur bearers, the chief problem besetting Russian occupation and exploitation of the region was the difficulty of provisionment. The grain salary of the state servitors had to be met somehow. The region's remote location impeded importation of foodstuffs (and engendered maladministration), while agriculture was restricted by the harsh physical environment (especially by the severe climate) and the backward cultural environment (particularly by the lack of native cultivation). The Okhotsk Seaboard and the Kamchatka Peninsula lacked not only aboriginal farmers but also bison (whose dried and pounded meat sustained the Canadian fur trade), although some reindeer and abundant fish were present. But fish runs were sometimes light, the preservation of fish was often difficult, and dogs needed much of the fish catch, while the Russians both desired and required customary provisions, especially grain, which in any case were nutritionally superior.

Five solutions to the problem of food supply of the seaboard and the peninsula were attempted: overland-oversea supply from Eastern Siberia, farming in Okhotsk-Kamchatka Kray itself, trade with foreign sources of foodstuffs, overseas supply around the Cape or the Horn from European Russia, and farming in extraterritorial colonies. The Russians relied overwhelmingly on overland-oversea supply, in particular, and local agriculture. Overland-oversea provisionment was merely an extension of the Siberian deliveries. The main source regions for the Okhotsk–Kamchatka delivery were the Yakutsk district (livestock) and Ilimsk Uyezd and Baikalia (grain), where agricultural products were obtained by the state through taxation of peasants until 1772 and thereafter through purchases from peasant and merchant contractors. Grain was carted in late winter to landings on the upper Lena River, whence it was boated downstream in early spring to Yakutsk. At least half of all freight (by value) that reached Yakutsk was then forwarded to Kamchatka and Okhotsk, principally via the spring-summer land route linking Yakutsk and Okhotsk. This track, which was shorter, easier, and cheaper than the rather circuitous and largely upstream river route, carried mostly provisions, especially in spring, when the unthawed track was safer and cheaper than in summer. Cattle were driven and grain was hauled to Okhotsk by Yakut conductors, chiefly on behalf of the state. Grain was transported in rawhide bags by pack trains of Yakut horses, which within two months reached Okhotsk, whence the provisions were shipped in late summer on three or four brigs and galiots to Gizhiga and the ports of Kamchatka. Annually thousands of horses packed hundreds of tons of state (especially) and private freight, largely provisions, to Okhotsk. Usually enough provisions were thus received on the seaboard and the peninsula but only at great cost, in accordance with the difficulty of transport, so that in Kamchatka provisions cost up to thirty-two times as much as in Irkutsk, thanks mainly to the Yakutsk–Okhotsk Track, the worst section of the supply line. This notorious stretch was marred by myriad streams, rough terrain, extensive bogs, dense woods, rocky ground, weak horses, swarms of mosquitoes and midges, ravenous dogs, snow and ice, and infectious diseases; thousands of horses perished on it every year, lining the track with their flesh and bones. Sparse settlement, plundering convicts, untrustworthy conductors, corrupt officials, and improper building and repairing further impeded transport on the Yakutsk-Okhotsk Track. Transport by sea from Okhotsk was hampered by the inadequacies of Okhotsk Port and the ports of Kamchatka and Gizhiga, as well as by the adverse marine conditions, the unseaworthy ships, and incompetent crews, so that many ships were wrecked. Consequently, it could take grain as long as six years to reach Kamchatka from Irkutsk, if it got there at all. The authorities responded by trying to improve or relocate the Yakutsk–Okhotsk Track and Okhotsk Port, but the difficulties continued; hence a new tack—local agricultural production—was attempted early in order to compensate for the shortcomings of overland-oversea supply.

The introduction of agriculture onto the Okhotsk Seaboard and especially onto the Kamchatka Peninsula in the second quarter of the eighteenth century represented an extension of Russian agricultural colonization of Siberia, which had also been instituted in order to meet the deficiencies of the Siberian deliveries. Agriculture was first begun in the late 1710's in Kamchatka, since provisions were scarcer and dearer there and the climate was more amenable than on the seaboard. In response to the findings of the First and Second Kamchatka Expeditions, the government transferred Russian Crown peasants from Ilimsk Uyezd and Yakut stockbreeders from Yakutsk to the seaboard and the peninsula in the 1730's and 40's. Although not all of these transmigrants arrived, by the mid-eighteenth century there were some hundred families of agriculturalists in the region, mainly in the Kamchatka River Valley at Milkovo and Klyuchi, where they engaged communally in mixed farming, particularly in grain cultivation, the entire output of which belonged to the state (until 1764). Despite initial optimism, agriculture did not flourish. Grain yields were sometimes high but usually low, and cattle propagated slowly, although vegetables, especially roots and tubers, succeeded. The failure of agriculture stemmed from various physical and cultural obstacles, particularly the shortness of the growing season and the disinterest and scarcity of the peasants. These sought higher and surer returns in trapping and fishing, which competed not only economically but also, respectively, spatially and temporally with farming. The neglect of agriculture went uncorrected by lax officials, who feared that diligent and productive farming would diminish their profits from the fur trade and the grain trade. The government responded by trying long and hard to improve agriculture in Kamchatka in particular by various measures. Despite its stubborn and costly efforts the Okhotsk Seaboard and the Kamchatka Peninsula never became self-supporting in foodstuffs; overland-oversea supply remained the basic response to the region's alimentary problem. Overland-oversea supply, supplemented by local agriculture, managed barely to meet but not really to overcome the problem, since foodstuffs remained sometimes deficient, often unpalatable, and usually expensive. Consequently, there was physical suffering and economic loss.

The Role of Provisionment

Thus for provisionment of the Okhotsk Seaboard and the Kamchatka Peninsula the Russians relied principally on importation but also on local agriculture. The spatial manifestations of these solutions—transport and settlement—were salient features of the region's geography between 1639 and 1856 and were mentioned emphatically by residents and visitors alike. Neither approach succeeded in satisfying the region's food needs in terms of amount, quality, or cost. Local agriculture rarely yielded surpluses; overland-oversea provisionment did furnish much food, but it was not always adequate in quantity or quality and was usually exorbitant in price.

The high price was especially crucial, for even when palatable provisions were available many Russians, especially the poorer ones, could not afford them. In 1769 at Nizhne-Kamchatsk grain (flour and groats) cost 40 to 71 times as much as at Yakutsk and 48 to 106 times as much as in Western Siberia (Barnaul and Yekaterinburg). Fresh beef in 1772 in Kamchatka cost ten times as much as in Western Siberia (Kungur and Yekaterinburg) and four times as much as in Moscow. In 1787 provisions and wares were ten times as costly at Bolsheretsk as at Moscow. And in 1828–30 a pud of rye flour cost 55 kopeks at Irkutsk; 1 ruble, 10 kopeks to 1 ruble, 25 kopeks at Yakutsk; 8 rubles, 75 kopeks to 10 rubles at Udsk; 10 rubles and more at Okhotsk; and at least 15 rubles, 25 kopeks in Kamchatka.[1] The shortage of provisions sometimes necessitated paying state servitors money in lieu of grain salary, but provisions were so expensive that the state servitors with cash still could not afford to buy grain from private traders—and this dilemma encouraged embezzlement.

Grain and beef were too expensive on the seaboard and the peninsula to be eaten often. Shakhovskoy, who inspected Gizhiga Kray in 1819, found that the Russian inhabitants did not eat bread, although those near Okhotsk sometimes had flour, which they used to flavor dishes and thicken soups.[2]* Provisions were so expensive that most Russians refrained from buying them and instead used fish in all forms. Fish dominated the diet of Russians and natives alike, especially at Okhotsk and Gizhiga, where agriculture was almost nonexistent.[3] The dearth of varied foodstuffs engendered malnutrition and disease, especially at Okhotsk, where fresh fruits and vegetables were particularly scarce. Scurvy and perhaps pellagra and beriberi were commonplace. In April of 1786 Sarychev was unable to obtain many men for felling timber at Okhotsk because most of them were incapacitated by scurvy. He noted that "to this sickness people of scanty means here were generally subject."[4] This observation was confirmed in 1806 by Academician Redovsky, who found that only a few wealthy residents of Okhotsk could afford to eat meat or to mix flour or groats with fish, and even these few lacked bread.[5] In the summer of 1849 another visitor noted that 60 to 65 of Okhotsk's 300 sailors were sick in hospital.[6] Scurvy was particularly prevalent in spring, when the winter stocks of fish had been exhausted and the summer runs had not yet begun; in March, April, May, and June often two-thirds of the populace of Okhotsk were stricken.[7] Scurvy was also common in Kamchatka. Captain King, Cook's second-in-command, found in April, 1779 that all the residents of Petropavlovsk were scorbutic.[8]

The Problem of Rationale

On the Okhotsk Seaboard and the Kamchatka Peninsula, then, the Russians encountered inimical physical and cultural conditions in a remote region and an unfamiliar maritime setting, with a resultant chronic problem of provisionment. Hunting-trapping forays were protracted by the search for substitute foodstuffs; profits from the fur trade were eroded by the high cost of provisions; and occupation was rendered both more costly and less secure.

Why did Russia doggedly maintain its presence in the face of

* Grain was even scarcer at Anadyrsk. In the late 1720's the Senate informed Tsar Peter II that for seventy-eight years (1649–1726) the Russians of Anadyrsk had lacked "grain provisions" and had lived on fish and game (Alexsandr Shakhovskoy, "Izvestiya o Gizhiginskoy kreposti" ["Information about Gizhiga Fortress"], *Severny arkhiv*, pt. 4 [1822], p. 302).

such adverse circumstances? The reasons that operated while the fur trade flourished are not difficult to discern. Handicaps were tolerable so long as there was an ample supply of, and a sizable demand for, sable and sea otter pelts, with their very high value per unit of weight. The rewards of the fur trade went largely to the upper mercantile and aristocratic classes of European Russia, who exerted much influence on state affairs. It is reasonable to expect that these classes would strongly favor an occupation that permitted them to acquire handsome profits and luxurious, fashionable attire. The fur trade was also a lucrative source of both state revenue and foreign goods, for not only did the Russian Government exact 10 percent of the catch of Siberian trappers but at Kyakhta, where Russian furs were traded for Chinese products, it also levied duties of up to 25 percent on exports and imports, amounting during the early 1770's to 550,000 rubles annually.[9] Fear of disrupting this profitable commerce long kept Russia from annexing China's Amur Valley, which it did not seize until the mid-nineteenth century.

By the second quarter of the 1800's, however, the fur trade had waned with the depletion of the fur resource and the decline of the fur market, so that Russia's presence on the seaboard and peninsula became unprofitable as well as tenuous. In Gizhiga Kray in 1828, for example, state expenses totaled 45,004 rubles, 85 kopeks (including 34,967 rubles, 75 kopeks for provisions alone), while state revenues were only 2,153 rubles, 50 kopeks.[10] The reasons for persisting under such conditions are less certain. Undoubtedly territory was not easily relinquished at an imperialistic time when the sheer size of a state enhanced its prestige. While the maritime nations of Western Europe were finding glory and prestige (as well as riches) overseas in the New World, continental Russia was forming its own new world inland. Withdrawal would have meant an inglorious loss of prestige, something that any self-respecting power would have tried to avoid, particularly if, like Russia, it had a national inferiority complex. Perhaps, too, Russia wished to reach and to hold what it considered its natural eastern frontier in the form of the edge of the continental land mass. This juncture of land and sea provided a sharp and definite boundary, leaving little doubt about its delineation and less fear of a foreign beachhead. Fear of a power vacuum was probably another reason for Russia's persisting presence, for the Okhotsk Seaboard and the Kamchatka Peninsula bordered the North Pacific sphere of international rivalry among Russia, Spain, Great Britain, and the United States. In the mid-nineteenth century, when **Commodore Perry** was forcibly reopening Japan, Yankee whaling, sealing, and trading vessels were active off Siberia's Pacific Coast,* and during the Crimean War Petropavlovsk and Ayan were attacked by Anglo-French squadrons. Now the European scramble for colonies and Russia's rebuffs in European affairs (such as defeat in the Crimean War) reinforced her interest in Asia, where she was determined to share in imperialism's spoils. Stronger opposition (from, say, an aggressive China or Japan) might have broken Russia's precarious foothold, but any such threat on the part of China or Japan was removed by their policies of isolation, imposed by the Manchu Dynasty and by the Tokugawa Shogunate in the second quarter of the seventeenth century, just as Russia was entering the Far East.

By contrast, on the Northwest Coast of America, where native resistance (Tlingit) was stouter and foreign competition (British and American) was stronger, Russia, again with a weak food base, ultimately felt compelled to withdraw. In the Pacific Northwest, incidentally, the Canadian fur trade managed to overcome a similar problem of provisionment, thanks to a milder climate and more willing farmers. Closer to the Okhotsk Seaboard and the Kamchatka Peninsula, in Chukotka, where native opposition was stronger and the food base was weaker than on the seaboard and the peninsula, the Russians were not completely victorious until 1869, over two centuries after their first contact with the Chukchi. Even in the Amur Valley, where provisionment had not been problematical, powerful Chinese opposition had forced faraway Moscow to retreat in 1689.

Finally, Russian occupation of the Okhotsk Seaboard and the Kamchatka Peninsula may have persisted from sheer inertia. Russia's large bureaucracy was not noted for close coordination, high efficiency, or rapid innovation; any radical change in policy with respect to Okhotsk–Kamchatka Kray would have been formulated, legislated, and executed very slowly. Indecision may have been reinforced by the stoical optimism of the Russians, who seemed almost to expect adversity, which, they felt, would somehow be overcome eventually. Inaction may have been further complemented by outright neglect. Siberia, after all, really mattered little at the Imperial court, and rightly so; and the Okhotsk Seaboard and the Kamchatka Peninsula probably mattered

* In 1846, for example, up to 500 American vessels were sealing in the Okhotsk and Bering seas (Sgibnev, "Istorichesky ocherk," 103 [August, 1869] : 81).

even less, particularly since there was usually no serious foreign competition for the region. Consequently, there would have been little reason for altering its status quo.

Probably a combination of these reasons contributed to Russia's maintaining its burdensome presence in a region once blessed with abundant fur bearers and fish but otherwise shortchanged by both Nature and man. It was such deprivation in terms of harsh physical conditions and meager cultural resources that long made most Russians perceive Siberia in general and the Okhotsk Seaboard and the Kamchatka Peninsula in particular as a blighted wilderness suited mainly for the cold storage of wrongdoers. In the words of a Tsarist general, Siberia was "the most extensive waste-land in the world—tailor-made for deportation."[11] And a Tsarist statesman declared that "Neva Avenue [St. Petersburg's main street] alone is worth at least five times as much as all of Siberia."[12]

Lastly, the plight of the Russian Far East should be put in proper perspective. The persistence of the Russians in the face of formidable difficulties testifies to that hardiness and fatalism so often noted in Russian behavior.[13] Both physically and culturally the Russian Empire was a "hard" land, a land that required much effort and offered little reward, as the historian Klyuchevsky repeatedly stressed. "No people in Europe," he wrote, "is less spoiled and less pretentious, is accustomed to expecting less from nature and fate, and is hardier."[14] Another noted Russian historian, Solovyov, felt that Nature had been a mother to Western Europe but merely a stepmother to Eastern Europe.[15] The Russian Far East exemplified the generalization that Nature in Russia yielded grudgingly and niggardly; "to eke out a livelihood" was no mere cliché but a hard fact of life. And the land was anything but softened by man, which in Russia meant draconian autocracy, with its selfish aristocracy, corrupt bureaucracy, strict Orthodoxy, oppressive serfdom, and backward technology. Little wonder that the Russian masses, whether in Primorye or Pomorye, were conditioned to endure privation and to accept fate, for they had virtually no control over either. Such control was especially minimal in the Russian Far East, where privation was more severe and fate was more cruel. It is no accident that one of the chief intentions and major accomplishments of the Soviet regime has been to increase man's control over capricious Nature through political, economic, and cultural modernization, and thereby to reduce privation and minimize fate.

❖ *Reference Material*

ABBREVIATIONS

AIE   Arkhiv Instituta etnografii imeni N. N. Miklukho-Maklaya Akademii nauk SSSR [Archive of the Miklukho-Maklay Institute of Ethnography of the Academy of Sciences of the USSR (Leningrad)]

d.   *delo* ["file" or "dossier"]

f.   *fond* ["fund" or "stock"]

GPB OR   Gosudarstvennaya publichnaya biblioteka, Otdel rukopisey [Saltykov-Shchedrin State Public Library, Manuscript Division (Leningrad)]

op.   *opis* ["inventory" or "account"]

port.   *portfel* ["portfolio"]

st.   *stolbets* ["roll"]

sv.   *svyazka* ["sheaf" or "bunch"]

TsGADA   Tsentralny gosudarstvenny arkhiv drevnikh aktov [Central State Archive of Ancient Acts (Moscow)]

TsGIAL   Tsentralny gosudarstvenny istorichesky arkhiv v Leningrade [Central State Historical Archive in Leningrad]

NOTES

Chapter 1: HISTORICAL BACKGROUND

1 Quoted in Raymond Beazley, Nevill Forbes, and G. A. Birkett, *Russia from the Varangians to the Bolsheviks* (Oxford: The Clarendon Press, 1918), p. 66.

2 George V. Lantzeff, "Russian Eastward Expansion before the Mongol Invasion," *American Slavic and East European Review*, 6, nos. 18–19 (December, 1947) : 1.

3 Robert Michell and Nevill Forbes, eds., *The Chronicle of Novgorod 1016–1471*, "Camden Third Series," vol. 25 (London: Camden Society, 1914), p. 6.

4 S. F. Platonov, *Proshloye russkovo severa* [*The Past of the Russian North*] (Peterburg: Izdatelstvo "Vremya," 1923), p. 15.

5 Robert J. Kerner, *The Urge to the Sea* (Berkeley and Los Angeles: University of California Press, 1946), pp. 68–69.

6 [P. A. Slovtsov], *Istoricheskoye obozrenie Sibiri* [*Historical Survey of Siberia*] (St. Petersburg: Tipografiya I. N. Skorokhodova, 1886), 1 : 84–85.

7 Peter I. Lyashchenko, *History of the National Economy of Russia to the 1917 Revolution*, trans. L. M. Herman (New York: The Macmillan Company, 1949), p. 237.

8 Philip J. Von Strahlenburg, *An Historico-Geographical Description of the North and Eastern Parts of Europe and Asia . . .* (London: W. Innys and R. Manby, 1738), p. 361.

9 N. S. Orlova, comp., *Otkrytiya russkikh zemleprokhodtsev i polyarnykh morekhodov XVII veka na severo-vostoke Azii: sbornik dokumentov* [*Discoveries of Russian Landsmen and Polar Seafarers of the XVIIth Century in the North-East of Asia: A Collection of Documents*] (Moscow: Gosudarstvennoye izdatelstvo geograficheskoy literatury, 1951), doc. 33, pp. 139–144.

10 M. I. Belov, comp., *Russkie morekhody v Ledovitom i Tikhom oke-anakh: sbornik dokumentov* . . . [*Russian Seafarers in the Arctic and the Pacific Oceans: A Collection of Documents* . . .] (Leningrad and Moscow: Izdatelstvo Glavsevmorputi, 1952), doc. 7, pp. 50–55.

11 Russia, Arkheograficheskaya kommissiya, *Dopolneniya k Aktam istoricheskim* . . . [*Supplements to Historical Acts* . . .] (St. Petersburg: Tipografiya Eduarda Pratsa, 1846–72), vol. 3, doc. 52, pp. 175–176.

12 *Ibid.*, doc. 86, pp. 320–321.

13 S. P. Krasheninnikov, *Opisanie zemli Kamchatki* [*Description of the Land of Kamchatka*] (Moscow and Leningrad: Izdatelstvo Glavsevmorputi, 1949), p. 476.

14 Shteller, "Opisanie strany Kamchatki" ["Description of the Country of Kamchatka"], AIE, f. K–II, op. 1, d. 304, pp. 153–154.

15 *Ibid.*, p. 151.

16 *Ibid.*, p. 150.

17 V. K. Andriyevich, *Sibir v XIX stoletii* [*Siberia in the XIXth Century*] (St. Petersburg: Tipografiya V. V. Komarova, 1889), pt. 2, pp. 370–371.

18 Krasheninnikov, *Opisanie zemli Kamchatki,* pp. 516–517; Shteller, "Opisanie strany Kamchatki," pp. 473–474, 476–479, 481.

19 N. N. Ogloblin, *Obozrenie stolbtsov i knig Sibirskavo prikaza (1592–1768 gg.)* [*Survey of the Rolls and the Books of the Siberian Office (1592–1768)*] (Moscow: Universitetskaya tipografiya, 1895), pt. 1, p. 199; A. A. Ionina, *Noviya danniya k istorii Vostochnoy Sibiri XVII veka* [*New Data on the History of Eastern Siberia of the XVIIth Century*] (Irkutsk: Tipo-litografiya P. I. Makushkina, 1895), p. 199.

20 A. Sgibnev, "Okhotsky port s 1649 po 1852 g." ["Okhotsk Port from 1649 to 1852"], *Morskoy sbornik,* 105, no. 11 (November, 1869) : 2, 4; Russia, Arkheograficheskaya kommissiya, *Dopolneniya k Aktam istoricheskim,* vol. 4, doc. 2, pp. 2–7.

21 Ya. P. Alkor and B. D. Grekov, eds., *Kolonialnaya politika Moskovskovo gosudarstva v Yakutii XVII v.* [*Colonial Policy of the Muscovite State in Yakutia of the XVIIth Century*] (Leningrad: Izdatelstvo Instituta narodov severa TsIK SSSR imeni P. G. Smidovicha, 1936), doc. 197, pp. 244–245.

22 Krasheninnikov, *Opisanie zemli Kamchatki,* pp. 489, 518–520; S. [sic: G. F.] Muller, *Voyages from Asia to America* . . . (London: T. Jefferys, 1761), p. xli; Ya. P. Alkor and A. K. Drezen, eds., *Kolonialnaya politika tsarizma na Kamchatke i Chukotke v XVIII veke* [*Colonial Policy of Tsarism in Kamchatka and Chukotka in the XVIIIth Century*] (Leningrad: Izdatelstvo Instituta narodov severa TsIK SSSR, 1935), p. 6; S. B. Okun, *Ocherki po istorii kolonialnoy politiki tsarizma v Kamchatskom kraye* [*Sketches on the History of the Colonial Policy of Tsarism in Kamchatka Kray*] (Leningrad: Ogiz, 1935), p. 19; Pervy sibirsky komitet, "O predpolozheniyakh Nachalnika Kamchatki ob

ustroistve sevo kraya" ["Concerning the Proposals of the Commandant of Kamchatka on the Organization of This Kray"], TsGIAL, f. 1,264, op. 1, d. 167, fol. 15ᵛ.

23 Russia, Arkheograficheskaya kommissiya, *Pamyatniki sibirskoy istorii XVIII veka* [*Memorials of Siberian History of the XVIIIth Century*] (St. Petersburg: Tipografiya Ministerstva vnutrennikh del, 1882–85), vol. 1, doc. 99, p. 427.

24 *Ibid.*, vol. 2, doc. 121, p. 522.

25 Muller, *Voyages from Asia to America,* p. xli; I. V. Shcheglov, *Kronologichesky perechen vazhneishikh dannykh iz istorii Sibiri 1032–1882 gg.* [*Chronological List of the Major Facts from the History of Siberia 1032–1882*] (Irkutsk: Tipografiya Shtaba Vostochnavo Sibirskavo voyennavo okruga, 1883), p. 160.

26 Okun, *Ocherki po istorii,* p. 19.

27 Russia, Arkheograficheskaya kommissiya, *Pamyatniki sibirskoy istorii,* vol. 2, doc. 12, pp. 37–39.

28 Muller, *Voyages from Asia to America,* pp. xli–xliii; Krasheninnikov, *Opisanie zemli Kamchatki,* pp. 158, 489, 520, 745, 757; Sgibnev, "Okhotsky port," 105, no. 11 : 9.

29 A. S. Pushkin, *A. S. Pushkin: polnoye sobranie sochineny v shesti tomakh* [*A. S. Pushkin: Complete Collection of Works in Six Volumes*] (Moscow and Leningrad: Academia, 1935), 5 : 444.

30 Krasheninnikov, *Opisanie zemli Kamchatki,* p. 151.

31 Okun, *Ocherki po istorii,* p. 21.

32 Krasheninnikov, *Opisanie zemli Kamchatki,* pp. 479–488.

33 [Vitus Bering], "Donesenie flota kapitana Beringa ob ekspeditsii yevo k vostochnym beregam Sibiri" ["Report of Fleet Captain Bering about his Expedition to the Eastern Shores of Siberia"], *Zapiski Voyenno-topograficheskavo depo,* vol. 10, pt. 1 (1847), 2d suppl., pp. 71–73; Vasily Berkh, *Pervoye morskoye puteshestvie rossiyan . . .* [*The First Sea Voyage of a Russian . . .*] (St. Petersburg: Imperatorskaya akademiya nauk, 1823), pp. 8, 11–12, 24, 26–27; V. Vakhtin, *Russkie truzheniki morya* [*Russian Toilers of the Sea*] (St. Petersburg: Tipografiya Morskavo ministerstva, 1890), pp. 11, 23, 47, 49; G. F. Muller, "Geografiya ili nyneshnoye sostoyanie zemli Kamchatki 1737 goda" ["The Geography or the Present Condition of the Land of Kamchatka of 1737"], TsGADA, f. 199, port. 527, d. 3, fols. 24ᵛ–26.

34 Sven Waxell, *The Russian Expedition to America,* trans. M. A. Michael (New York: Collier Books, 1962), p. 61.

35 L. N. Maikov, *Razskazy Nartova o Petre velikom* [*Nartov's Narrations about Peter the Great*] (St. Petersburg: Tipografiya Imperatorskoy akademii nauk, 1891), p. 99.

36 Russia, *Polnoye sobranie zakonov rossiiskoy imperii* [*Complete Collection of Laws of the Russian Empire*], 1st ser. (1649–1825) (St. Petersburg: Kantselyariya Yevo Imperatorskavo Velichestva, 1830), vol. 8, doc. 6,041, p. 770.

37 *Ibid.*, doc. 5,753, p. 461, doc. 5,813, pp. 520–524, doc. 6,041, pp. 770–774; Timofey Shmalev, "Ukaz i Instruktsiya opredelyonnomu v Okhotsk Glavnym Komandirom Grigoryu Pisarevu 1 Aprel 1732 goda" ["Decree and Instructions Appointing Grigory Pisarev Chief Commander of Okhotsk on April 1, 1732"], TsGADA, f. 199, port. 528, pt. 1, d. 1, fols. 1ʳ–5ʳ.

38 Ivan Borisov, "Vedomost sochineniya v Yakutskoy voyevodskoy kantselyarii po trebovaniyu Akademii Nauk professora Gerarda Fridrikha Gospodina Millera o sostoyanii goroda Yakutska i Yakutskovo vedomstva . . ." ["List of Works in the Yakutsk Gubernatorial Office Relating to the Request of Professor of the Academy of Sciences Mr. Gerhard Friedrich Muller about the Condition of the Town of Yakutsk and Yakutsk Province . . ."], TsGADA, f. 199, port. 528, pt. 7, d. 481, fol. 335; A. S. Sgibnev, "Skornyakov-Pisarev i Devyer v Sibiri" ["Skornyakov-Pisarev and Devier in Siberia"], *Russkaya starina*, 15, no. 2 (February, 1876) : 445; Kanagev, "Okhotsk," *Severnoye obozrenie*, 3 (1850) : 366–367; A. P. [A. S. Polonsky], "Okhotsk," *Otechestvennia zapiski*, no. 6, pt. 8 (June, 1850), pp. 136–137.

39 Borisov, "Vedomost sochineniya," fols. 228ʳ, 337ʳ.

40 *Ibid.*, fol. 335.

41 Waxell, *Russian Expedition to America*, pp. 139–140.

42 Krasheninnikov, *Opisanie zemli Kamchatki*, p. 152.

43 Anonymous, "Chernovie opisi kazyonnikh stroyeny g. Gizhiginska i svedeniya o chisle zhiteley" ["Rough Inventories of the State Buildings of the Town of Gizhiga and Information about the Number of Inhabitants"], TsGADA, f. 1,096, op. 1, d. 53, fol. 1; A. Shakhovskoy, "O nachale postroyeniya Gizhiginskoy kreposti" ["Concerning the Beginning of the Construction of Gizhiga Fortress"], *Vestnik Yevropy*, no. 24, pt. 102 (December, 1818), pp. 281–282; Aleksandr Shakhovskoy, "Izvestiya o Gizhiginskoy kreposti" ["Information about Gizhiga Fortress"], *Severny arkhiv*, pt. 4 (1822), pp. 284–285; Timofey Shmalev, "Statisticheskiya i Geograficheskiya Primechaniya Kapitana Tim. Shmaleva ob otdalyonnykh onykh mest krepostyakh, o khlebopashestve i pr. s pribavleniyami" ["Statistical and Geographical Notes of Captain Tim Shmalev about the Fortresses, Grain Cultivation, etc. of the Aforementioned Remote Places with Supplements"], TsGADA, f. 199, port. 528, pt. 1, d. 19, fol. 2ʳ; Anonymous, "Iskhodyashchy zhurnal Gizhiginskoy kreposti za 1767 god" ["Outgoing Journal of Gizhiga Fortress for 1767"], TsGADA, f. 1,096, op. 1, d. 24, fol. 138ʳ.

44 Shmalev, "Statisticheskiya i Geograficheskiya Primechaniya," fols. 13–14ʳ, 15ʳ; Sgibnev, "Okhotsky port," 105, no. 12 : 39; N. V. Sushkov, "O sibirskikh solyanykh promyslakh" ["Concerning the Siberian Salt Industries"], *Sibirsky vestnik*, pt. 15, bk. 7 (July, 1821), p. 88; Pervy sibirsky komitet, "O predpolozheniyakh Nachalnika Kamchatki," d. 166, fols. 8–8ʳ, 36, 66, 182ʳ–183.

45 N. P. Rezanov, "Zapiska gorodnichevo Nizhne-Kamchatska Voyevod-

skovo o sostoyanii Kamchatki i vygodnosti yeyo ekspluatatsii dlya kazny" ["Note of Mayor Voyevodsky of Nizhne-Kamchatsk on the Condition of Kamchatka and the Advantages of Its Exploitation for the State"], TsGADA, f. 796, op. 1, d. 285, fol. 5.

46 Anonymous, "Zapiski o Chukotskom narode . . . iz imeyushchikhsya v Senatskom sekretnom Arkhive svedeny" ["Notes on the Chukot People . . . from Information Available in the Senate's Secret Archive"], *Chteniya v Obshchestve istorii i drevnostey rossiiskikh pri Moskovskom universitete,* bk. 4, pt. 5 (1858), pp. 102; Timofey Shmalev, "Vypiski o raspolozhenii v Sibirskoy Gubernii vnov yasak" ["Excerpts on the Re-establishment of Yasak in the Province of Siberia"], TsGADA, f. 199, port. 528, pt. 1, d. 18, fol. 11ᵛ.

47 [Bering], "Donesenie flota kapitana Beringa," p. 71; Kanagev, "Okhotsk," p. 368; A. P., "Okhotsk," pp. 135–136, 138; Sgibnev, "Okhotsky port," 105, no. 11 : 32; Sgibnev, "Skornyakov-Pisarev i Devyer," p. 447.

48 Savin, "Okhotsk," *Zapiski Gidrograficheskavo departamenta Morskavo ministerstva,* pt. 9 (1851), pp. 154–155.

49 Russia, Pravitelstvuyushchy senat, *Senatsky arkhiv [Senate Archive]* (St. Petersburg: Tipografiya Pravitelstvuyushchavo senata, 1892–1901), 8 : 210.

50 V. Berkh, "Izvestie o mekhovoy torgovle, proizvodimoy rossiyanami pri ostrovakh Kurilskikh, Aleutskikh i severozapadnom beregu Ameriki" ["Information on the Fur Trade Conducted by the Russians along the Kurile and Aleutian Islands and the Northwestern Coast of America"], *Syn otechestva,* pt. 88, no. 39 (1823), pp. 245, 251; Vasily Berkh, *The Chronological History of the Discovery of the Aleutian Islands . . . ,* trans. Dimitri Krenov (Seattle: Works Progress Administration, 1938), pp. 1, 102; Frank A. Golder, *Bering's Voyages* (New York: American Geographical Society, 1922–25), 2 : 216–217, 220; Muller, *Voyages from Asia to America,* p. 59; A. Pokrovsky, ed., *Ekspeditsiya Beringa: sbornik dokumentov [Bering's Expedition: A Collection of Documents]* (Moscow: Glavnoye arkhivnoye upravlenie NKVD SSSR, 1941), p. 370.

51 Captain James Cook [and Captain James King], *A Voyage to the Pacific Ocean . . .* (London: G. Nichol and T. Cadell, 1784), 3 : 497.

52 *Ibid.,* p. 509.

53 Carol Urness, ed., *A Naturalist in Russia* (Minneapolis: University of Minnesota Press, 1967), p. 118.

54 R. V. Makarova, *Russkie na Tikhom okeane vo vtoroy polovine XVIII v. [Russians on the Pacific Ocean in the Second Half of the XVIIIth Century]* (Moscow: Izdatelstvo "Nauka," 1968), pp. 113, 182–188; K. F. German, "Statisticheskiya svedeniya o lovle zverey i ptits v Rossii i Sibiri" ["Statistical Information on the Catching of Animals and Birds in Russia and Siberia"], *Sibirsky vestnik,* pt. 11, bk. 9 (1820), p. 85.

55 Frank A. Golder, "A Survey of Alaska, 1743–1799," *Washington Historical Quarterly*, 4, no. 2 (April, 1913) : 92; P. N. Pavlov, ed., *K istorii Rossiisko-Amerikanskoy kompanii: sbornik dokumentalnykh materialov* [*Concerning the History of the Russian-American Company: A Collection of Documentary Materials*] (Krasnoyarsk: Krasnoyarsky krayevoy gosudarstvenny arkhiv i Krasnoyarsky gosudarstvenny pedagogichesky institut, 1957), pp. 9–15, 20–21; Akademiya nauk SSSR, Institut literatury (Pushkinsky dom), *A. N. Radishchev: polnoye sobranie sochineny* [*A. N. Radishchev: Complete Collection of Works*] (Moscow and Leningrad: Izdatelstvo Akademii nauk SSSR, 1938–52), 3 : 140; G. F. Muller and Peter Simon Pallas, *Conquest of Siberia, and the History of the Transactions, Wars, Commerce, etc. etc. Carried on Between Russia and China, from the Earliest Period* (London: Smith, Elder, and Co., 1842), p. 116.

56 Krasheninnikov, *Opisanie zemli Kamchatki*, pp. 514, 515; Shteller, "Opisanie strany Kamchatki," p. 473.

57 Kapitan-Leitenant Minitsky, "Nekotoria izvestiya ob Okhotskom porte i uyezde onavo, dostavlennia Kapitan-Leitenantom Minitskim v 1809 godu" ["Some Information about Okhotsk Port and Its Uyezd, Supplied by Captain-Lieutenant Minitsky in 1809"], *Zapiski, izdavayemia Gosudarstvennym admiralteiskim departamentom*, pt. 3 (1815), p. 91; Shmalev, "Statisticheskiya i Geograficheskiya Primechaniya," fols. 66–67; Grigory Skornyakov–Pisarev, "Promemoriya is kantselyarii Okhotskovo porta blagorodnomu Gospodinu Akademii Nauk professoru Gerardu Fridrikhu Milleru . . ." ["Memorandum from the Office of Okhotsk Port to Professor of the Academy of Sciences Noble Mr. Gerhard Friedrich Muller . . ."], TsGADA, f. 199, port. 528, pt. 7, d. 481, fols. 335, 337ᵛ.

58 I. P. Shaskolsky, ed., *Geograficheskoye izuchenie Sibiri XVII–XIX v.v.* [*The Geographical Study of Siberia of the XVIIth–XIXth Centuries*], "Materialy Otdeleniya istorii geograficheskikh znany Geograficheskovo obshchestva Soyuza SSR," no. 1 (Leningrad: Geograficheskoye obshchestvo SSSR, 1962), p. 26.

59 Capt. John Dundas Cochrane, *Narrative of a Pedestrian Journey through Russia and Siberian Tartary . . .* (Philadelphia: H. C. Carey, I. Lea, and A. Small, 1824), pp. 251, 318.

60 Shaskolsky, *Geograficheskoye izuchenie Sibiri*, pp. 30, 33; Shmalev, "Statisticheskiya i Geograficheskiya Primechaniya," fols. 6–6ᵛ.

61 Robert J. Kerner, "The Russian Eastward Movement: Some Observations on Its Historical Significance," *Pacific Historical Review*, 17, no. 5 (May, 1948) : 137.

62 R. V. Makarova, "Ekspeditsii russkikh promyshlennykh lyudey v Tikhom okeane v XVIII veke" ["Expeditions of Russian Promyshlenniks in the Pacific Ocean in the XVIIIth Century"], *Voprosy geografii*, no. 17 (1950), p. 28.

63 Alexander De Humboldt, *Political Essay on the Kingdom of New*

Spain, trans. John Black (London: Longman, Hurst, Rees, Orme, and Brown and H. Colburn, 1811), 2 : 389.

64 Pavlov, *K istorii Rossiisko-Amerikanskoy kompanii*, pp. 19–20, 27–32, 34–35.

65 Raymond H. Fisher, *The Russian Fur Trade 1550–1700*, "University of California Publications in History," vol. 31 (Berkeley and Los Angeles: University of California Press, 1943), p. 34.

66 N. Yanitsky, "Torgovlya pushnym tovarom v XVII v." ["The Fur Trade in the XVIIth Century"], *Universitetskiya izvestiya*, 52, no. 2 (September, 1912) : 1.

67 Urness, *Naturalist in Russia*, p. 66.

68 Fisher, *Russian Fur Trade*, p. 47.

69 *Ibid.*, pp. 56, 61, 119–120, 123, 184, 187, 196–197.

70 Zoologichesky institut Akademii nauk SSSR, *Atlas okhotnichikh i promyslovykh ptits i zverey SSSR* [*Atlas of Game Birds and Animals of the USSR*] (Moscow: Izdatelstvo Akademii nauk SSSR, 1950–53), 2 : 153; G. F. Muller, "Izvestie o torgakh sibirskikh" ["Information on Siberian Trade"], *Yezhemesyachnia sochineniya* . . . , 3 (February, 1756) : 181; German, "Statisticheskiya svedeniya," pt. 11, bk. 8, p. 42.

71 Zoologichesky institut Akademii nauk SSSR, *Atlas*, 2 : 156.

72 *Ibid.*, p. 154; I. F. Kilberger, *Kratkoye izvestie o russkoy torgovle, kakim obrazom onaya proizvodilas chrez vsyu Rossiyu v 1674 godu* [*Brief Information on Russian Trade and on the Way It Is Conducted throughout Russia in 1674*] (St. Petersburg: Tipografiya Departamenta narodnavo prosveshcheniya, 1820), pp. 170, 172; [Muller], "Izvestie o torgakh sibirskikh," 3 (March, 1756) : 196.

73 Yanitsky, "Torgovlya pushnym tovarom," pp. 7, 28; Muller, "Geografiya ili nyneshnoye sostoyanie," fol. 32ᵛ.

74 J. B. Du Halde, *Description Geographique, Historique, Chronologique, Politique, et Physique de l'Empire de la Chine et de la Tartarie Chinoise* . . . , 2d ed. (La Haye: Henri Scheurleer, 1736), 2 : 97.

75 Yanitsky, "Torgovlya pushnym tovarom," p. 28; Muller and Pallas, *Conquest of Siberia*, p. 121; Von Strahlenburg, *Historico-Geographical Description*, p. 335.

76 Pavlov, *K istorii Rossiisko-Amerikanskoy kompanii*, pp. 27, 34; Martin Sauer, *An Account of a Geographical and Astronomical Expedition to the Northern Parts of Russia* . . . (London: T. Cadell, Jr. and W. Davies, 1802), pp. 15, 15n.

77 Von Strahlenburg, *Historico-Geographical Description*, p. 341.

78 Pyotr Simon Pallas, *Puteshestvie po raznym provintsiyam rossiiskavo gosudarstva* [*Journey through Various Provinces of the Russian State*], trans. Vasily Zuyev, vol. 3 (St. Petersburg: Imperatorskaya Akademiya nauk, 1788), pt. 1, pp. 183, 185–186.

79 Golder, *Bering's Voyages*, 2 : 220; [Muller], "Izvestie o torgakh sibirskikh," 3 (March, 1756) : 213; [F. I. Soimonov], "Drevnyaya poslovitsa Sibir zolotoye dno" ["The Old Proverb Siberia Is a Gold Mine"],

Sochineniya i perevody . . . , 14 (November, 1761) : 466, and *Yezhemesyachnia sochineniya* . . . , 11 (January, 1764) : 52, 52n; Waxell, *Russian Expedition to America*, p. 154; Muller and Pallas, *Conquest of Siberia*, pp. 120–121, 123; Krasheninnikov, *Opisanie zemli Kamchatki*, pp. 515, 517.

80 Akademiya nauk SSSR, Institut literatury (Pushkinsky dom), *A. N. Radishchev*, 2 : 15, 21, 30; Pallas, *Puteshestvie po raznym provintsiyam*, vol. 3, pt. 1, pp. 184, 207; Urness, *Naturalist in Russia*, p. 113.

81 Adele Ogden, *The California Sea Otter Trade 1784–1848*, "University of California Publications in History," vol. 26 (Berkeley and Los Angeles: University of California Press, 1941), p. 8; Zoologichesky institut Akademii nauk SSSR, *Atlas*, 2 : 151; Shteller, "Opisanie strany Kamchatki," p. 17.

82 Zoologichesky institut Akademii nauk SSSR, *Atlas*, 2 : 152.

83 *Ibid.*, p. 153; Berkh, "Izvestie o mekhovoy torgovle," pt. 88, no. 39, p. 245; Ogden, *California Sea Otter Trade*, p. 4.

84 Elliot C. Cowdin, "The Northwest Fur Trade," *Hunt's Merchants' Magazine*, 14 (June, 1846) : 534.

85 Muller, "Geografiya ili nyneshnoye sostoyanie," fols. 31ᵛ–32; Timofey Shmalev, "Pribavlenie, uchinyonnoye Kap. T. Shmalevym, kasayushchusya do raznykh proisshestvy v Okhotskom porte, Kamchatke i okolo onykh otdalyonnykh mest" ["Supplement Made by Capt. T. Shmalev Concerning Various Occurrences in Okhotsk Port and Kamchatka and Remote Places near Them"], TsGADA, f. 199, port. 528, pt. 1, d. 12, fol. 2ᵛ; Pavlov, *K istorii Rossiisko-Amerikanskoy kompanii*, pp. 33–34.

86 Sauer, *Account of an Expedition*, p. 181.

87 M. De Lesseps, *Travels in Kamtschatka, during the Years 1787 and 1788* (London: J. Johnson, 1790), 2 : 240–241; Muller and Pallas, *Conquest of Siberia*, p. 115; Sauer, *Account of an Expedition*, p. 275; [Soimonov], "Drevnyaya poslovitsa," *Sochineniya i perevody*, 14 : 465.

88 A. I. Alekseyev, *Okhotsk—kolybel russkovo Tikhookeanskovo flota* [*Okhotsk—Cradle of the Russian Pacific Fleet*] (Khabarovsk: Khabarovskoye knizhnoye izdatelstvo, 1958), p. 77; De Lesseps, *Travels in Kamtschatka*, 1 : 94, 128; Kanagev, "Okhotsk," pp. 378–379; [K. T. Khlebnikov], "Pisma o Kamchatke" ["Letters about Kamchatka"], GPB OR, f. 4, no. 815, fol. 26; A. P., "Okhotsk," p. 140; P. Tikhmenev, *The Historical Review of Formation of the Russian-American Company* . . . , trans. Dimitri Krenov (Seattle: Works Progress Administration, 1939–40), pt. 2, pp. 4–5.

89 Berkh, *Chronological History*, pp. 17, 94–95, *passim;* J. F. G. De La Perouse, *A Voyage Round the World* . . . (London: J. Johnson, 1798), 3 : 40; V. Mamyshev, "Amerikanskiya vladeniya Rossii" ["Russia's American Possessions"], *Biblioteka dlya chteniya*, vol. 130, pts. 3–4 (March–April, 1855), p. 212; James R. Masterson and Helen Brower,

Bering's Successors 1745–1780 (Seattle: University of Washington Press, 1948), p. 31; [Soimonov], "Drevnyaya poslovitsa," *Yezhemesyachnia sochineniya,* 11 : 45.

90 De La Perouse, *Voyage Round the World,* 3 : 40. See also Akademiya nauk SSSR, Institut literatury (Pushkinsky dom), *A. N. Radishchev,* 3 : 40; Masterson and Brower, *Bering's Successors,* p. 31; Muller and Pallas, *Conquest of Siberia,* p. 114; [Soimonov], "Drevnyaya poslovitsa," *Sochineniya i perevody,* 14 : 465.

91 Berkh, *Chronological History,* p. 15; Mamyshev, "Amerikanskiya vladeniya Rossii," pp. 212, 213; [Soimonov], "Drevnyaya poslovitsa," *Sochineniya i perevody,* 14 : 465, *Yezhemesyachnia sochineniya,* 11 : 47; Masterson and Brower, *Bering's Successors,* p. 32; Muller and Pallas, *Conquest of Siberia,* p. 114.

92 De Lesseps, *Travels in Kamtschatka,* 2 : 240; Masterson and Brower, *Bering's Successors,* p. 32; Sauer, *Account of an Expedition,* p. 275; [Soimonov], "Drevnyaya poslovitsa," *Sochineniya i perevody,* 14 : 465, *Yezhemesyachnia sochineniya,* 11 : 46–47; Muller and Pallas, *Conquest of Siberia,* p. 114; [Slovtsov], *Istoricheskoye obozrenie Sibiri,* 2 : 216.

93 Masterson and Brower, *Bering's Successors,* p. 32; [Soimonov], "Drevnyaya poslovitsa," *Sochineniya i perevody,* 14 : 465; Mamyshev, "Amerikanskiya vladeniya Rossii," p. 213.

94 [Soimonov], "Drevnyaya poslovitsa," *Yezhemesyachnia sochineniya,* 11 : 50.

95 Shteller, "Opisanie strany Kamchatki," p. 152.

96 [Soimonov], "Drevnyaya poslovitsa," *Yezhemesyachnia sochineniya,* 11 : 49; A. I. Andreyev, ed., *Russian Discoveries in the Pacific and in North America in the Eighteenth and Nineteenth Centuries,* trans. Carl Ginsburg (Ann Arbor: J. W. Edwards, 1952), p. 88; Stewart Culin, ed., "The Wonderful News of the Circumnavigation," *Asia,* 20 (1920) : 372; Sauer, *Account of an Expedition,* p. 179; P. Tikhmenev, *Supplement of some Historical Documents to the Historical Review of the Formation of the Russian-American Company . . . ,* trans. Dimitri Krenov (Seattle: Works Progress Administration, 1938), p. 33; United States, Congress, Senate, *Russian Administration of Alaska and the Status of the Alaskan Natives,* 81st Cong., 2d sess., 1950, Sen. Doc. 152, p. 4.

97 Berkh, *Chronological History,* p. 16; De Lesseps, *Travels in Kamtschatka,* 2 : 241; [Soimonov], "Drevnyaya poslovitsa," *Sochineniya i perevody,* 14 : 465, *Yezhemesyachnia sochineniya,* 11 : 51; Mamyshev, "Amerikanskiya vladeniya Rossii," p. 213.

98 De Lesseps, *Travels in Kamtschatka,* 2 : 240; Masterson and Brower, *Bering's Successors,* p. 31; Muller and Pallas, *Conquest of Siberia,* p. 115; [Soimonov], "Drevnyaya poslovitsa," *Sochineniya i perevody,* 14 : 465, *Yezhemesyachnia sochineniya,* 11 : 51–52.

99 Masterson and Brower, *Bering's Successors,* p. 31, *passim;* Muller and Pallas, *Conquest of Siberia,* p. 116; Mamyshev, "Amerikanskiya vladeniya Rossii," p. 213.

100 Berkh, "Izvestie o mekhovoy torgovle," pt. 88, no. 39, pp. 247, 249, 251; Berkh, *Chronological History,* pp. 103–104, 106, 107; Sauer, *Account of an Expedition,* p. 181.

101 Akademiya nauk SSSR, Institut literatury (Pushkinsky dom), *A. N. Radishchev,* 3 : 140; Golder, "Survey of Alaska," p. 93; G. A. Sarychev, *Puteshestvie po severo-vostochnoy chasti Sibiri, Ledovitomu moryu i Vostochnomu okeanu* [*Journey through the Northeastern Part of Siberia, the Arctic Sea and the Eastern Ocean*] (Moscow: Gosudarstvennoye izdatelstvo geograficheskoy literatury, 1952), p. 52.

102 Urness, *Naturalist in Russia,* p. 118.

103 Sarychev, *Puteshestvie,* p. 52.

104 Cowdin, "Northwest Fur Trade," p. 533; Berkh, "Izvestie o mekhovoy torgovle," pt. 88, no. 39, p. 254; Berkh, *Chronological History,* p. 109.

105 Sauer, *Account of an Expedition,* Appendices, pp. 55–56.

106 Andreyev, *Russian Discoveries,* p. 71.

107 Berkh, "Izvestie o mekhovoy torgovle," pt. 88, no. 39, p. 252; Berkh, *Chronological History,* p. 107.

108 United States, Congress, Senate, *Proceedings of the Alaska Boundary Tribunal* . . . (Washington: Government Printing Office, 1904), 2 : 23–24.

Chapter 2: GEOGRAPHICAL BACKGROUND

1 This section is based largely on the following works: L. S. Berg, *Natural Regions of the U.S.S.R.,* trans. Olga Adler Titelbaum (New York: The Macmillan Company, 1950); and S. P. Suslov, *Physical Geography of Asiatic Russia,* trans. Noah D. Gershevsky (San Francisco and London: W. H. Freeman and Company, 1961).

2 G. P. Gorskov and V. V. Popov, "A Short Review of the Seismicity of the Kamchatka Peninsula," *Bulletin of the Kamchatka Volcanological Station,* no. 4 (1938), p. 25.

3 M. P. De Semenov, *La Russie Extra-Européene et Polaire* (Paris: Paul Dupont, 1900), p. 91.

4 Byvaly, "Pochva i klimat Kamchatki" ["The Soil and Climate of Kamchatka"], *Zemledelchesky zhurnal* . . . , no. 2 (1836), p. 191; Suslov, *Physical Geography,* p. 392.

5 Byvaly, "Pochva i klimat Kamchatki," p. 189.

6 Anton Chekhov, *The Island: A Journey to Sakhalin,* trans. Luba and Michael Terpak (New York: Washington Square Press, 1967), p. 80.

7 Berg, *Natural Regions,* p. 340; Suslov, *Physical Geography,* p. 395.

8 Berg, *Natural Regions,* p. 342; Suslov, *Physical Geography,* p. 399.

9 This section is based largely on the following works: M. G. Levin and L. P. Potapov, eds., *Narody Sibiri* [*Peoples of Siberia*] (Moscow and

Leningrad: Izdatelstvo Akademii nauk SSSR, 1956); and S. A. Tokarev, *Etnografiya narodov SSSR* [*Ethnography of the Peoples of the USSR*] (Moscow: Izdatelstvo Moskovskovo universiteta, 1958).

10 Muller and Pallas, *Conquest of Siberia*, p. 110.

11 Adolph Erman, *Travels in Siberia* . . . , trans. W. D. Cooley (Philadelphia: Lea and Blanchard, 1850), 1 : 295.

12 Lillian Hellman, ed., *The Selected Letters of Anton Chekhov*, trans. Sidonie Lederer (New York: Farrar, Straus and Company, 1955), p. 113.

13 Erman, *Travels in Siberia*, p. 249.

14 F. Veselago, ed., *Materialy dlya istorii russkavo flota* [*Materials for the History of the Russian Fleet*] (St. Petersburg: Tipografiya Morskavo ministerstva, 1880–1904), 17 : 314.

15 Peter Dobell, *Travels in Kamtchatka and Siberia* . . . (London: Henry Colburn and Richard Bentley, 1830), 1 : 68, 2 : 121.

16 [Nikolay V. Semivsky], *Noveishiya, lyubopytnia i dostovernia povestvovaniya o Vostochnoy Sibiri* . . . [*The Latest Interesting and Authentic Accounts about Eastern Siberia* . . .] (St. Petersburg: Voyennaya tipografiya Glavnavo shtaba, 1817), pp. 224–225.

17 Cochrane, *Narrative of a Pedestrian Journey*, p. 55.

18 Yuri Semyonov, *The Conquest of Siberia*, trans. E. W. Dickes (London: George Routledge & Sons Ltd., 1944), p. 147.

19 De Lesseps, *Travels in Kamtschatka*, 2 : 222.

20 A. Lobanov-Rostovsky, *Russia and Asia* (Ann Arbor: The George Wahr Publishing Co., 1951), p. 135.

21 A. Silnitsky, "Mery pravitelstva dlya podnyatiya blagosostoyaniya Gizhiginskavo kraya, s 1819–1840 g." ["Measures of the Government for Improving the Well-Being of Gizhiga Kray, 1819–1840"], *Zapiski Priamurskavo otdela Imperatorskavo russkavo geograficheskavo obshchestva*, 4, no. 1 (1898) : 53–73.

22 *Sibirskaya sovetskaya entsiklopediya* [*Siberian Soviet Encyclopedia*] (Novosibirsk: Zapadno-Sibirskoye otdelenie Ogiz, 1929–32), 1 : 21.

23 De Lesseps, *Travels in Kamtschatka*, 2 : 239n.

24 Lobanov-Rostovsky, *Russia and Asia*, pp. 135, 141.

25 M. L'Abbé Chappe D'Auteroche, *A Journey into Siberia, Made by the Order of the King of France*, 2d ed. (London: Faden and Jefferys, 1774), p. 372.

26 Akademiya nauk SSSR, Institut literatury (Pushkinsky dom), *A. N. Radishchev*, 3 : 137.

27 F. Veselago, *Kratkaya istoriya russkavo flota* [*Brief History of the Russian Fleet*] (St. Petersburg: Tipografiya V. Demakova, 1893), pt. 1, p. 290.

28 A. P., "Okhotsk," p. 138; Russia, Pravitelstvuyushchy senat, *Senatsky arkhiv*, 5 : 206.

29 A. R. Cederberg, ed., "Heinrich Fick. Ein Beitrag zur russischen Geschichte des XVIII. Jahrhunderts" ["Heinrich Fick. A Contribu-

tion to Russian History of the XVIIIth Century"], *Acta et Commentationes Universitatis Tartuensis (Dorpatensis)*, ser. B, 17 (1930) : 136.
30 F. Vrangel, "Putevia zapiski admirala barona F. P. Vrangelya" ["Travel Notes of Admiral Baron F. P. Wrangel"], *Istorichesky vestnik*, 18 (1884) : 172.
31 Flot Leitenant Golovnin, *Puteshestvie na shlyupe "Diana" iz Kronshtadta v Kamchatku . . . [Voyage on the Sloop "Diana" from Kronstadt to Kamchatka . . .]* (Moscow: Gosudarstvennoye izdatelstvo geograficheskoy literatury, 1961), p. 351.
32 Cochrane, *Narrative of a Pedestrian Journey*, p. 294.
33 Sir George Simpson, *Narrative of a Journey Round the World . . .* (London: Henry Colburn, 1847), 2 : 233.
34 Golovnin, *Puteshestvie na shlyupe "Diana,"* p. 351n.
35 Byvaly, "Pochva i klimat Kamchatki," p. 187.

Chapter 3: THE PROBLEM OF PROVISIONMENT

1 V. I. Ogorodnikov, *Ocherk istorii Sibiri do nachala XIX st. [A Sketch of the History of Siberia up to the Beginning of the XIXth Century]* (Irkutsk: n.p., 1921), pt. 2, no. 3, p. 11.
2 G. F. Miller [Muller], *Istoriya Sibiri [History of Siberia]* (Moscow and Leningrad: Izdatelstvo Akademii nauk SSSR, 1937–41), 2 : 14.
3 *Ibid.*, p. 51.
4 Von Strahlenburg, *Historico-Geographical Description*, pp. 444–445.
5 Chappe D'Auteroche, *Journey into Siberia*, p. 57.
6 Pervy sibirsky komitet, "O predpolozheniyakh Nachalnika Kamchatki," d. 167, fols. 2ᵛ, 10ᵛ; V. Vagin, *Istoricheskiya svedeniya o deyatelnosti grafa M. M. Speranskavo v Sibiri s 1819 po 1822 god [Historical Information about the Activities of Count M. M. Speransky in Siberia from 1819 to 1822]* (St. Petersburg: Tipografiya Vtoravo otdeleniya Sobstvennoy Ye. I. V. Kantselyarii, 1872), vol. 2, p. 90, suppl., p. 473.
7 Cochrane, *Narrative of a Pedestrian Journey*, p. 304.
8 Pervy sibirsky komitet, "O predpolozheniyakh Nachalnika Kamchatki," d. 166, fols. 9ᵛ, 36, 183, d. 168, fols. 105ᵛ, 109ᵛ.
9 Timofey Shmalev, "Kratkoye o Kamchatke obyasnenie uchinyonnoye Kapitanom Timofeiyem Shmalevym" ["Brief Explanation about Kamchatka Made by Captain Timofey Shmalev"], TsGADA, f. 199, port. 539, pt. 1, d. 8, fol. 1ᵛ; Timofey Shmalev, "Kratkoye opisanie o Kamchatke . . ." ["Brief Description of Kamchatka . . ."], *Opyt trudov Volnavo rossiiskavo sobraniya pri Imperatorskom moskovskom universitete*, pt. 1 (1774), p. 198.
10 Grigory Spassky, "Izvestie o Kamchatskoy dukhovnoy missii" ["Information about the Kamchatka Ecclesiastical Mission"], *Sibirsky vestnik*, pt. 17 (1822), p. 89; Russia, *Polnoye sobranie zakonov*, 1st ser., vol. 15, doc. 10,820, p. 187.

11 V. A. Divin, "Vtoraya Sibirsko-tikhookeanskaya ekspeditsiya i voprosy khozyaistvennavo osvoyeniya Dalnevo Vostoka" ["The Second Siberia-Pacific Ocean Expedition and Questions of the Economic Development of the Far East"], *Letopis Severa*, 2 (1957) : 168–169.

12 Arktichesky nauchno-issledovatelsky institut, *Istorichesky pamyatnik russkovo arkticheskovo moreplavaniya XVII veka* [*Historical Memorial of Russian Arctic Navigation of the XVIIth Century*] (Moscow and Leningrad: Izdatelstvo Glavsevmorputi, 1951), p. 90; Krasheninnikov, *Opisanie zemli Kamchatki*, p. 258.

13 Waxell, *Russian Expedition to America*, p. 143.

14 *Doklad komiteta ob ustroistve russkikh amerikanskikh kolony* [*Report of the Committee on the Organization of the Russian American Colonies*] (St. Petersburg: Tipografiya Departamenta vneshney torgovli, 1863–64), pt. 1, p. 379.

15 This section is based largely on Russell Blair, "The Food Habits of the East Slavs" (Ph.D. diss., University of Pennsylvania, Department of Slavic and Baltic Studies, 1956).

16 Simpson, *Narrative of a Journey*, 1 : 269.

17 De Lesseps, *Travels in Kamtschatka*, 2 : 269; Captain A. J. Von Krusenstern, *Voyage Round the World in the Years 1803, 1804, 1805, & 1806*, trans. Richard Belgrave Hoppner (London: John Murray, 1813), 2 : 110; Sarychev, *Puteshestvie*, p. 54; Waxell, *Russian Expedition to America*, p. 124; Erman, *Travels in Siberia*, 1 : 290; Pavel Kuzmishchev, "O lesakh i kustarnikakh, rastushchikh v Kamchatke" ["Concerning the Trees and Shrubs Growing in Kamchatka"], *Lesnoy zhurnal* . . . , 4 (1836) : 119.

18 Waxell, *Russian Expedition to America*, p. 120.

19 Golder, *Bering's Voyages*, 2 : 5; Pyotr Pekarsky, *Istoriya Imperatorskoy akademii nauk* [*History of the Imperial Academy of Sciences*] (St. Petersburg: Tipografiya Imperatorskoy akademii nauk, 1870), 1 : 598–599.

20 Krasheninnikov, *Opisanie zemli Kamchatki*, p. 205.

21 *Ibid.*, p. 300; Shteller, "Opisanie strany Kamchatki," pp. 50–51, 177, 207.

22 Krasheninnikov, *Opisanie zemli Kamchatki*, p. 300; Shteller, "Opisanie strany Kamchatki," pp. 50–51; Anonymous, "Poluostrov Kamchatka" ["The Kamchatka Peninsula"], *Rusky invalid*, no. 94 (November 24/December 6, 1815), p. 375.

23 [Khlebnikov], "Pisma o Kamchatke," fol. 18ᵛ.

24 Jacob Lindenau, "Opisanie sukhoputnovo puteshestviya iz Yakutska v Okhotsk 1741 g." ["Description of a Land Journey from Yakutsk to Okhotsk of 1741"] (in German), TsGADA, f. 199, port. 511, pt. 1, d. 1, fol. 16ᵛ; Sarychev, *Puteshestvie*, pp. 55–56.

25 Vagin, *Istoricheskiya svedeniya*, vol. 2, suppl., p. 418; Shteller, "Opisanie strany Kamchatki," pp. 199, 213, 250; [Khlebnikov], "Pisma o Kamchatke," fol. 18; Krasheninnikov, *Opisanie zemli Kamchatki*, p.

304; Anonymous, "Okhotsky kray," ["Okhotsk kray"], *Vostochnoye Pomorye*, no. 23 (November 6/18, 1865), p. 135; Sarychev, *Puteshestvie*, p. 55.

26 Muller, *Voyages from Asia to America*, p. 61.

27 Andreyev, *Russkie otkrytiya v Tikhom okeane i Severnoy Amerike v XVIII veke* [*Russian Discoveries in the Pacific Ocean and in North America in the XVIIIth Century*] (Moscow: Gosudarstvennoye izdatelstvo geograficheskoy literatury, 1948), pp. 114–115; Sven Vaksel, *Vtoraya kamchatskaya ekspeditsiya Vitusa Beringa* [*Vitus Bering's Second Kamchatka Expedition*] (Leningrad and Moscow: Izdatelstvo Glavsevmorputi, 1940), p. 149; Waxell, *Russian Expedition to America*, p. 158.

28 Krasheninnikov, *Opisanie zemli Kamchatki*, p. 250.

29 Shteller, "Opisanie strany Kamchatki," p. 141.

30 Flot Kapitan Rikord, "O sostoyanii poluostrova Kamchatki i o blagotvoritelnykh zavedeniyakh v onoy uchrezhdayemykh" ["Concerning the Condition of the Peninsula of Kamchatka and the Charitable Institutions Founded in It"], *Zhurnal Imperatorskavo chelovekolyubivavo obshchestva*, 8 (April, 1819) : 9; Vagin, *Istoricheskiya svedeniya*, 2 : 27; P. K., "O vozmozhnosti uluchsheniya Selskavo Khozyaistva v Kamchatke i bliz Tigilskoy kreposti" ["Concerning the Possibility of Improving Agriculture in Kamchatka and Near Tigilsk Fortress"], *Zemledelchesky zhurnal . . .* , no. 2 (1833), p. 301.

31 Shteller, "Opisanie strany Kamchatki," p. 160.

32 Waxell, *Russian Expedition to America*, p. 145.

33 Krasheninnikov, *Opisanie zemli Kamchatki*, p. 321; Sarychev, *Puteshestvie*, p. 56.

34 Sauer, *Account of an Expedition*, p. 36.

35 [Khlebnikov], "Pisma o Kamchatke," fol. 20ᵛ.

36 [Captain Golovnin], *Sochineniya i perevody Vasiliya Mikhailovicha Golovnina* [*The Writings and the Translations of Vasily Mikhailovich Golovnin*], vol. 5 (St. Petersburg: Tipografiya Morskavo ministerstva, 1865), p. 48.

37 Shmalev, "Kratkoye opisanie o Kamchatke," p. 196; N. Shch. [Shchukin], *Poyezdka v Yakutsk* [*Journey to Yakutsk*] (St. Petersburg: Tipografiya Konrada Vingebera, 1833), p. 126.

38 Krasheninnikov, *Opisanie zemli Kamchatki*, pp. 228, 230, 506, 517, 689–690; Shteller, "Opisanie strany Kamchatki," pp. 94–95, 105–106, 113; Cochrane, *Narrative of a Pedestrian Journey*, pp. 146, 225, 289; Cook [and King], *Voyage to the Pacific Ocean*, 3 : 336; De Lesseps, *Travels in Kamtschatka*, 1 : 92; [Khlebnikov], "Pisma o Kamchatke," fol. 10ᵛ; Waxell, *Russian Expedition to America*, pp. 142–143.

39 Krasheninnikov, *Opisanie zemli Kamchatki*, p. 228.

40 *Ibid.*, pp. 178, 227; [Khlebnikov], "Pisma o Kamchatke," fol. 21; Sauer, *Account of an Expedition*, p. 299; Muller, "Geografiya ili nyneshnoye sostoyanie," fols. 28ᵛ–29.

41 Sauer, *Account of an Expedition,* p. 181; A. Sgibnev, "Istorichesky ocherk glavneishikh sobyty v Kamchatke" ["Historical Sketch of the Main Events in Kamchatka"], *Morskoy sbornik,* 102 (June, 1869) : 50, 103 (August, 1869) : 33; Sgibnev, "Okhotsky port," 105, no. 12 : 18.

42 Krasheninnikov, *Opisanie zemli Kamchatki,* p. 502.

43 Alekseyev, *Okhotsk,* p. 122; De Lesseps, *Travels in Kamtschatka,* 1 : 147–148.

44 Krasheninnikov, *Opisanie zemli Kamchatki,* pp. 304, 501.

45 Waxell, *Russian Expedition to America,* p. 140.

46 Krasheninnikov, *Opisanie zemli Kamchatki,* p. 201.

47 Rezanov, "Zapiska gorodnichevo Nizhne-Kamchatska Voyevodskovo," fol. 4.

48 Krasheninnikov, *Opisanie zemli Kamchatki,* p. 303; Waxell, *Russian Expedition to America,* p. 141.

49 G. I. Davydov, *Dvukratnoye puteshestvie v Ameriku morskikh ofitserov Khvostova i Davydova* [*Double Voyage to America of the Naval Officers Khvostov and Davydov*] (St. Petersburg: Morskaya tipografiya, 1810), 1 : 144; Krasheninnikov, *Opisanie zemli Kamchatki,* pp. 205, 517.

50 Krasheninnikov, *Opisanie zemli Kamchatki,* p. 501; Shteller, "Opisanie strany Kamchatki," p. 73.

51 Rezanov, "Zapiska gorodnichevo Nizhne-Kamchatska Voyevodskovo," fol. 4.

52 Shteller, "Opisanie strany Kamchatki," pp. 165, 462.

53 *Ibid.,* pp. 170, 463; Krasheninnikov, *Opisanie zemli Kamchatki,* p. 400.

54 Krasheninnikov, *Opisanie zemli Kamchatki,* p. 253; Shteller, "Opisanie strany Kamchatki," pp. 165*n,* 171.

55 Dr. Langsdorff, "Remarques sur le Kamtschatka et sur ses productions naturelles" ["Remarks on Kamchatka and on Its Natural Productions"], *Memoires de la Société Impériale des Naturalistes de Moscou,* 3 (1812) : 101; Rikord, "O sostoyanii poluostrova Kamchatki," p. 9.

56 Cochrane, *Narrative of a Pedestrian Journey,* pp. 252, 292.

57 De Lesseps, *Travels in Kamtschatka,* 1 : 116.

58 H. Beaumont, "Essais d'agriculture dans le Kamchatka" ["Attempts at Agriculture in Kamchatka"], *Memoires de la Société de Géographie de Genève,* 1 (1860) : 126; K. A. Shakhovskoy, "Mnenie, o sposobakh prodovolstviya zhiteley Okhotskavo i Gizhiginskavo uyezdov" ["Opinion on the Ways of Provisioning the Inhabitants of Okhotsk and Gizhiga Uyezds"], *Severny arkhiv,* pt. 5 (1823), p. 351; Silnitsky, "Mery pravitelstva," p. 28; Vagin, *Istoricheskiya svedeniya,* vol. 2, suppl., p. 417.

Chapter 4: INTRODUCTION

1 Russia, Gosudarstvenny sovet, *Arkhiv Gosudarstvennavo soveta* [*Archive of the State Council*] (St. Petersburg: Tipografiya Vtoravo otde-

leniya Sobstvennoy Ye. I. V. Kantselyarii, 1869–1904), vol. 1, pt. 2, p. 79.

2 V. I. Shunkov, "Geografiya khlebnykh tsen Sibiri XVII v." ["Geography of the Grain Prices of Siberia of the XVIIth Century"], *Voprosy geografii*, no. 31 (1953), p. 178.

3 Akademiya nauk SSSR, Institut literatury (Pushkinsky dom), *A. N. Radishchev*, 2 : 158.

4 Komitet Severa pri Russkom geograficheskom obshchestve i Severnaya kolonizatsionnaya ekspeditsiya, *Ocherki po istorii kolonizatsii Severa i Sibiri* [*Sketches on the History of the Colonization of the North and Siberia*], 2d ed. (Petrograd: Redaktsionno-izdatelsky komitet Narodnovo komissariata zemledeliya, 1922), p. 56; N. N. Kozmin, *Ocherki proshlavo i nastoyashchavo Sibiri* [*Sketches of Past and Present Siberia*] (St. Petersburg: Tipografiya "Pechatny trud," 1910), pp. 1–2; Shunkov, "Geografiya khlebnykh tsen," pp. 170–178.

5 Russia, Arkheograficheskaya kommissiya, *Russkaya istoricheskaya biblioteka* [*Russian Historical Library*] (St. Petersburg: Tipografiya Br. Panteleyevykh, 1872–1927), vol. 2, doc. 60, pp. 126–137.

6 Orlova, *Otkrytiya russkikh zemleprokhodtsev*, doc. 15, pp. 84–89; Russia, Arkheograficheskaya kommissiya, *Dopolneniya k Aktam istoricheskim*, vol. 4, doc. 77, pp. 196–197, vol. 7, doc. 16, pp. 103–122; K. Rozhdestvenskaya, "Dorogi v Sibir" ["Roads to Siberia"], *Uralsky sovremennik*, 9 (1944) : 110.

7 Kozmin, *Ocherki Sibiri*, p. 1; V. I. Ogorodnikov, *Tuzemnoye i russkoye zemledelie na Amure v XVII v.* [*Aboriginal and Russian Agriculture on the Amur in the XVIIth Century*], "Trudy Gosudarstvennovo dalnevostochnovo universiteta," 3d ser., no. 4 (Vladivostok: Tipografiya Gosudarstvennovo dalnevostochnovo universiteta, 1927), p. 8.

8 Orlova, *Otkrytiya russkikh zemleprokhodtsev*, doc. 15, pp. 84–89.

9 Shunkov, "Geografiya khlebnykh tsen," pp. 178, 187, 200.

10 Ogorodnikov, *Tuzemnoye i russkoye zemledelie*, p. 8.

11 Russia, Arkheograficheskaya kommissiya, *Akty istoricheskie* [*Historical Acts*] (St. Petersburg: Tipografiya Vtorova otdeleniya Sobstvennoy Ye. I. V. Kantselyarii, 1841–42), vol. 2, doc. 261, pp. 313–314.

12 *Ibid.*, vol. 5, doc. 120, p. 190.

13 A. N. Kopylov, "Yeniseisky zemledelchesky raion v seredine XVII v. i yevo znachenie dlya snabzheniya Vostochnoy Sibiri khlebom" ["The Yeniseisk Agricultural Region in the Middle of the XVIIth Century and Its Significance for the Supply of Eastern Siberia with Grain"], *Trudy Moskovskovo gosudarstvennovo istoriko-arkhivnovo instituta*, 10 (1957) : 118, 122, 126–127, 131–132, 134.

14 Ilimskaya voyevodskaya kantselyariya, "Sbornik del, tom I" ["Collection of Files, Volume I"], TsGADA, f. 494, op. 2, d. 285, sv. 39, fols. 38–40ᵛ; V. N. Sherstoboyev, "Zemledelie severnovo Predbaikalya v XVII–XVIII vv." ["The Agriculture of Northern Prebaikalia in the

XVIIth–XVIIIth Centuries"], in *Materialy po istorii zemledeliya SSSR,* ed. B. D. Grekov (Moscow and Leningrad: Izdatelstvo Akademii nauk SSSR, 1952), collection 1, pp. 281–286, 291–292, 299.

15 V. N. Sherstoboyev, *Ilimskaya pashnya* [*The Ilimsk Plowland*] (Irkutsk: Irkutskoye oblastnoye gosudarstvennoye izdatelstvo i Irkutskoye knizhnoye izdatelstvo, 1949–57), 2 : 289; Sherstoboyev, "Zemledelie severnovo Predbaikalya," p. 281.

16 Vasily Myatlev, "Instruktsiya ot General-Leitenanta, Kavelera i Sibirskavo Gubernatora Myatleva opredelyonnomu v Okhotsk Glavnomu Komandiru Kollezhskomu Sovetniku Shapilovu 22 fevr. 1757 g." ["Instructions from General-Lieutenant, Cavalier and Siberian Governor Myatlev Appointing Collegiate Councillor Shapilov Chief Commander at Okhotsk Feb. 22, 1757"], TsGADA, f. 199, port. 528, pt. 1, d. 2, fol. 12^{v}.

17 Sherstoboyev, *Ilimskaya pashnya,* 2 : 289.

18 *Ibid.,* p. 300.

19 Alkor and Grekov, *Kolonialnaya politika Moskovskovo gosudarstva,* doc. 38, pp. 87–90; A. Izbekova, "Materialy o razvitii khlebopashestva v Yakutii v XVIII–XIX vekakh" ["Materials on the Development of Grain Cultivation in Yakutia in the XVIIIth–XIXth Centuries"], *Uchyonie zapiski Instituta yazyka, literatury i istorii Yakutskovo filiala Akademii nauk SSSR,* no. 3 (1955), p. 80.

20 Sherstoboyev, *Ilimskaya pashnya,* 2 : 289.

21 [Slovtsov], *Istoricheskoye obozrenie Sibiri,* 2 : 198n.

22 O. I. Kashik, "Torgovlya v Vostochnoy Sibiri v XVII–nachale XVIII vv." ["Trade in Eastern Siberia in the XVIIth to the Beginning of the XVIIIth Centuries"], in *Voprosy istorii Sibiri i Dalnevo Vostoka,* ed. Akademiya nauk SSSR, Sibirskoye otdelenie (Novosibirsk: Izdatelstvo Sibirskovo otdeleniya AN SSSR, 1961), p. 190.

23 Sherstoboyev, "Zemledelie severnovo Predbaikalya," pp. 289–290.

24 *Ibid.,* pp. 281, 295–296; Sherstoboyev, *Ilimskaya pashnya,* 2 : 447.

25 Dobell, *Travels in Kamtchatka and Siberia,* 2 : 21, 69–70; M. Gedenstrom, *Otryvki o Sibiri* [*Excerpts on Siberia*] (St. Petersburg: Ministerstvo vnutrennikh del, 1830), p. 80; Al. Markov, *Russkie na Vostochnom okeane* [*Russians on the Eastern Ocean*], 2d ed. (St. Petersburg: Tipografiya A. Dmitriyeva, 1856), pp. 10–11; Sauer, *Account of an Expedition,* pp. 22, 27; Vrangel, "Putevia zapiski," p. 169; Ferdinand Von Wrangell, *Narrative of an Expedition to the Polar Sea . . .* (London: James Madden and Co., 1840), pp. 8, 9n.

26 Vagin, *Istoricheskiya svedeniya,* 2 : 22.

27 V. I. Shunkov, "Geograficheskoye razmeshchenie sibirskovo zemledeliya v XVII veke" ["Geographical Distribution of Siberian Agriculture in the XVIIth Century"], *Voprosy geografii,* no. 20 (1950), p. 235.

28 Shcheglov, *Kronologichesky perechen,* p. 331.

29 F. G. Safronov, *Russkie krestyane v Yakutii (XVII–nachalo XX vv.)* [*Russian Peasants in Yakutia (XVIIth to the Beginning of the XXth*

Centuries)] (Yakutsk: Yakutskoye knizhnoye izdatelstvo, 1961), p. 318.

30 [Yekaterina Avdeyeva], *Zapiski i zamechaniya o Sibiri* [*Notes and Remarks about Siberia*] (Moscow: Tipografiya Nikolaya Stepanova, 1837), p. 21.

31 *Ibid.,* p. 28.

32 Perry McDonough Collins, *Siberian Journey: Down the Amur to the Pacific, 1856–1857,* ed. Charles Vevier (Madison: University of Wisconsin Press, 1962), p. 167.

33 Akademiya nauk SSSR, Institut yazyka, literatury i istorii Yakutskovo filiala AN SSSR, *Istoriya Yakutskoy ASSR* [*History of the Yakut ASSR*], vol. 2 (Moscow: Izdatelstvo Akademii nauk SSSR, 1957), pp. 14–16; S. V. Bakhrushin and S. A. Tokarev, eds., *Yakutiya v XVII veke* [*Yakutia in the XVIIth Century*] (Yakutsk: Yakutskoye knizhnoye izdatelstvo, 1953), pp. 67, 72–73; Levin and Potapov, *Narody Sibiri,* pp. 271, 272.

34 Anonymous, "Opisanie Yakutskoy provintsii" ["Description of Yakutsk Province"], GPB OR, Ermitazhnoye sobranie, no. 238 6-f, pp. 67–68.

35 Levin and Potapov, *Narody Sibiri,* pp. 272–274; Dobell, *Travels in Kamtchatka and Siberia,* 1 : 345, 2 : 36–37.

36 Bakhrushin and Tokarev, *Yakutiya,* pp. 67–69; Levin and Potapov, *Narody Sibiri,* p. 281.

37 For example: Cochrane, *Narrative of a Pedestrian Journey,* p. 327; Davydov, *Dvukratnoye puteshestvie v Ameriku,* 1 : 63; Sauer, *Account of an Expedition,* p. 114.

38 Gedenstrom, *Otryvki o Sibiri,* p. 93; Rear-Admiral Minitsky, "Opisanie Yakutskoy oblasti" ["Description of Yakutsk Oblast"], *Zhurnal Ministerstva vnutrennikh del,* bk. 6 (1830), p. 159; Levin and Potapov, *Narody Sibiri,* p. 272.

39 Safronov, *Russkie krestyane v Yakutii,* pp. 243, 262; V. I. Shunkov, "K voprosu o kharaktere khlebooborota Sibiri v XVII v." ["Concerning the Question of the Character of Siberia's Grain Turnover in the XVIIth Century"], in *Voprosy sotsialno-ekonomicheskoy istorii i istochnikovedeniya perioda feodalizma v Rossii,* ed. Akademiya nauk SSSR, Institut istorii (Moscow: Izdatelstvo Akademii nauk SSSR, 1961), pp. 79–80.

Chapter 5: ROUTES AND CARRIERS

1 Myatlev, "Instruktsiya ot General-Leitenanta," fol. 12ᵛ.

2 Vrangel, "Putevia zapiski," p. 169; [Slovtsov], *Istoricheskoye obozrenie Sibiri,* 2 : 140; Major Termin, "Kratkoye obozrenie reki Leny i sudokhodstva po onoy" ["Brief Survey of the Lena River and of Navigation on It"], *Zhurnal putey soobshcheniya,* no. 32 (1835), p. 83.

3 Anonymous, "Opisanie Yakutskoy provintsii," p. 5.

4 Dobell, *Travels in Kamtschatka and Siberia,* 2 : 79.

5 Akademiya nauk Soyuza Sovetskikh Sotsialisticheskikh Respublik (SSSR), *Pamyati Dekabristov* [*Remembrances of the Decembrists*] (Leningrad: Izdatelstvo Akademii nauk SSSR, 1926), 2 : 195.

6 [Avdeyeva], *Zapiski i zamechaniya,* p. 20; Markov, *Russkie na Vostochnom okeane,* pp. 7–8.

7 [Avdeyeva], *Zapiski i zamechaniya,* p. 28.

8 Markov, *Russkie na Vostochnom okeane,* pp. 7–8.

9 Ivan Miller, "Moy put iz Irkutska v Kirensk (v 1814 godu)" ["My Route from Irkutsk to Kirensk (in 1814)"], *Kazanskaya izvestiya,* no. 52 (June 28/July 10, 1816), p. 259.

10 Termin, "Kratkoye obozrenie reki Leny," p. 77.

11 Sherstoboyev, *Ilimskaya pashnya,* 1 : 570.

12 Yu. A. Gagemeister, *Statisticheskoye obozrenie Sibiri* [*Statistical Survey of Siberia*] (St. Petersburg: Tipografiya II otdeleniya Sobstvennoy Yevo Imperatorskavo Velichestva Kantselyarii, 1854), pt. 2, p. 653; Orlova, *Otkrytiya russkikh zemleprokhodtsev,* doc. 173, pp. 448–450; Sauer, *Account of an Expedition,* p. 20*n;* Shch., *Poyezdka v Yakutsk,* p. 109; Termin, "Kratkoye obozrenie reki Leny," pp. 81–82.

13 Dobell, *Travels in Kamtchatka and Siberia,* 2 : 4*n;* Gagemeister, *Statisticheskoye obozrenie Sibiri,* pt. 2, p. 653; Minitsky, "Opisanie Yakutskoy oblasti," pp. 173–174; Shch., *Poyezdka v Yakutsk,* pp. 101–111; Sherstoboyev, *Ilimskaya pashnya,* 2 : 299; Termin, "Kratkoye obozrenie reki Leny," p. 82; Vrangel, "Putevia zapiski," p. 169.

14 Gagemeister, *Statisticheskoye obozrenie Sibiri,* pt. 2, p. 653; Shch., *Poyezdka v Yakutsk,* pp. 26–27, 110; Termin, "Kratkoye obozrenie reki Leny," p. 82.

15 Ivan Islenyev, "Perechen dnevnoy zapiski g. Islenyeva" ["List of the Daily Notes of Mr. Islenyev"], *Novia yezhemesyachnia sochineniya,* pt. 23 (1788), p. 13; Minitsky, "Opisanie Yakutskoy oblasti," p. 174; Safronov, *Russkie krestyane v Yakutii,* pp. 258, 319; Sherstoboyev, *Ilimskaya pashnya,* 2 : 296.

16 Minitsky, "Opisanie Yakutskoy oblasti," p. 174.

17 *Ibid.,* p. 173; Safronov, *Russkie krestyane v Yakutii,* pp. 258, 263–264; Shch., *Poyezdka v Yakutsk,* pp. 29–30, 111; Sherstoboyev, *Ilimskaya pashnya,* 1 : 570, 2 : 291; Termin, "Kratkoye obozrenie reki Leny," p. 83.

18 Shch., *Poyezdka v Yakutsk,* p. 24.

19 I. Bulychev, *Puteshestvie po Vostochnoy Sibiri* [*Journey through Eastern Siberia*] (St. Petersburg: n.p., 1856), pt. 1, p. 70; G. I. Granik, "Letopis sudokhodstva na rekakh Yakutii" ["A Chronicle of Navigation on the Rivers of Yakutia"], *Letopis Severa,* 3 (1962) : 213; Markov, *Russkie na Vostochnom okeane,* p. 9; Minitsky, "Opisanie Yakutskoy oblasti," p. 174.

20 M. I. Belov, *Arkticheskoye moreplavanie s drevneishikh vremen do serediny XIX veka* [*Arctic Navigation from Antiquity until the Middle of the XIXth Century*], vol. 1 of *Istoriya otkrytiya i osvoyeniya Sever-*

novo morskovo puti, ed. Ya. Ya. Gakkel, A. P. Okladnikov, and M. B. Chernenko (Moscow: Izdatelstvo "Morskoy transport," 1956), p. 199; Russia, Arkheograficheskaya kommissiya, *Dopolneniya k Aktam istoricheskim,* vol. 10, doc. 14, p. 37; Sherstoboyev, *Ilimskaya pashnya,* 1 : 570.

21 Anonymous, "Opisanie Irkutskoy gubernii" ["Description of Irkutsk Province"], TsGIAL, f. 1,350, op. 312, d. 239, fol. 44ʳ.

22 [Semivsky], *Noveishiya, lyubopytnia i dostovernia povestvovaniya,* p. 149; Shch., *Poyezdka v Yakutsk,* p. 141.

23 Safronov, *Russkie krestyane v Yakutii,* p. 265; Belov, *Arkticheskoye moreplavanie,* p. 203.

24 Sherstoboyev, *Ilimskaya pashnya,* 2 : 295-296.

25 *Ibid.,* p. 289; F. G. Safronov, *Gorod Yakutsk v XVII–nachale XIX vekov* [*The Town of Yakutsk in the XVIIth to the Beginning of the XIXth Centuries*] (Yakutsk: Yakutskoye knizhnoye izdatelstvo, 1957), p. 59; Safronov, *Russkie krestyane v Yakutii,* p. 318.

26 Islenyev, "Perechen dnevnoy zapiski," p. 13.

27 G. F. Muller, "Opisanie reki Leny ot Verkholenskavo ostroga vniz do goroda Yakutska" ["Description of the Lena River from Verkholensk Ostrog Downstream to the Town of Yakutsk"], TsGADA, f. 199, port. 517, pt. 1, d. 20, fols. 52ʳ-53ʳ; Anonymous, "Opisanie Yakutskoy provintsii," pp. 34-36.

28 Termin, "Kratkoye obozrenie reki Leny," pp. 78-79.

29 Islenyev, "Perechen dnevnoy zapiski," pp. 7-8.

30 Minitsky, "Opisanie Yakutskoy oblasti," pp. 5, 174; Sauer, *Account of an Expedition,* p. 28.

31 Shch., *Poyezdka v Yakutsk,* p. 141.

32 Anonymous, "Opisanie Yakutskoy provintsii," p. 40.

33 [Semivsky], *Noveishiya, lyubopytnia i dostovernia povestvovaniya,* p. 149; Termin, "Kratkoye obozrenie reki Leny," pp. 77, 79-80, 82-83; Davydov, *Dvukratnoye puteshestvie v Ameriku,* 1 : 24; Minitsky, "Opisanie Yakutskoy oblasti," pp. 174-175; Von Wrangell, *Narrative of an Expedition,* p. 4.

34 Minitsky, "Opisanie Yakutskoy oblasti," pp. 167, 169.

35 Culin, "Wonderful News of the Circumnavigation," pp. 505-506.

36 L. I. Rikord, "Vospominaniya L. I. Rikord" ["Recollections of L. I. Rikord"], *Russkaya starina,* 24 (1879) : 44.

37 De Lesseps, *Travels in Kamtschatka,* 2 : 266.

38 Akademiya nauk SSSR, Institut istorii, *S. V. Bakhrushin: nauchnie trudy* [*S. V. Bakhrushin: Scientific Works*] (Moscow: Izdatelstvo Akademii nauk SSSR, 1952–59), vol. 3, pt. 1, p. 136; Kanagev, "Okhotsk," p. 369; A. Sgibnev, "Bolshoy kamchatsky naryad" ["The Great Kamchatka Detail"], *Morskoy sbornik,* vol. 99, pt. 2 (December, 1868), pp. 131, 133-134; Timofey Shmalev, "Izvestiya Kap. Shmaleva o byvshikh prezhde v Sibirskikh otdalyonnykh mestakh sukhoputnykh i vodnykh soobshcheniyakh" ["Capt. Shmalev's Information about

Former Land and Water Communications in Remote Siberian Places"],
TsGADA, f. 199, port. 539, pt. 1, d. 13, fol. 40.

39 Kanagev, "Okhotsk," pp. 368–369, 371; A. P., "Okhotsk," pp. 135, 146;
Sgibnev, "Okhotsky port," 105, no. 11 : 81.

40 P. Gorip, ed., "Iz istorii osvoyeniya Severnovo morskovo puti" ["From
the History of the Opening of the Northern Sea Route"], *Krasny arkhiv,* 71 (1935) : 148; Kanagev, "Okhotsk," pp. 371–372; Krasheninnikov, *Opisanie zemli Kamchatki,* p. 520; A. P., "Okhotsk," p. 146;
Pokrovsky, *Ekspeditsiya Beringa,* p. 128; Sgibnev, "Okhotsky port,"
105, no. 11 : 81–82; Vagin, *Istoricheskiya svedeniya,* vol. 2, p. 1,
suppl., pp. 408, 411.

41 Markov, *Russkie na Vostochnom okeane,* p. 247.

42 F. G. Safronov, *Okhotsko–Kamchatsky kray (Puty soobshcheniya,
naselenie, snabzhenie i zemledelie do revolyutsii)* [*Okhotsk–Kamchatka
Kray (Routes of Communication, Population, Supply and Agriculture
before the Revolution)*] (Yakutsk: Yakutskoye knizhnoye izdatelstvo,
1958), p. 11.

43 Belov, *Russkie morekhody,* doc. 7, pp. 50–55.

44 Akademiya nauk SSSR, Institut istorii, *S. V. Bakhrushin,* vol. 3,
pt. 1, p. 135; Orlova, *Otkrytiya russkikh zempleprokhodtsev,* doc. 101,
pp. 298–300; Russia, Arkheograficheskaya kommissiya, *Pamyatniki
sibirskoy istorii,* vol. 2, doc. 20, pp. 62–63; Okun, *Ocherki po istorii,*
p. 20.

45 Imperatorskoye russkoye istoricheskoye obshchestvo, *Protokoly,
zhurnaly i ukazy Verkhovnavo tainavo soveta, 1726–1730* [*Minutes,
Journals and Decrees of the Supreme Privy Council, 1726–1730*], vol.
63 of *Sbornik Imperatorskavo russkavo istoricheskavo obshchestva* (St.
Petersburg: Imperatorskoye russkoye istoricheskoye obshchestvo,
1888), p. 290.

46 Davydov, *Dvukratnoye puteshestvie v Ameriku,* 1 : 57; [Johann
George] Gmelin, *Voyage en Siberie . . .* (Paris: Desaint, 1767),
1 : 417; Kanagev, "Okhotsk," p. 370; Krasheninnikov, *Opisanie zemli
Kamchatki,* pp. 159, 520; [Muller], "Izvestie o torgakh sibirskikh," 2
(September, 1755) : 247; G. P. [*sic*] Muller, *Voyages et découvertes
faites par les Russes . . . ,* trans. C. G. F. Dumas (Amsterdam: Marc
Michel Rey, 1766), 1 : 209; A. P., "Okhotsk," pp. 145–146; Sauer,
Account of an Expedition, p. 102; A. Sokolov, "Severnaya ekspedi-
tsiya 1733–43 godu" ["The Northern Expedition 1733–43"], *Zapiski
Gidrograficheskavo departamenta,* 9 (1851) : 460.

47 Shmalev, "Ukaz i Instruktsiya," fol. 3ᵛ.

48 Johannis Georgii Gmelini, *Reliquias quae supersunt commercii epistolici . . . [Fragments concerning Letters of Commerce . . .]* (Stuttgartiae: Typis C. F. Heringianis, 1861), p. 175.

49 Kanagev, "Okhotsk," pp. 370–371; [Muller], "Izvestie o torgakh sibirskikh," 2 (September, 1755) : 246.

50 Muller, *Voyages et découvertes,* 1 : 208; [Slovtsov], *Istoricheskoye*

obozrenie Sibiri, 2 : 152; Gmelin, *Voyage en Siberie,* 1 : 416; A. P., "Okhotsk," p. 145.

51 L. A. Goldenberg, *Fyodor Ivanovich Soimonov (1692–1780)* (Moscow: Izdatelstvo "Nauka," 1966), p. 161.

52 V. A. Divin, *Veliky russky moreplavatel A. I. Chirikov [The Great Russian Navigator A. I. Chirikov]* (Moscow: Gosudarstvennoye izdatelstvo geograficheskoy literatury, 1953), p. 211.

53 [Bering], "Donesenie flota kapitana Beringa," p. 71.

54 Goldenberg, *Fyodor Ivanovich Soimonov,* p. 161.

55 *Ibid.*

56 Ye. D. Strelov, *Akty arkhivov Yakutskoy oblasti (s 1650 g. do 1800 g.) [Archival Acts of Yakutsk Oblast (from 1650 to 1800)]* (Yakutsk: Yakutskaya oblastnaya uchyonaya arkhivnaya kommissiya, 1916), vol. 1, doc. 49, pp. 225–228; Sauer, *Account of an Expedition,* p. 107.

57 Davydov, *Dvukratnoye puteshestvie v Ameriku,* 1 : 57.

58 Anonymous, "Opisanie Yakutskoy provintsii," p. 54.

59 Davydov, *Dvukratnoye puteshestvie v Ameriku,* 1 : 96; Gedenstrom, *Otryvki o Sibiri,* pp. 45, 103; Shmalev, "Izvestiya Kap. Shmaleva," fol. 30^r; Erman, *Travels in Siberia,* 2 : 303.

60 Anonymous, "Opisanie Udskavo ostroga" ["Description of Udsk Ostrog"], *Moskovsky telegraf,* pt. 1 (1825), pp. 327–328, 333; Al. Sk. [A. Sokolov], "Opis Udskavo berega i Shantarskikh ostrovov, poruchika Kozmina" ["Lieutenant Kozmin's Inventory of the Udsk Coast and the Shantar Islands"], *Zapiski Gidrograficheskavo departamenta,* pt. 4 (1846), pp. 23–26, 70–71; N. S. Shchukin, "Udskoye selenie" ["Udsk Settlement"], *Zhurnal Ministerstva vnutrennikh del,* pt. 22 (1848), p. 460.

61 Shchukin, "Udskoye selenie," *Zhurnal Ministerstva vnutrennikh del,* p. 460.

62 Shch., *Poyezdka v Yakutsk,* p. 147.

63 Shcheglov, *Kronologichesky perechen,* pp. 540–541; Gagemeister, *Statisticheskoye obozrenie Sibiri,* pt. 2, p. 662; Rossiisko-Amerikanskaya kompaniya, *Otchyot Rossiisko-Amerikanskoy kompanii Glavnavo pravleniya [Report of the Main Administration of the Russian-American Company]* (St. Petersburg: Tipografiya Fishera, 1845), pp. 21–22; Bulychev, *Puteshestvie po Sibiri,* pt. 1, pp. 270–272; Akademiya nauk SSSR, Institut yazyka, literatury i istorii Yakutskovo filiala AN SSSR, *Istoriya Yakutskoy ASSR,* 2 : 269–270.

64 Russia, Ministerstvo vnutrennikh del, *Statisticheskoye obozrenie Sibiri [Statistical Survey of Siberia]* (St. Petersburg: Tipografiya Shnora, 1810), p. 32.

65 Vagin, *Istoricheskiya svedeniya,* vol. 2, suppl., pp. 409, 411.

66 Termin, "Kratkoye obozrenie reki Leny," p. 88.

67 Anonymous, "Opisanie Irkutskoy gubernii," fols. 44^v–45; Vladimir Dal, *Tolkovy slovar zhivovo velikorusskovo yazyka [Explanatory Dic-*

tionary of the Living Great Russian Language] (Moscow: Gosudarstvennoye izdatelstvo inostrannykh i natsionalnykh slovarey, 1955), 3 : 120; Davydov, *Dvukratnoye puteshestvie v Ameriku,* 1 : 72; Flot Kapitan Minitsky, "Ob Okhotskom porte" ["Concerning Okhotsk Port"], *Severnaya pochta,* no. 50 (June 20/July 2, 1812), p. [4]; Rear-Admiral Minitsky, "Opisanie Okhotskavo porta" ["Description of Okhotsk Port"], *Syn otechestva i severny arkhiv,* 5 (1829) : 209–210; Minitsky, "Opisanie Yakutskoy oblasti," p. 170; Sgibnev, "Okhotsky port," 105, no. 12 : 31.

68 Davydov, *Dvukratnoye puteshestvie v Ameriku,* 1 : 72; Markov, *Russkie na Vostochnom okeane,* p. 18; Anonymous, "Opisanie Irkutskoy gubernii," fol. 45; Anonymous, "Opisanie Yakutskoy provintsii," p. 51; L. A. Zagoskin, *Puteshestviya i issledovaniya leitenanta Lavrentiya Zagoskina v Russkoy Amerike v 1842–1844 g.g.* [*Travels and Explorations of Lieutenant Lavrenty Zagoskin in Russian America in the Years 1842–1844*] (Moscow: Gosudarstvennoye izdatelstvo geograficheskoy literatury, 1956), p. 339; A., "Myorzly kray. Ocherki severovostochnoy Sibiri" ["The Frozen Kray. Sketches of Northeastern Siberia"], *Vsemirny puteshestvennik,* 12 (December, 1877): 238; Dobell, *Travels in Kamtchatka and Siberia,* 1 : 351; Krasheninnikov, *Opisanie zemli Kamchatki,* p. 520; Sauer, *Account of an Expedition,* p. 28; Minitsky, "Ob Okhotskom porte," *Severnaya pochta,* no. 50, p. [4]; Sgibnev, "Okhotsky port," 105, no. 12 : 31.

69 Vagin, *Istoricheskiya svedeniya,* vol. 2, pp. 8, 22, suppl., pp. 409, 412, 437, 447; Stefan Kiselev, "Zamechaniya uchinyonnia na puti iz Yakutska v Okhotsk, o perevozke tovarov Yakutami" ["Observations Made on the Route from Yakutsk to Okhotsk about the Transport of Goods by the Yakuts"], *Trudy Volnavo ekonomicheskavo obshchestva,* vol. 52, pt. 3 (1798), p. 131; Minitsky, "Opisanie Yakutskoy oblasti," p. 175.

70 Anonymous, "Opisanie Irkutskoy gubernii," fol. 51ᵛ; Vrangel, "Putevia zapiski," p. 179.

71 [Bering], "Donesenie flota kapitana Beringa," p. 71; Davydov, *Dvukratnoye puteshestvie v Ameriku,* 1 : 55; Dobell, *Travels in Kamtchatka and Siberia,* 2 : 123.

72 G. P. Basharin, *Istoriya agrarnykh otnosheny v Yakutii (60-ye gody XVIII–seredina XIX v.)* [*History of Agrarian Relations in Yakutia (1760's to the Middle of the XIXth Century)*] (Moscow: Izdatelstvo Akademii nauk SSSR, 1956), pp. 235, 236; Sgibnev, "Okhotsky port," 105, no. 12 : 30; Erman, *Travels in Siberia,* 2 : 282; Markov, *Russkie na Vostochnom okeane,* p. 18; D. M. Pavlinov, N. A. Vitashevsky, and L. G. Levental, *Materialy po obychnomu pravu i po obshchestvennomu bytu Yakutov* [*Materials on the Customary Law and on the Social Life of the Yakuts*], "Trudy Komissii po izucheniyu Yakutskoy Avtonomnoy Sovetskoy Respubliki," vol. 4 (Leningrad: Izdatelstvo

Akademii nauk SSSR, 1929), pp. 308–309; Kiselev, "Zamechaniya uchinyonnia na puti," p. 132; Zagoskin, *Puteshestviya i issledovaniya,* pp. 339–340.

73 Basharin, *Istoriya agrarnykh otnosheny,* pp. 231–234; Akademiya nauk SSSR, Institut yazyka, literatury i istorii Yakutskovo filiala AN SSSR, *Istoriya Yakutskoy ASSR,* 2 : 149; Pavlinov, Vitashevsky, and Levental, *Materialy po obychnomu pravu,* pp. 309, 313; Vagin, *Istoricheskiya svedeniya,* vol. 2, pp. 1–2, suppl., pp. 408, 411; Fyodor Shemelin, *Zhurnal pervavo puteshestviya rossiyan vokrug zemnavo shara . . . [Journal of the First Voyage of a Russian around the Globe . . .]* (St. Petersburg: Meditsinskaya tipografiya, 1818), pt. 2., pp. 202–203.

74 Akademiya nauk SSSR, Institut yazyka, literatury i istorii Yakutskovo filiala AN SSSR, *Istoriya Yakutskoy ASSR,* 2 : 149; Vagin, *Istoricheskiya svedeniya,* vol. 2, pp. 2–3, suppl., pp. 408–409, 411–412.

75 Pavlinov, Vitashevsky, and Levental, *Materialy po obychnomu pravu,* pp. 315–316.

76 *Ibid.,* pp. 316–317; Akademiya nauk SSSR, Institut yazyka, literatury i istorii Yakutskovo filiala AN SSSR, *Istoriya Yakutskoy ASSR,* 2 : 148–149; Erman, *Travels in Siberia,* 2 : 145; S. A. Tokarev, *Ocherk istorii yakutskovo naroda [Sketch of the History of the Yakut People]* (Moscow: Gosudarstvennoye sotsialno-ekonomicheskoye izdatelstvo, 1940), pp. 126–127.

77 Vagin, *Istoricheskiya svedeniya,* vol. 2, suppl., pp. 409, 412.

78 *Ibid.,* p. 448.

79 *Ibid.,* p. 3, suppl., pp. 409, 412; Pavlinov, Vitashevsky, and Levental, *Materialy po obychnomu pravu,* p. 316; Davydov, *Dvukratnoye puteshestvie v Ameriku,* 1 : 72; Termin, "Kratkoye obozrenie reki Leny," p. 88.

80 Davydov, *Dvukratnoye puteshestvie v Ameriku,* 1 : 72–73; Kiselev, "Zamechaniya uchinyonnia na puti," pp. 132–133.

81 Sauer, *Account of an Expedition,* pp. 25–26; Minitsky, "Opisanie Okhotskavo porta," pp. 208–209.

82 Russia, *Polnoye sobranie zakonov,* 1st ser., vol. 16, doc. 11,827, p. 259; Kiselev, "Zamechaniya uchinyonnia na puti," p. 135.

83 Yu. Dzhuliyani, "O Yakutakh" ["Concerning the Yakuts"], *Syn otechestva,* vol. 4, pt. 178 (1836), p. 159; Kiselev, "Zamechaniya uchinyonnia na puti," pp. 131–132; G. Peizen, "Istorichesky ocherk kolonizatsii Sibiri" ["Historical Sketch of the Colonization of Siberia"], *Sovremennik,* 77, no. 9 (1859) : 26n; Vagin, *Istoricheskiya svedeniya,* vol. 2, suppl., pp. 407, 413.

84 Akademiya nauk Soyuza Sovetskikh Sotsialisticheskikh Respublik, *Pamyati Dekabristov,* 2 : 196.

85 Dobell, *Travels in Kamtchatka and Siberia,* 2 : 37; Erman, *Travels in Siberia,* 2 : 321; V. Golman, "Zametki o konevodstve v Yakutskoy oblasti" ["Notes on Horsebreeding in Yakutsk Oblast"], *Pamyatnaya knizhka Yakutskoy oblasti na 1871 god* (St. Petersburg: Yakutsky oblastnoy statistichesky komitet, 1877), p. 122; S. S. Hill, *Travels in*

Siberia (London: Longman, Brown, Green, and Longmans, 1854), 2 : 242; V. Kalinin, "Severnie mestnie porody loshadey" ["Northern Local Breeds of Horses"], *Selskokhozyaistvennaya entsiklopediya,* 3d ed. (Moscow: Gosudarstvennoye izdatelstvo selskokhozyaistvennoy literatury, 1955), 4 (1955) : 417–418; G. V. Naumov, *Yakutskaya loshad i yeyo khozyaistvennoye znachenie* [*The Yakut Horse and Its Economic Significance*] (Yakutsk: Yakutskoye knizhnoye izdatelstvo, 1953), p. 5; Alexander Rowand, *Notes of a Journey in Russian America and Siberia . . .* (Edinburgh [?] : n.p., n.d.), pp. 24, 32; Simpson, *Narrative of a Journey,* 2 : 273.

86 Kiselev, "Zamechaniya uchinyonnia na puti," p. 134.

87 Von Wrangell, *Narrative of an Expedition,* p. 28n.

88 I. A. Goncharov, *Sobranie sochineny* [*Collected Works*] (Moscow: Gosudarstvennoye izdatelstvo khudozhestvennoy literatury, 1952–53), 3 : 343.

89 Dobell, *Travels in Kamtchatka and Siberia,* 1 : 350.

90 *Ibid.,* 2 : 8n, 37; Rowand, *Notes of a Journey,* p. 24; Charles Herbert Cottrell, *Recollections of Siberia . . .* (London: John W. Parker, 1842), p. 328.

91 Dobell, *Travels in Kamtchatka and Siberia,* 1 : 300, 2 : 25; Erman, *Travels in Siberia,* 2 : 305; Protoiyerey Prokopy Gromov, "Put ot Irkutska v Kamchatku" ["The Route from Irkutsk to Kamchatka"], *Pribavleniya k Irkutskim yeparkhialnym vedomostyam,* 7, no. 5 (February, 1869) : 57n. Markov, *Russkie na Vostochnom okeane,* p. 16.

92 Anonymous, "Opisanie Yakutskoy provintsii," p. 54; Davydov, *Dvukratnoye puteshestvie v Ameriku,* 1 : 55–56; De Lesseps, *Travels in Kamtschatka,* 2 : 258n; Erman, *Travels in Siberia,* 2 : 321; Gromov, "Put ot Irkutska," 7, no. 5 : 57n; Kiselev, "Zamechaniya uchinyonnia na puti," p. 132; Krasheninnikov, *Opisanie zemli Kamchatki,* pp. 520–521; Minitsky, "Ob Okhotskom porte," *Severnaya pochta,* no. 50, p. [4]; Minitsky, "Opisanie Okhotskavo porta," p. 208; Minitsky, "Opisanie Yakutskoy oblasti," p. 169; Pokrovsky, *Ekspeditsiya Beringa,* pp. 136–137, 207; Sgibnev, "Okhotsky port," 105, no. 12 : 31; Vagin, *Istoricheskiya svedeniya,* vol. 2, pp. 2–3, suppl., pp. 409, 412; G. H. Von Langsdorff, *Voyages and Travels in Various Parts of the World . . .* (London: Henry Colburn, 1814), pt. 2, p. 334; Waxell, *Russian Expedition to America,* p. 53; Zagoskin, *Puteshestviya i issledovaniya,* p. 339.

93 Davydov, *Dvukratnoye puteshestvie v Ameriku,* 1 : 55–57; De Lesseps, *Travels in Kamtschatka,* 2 : 258, 258n; Dobell, *Travels in Kamtchatka and Siberia,* 2 : 7; Gromov, "Put ot Irkutska," 7, no. 5 : 56n; I. F. Kruzenshtern, *Puteshestvie vokrug sveta . . .* [*Voyage around the World . . .*] (Moscow: Gosudarstvennoye izdatelstvo geograficheskoy literatury, 1950), p. 8; Levin and Potapov, *Narody Sibiri,* p. 281; Lyudmila Rikord, "Pismo k g. Predsedatelyu Obshchestva" ["A Letter to Mr. President of the Society"], *Trudy Vsyochaishe utverzhdennavo Volnavo obshchestva lyubiteley rossiiskoy slovesnosti,* pt. 23 (1823),

p. 99; Rowand, *Notes of a Journey,* p. 24; Sgibnev, "Okhotsky port," 105, no. 11 : 81; Veselago, *Kratkaya istoriya russkavo flota,* pt. 1, p. 290; Zagoskin, *Puteshestviya i issledovaniya,* pp. 340, 345.

94 A., "Myorzly kray," pp. 238–239; Akademiya nauk SSSR, Institut yazyka, literatury i istorii Yakutskovo filiala AN SSSR, *Istoriya Yakutskoy ASSR,* 2 : 148; Bulychev, *Puteshestvie po Sibiri,* pt. 1, p. 71; Davydov, *Dvukratnoye puteshestvie v Ameriku,* 1 : 56; Dobell, *Travels in Kamtchatka and Siberia,* 1 : 299; Gedenstrom, *Otryvki o Sibiri,* p. 104; Markov, *Russkie na Vostochnom okeane,* pp. 19, 22; Minitsky, "Opisanie Okhotskavo porta," pp. 208–209; Minitsky, "Opisanie Yakutskoy oblasti," p. 169; Pavlinov, Vitashevsky, and Levental, *Materialy po obychnomu pravu,* p. 306; Rowand, *Notes of a Journey,* p. 24; V. V. Struve, *Vospominaniya o Sibiri, 1848–1854* [*Reminiscences about Siberia, 1848–1854*] (St. Petersburg: Tipografiya Tovarishchestva "Obshchestvennaya polza," 1889), p. 71*n;* Zagoskin, *Puteshestviya i issledovaniya,* p. 340.

95 Davydov, *Dvukratnoye puteshestvie v Ameriku,* 1 : 72; Dobell, *Travels in Kamtchatka and Siberia,* 2 : 8*n;* Gromov, "Put ot Irkutska," 7, no. 7 : 82–83; Kiselev, "Zamechaniya uchinyonnia na puti," p. 138; Markov, *Russkie na Vostochnom okeane,* pp. 18, 21, 162; Minitsky, "Nekotoria izvestiya," pp. 92–93; Minitsky, "Opisanie Okhotskavo porta," pp. 209–210; Minitsky, "Opisanie Yakutskoy oblasti," pp. 169–170; Safronov, *Okhotsko-Kamchatsky kray,* p. 11; Sauer, *Account of an Expedition,* p. 26; Simpson, *Narrative of a Journey,* 2 : 268.

96 Anonymous, "Opisanie Irkutskoy gubernii," fol. 51ᵛ.

97 *Ibid.;* Khersonsky, "Neskolko slov o proshlom i nastoyashchem g. Okhotska" ["Several Words about the Past and the Present of the Town of Okhotsk"], *Priamurskiya vedomosti,* no. 39 (September 25/October 7, 1894), pp. 11–12; Minitsky, "Nekotoria izvestiya," p. 91; Minitsky, "Ob Okhotskom porte," *Severnaya pochta,* no. 50, p. [4]; Minitsky, "Opisanie Okhotskavo porta," p. 212; Shmalev, "Izvestiya Kap. Shmaleva," fols. 36ᵛ–37, 38; [Slovtsov], *Istoricheskoye obozrenie Sibiri,* 2 : 85.

98 Davydov, *Dvukratnoye puteshestvie v Ameriku,* 1 : 72–73; Gmelin, *Voyage en Siberie,* 1 : 416–417; Minitsky, "Opisanie Okhotskavo porta," pp. 210, 212.

99 Pokrovsky, *Ekspeditsiya Beringa,* pp. 136, 207.

100 Gmelin, *Voyage en Siberie,* 1 : 417.

101 Cochrane, *Narrative of a Pedestrian Journey,* p. 305.

102 Simpson, *Narrative of a Journey,* 2 : 270.

103 Gagemeister, *Statisticheskoye obozrenie Sibiri,* pt. 2, p. 667; Peizen, "Istorichesky ocherk," p. 26*n;* Rowand, *Notes of a Journey,* p. 22; P. P. Semyonov, ed., *Zhivopisnaya Rossiya* [*Picturesque Russia*], vol. 12 (St. Petersburg and Moscow: Izdanie Tovarishchestva M. O. Volf, 1895), pt. 2, p. 53; Sgibnev, "Okhotsky port," 105, no. 11 : 81; Veselago, *Kratkaya istoriya russkavo flota,* pt. 1, p. 290.

104 Pavlinov, Vitashevsky and Levental, *Materialy po obychnomu pravu,*
pp. 36, 317–318; Shemelin, *Zhurnal pervavo puteshestviya rossiyan,*
pt. 2, pp. 203–204.

105 Shemelin, *Zhurnal pervavo puteshestviya rossiyan,* pt. 2, p. 203; Vagin,
Istoricheskiya svedeniya, vol. 2, p. 8, suppl., pp. 409, 412, 437, 447.

106 Anonymous, "Vzglyad na torgovlyu, proizvodimuyu chrez Okhotsky
port" ["A Glance at the Trade Conducted through Okhotsk Port"],
Severny arkhiv, pt. 7 (1823), pp. 42, 45; Termin, "Kratkoye obozrenie
reki Leny," p. 88.

107 Kanagev, "Okhotsk," p. 370; A. P., "Okhotsk," p. 145.

108 Pokrovsky, *Ekspeditsiya Beringa,* pp. 136, 207.

109 Sarychev, *Puteshestvie,* p. 96.

110 Kanagev, "Okhotsk," p. 370; A. P., "Okhotsk," p. 145.

111 Minitsky, "Opisanie Okhotskavo porta," p. 140; Shmalev, "Kratkoye
opisanie," pp. 196, 199.

112 Minitsky, "Ob Okhotskom porte," *Severnaya pochta,* no. 50, p. [4].

113 Alaska History Research Project, *Documents Relative to the History
of Alaska* (College: University of Alaska, 1938), 3 : 277; De Lesseps,
Travels in Kamtschatka, 2 : 293; Krasheninnikov, *Opisanie zemli
Kamchatki,* pp. 156, 199, 223–224; Minitsky, "Nekotoria izvestiya,"
p. 99; Minitsky, "Ob Okhotskom porte," *Severnaya pochta,* no. 49, p.
[4]; Minitsky, "Opisanie Okhotskavo porta," pp. 140, 217–218; Shmalev, "Kratkoye o Kamchatke obyasnenie," fol. 4; Sokolov, "Severnaya
ekspeditsiya," p. 425n; Waxell, *Russian Expedition to America,* p. 139.

114 Sarychev, *Puteshestvie,* p. 54.

115 Dobell, *Travels in Kamtchatka and Siberia,* 1 : 298.

116 Anonymous, "Razniya izvestiya iz Okhotska ot 30 noyabrya po 17
dekabre 1775 g." ["Various Information from Okhotsk from November 30 to December 17 of 1775"], TsGADA, f. 199, port. 528, pt. 1,
d. 24, fol. 1ʳ.

117 Sarychev, *Puteshestvie,* p. 52; A. P., "Okhotsk," p. 142.

118 Veselago, *Materialy dlya istorii,* 17 : 143–144.

119 Alaska History Research Project, *Documents Relative to Alaska,*
3 : 277; N. P. Rezanov, "Pismo Bukharina Ivana neustanovlennomu
litsu s opisaniem sostoyaniya transportnikh sudov v Okhotske; zapiska
neustanovlennovo litsa o deyatelnosti Bukharina Ivana" ["A Letter of
Ivan Bukharin to an Unidentified Person with a Description of the
Condition of the Transport Vessels at Okhotsk; A Note of an Unidentified Person about the Activities of Ivan Bukharin"], TsGADA, f. 796,
op. 1, d. 290, fol. 2.

120 Shaskolsky, *Geograficheskoye izuchenie Sibiri,* p. 26.

121 Minitsky, "Nekotoria izvestiya," p. 89; Minitsky, "Ob Okhotskom
porte," *Severnaya pochta,* no. 50, p. [4]; Minitsky, "Opisanie Okhotskavo porta," pp. 137–138; A. P., "Okhotsk," p. 142; [Semivsky],
Noveishiya, lyubopytnia i dostovernia povestvovaniya, p. 201; Timofey
Shmalev, "Vedomost o nakhodyashchemsya proviante v Okhotskom

porte" ["List of Provisions Found at Okhotsk Port"], TsGADA, f. 199, port. 528, pt. 1, d. 13, fol. 1; Vagin, *Istoricheskiya svedeniya*, vol. 2, p. 34, suppl., pp. 417, 421, 423.

122 Bulychev, *Puteshestvie po Sibiri*, pt. 1, p. 54; Krasheninnikov, *Opisanie zemli Kamchatki*, p. 159; Minitsky, "Opisanie Okhotskavo porta," pp. 140–141, 149; Muller, "Geografiya ili nyneshnoye sostoyanie," fol. 26; [Muller], "Izvestie o torgakh sibirskikh," 2 (September, 1755) : 248–249; [Semivsky], *Noveishiya, lyubopytnia i dostovernia povestvovaniya*, pp. 224–225; Shmalev, "Kratkoye opisanie," p. 199.

123 Shmalev, "Izvestiya Kap. Shmaleva," fols. 8, 12ᵛ, 15.

124 Russia, *Polnoye sobranie zakonov*, 1st ser., vol. 32, doc. 25,423, pp. 597–599; Sarychev, *Puteshestvie*, p. 52.

Chapter 6: PERFORMANCE

1 Pokrovsky, *Ekspeditsiya Beringa*, pp. 261, 365, 370.

2 Russia, Pravitelstvuyushchy senat, *Senatsky arkhiv*, 9 : 137.

3 Myatlev, "Instruktsiya ot General-Leitenanta," fols. 12ᵛ–13.

4 Sgibnev, "Okhotsky port," 105, no. 11 : 82.

5 *Ibid.*, p. 77.

6 Shemelin, *Zhurnal pervavo puteshestviya rossiyan*, pt. 2, p. 203.

7 Graf Nikolay Rumyantsov et al., "Doklad ob ustroyenii Kamchatki i Okhotska" ["Report on the Organization of Kamchatka and Okhotsk"], *Sanktpeterburgsky zhurnal*, no. 5 (May, 1804), pp. 35–36; Veselago, *Materialy dlya istorii*, 17 : 313.

8 Sgibnev, "Istorichesky ocherk," 103 (July, 1869) : 68.

9 Golovnin, *Puteshestvie na shlyupe "Diana,"* pp. 266–267n, 268.

10 Vagin, *Istoricheskiya svedeniya*, 2 : 43; Veselago, *Materialy dlya istorii*, 17 : 38, 143.

11 Vagin, *Istoricheskaya svedeniya*, 2 : 26, 28, suppl., pp. 417, 422; Anonymous, "Delo o zapiske v prikhod kazyonnovo provianta 1784 goda" ["File Noting the Arrival of State Provisions of 1784"], TsGADA, f. 1,096, op. 1, d. 47, fol. 19.

12 Pervy sibirsky komitet, "O predpolozheniyakh Nachalnika Kamchatki," d. 167, fol. 13.

13 Anonymous, "Vzglyad na torgovlyu," p. 42.

14 Vagin, *Istoricheskiya svedeniya*, vol. 2, suppl., p. 410.

15 Peizen, "Istorichesky ocherk," p. 26n; Bulychev, *Puteshestvie po Sibiri*, pt. 1, p. 118.

16 Vagin, *Istoricheskiya svedeniya*, vol. 2, suppl., p. 473.

17 Pokrovsky, *Ekspeditsiya Beringa*, p. 370.

18 Russia, Gosudarstvenny sovet, *Arkhiv Gosudarstvennavo soveta*, vol. 1, pt. 2, p. 78.

19 Ministerstvo inostrannykh del SSSR, *Vneshnyaya politika Rossii XIX i nachala XX veka* [*The Foreign Policy of Russia of the XIXth and Beginning of the XXth Centuries*] (Moscow: Izdatelstvo politicheskoy literatury, 1960–), 1st ser., vol. 1, doc. 99, pp. 266–269.

20 P. I. Lyashchenko, *Istoriya narodnovo khozyaistva SSSR* [*History of the National Economy of the USSR*], 4th ed. (Moscow: Gosudarstvennoye izdatelstvo politecheskoy literatury, 1956), 1 : 448.

21 Termin, "Kratkoye obozrenie reki Leny," p. 89; Sgibnev, "Okhotsky port," 105, no. 12, p. 50.

22 N. N. Firsov, "Istoricheskaya zapiska o Kamchatke" ["An Historical Note on Kamchatka"], *Izvestiya Obshchestva arkheologii, istorii i etnografii pri Kazanskom gosudarstvennom universitete,* 33 (1926) : 179.

23 Pervy sibirsky komitet, "O predpolozheniyakh Nachalnika Kamchatki," d. 167, fol. 26.

24 Divin, "Vtoraya Sibirsko-tikhookeanskaya ekspeditsiya," p. 173.

25 Shaskolsky, *Geograficheskoye izuchenie Sibiri,* p. 26.

26 Myatlev, "Instruktsiya ot General-Leitenanta," fol. 16^v; Alaska History Research Project, *Documents Relative to Alaska,* 3 : 217; V. G. Sirotkin, "Dokumenty o politike Rossii na Dalnem Vostoke v nachale XIX v." ["Documents on the Policy of Russia in the Far East in the Beginning of the XIXth Century"], *Istorichesky arkhiv,* 6 (November–December, 1962) : 88; Shemelin, *Zhurnal pervavo puteshestvie rossiyan,* pt. 2, p. 204; Markov, *Russkie na Vostochnom okeane,* p. 162.

27 Stary pochtalion, "Vospominaniya Lenskavo pochtaliona" ["Reminiscences of a Lena Postman"], *Sibirskaya gazeta,* no. 24 (June 13/25, 1882), p. 585.

28 *Ibid.*

29 Vagin, *Istoricheskiya svedeniya,* 2 : 34.

30 A. P., "Okhotsk," p. 137.

31 Shmalev, "Kratkoye o Kamchatke obyasnenie," fols. 1, 4; Shmalev, "Kratkoye opisanie," pp. 196, 207; De Lesseps, *Travels in Kamtschatka,* 1 : 85.

32 Krasheninnikov, *Opisanie zemli Kamchatki,* pp. 504, 517; Shteller, "Opisanie strany Kamchatki," pp. 252, 479.

33 Shteller, "Opisanie strany Kamchatki," p. 254.

34 Shmalev, "Kratkoye o Kamchatke obyasnenie," fols. 1, 3^v; Shmalev, "Kratkoye opisanie," pp. 196, 205–206; Russia, *Polnoye sobranie zakonov,* 1st ser., vol. 35, doc. 27,575, pp. 613–615.

35 Shmalev, "Kratkoye o Kamchatke obyasnenie," fol. 3^v.

36 Krasheninnikov, *Opisanie zemli Kamchatki,* p. 517.

37 Simpson, *Narrative of a Journey,* 2 : 253.

38 Myatlev, "Instruktsiya ot General-Lietenanta," fols. 16–16^v.

39 Dobell, *Travels in Kamtchatka and Siberia,* 2 : 24, 26–27; Erman, *Travels in Siberia,* 2 : 145.

40 Pervy sibirsky komitet, "O predpolozheniyakh Nachalnika Kamchatki," d. 167, fols. 13, 14; Vagin, *Istoricheskiya svedeniya,* vol. 2, suppl., p. 410; Russia, *Polnoye sobranie zakonov,* 1st ser., vol. 29, doc. 22,187, p. 394.

41 Sirotkin, "Dokumenty o politike Rossii," p. 87.

42 Myatlev, "Instruktsiya ot General-Leitenanta," fols. 16–16^v.

43 Pavlinov, Vitashevsky, and Levental, *Materialy po obychnomu pravu,* p. 230; Tokarev, *Ocherk istorii,* p. 126.

Chapter 7: TRANSPORT PROBLEMS

1 Anonymous, "Opisanie Irkutskoy gubernii," fol. 3ᵛ; Termin, "Kratkoye obozrenie reki Leny," p. 83.

2 Russia, Arkheograficheskaya kommissiya, *Dopolneniya k Aktam istoricheskim,* vol. 6, doc. 136, pp. 403–404.

3 Ilimskaya voyevodskaya kantselyariya, "Sbornik del," fol. 88; Ilimskaya voyevodskaya kantselyariya, "Splav po Lene i na Kamchatku, tom I" ["Shipping along the Lena and to Kamchatka, Volume 1"], TsGADA, f. 494, op. 2, d. 297, sv. 30, fol. 9.

4 Sherstoboyev, *Ilimskaya pashnya,* 2 : 297.

5 Shch., *Poyezdka v Yakutsk,* p. 111.

6 Pavlinov, Vitashevsky, and Levental, *Materialy po obychnomu pravu,* p. 307.

7 Peizen, "Istorichesky ocherk," p. 26; Mauritius Augustus Count De Benyowsky, *Memoirs and Travels . . .* (Dublin: P. Wogan, L. White, P. Byrne et al., 1790), 1 : 252; Gmelin, *Voyage en Siberie,* 1 : 417; Kanagev, "Okhotsk," p. 373; Simpson, *Narrative of a Journey,* 2 : 279.

8 De Benyowsky, *Memoirs and Travels,* 1 : 252.

9 [Muller], "Izvestie o torgakh sibirskikh," 2 (September, 1755) : 246.

10 Dobell, *Travels in Kamtchatka and Siberia,* 2 : 52.

11 D. I. Zavalishin, *Zapiski Dekabrista* [*Notes of a Decembrist*] (St. Petersburg: Tipografiya "Sirius," 1906), p. 79.

12 Gedenstrom, *Otryvki o Sibiri,* pp. 22, 102.

13 Vrangel, "Putevia zapiski," p. 172.

14 Ivan Barsukov, *Graf Nikolay Nikolayevich Muravyov-Amursky . . .* [*Count Nikolay Nikolayevich Muravyov-Amursky . . .*] (Moscow: Sinodalnaya tipografiya, 1891), vol. 1, pt. 1, p. 217.

15 V. A. Bilbasov, ed., *Arkhiv grafov Mordvinovykh* [*Archive of the Counts Mordvinov*] (St. Petersburg: Tipografiya I. N. Skorokhodova, 1901–3), 3 : 578–579.

16 Cochrane, *Narrative of a Pedestrian Journey,* p. 320.

17 *Ibid.;* Markov, *Russkie na Vostochnom okeane,* p. 23.

18 Gromov, "Put ot Irkutska," 7, no. 7 : 82, 87.

19 Termin, "Kratkoye obozrenie reki Leny," p. 87.

20 Anonymous, "Delo po predlozheniyu . . . Irkutskovo gubernatora . . . o sostoyanii zdeshnevo vedomstva 1782 goda aprelya 16 chislo" ["File on the Proposal . . . of the Irkutsk Governor . . . about the Condition of the Local Department, April 16, 1782"], TsGADA, f. 416, op. 1, d. 24, fols. 19ᵛ–20; Anonymous, "Opisanie Yakutskoy provintsii," p. 49.

21 Vagin, *Istoricheskiya svedeniya,* vol. 2, suppl., p. 407.

22 Simpson, *Narrative of a Journey,* 2 : 265.

23 De Lesseps, *Travels in Kamtschatka*, 2 : 218*n*, 261*n;* A. P., "Okhotsk," p. 147; Termin, "Kratkoye obozrenie reki Leny," p. 87; Gromov, "Put ot Irkutska," 7, no. 9 : 107.

24 Andreyev, *Russkie otkrytiya*, p. 364.

25 Shmalev, "Statisticheskiya i Geograficheskiya Primechaniya," fol. 65.

26 Cochrane, *Narrative of a Pedestrian Journey*, p. 326; Dobell, *Travels in Kamtchatka and Siberia*, 1 : 336–337; Kanagev, "Okhotsk," p. 373; A. P., "Okhotsk," p. 147.

27 Krasheninnikov, *Opisanie zemli Kamchatki*, p. 529.

28 Gromov, "Put ot Irkutska," 7, no. 7 : 86.

29 *Ibid.*, 7, no. 5 : 59, 62; Krasheninnikov, *Opisanie zemli Kamchatki*, p. 529; Shemelin, *Zhurnal pervavo puteshestviya rossiyan*, pt. 2, pp. 204–205; Gedenstrom, *Otryvki o Sibiri*, pp. 103–104; Dobell, *Travels in Kamtchatka and Siberia*, 1 : 332.

30 Dobell, *Travels in Kamtchatka and Siberia*, 1 : 332, 337*n;* Kanagev, "Okhotsk," p. 372; A. P., "Okhotsk," p. 147; Vrangel, "Putevia zapiski," p. 177; Cochrane, *Narrative of a Pedestrian Journey*, p. 325; Simpson, *Narrative of a Journey*, 2 : 280–281.

31 Hill, *Travels in Siberia*, 2 : 236; Zagoskin, *Puteshestviya i issledovaniya*, p. 343.

32 Rowand, *Notes of a Journey*, p. 34; Markov, *Russkie na Vostochnom okeane*, p. 23.

33 Cochrane, *Narrative of a Pedestrian Journey*, p. 321; Markov, *Russkie na Vostochnom okeane*, pp. 22–23.

34 De Lesseps, *Travels in Kamtschatka*, 2 : 257–258.

35 Dobell, *Travels in Kamtchatka and Siberia*, 2 : 7; Kanagev, "Okhotsk," pp. 373–374; A. P., "Okhotsk," p. 147; Markov, *Russkie na Vostochnom okeane*, p. 22; Shemelin, *Zhurnal pervavo puteshestviya rossiyan*, pt. 2, p. 205; Gromov, "Put ot Irkutska," 7, no. 7 : 86; Kiselev, "Zamechaniya uchinyonnia na puti," p. 131.

36 Krasheninnikov, *Opisanie zemli Kamchatki*, p. 529.

37 Pokrovsky, *Ekspeditsiya Beringa*, pp. 216–217.

38 Termin, "Kratkoye obozrenie reki Leny," p. 86.

39 A. Marlinsky, *Polnoye sobranie sochineny [Complete Collection of Works]* (St. Petersburg: Tipografiya N. Grecha, 1832), 1 : 220.

40 Simpson, *Narrative of a Journey*, 2 : 265.

41 De Lesseps, *Travels in Kamtschatka*, 2 : 260*n*, 265; Shch., *Poyezdka v Yakutsk*, pp. 157–158; Shemelin, *Zhurnal pervavo puteshestviya rossiyan*, pt. 2, p. 205; Zagoskin, *Puteshestviya i issledovaniya*, p. 348.

42 Sauer, *Account of an Expedition*, p. 41.

43 Gedenstrom, *Otryvki o Sibiri*, p. 104; Shemelin, *Zhurnal pervavo puteshestviya rossiyan*, pt. 2, p. 205; Captain John D'Wolf, *A Voyage to the North Pacific and A Journey through Siberia . . .* (Cambridge, Mass.: Welch, Bigelow, and Company, 1861), p. 95.

44 Vagin, *Istoricheskiya svedeniya*, vol. 2, suppl., pp. 407, 412; Chappe

D'Auteroche, *Journey into Siberia,* p. 253; Gmelin, *Voyage en Siberie,* 1 : 417.
45 Culin, "Wonderful News of the Circumnavigation," pp. 505, 506; Termin, "Kratkoye obozrenie reki Leny," p. 86.
46 Von Langsdorff, *Voyages and Travels,* pt. 2, p. 346.
47 Dobell, *Travels in Kamtchatka and Siberia,* 2 : 8*n;* Sgibnev, "Okhotsky port," 105, no. 12 : 32, 36–37; Pavlinov, Vitashevsky, and Levental, *Materialy po obychnomu pravu,* pp. 316, 414*n;* Vagin, *Istoricheskiya svedeniya,* 2 : 5, 5*n.*
48 Shch., *Poyezdka v Yakutsk,* p. 226.
49 Alekseyev, *Okhotsk,* p. 122; Sgibnev, "Okhotsky port," 105, no. 12 : 36; Vagin, *Istoricheskiya svedeniya,* 2 : 5*n.*
50 Gedenstrom, *Otryvki o Sibiri,* p. 104.
51 A. P., "Okhotsk," p. 147.
52 Shmalev, "Statisticheskiya i Geograficheskiya Primechaniya," fol. 65.
53 *Ibid.*
54 *Ibid.,* fols. 64^v–65.
55 Andreyev, *Russkie otkrytiya,* p. 364.
56 De Lesseps, *Travels in Kamtschatka,* 2 : 261*n.*
57 Pervy sibirsky komitet, "O predpolozheniyakh Nachalnika Kamchatki," d. 167, fols. 26–26^v; Vagin, *Istoricheskiya svedeniya,* vol. 2, suppl., p. 404.
58 Pervy sibirsky komitet, "O predpolozheniyakh Nachalnika Kamchatki," d. 167, fols. 13–13^v.
59 Vagin, *Istoricheskiya svedeniya,* vol. 2, suppl., p. 407.
60 Shemelin, *Zhurnal pervavo puteshestviya rossiyan,* pt. 2, p. 204.
61 Pokrovsky, *Ekspeditsiya Beringa,* p. 370.
62 Marlinsky, *Polnoye sobranie sochineny,* 1 : 221.
63 Zagoskin, *Puteshestviya i issledovaniya,* p. 340.
64 Vagin, *Istoricheskiya svedeniya,* 2 : 23; Minitsky, "Opisanie Yakutskoy oblasti," pp. 170–171.
65 Kiselev, "Zamechaniya uchinyonnia na puti," p. 133; Naumov, *Yakutskaya loshad,* p. 11; Shemelin, *Zhurnal pervavo puteshestviya rossiyan,* pt. 2, p. 205; A., "Myorzly kray," p. 239; Vagin, *Istoricheskiya svedeniya,* vol. 2, suppl., pp. 409–413.
66 Anonymous, "Opisanie Udskavo ostroga," pp. 323–324; Sarychev, *Puteshestvie,* p. 94.
67 Cochrane, *Narrative of a Pedestrian Journey,* pp. 260, 305.
68 Anonymous, "Opisanie Udskavo ostroga," p. 329.
69 De Lesseps, *Travels in Kamtschatka,* 2 : 260–261*n.*
70 Gromov, "Put ot Irkutska," 7, no. 7 : 87.
71 Sgibnev, "Okhotsky port," 105, no. 12 : 30.
72 Cochrane, *Narrative of a Pedestrian Journey,* p. 325; Gromov, "Put ot Irkutska," 7, no. 7 : 87; Vrangel, "Putevia zapiski," p. 179.
73 Simpson, *Narrative of a Journey,* 2 : 264–265.
74 Vagin, *Istoricheskiya svedeniya,* vol. 2, pp. 5–7, suppl., p. 404.

75 Anonymous, "Delo po predlozheniyu," fol. 15ᵛ; E. [E. I. Stogov], "Ssylno-katorzhnie v Okhotskom solevarennom zavode" ["Hard-Labor Exiles at the Okhotsk Saltworks"], *Russkaya starina,* 22 (August, 1878) : 623; Gromov, "Put ot Irkutska," 7, no. 5 : 63, no. 12 : 149, no. 16 : 195; Markov, *Russkie na Vostochnom okeane,* p. 21; Pavlinov, Vitashevsky, and Levental, *Materialy po obychnomu pravu,* p. 320; Rumyantsov et al., "Doklad ob ustroyenii," p. 39; Russia, *Polnoye sobranie zakonov rossiiskoy imperii,* 2d ser. (1825–81) (St. Petersburg: Kantselyariya Yevo Imperatorskavo Velichestva, 1830–84), vol. 11, pt. 1, doc. 9,350, p. 768; Veselago, *Materialy dlya istorii,* 17 : 314; Vrangel, "Putevia zapiski," pp. 179–180.

76 Vagin, *Istoricheskiya svedeniya,* 1 : 420.

77 Pervy sibirsky komitet, "O predpolozheniyakh Nachalnika Kamchatki," d. 166, fols. 8–8ᵛ, 35ᵛ, 183.

78 Von Langsdorff, *Voyages and Travels,* pt. 2, p. 341.

79 Dobell, *Travels in Kamtchatka and Siberia,* 1 : 307; Markov, *Russkie na Vostochnom okeane,* p. 18.

80 Vagin, *Istoricheskiya svedeniya,* vol. 2, suppl., p. 404.

81 I. S. Moskvin, "Voyevody i Nachalniki g. Yakutska i ikh deistviya" ["Governors and Commandants of the Town of Yakutsk and Their Activities"], in *Pamyatnaya knizhka Yakutskoy oblasti za 1863 god* (St. Petersburg: Yakutsky oblastnoy statistichesky komitet, 1864), p. 179.

82 Dobell, *Travels in Kamtchatka and Siberia,* 2 : 24.

83 Sgibnev, "Okhotsky port," 105, no. 12 : 30; Akademiya nauk SSSR, Institut yazyka, literatury i istorii Yakutskovo filiala AN SSSR, *Istoriya Yakutskoy ASSR,* 2 : 148; Tokarev, *Ocherk istorii,* pp. 127–129.

84 Pavlinov, Vitashevsky, and Levental, *Materialy po obychnomu pravu,* p. 317.

85 Basharin, *Istoriya agrarnykh otnosheny,* p. 236.

86 Pavlinov, Vitashevsky, and Levental, *Materialy po obychnomu pravu,* p. 312.

87 Dobell, *Travels in Kamtchatka and Siberia,* 2 : 25–26.

88 Alaska History Research Project, *Documents Relative to Alaska,* 3 : 217.

89 Sgibnev, "Okhotsky port," 105, no. 11 : 82.

90 Dobell, *Travels in Kamtchatka and Siberia,* 2 : 106.

91 Termin, "Kratkoye obozrenie reki Leny," p. 85.

92 Bilbasov, *Arkhiv grafov Mordvinovykh,* 3 : 578.

93 Krasheninnikov, *Opisanie zemli Kamchatki,* pp. 159, 520, 531; [Muller], "Izvestie o torgakh sibirskikh," 2 (September, 1755) : 246; Sarychev, *Puteshestvie,* pp. 96–100, 106–107; Anonymous, "Opisanie Irkutskoy gubernii," fol. 52; De Lesseps, *Travels in Kamtschatka,* 2 : 278; Gmelin, *Voyage en Siberie,* 1 : 416; N. P. Rezanov, "Opisanie morskavo berega ot Okhotska do rechki Ulkan, s pokazaniem glubin

farvaterov i opisaniem flory i fauny po rekam, predstavlennoye Britovym i Ocheredinym" ["Description of the Coast from Okhotsk to the Ulkan River, with an Indication of the Depths of Channels and a Description of the Flora and the Fauna along the Rivers, Submitted by Britov and Ocheredin"], TsGADA, f. 796, op. 1, d. 284, fol. 2; Waxell, *Russian Expedition to America*, p. 56.

94 Shmalev, "Izvestiya Kap. Shmaleva," fol. 30^v.

95 Bilbasov, *Arkhiv grafov Mordvinovykh*, 3 : 578.

96 Krasheninnikov, *Opisanie zemli Kamchatki*, p. 159; Sarychev, *Puteshestvie*, p. 100; Waxell, *Russian Expedition to America*, p. 57; Gmelin, *Voyage en Siberie*, 1 : 416; Pokrovsky, *Ekspeditsiya Beringa*, p. 305.

97 A. P., "Okhotsk," p. 139; Kanagev, "Okhotsk," p. 370.

98 [Muller], "Izvestie o torgakh sibirskikh," 2 (September, 1755) : 347.

99 Bilbasov, *Arkhiv grafov Mordvinovykh*, 3 : 576; Dobell, *Travels in Kamtchatka and Siberia*, 1 : 301; Minitsky, "Nekotoria izvestiya," p. 88; Minitsky, "Ob Okhotskom porte," *Severnaya pochta*, no. 49, p. [4]; Kapitan-Leitenant Minitsky, "Prodolzhenie izvesty ob Okhotskom porte, dostavlennykh Kapitan-Leitenantom Minitskim v 1811 godu" ["Continuation of Information about Okhotsk Port, Supplied by Captain-Lieutenant Minitsky in 1811"], *Zapiski, izdavayemia Gosudarstvennym admiralteiskim departamentom*, pt. 3 (1815), p. 144.

100 De Lesseps, *Travels in Kamtschatka*, 2 : 251; Sgibnev, "Okhotsky port," 105, no. 11 : 65, no. 12 : 15; Shmalev, "Primechanie uchinyonnoye Kapitanom Timofeiyem Shmalevym," fols. 1^v, 2^v, 3^v–5; Shmalev, "Statisticheskiya i Geograficheskiya Primechaniya," fols. 3^v–4; Von Langsdorff, *Voyages and Travels*, pt. 2, p. 332; Veselago, *Materialy dlya istorii*, 8 : 291–292.

101 Shmalev, "Primechanie uchinyonnoye Kapitanom Timofeiyem Shmalevym," fol. 8; Vasily Shmalev, "Nachalo izyskaniya novavo trakta ot Yakutska k Okhotsku" ["The Beginning of the Search for a New Track from Yakutsk towards Okhotsk"], TsGADA, f. 199, port. 528, pt. 1, d. 9, fol. 5.

102 Anonymous, "Razniya izvestiya iz Okhotska," fol. 1.

103 *Ibid.*, fols. 1–1^v; Bilbasov, *Arkhiv grafov Mordvinovykh*, 3 : 577; Dobell, *Travels in Kamtchatka and Siberia*, 1 : 296–297; Minitsky, "Ob Okhotskom porte," *Severnaya pochta*, no. 49, p. [4]; Tikhmenev, *Historical Review*, pt. 2, p. 5.

104 Minitsky, "Ob Okhotskom porte," *Severnaya pochta*, no. 49, p. [4]; Sarychev, *Puteshestvie*, p. 110; Sauer, *Account of an Expedition*, p. 42; Savin, "Okhotsk," pp. 157–158; Shmalev, "Primechanie uchinyonnoye Kapitanom Timofeiyem Shmalevym," fol. 8.

105 Bulychev, *Puteshestvie po Sibiri*, pt. 1, p. 145; D'Wolf, *Voyage to the North Pacific*, p. 91; M. I. Minitsky, "Ob Okhotskom porte" ["Concerning Okhotsk Port"], *Zapiski, izdavayemia Gosudarstvennym admiralteiskim departamentom*, pt. 7 (1824), p. 97; Von Langsdorff, *Voyages and Travels*, pt. 2, p. 331.

106 Sauer, *Account of an Expedition,* p. 42; Minitsky, "Nekotoria izvestiya," p. 98; Minitsky, "Prodolzhenie izvesty," p. 145; Bilbasov, *Arkhiv grafov Mordvinovykh,* 3 : 577–578; Dobell, *Travels in Kamtchatka and Siberia,* 1 : 301; Waxell, *Russian Expedition to America,* pp. 62, 135; Savin, "Okhotsk," p. 157; Bulychev, *Puteshestvie po Sibiri,* pt. 1, p. 119; Shmalev, "Primechanie uchinyonnoye Kapitanom Timofeiyem Shmalevym," fol. 8.

107 Minitsky, "Ob Okhotskom porte," *Zapiski,* pt. 7, p. 87; Sarychev, *Puteshestvie,* p. 111; Sauer, *Account of an Expedition,* p. 42; Savin, "Okhotsk," p. 158; Veselago, *Kratkaya istoriya russkavo flota,* pt. 1, p. 291.

108 Bulychev, *Puteshestvie po Sibiri,* pt. 1, pp. 118–119; Tikhmenev, *Historical Review,* pt. 2, p. 6.

109 Andreyev, *Russkie otkrytiya,* p. 365.

110 Bulychev, *Puteshestvie po Sibiri,* pt. 1, p. 120.

111 Tikhmenev, *Historical Review,* pt. 2, pp. 5–6.

112 Waxell, *Russian Expedition to America,* p. 62.

113 Savin, "Okhotsk," p. 159.

114 Gromov, "Put ot Irkutska," nos. 17–18, 217.

115 Struve, *Vospominaniya o Sibiri,* p. 73.

116 Bilbasov, *Arkhiv grafov Mordvinovykh,* 3 : 577.

117 Alaska History Research Project, *Documents Relative to Alaska,* 3 : 278; Rezanov, "Pismo Bukharina Ivana," fol. 2.

118 Peter Lauridsen, *Vitus Bering: The Discoverer of Bering Strait,* trans. Julius E. Olson (Chicago: S. C. Griggs & Company, 1889), p. 199.

119 Savin, "Okhotsk," p. 160; Shmalev, "Primechanie uchinyonnoye Kapitanom Timofeiyem Shmalevym," fols. 8ᵛ–9ᵛ.

120 Krasheninnikov, *Opisanie zemli Kamchatki,* pp. 500–502; [Muller], "Izvestie o torgakh sibirskikh," 2 (September, 1755) : 249–250; Shmalev, "Kratkoye o Kamchatke obyasnenie," fols. 1, 3.

121 Muller, "Geografiya ili nyneshnoye sostoyanie," fol. 26.

122 Shteller, "Opisanie strany Kamchatki," p. 18.

123 Sauer, *Account of an Expedition,* p. 301; Waxell, *Russian Expedition to America,* p. 137.

124 Sauer, *Account of an Expedition,* p. 294.

125 Sarychev, *Puteshestvie,* pp. 129–130.

126 [Slovtsov], *Istoricheskoye obozrenie Sibiri,* 2 : 154; Waxell, *Russian Expedition to America,* p. 79.

127 Waxell, *Russian Expedition to America,* p. 79.

128 *Ibid.,* pp. 79, 136.

129 Muller, *Voyages from Asia to America,* p. 37.

130 Bilbasov, *Arkhiv grafov Mordvinovykh,* 3 : 571.

131 Muller, *Voyages from Asia to America,* p. xli; Sgibnev, "Istorichesky ocherk," 103 (August, 1869) : 82.

132 De Lesseps, *Travels in Kamtschatka,* 1 : 22*n;* Divin, "Vtoraya Sibirsko-tikhookeanskaya ekspeditsiya," p. 167; Golder, "Survey of

Alaska," p. 84; Muller and Pallas, *Conquest of Siberia*, pp. 113–114; Sauer, *Account of an Expedition*, p. xvi; [Slovtsov], *Istoricheskoye obozrenie Sibiri*, 2 : 216; [F. Veselago], *Russkoy morskoy istorii* [*Of Russian Naval History*] (St. Petersburg: Tipografiya Demakova, 1875), pt. 1, p. 53; N. P. Zagoskin, *Russkie vodnie puti i sudovoye delo v do-Petrovskoy Rossii* [*Russian Waterways and Shipping in Pre-Petrine Russia*] (Kazan: Lito-tipografiya I. N. Kharitonova, 1910), p. 454.

133 Divin, "Vtoraya Sibirsko-tikhookeanskaya ekspeditsiya," p. 167.

134 Veselago, *Materialy dlya istorii*, 17 : 144.

135 Davydov, *Dvukratnoye puteshestvie v Ameriku*, 1 : 141.

136 *Ibid.*, p. 142.

137 Sgibnev, "Istorichesky ocherk," 103 (July, 1869) : 53.

138 Ministerstvo inostrannykh del SSSR, *Vneshnyaya politika Rossi*, vol. 1, doc. 99, pp. 266–269; Alaska History Research Project, *Documents Relative to Alaska*, 3 : 178.

139 Von Langsdorff, *Voyages and Travels*, pt. 2, pp. 332–333.

140 Sokolov, "Severnaya ekspeditsiya," p. 430.

141 Sauer, *Account of an Expedition*, 231n.

142 Sarychev, *Puteshestvie*, p. 113.

143 *Ibid.*, p. 110.

144 Davydov, *Dvukratnoye puteshestvie v Ameriku*, 1 : 142.

145 Von Langsdorff, *Voyages and Travels*, pt. 2, p. 12.

146 N. I. Barbashev, *K istorii morekhodnovo obrazovaniya v Rossii* [*Toward a History of Naval Education in Russia*] (Moscow: Izdatelstvo Akademii nauk SSSR, 1959), p. 73.

147 *Ibid.*, pp. 73, 74; A. P., "Okhotsk," p. 137; Myatlev, "Instruktsiya ot General-Leitenanta," fol. 8ᵛ; A. Sgibnev, "Navigatskiya shkoly v Sibiri" ["Navigational Schools in Siberia"], *Morskoy sbornik*, 87, no. 11 (1866) : 11, 13, 23.

148 Barbashev, *K istorii morekhodnovo obrazovaniya*, pp. 73, 73n; Sgibnev, "Navigatskiya shkoly," p. 7.

149 Aleksey Martos, *Pisma o Vostochnoy Sibiri* [*Letters about Eastern Siberia*] (Moscow: Universitetskaya tipografiya, 1827), p. 170; Shcheglov, *Kronologichesky perechen*, p. 251; Sirotkin, "Dokumenty o politike Rossii," p. 87n.

150 [Khlebnikov], "Pisma o Kamchatke," fol. 3.

151 Shteller, "Opisanie strany Kamchatki," pp. 25–26.

152 Cochrane, *Narrative of a Pedestrian Journey*, p. 314.

153 J. M. Tronson, *Personal Narrative of a Voyage to Japan, Kamtschatka, Siberia, Tartary* . . . (London: Smith, Elder & Co., 1859), p. 110.

154 Krasheninnikov, *Opisanie zemli Kamchatki*, pp. 180, 202.

155 Timofey Shmalev, "Izvestiya Kapitana Shmaleva ob Okhotskom porte; o stroyenii sudov i o pr." ["Captain Shmalev's Information about Okhotsk Port; about Shipbuilding, etc."], TsGADA, f. 199, port. 539, pt. 1, d. 12, fol. 10ᵛ.

156 De Lesseps, *Travels in Kamtschatka*, 1 : 9–10n.

157 Krasheninnikov, *Opisanie zemli Kamchatki*, pp. 530–531.

158 Rezanov, "Zapiska gorodnichevo Nizhne-Kamchatska Voyevodskovo," fol. 4.

159 Sgibnev, "Okhotsky port," 105, no. 12 : 55–63.

160 Veselago, *Kratkaya istoriya russkavo flota*, pt. 1, p. 291; Shmalev, "Izvestiya Kapitana Shmaleva," fols. 1–10; Alekseyev, *Okhotsk*, p. 68.

161 Rowand, *Notes of a Journey*, p. 22.

162 Dobell, *Travels in Kamtchatka and Siberia*, 1 : 297–298.

163 Hill, *Travels in Siberia*, 2 : 348.

164 Simpson, *Narrative of a Journey*, 2 : 233.

165 Dobell, *Travels in Kamtchatka and Siberia*, 2 : 27–35.

166 Sauer, *Account of an Expedition*, pp. 274–275.

167 Kruzenshtern, *Puteshestvie vokrug sveta*, p. 6.

168 Divin, "Vtoraya Sibirsko-tikhookeanskaya ekspeditsiya," p. 167.

169 Vagin, *Istoricheskiya svedeniya*, vol. 2, pp. 17–18, 27, suppl., p. 419.

170 Pervy sibirsky komitet, "O predpolozheniyakh Nachalnika Kamchatki," d. 167, fol. 10^v.

171 *Ibid.*, d. 168, fols. 199^v–200.

172 *Ibid.*, fol. 200^v, d. 167, fol. 10.

173 Veselago, *Materialy dlya istorii*, 17 : 313.

174 Andreyev, *Russian Discoveries*, pp. 92–93; Tikhmenev, *Supplement of Documents*, p. 33; Vagin, *Istoricheskiya svedeniya*, 2 : 17.

175 Anonymous, "Vzglyad na torgovlyu," pp. 43–44; Pervy sibirsky komitet, "O predpolozheniyakh Nachalnika Kamchatki," d. 167, fols. 12–13; Silnitsky, "Mery pravitelstva," p. 29; Vagin, *Istoricheskiya svedeniya*, 2 : 22.

176 Dobell, *Travels in Kamtchatka and Siberia*, 2 : 24–27.

177 Anonymous, "Vzglyad na torgovlyu," p. 44; Markov, *Russkie na Vostochnom okeane*, pp. 162–163; Shemelin, *Zhurnal pervavo puteshestviya rossiyan*, pt. 2, pp. 265–266.

178 A. P., "Okhotsk," p. 138*n;* Sgibnev, "Bolshoy kamchatsky naryad," p. 135; Shmalev, "Primechanie uchinyonnoye Kapitanom Timofeiyem Shmalevym," fol. 4.

179 Kapitan Vasily Shmalev, "Ukazy i raporty ob Okhotskom porte s prilozhennym planom" ["Decrees and Reports about Okhotsk Port with an Appended Plan"], TsGADA, f. 199, port. 528, pt. 1, d. 11, fols. 1^v–2.

180 Von Kruzenstern, *Voyage Round the World*, 2 : 198–201.

181 Rezanov, "Zapiska gorodnichevo Nizhne-Kamchatska Voyevodskovo," fol. 2.

182 Dobell, *Travels in Kamtchatka and Siberia*, 2 : 26.

183 Sgibnev, "Istorichesky ocherk," 103 (August, 1869) : 83–84.

Chapter 8: REACTIONS

1 Sgibnev, "Okhotsky port," 105, no. 11 : 81.

2 Gorip, "Iz istorii osvoyeniya," pp. 151–153; Pokrovsky, *Ekspeditsiya*

Beringa, pp. 97, 132, 135; Sokolov, "Severnaya ekspeditsiya," p. 226.

3 Sokolov, "Severnaya ekspeditsiya," p. 226.

4 *Ibid.,* pp. 246–249; Gorip, "Iz istorii osvoyeniya," pp. 151–153.

5 Pokrovsky, *Ekspeditsiya Beringa,* p. 133; Sokolov, "Severnaya ekspeditsiya," p. 249.

6 Kanagev, "Okhotsk," p. 376; A. P., "Okhotsk," pp. 138–139; Savin, "Okhotsk," p. 153; Tikhmenev, *Historical Review,* p. 4.

7 Kanagev, "Okhotsk," p. 376; A. P., "Okhotsk," p. 138; Savin, "Okhotsk," p. 153; Tikhmenev, *Historical Review,* p. 4.

8 Sgibnev, "Okhotsky port," 105, no. 11 : 82; Shcheglov, *Kronologichesky perechen,* p. 250.

9 Shmalev, "Izvestiya Kap. Shmaleva," fol. 31; Shmalev, "Nachalo izyskaniya," fol. 1.

10 Anonymous, "Delo o osvidetelstvovanii novoy i staroy dorogi ot Yakutska do Okhotska i mesta dlya postroiki gor. Aldana" ["File on the Examination of the New and the Old Road from Yakutsk to Okhotsk and the Places for the Construction of the Town of Aldan"], TsGADA, f. 416, op. 1, d. 16, fol. 1.

11 *Ibid.,* fols. 1–2; Sgibnev, "Okhotsky port," 105, no. 11 : 82–83; Shmalev, "Izvestiya Kap. Shmaleva," fols. 30–31.

12 A. P., "Okhotsk," p. 141; Shmalev, "Izvestiya Kap. Shmaleva," fols. 31^v–33; Shmalev, "Primechanie uchinyonnoye Kapitanom Timofeiyem Shmalevym," fol. 5^v; Shmalev, "Nachalo izyskaniya," fols. 1–3.

13 Shmalev, "Primechanie uchinyonnoye Kapitanom Timofeiyem Shmalevym," fols. 8–9^v.

14 Shmalev, "Statisticheskiya i Geograficheskiya Primechaniya," fol. 63; Anonymous, "Delo o osvidetelstvovanii," fol. 2.

15 Akademiya nauk SSSR, Institut yazyka, literatury i istorii Yakutskovo filiala AN SSSR, *Istoriya Yakutskoy ASSR,* 2 : 199; I. I. Mainov, *Russkie krestyane i osedlie inorodtsy Yakutskoy oblasti* [*Russian Peasants and Settled Natives of Yakutsk Oblast*], "Zapiski Imperatorskavo russkavo geograficheskavo obshchestva po Otdeleniyu statistiki," vol. 12 (St. Petersburg: Tipografiya V. F. Kirshbauma, 1912), p. 4; Pavlinov, Vitashevsky, and Levental, *Materialy po obychnomu pravu,* p. 310; Peizen, "Istorichesky ocherk," p. 26; Sgibnev, "Okhotsky port," 105, no. 11 : 83.

16 Andriyevich, *Sibir v XIX stoletii,* pt. 1, p. 74.

17 Sgibnev, "Okhotsky port," 105, no. 11 : 85–86; Andreyev, *Russkie otkrytiya,* pp. 278, 280, 365–367.

18 Bulychev, *Puteshestvie po Sibiri,* pt. 1, p. 111; Sarychev, *Puteshestvie,* pp. 106–107; Sgibnev, "Okhotsky port," 105, no. 11 : 84–86.

19 Russia, *Polnoye sobranie zakonov,* 1st ser., vol. 26, doc. 19,308, p. 68.

20 Sgibnev, "Okhotsky port," 105, no. 11 : 87; Kanagev, "Okhotsk," p. 380; A. P., "Okhotsk," p. 141.

21 Bilbasov, *Arkhiv grafov Mordvinovykh,* 3 : 580–587.

22 A. P., "Okhotsk," p. 142.

23 Sgibnev, "Okhotsky port," 105, no. 12 : 29.

24 *Ibid.*

25 Russia, *Polnoye sobranie zakonov,* 1st ser., vol. 31, suppl., doc. 24,803, pp. 5–6.

26 Sgibnev, "Okhotsky port," 105, no. 12 : 29; Safronov, *Okhotsko-Kamchatsky kray,* p. 17.

27 Sgibnev, "Okhotsky port," 105, no. 12 : 29; Minitsky, "Opisanie Okhotskavo porta," p. 211; Minitsky, "Opisanie Yakutskoy oblasti," p. 168.

28 Sgibnev, "Okhotsky port," 105, no. 12 : 30.

29 *Ibid.,* pp. 29–30; Akademiya nauk SSSR, Institut yazyka, literatury i istorii Yakutskovo filiala AN SSSR, *Istoriya Yakutskoy ASSR,* 2 : 199; Andriyevich, *Sibiri v XIX stoletii,* pt. 2, p. 321.

30 Alekseyev, *Okhotsk,* p. 114; Sgibnev, "Okhotsky port," 105, no. 12 : 31.

31 Sgibnev, "Okhotsky port," 105, no. 12 : 31–32.

32 *Ibid.*

33 Termin, "Kratkoye obozrenie reki Leny," pp. 89, 91.

34 Bulychev, *Puteshestvie po Sibiri,* pt. 1, pp. 112, 114–115; Savin, "Okhotsk," p. 160; Sgibnev, "Okhotsky port," 105, no. 12 : 16; Shmalev, "Primechanie uchinyonnoye Kapitanom Timofeiyem Shmalevym," fol. 2.

35 Al. Sk., "Opis Udskavo berega," p. 16n.

36 Bulychev, *Puteshestvie po Sibiri,* pt. 1, p. 112.

37 Sgibnev, "Okhotsky port," 105, no. 12 : 32.

38 Rossiisko-Amerikanskaya Kompaniya, "Po predstavleniyu Glavnavo Pravleniya Rossiisko-Amerikanskoy Kompanii o predpolozheniyakh onoy Kompanii ustanovit put iz Yakutska k Okhotskomu moryu i o promyshlennosti na Shantarskikh Ostrovakh" ["Concerning the Company's Proposals to Establish a Route from Yakutsk to the Okhotsk Sea and Concerning Business on the Shantar Islands, According to the Representation of the Main Administration of the Russian-American Company"], TsGIAL, f. 18, op. 5, d. 1,288, fols. 1–1ᵛ.

39 Al. Sk., "Opis Udskavo berega," pp. 17–18.

40 *Ibid.,* p. 18.

41 Sgibnev, "Okhotsky port," 105, no. 12 : 32.

42 Al. Sk., "Opis Udskavo berega," p. 72.

43 Sgibnev, "Okhotsky port," 105, no. 12 : 41–42; Tikhmenev, *Historical Review,* pt. 2, pp. 14–15.

44 Mamyshev, "Amerikanskiya vladeniya Rossii," p. 285.

45 *Ibid.,* p. 287; Bulychev, *Puteshestvie po Sibiri,* pt. 1, p. 123; Peizen, "Istorichesky ocherk," p. 39; Sgibnev, "Okhotsky port," 105, no. 12 : 42; [A. Sokolov], "Zaliv Ayan" ["Ayan Bay"], *Zapiski Gidrograficheskavo departamenta,* pt. 4 (1846), pp. 80–83; Tikhmenev, *Historical Review,* pt. 2, pp. 11–12, 23–25, 181.

46 Sgibnev, "Okhotsky port," 105, no. 12 : 42–43; [Sokolov], "Zaliv Ayan," p. 84.

47 Graf M. Tolstoy, "Missionerskaya deyatelnost pokoinavo mitropolita

Innokentiya" ["The Missionary Activity of the Late Metropolitan Innokenty"], *Russky arkhiv*, vol. 17, bk. 2 (1879), p. 283.

48 I. Barsukov, *Pisma Innokentiya mitropolita Moskovskavo i Kolomenskavo 1828–1853 [Letters of Metropolitan Innokenty of Moscow and Kolomna 1828–1853]* (St. Petersburg: Sinodalnaya tipografiya, 1897), bk. 1, p. 207.

49 Sgibnev, "Okhotsky port," 105, no. 12 : 50.

50 *Ibid.*, 51, 53; Barsukov, *Graf Nikolay Nikolayevich Muravyov-Amursky*, vol. 1, pt. 1, pp. 218–221.

51 Struve, *Vospominaniya o Sibiri*, p. 73.

52 Savin, "Okhotsk," p. 148.

53 *Ibid.*, p. 161; Anonymous, "Okhotsky kray," no. 23, p. 135; Khersonsky, "Neskolko slov," p. 12; Sgibnev, "Okhotsky port," 105, no. 12 : 54–55; Vtoroy sibirsky komitet, "Kopiya s otchyota Yakutskavo grazhdanskavo gubernatora o sostoyanii Yakutskoy oblasti za 1854 god" ["A Copy from the Report of the Civil Governor of Yakutsk on the Condition of Yakutsk Oblast for 1854"], TsGIAL, f. 1,265, op. 4, d. 109, fol. 69^v.

Chapter 9: INTRODUCTION

1 F. G. Safronov, "Popytki prodvizheniya granitsy sibirskovo zemledeliya do beregov Tikhovo okeana v XVIII v." ["Attempts at the Extension of the Boundary of Siberian Agriculture up to the Shores of the Pacific Ocean in the XVIIIth Century"], *Izvestiya Vsesoyuznovo geograficheskovo obshchestva*, 86, no. 6 (1954) : 516.

2 V. I. Shunkov, " 'Opyt' v selskom khozyaistve Sibiri XVII veka" [" 'Experimentation' in the Agriculture of Siberia of the XVIIth Century"], in *Materialy po istorii zemledeliya SSSR*, ed. B. D. Grekov (Moscow and Leningrad: Izdatelstvo Akademii nauk SSSR, 1952), collection 1, p. 228.

3 Miller, *Istoriya Sibiri*, 2 : 74; V. E. Pisarev, "K voprosu o proiskhozdenii zemledeliya i polevykh kultur Vostochnoy Sibiri" ["Concerning the Question about the Origin of Agriculture and Field Cropping of Eastern Siberia"], in *Materialy po istorii zemledeliya SSSR*, ed. B. D. Grekov (Moscow and Leningrad: Izdatelstvo Akademii nauk SSSR, 1956), collection 2, p. 196; Ogorodnikov, *Ocherk istorii Sibiri*, pt. 2, no. 3, pp. 11–12; Ogorodnikov, *Tuzemnoye i russkoye zemledelie*, p. 52.

4 Ogorodnikov, *Tuzemnoye i russkoye zemledelie*, p. 52.

5 Pisarev, "K voprosu o proiskhozdenii," p. 197.

6 *Ibid.*, p. 196.

7 Boris Nolde, *La formation de l'Empire russe: études, notes et documents*, "Collection historique de l'Institut d'Etudes slaves," vol. 15 (Paris: Institut d'Etudes slaves, 1952), 1 : 177.

8 Herbert J. Ellison, "Peasant Colonization of Siberia" (Ph.D. diss., Uni-

versity of London, 1955), p. 6; Kozmin, *Ocherki Sibiri,* p. 4; [Slovtsov], *Istoricheskoye obozrenie Sibiri,* 2 : 32.

9 Jerome Blum, *Lord and Peasant in Russia from the Ninth to the Nineteenth Century* (Princeton: Princeton University Press, 1961), p. 430; Pisarev, "K voprosu o proiskhozdenii," p. 197.

10 Pisarev, "K voprosu o proiskhozdenii," p. 197; *Sibirskaya sovetskaya entsiklopediya,* 1 : 727–728.

11 [Slovtsov], *Istoricheskoye obozrenie Sibiri,* 1 : 84–85.

12 Shunkov, "Geograficheskoye razmeshchenie," pp. 216–238.

13 *Ibid.,* p. 237.

Chapter 10: AGRICULTURAL SETTLEMENT

1 Krasheninnikov, *Opisanie zemli Kamchatki,* p. 158.

2 Russia, Pravitelstvuyushchy senat, *Senatsky arkhiv,* 5 : 206.

3 Krasheninnikov, *Opisanie zemli Kamchatki,* pp. 158, 517; Shteller, "Opisanie strany Kamchatki," p. 479.

4 Muller, "Geografiya ili nyneshnoye sostoyanie," fol. 33.

5 Krasheninnikov, *Opisanie zemli Kamchatki,* p. 158.

6 Semyon Baskin, ed., "Bolshoy chertyozh Kamchadalskoy zemli" ["The Great Map of the Kamchadal Land"], *Izvestiya Vsesoyuznovo geograficheskovo obshchestva,* 81, no. 2 (March–April, 1949) : 228; Shcheglov, *Kronologichesky perechen,* p. 158n.

7 Prokopy Gromov, "Istoriko-statisticheskoye opisanie Kamchatskikh tserkvey" ["An Historico-statistical Description of Kamchatkan Churches"], *Trudy Kiyevskoy dukhovnoy akademii,* 1 (1860) : 34.

8 Krasheninnikov, *Opisanie zemli Kamchatki,* p. 783n.

9 *Ibid.,* p. 107.

10 I. Bulychev, "Ob opytakh zemledeliya v Kamchatke" ["Concerning Agricultural Experiments in Kamchatka"], *Vestnik Imperatorskavo russkavo geograficheskavo obshchestva,* pt. 8 (1853), p. 77; Sgibnev, "Istorichesky ocherk," 102 (May, 1869) : 80.

11 [Bering], "Donesenie flota kapitana Beringa," p. 73.

12 *Ibid.*

13 *Ibid.*

14 *Ibid.*

15 Bulychev, "Ob opytakh zemledeliya," p. 78; Sgibnev, "Istorichesky ocherk," 102 (May, 1869) : 80.

16 Muller, "Geografiya ili nyneshnoye sostoyanie," fols. 28–28ᵛ.

17 Krasheninnikov, *Opisanie zemli Kamchatki,* p. 195.

18 Shteller, "Opisanie strany Kamchatki," p. 65.

19 Krasheninnikov, *Opisanie zemli Kamchatki,* p. 102; [Slovtsov], *Istoricheskoye obozrenie Sibiri,* 2 : 85, 205.

20 Imperatorskoye russkoye istoricheskoye obshchestvo, *Protokoly, zhurnaly i ukazy,* p. 290.

21 Sgibnev, "Istorichesky ocherk," 102 (May, 1869) : 80.
22 Sokolov, "Severnaya ekspeditsiya," p. 429.
23 *Ibid.*
24 Russia, *Polnoye sobranie zakonov,* 1st ser., vol. 8, doc. 5,753, p. 461.
25 Shmalev, "Statisticheskiya i Geograficheskiya Primechaniya," fol. 21; Shmalev, "Ukaz i Instruktsiya," fols. 1ᵛ–5ᵛ.
26 Pokrovsky, *Ekspeditsiya Beringa,* p. 214; Russia, *Polnoye sobranie zakonov,* 1st ser., vol. 8, doc. 5,813, pp. 520–524.
27 Russia, *Polnoye sobranie zakonov,* 1st ser., vol. 8, doc. 5,813, pp. 520–524; Sgibnev, "Istorichesky ocherk," 102 (May, 1869) : 80.
28 Russia, *Polnoye sobranie zakonov,* 1st ser., vol. 8, doc. 6,041, p. 771.
29 *Ibid.*
30 *Ibid.*
31 Sgibnev, "Istorichesky ocherk," 102 (May, 1869) : 81.
32 Russia, *Polnoye sobranie zakonov,* 1st ser., vol. 8, doc. 5,813, p. 524; Shmalev, "Ukaz i Instruktsiya," fol. 3ᵛ.
33 Pokrovsky, *Ekspeditsiya Beringa,* p. 216.
34 Bulychev, "Ob opytakh zemledeliya," p. 78; Sgibnev, "Istorichesky ocherk," 102 (May, 1869) : 80–81.
35 Krasheninnikov, *Opisanie zemli Kamchatki,* p. 194; Levin and Potapov, *Narody Sibiri,* p. 984; Semyonov, *Zhivopisnaya Rossiya,* vol. 12, pt. 2, p. 39; Shcheglov, *Kronologichesky perechen,* p. 199; Sgibnev, "Istorichesky ocherk," 102 (May, 1869) : 81; A. P., "Okhotsk," p. 138; Russia, Pravitelstvuyushchy senat, *Senatsky arkhiv,* 5 : 206; Waxell, *Russian Expedition to America,* p. 81.
36 Sgibnev, "Okhotsky port," 105, no. 11 : 31.
37 Shmalev, "Statisticheskiya i Geograficheskiya Primechaniya," fol. 22.
38 Sherstoboyev, *Ilimskaya pashnya,* 2 : 27; D. K. Chernykh, "Kratkoye istoricheskoye obozrenie zemledeliya v Kamchatke" ["A Brief Historical Review of Agriculture in Kamchatka"], *Zemledelchesky zhurnal* . . . , no. 1 (1833), p. 106; Yu. A. Gagemeister, "Khozyaistvenno-statistichesky obzor Kamchatki" ["Economico-statistical Survey of Kamchatka"], *Zhurnal Ministerstva vnutrennikh del,* pt. 42 (1853), p. 249; Peizen, "Istorichesky ocherk," p. 23; Semyonov, *Zhivopisnaya Rossiya,* vol. 12, pt. 2, pp. 38–39; Shcheglov, *Kronologichesky perechen,* pp. 199, 204; Sgibnev, "Okhotsky port," 105, no. 11 : 27.
39 Safronov, "Popytki prodvizheniya," p. 518.
40 Shmalev, "Statisticheskiya i Geograficheskiya Primechaniya," fol. 21ᵛ.
41 Ilimskaya voyevodskaya kantselyariya, "Delo o splavke khleba, semen i gorokha v Yakutsk i v kamchatskuyu ekspeditsiyu" ["File about the Shipping of Grain, Seed, and Peas to Yakutsk and to the Kamchatka Expedition"], TsGADA, f. 494, op. 2, d. 172, sv. 17, fol. 8; Sherstoboyev, *Ilimskaya pashnya,* 2 : 41–42.
42 Ilimskaya voyevodskaya kantselyariya, "Sbornik del," fols. 80–81; Safronov, "Popytki prodvizheniya," p. 518; Sherstoboyev, *Ilimskaya pashnya,* 2 : 43.

43 Safronov, "Popytki prodvizheniya," pp. 518, 519.
44 Ilimskaya voyevodskaya kantselyariya, "Splav khleba" ["Shipping of Grain"], TsGADA, f. 494, op. 2, d. 279, sv. 28, fol. 24; Pokrovsky, *Ekspeditsiya Beringa,* p. 370; Sgibnev, "Istorichesky ocherk," 102 (May, 1869) : 81; Shmalev, "Statisticheskiya i Geograficheskiya Primechaniya," fols. 21ᵛ–22.
45 Krasheninnikov, *Opisanie zemli Kamchatki,* p. 194.
46 Bulychev, "Ob opytakh zemledeliya," p. 78; Safronov, "Popytki prodvizheniya," p. 519.
47 Alkor and Drezen, *Kolonialnaya politika tsarizma,* doc. 53, pp. 143–149; Izbekova, "Materialy o razvitii khlebopashestva," p. 80.
48 Gagemeister, "Khozyaistvenno-statistichesky obzor Kamchatki," p. 249; Sauer, *Account of an Expedition,* p. 291; Semyonov, *Zhivopisnaya Rossiya,* vol. 12, pt. 2, pp. 38, 39; [Slovtsov], *Istoricheskoye obozrenie Sibiri,* 2 : 85; G. Spassky, "O peremenakh, proizshedshikh na Kamchatke so vremeni opisaniya onoy Krasheninnikovym" ["Concerning the Changes Wrought in Kamchatka since the Time of Its Description by Krasheninnikov"], *Sibirsky vestnik,* pt. 4, bks. 19–24 (1824), pp. 333, 337–339; M. Lyubarsky, "Kratkoye izvestie o Kamchatskom zemledelii" ["Brief Information about Kamchatkan Agriculture"], *Severny arkhiv,* pt. 6 (1823), pp. 111, 134n.
49 Anonymous, "Opisanie Udskavo ostroga," pp. 321–322; Divin, "Vtoraya Sibirsko-tikhookeanskaya ekspeditsiya," p. 164; Krasheninnikov, *Opisanie zemli Kamchatki,* p. 161; A. Middendorf, *Puteshestvie na severe i vostoke Sibiri* [*Journey in the North and the East of Siberia*] (St. Petersburg: Tipografiya Imperatorskoy akademii nauk, 1867), pt. 1, suppl. 3, p. xii; Semyonov, *Zhivopisnaya Rossiya,* vol. 12, pt. 2, pp. 164, 166.
50 Anonymous, "Opisanie Udskavo ostroga," p. 322.
51 Alekseyev, *Okhotsk,* p. 67; Krasheninnikov, *Opisanie zemli Kamchatki,* p. 158; Izbekova, "Materialy o razvitii khlebopashestva," p. 81; [Slovtsov], *Istoricheskoye obozrenie Sibiri,* 2 : 84; Shaskolsky, *Geograficheskoye izuchenie Sibiri,* p. 28; Shmalev, "Statisticheskiya i Geograficheskiya Primechaniya," fol. 6.
52 Strelov, *Akty arkhivov,* vol. 1, doc. 46, p. 217.
53 Shmalev, "Statisticheskiya i Geograficheskiya Primechaniya," fol. 23ᵛ.
54 Strelov, *Akty arkhivov,* vol. 1, doc. 46, pp. 217–219.
55 *Ibid.,* pp. 217, 219.
56 Safronov, "Popytki prodvizheniya," p. 521.
57 Middendorf, *Puteshestvie na Sibiri,* pt. 1, suppl. 3, p. xii; Semyonov, *Zhivopisnaya Rossiya,* vol. 12, pt. 2, p. 164.
58 Strelov, *Akty arkhivov,* vol. 1, doc. 46, p. 219.
59 Safronov, "Popytki prodvizheniya," p. 521.
60 Strelov, *Akty arkhivov,* vol. 1, doc. 46, p. 219.
61 Bulychev, "Ob opytakh zemledeliya," p. 81; Lyubarsky, "Kratkoye izvestie," pp. 111–112; Safronov, "Popytki prodvizheniya," p. 521;

Sgibnev, "Istorichesky ocherk," 102 (June, 1869) : 45; Shmalev, "Statisticheskiya i Geograficheskiya Primechaniya," fol. 24.

62 Krasheninnikov, *Opisanie zemli Kamchatki,* p. 255; Shteller, "Opisanie strany Kamchatki," p. 175.

Chapter 11: PRODUCTION

1 Krasheninnikov, *Opisanie zemli Kamchatki,* pp. 196–197; Sgibnev, "Istorichesky ocherk," 102 (May, 1869) : 81; Sokolov, "Severnaya ekspeditsiya," pp. 424–425n.

2 Krasheninnikov, *Opisanie zemli Kamchatki,* pp. 195–198.

3 Shteller, "Opisanie strany Kamchatki," pp. 62–64.

4 Krasheninnikov, *Opisanie zemli Kamchatki,* pp. 196–197.

5 *Ibid.,* p. 158.

6 *Ibid.,* p. 161.

7 *Ibid.,* p. 195.

8 *Ibid.,* p. 502.

9 *Ibid.,* p. 198.

10 Shteller, "Opisanie strany Kamchatki," p. 65.

11 *Ibid.,* p. 66.

12 Waxell, *Russian Expedition to America,* p. 140.

13 Sokolov, "Severnaya ekspeditsiya," pp. 424–425n.

14 Krasheninnikov, *Opisanie zemli Kamchatki,* p. 194.

15 *Ibid.,* p. 196.

16 Shteller, "Opisanie strany Kamchatki," p. 66.

17 *Ibid.,* pp. 66–67.

18 *Ibid.,* p. 67.

19 *Ibid.,* pp. 67–68.

20 Krasheninnikov, *Opisanie zemli Kamchatki,* p. 255.

21 *Ibid.*

22 Sokolov, "Severnaya ekspeditsiya," pp. 424–425n.

23 Beaumont, "Essais d'agriculture," p. 121; Bulychev, "Ob opytakh zemledeliya," pp. 78, 80; Sgibnev, "Istorichesky ocherk," 102 (May, 1869) : 81.

24 Bulychev, "Ob opytakh zemledeliya," pp. 79–80; G. Spassky, "O peremenakh," p. 337.

25 Shmalev, "Statisticheskiya i Geograficheskiya Primechaniya," fol. 22^{v}.

26 Lyashchenko, *History of the National Economy,* p. 324.

27 P. Pallas, "Izvestiya o vvedennom skotovodstve i zemlepashestve v Kamchatke i okolo Okhotska, pri Udskom ostroge lezhashchem podle Okhotskavo morya" ["Information about Stockbreeding and Cultivation Introduced into Kamchatka and around Okhotsk, Lying alongside the Okhotsk Sea near Udsk Ostrog"], *Prodolzhenie trudov Volnavo ekonomicheskavo obshchestva . . . ,* pt. 3 (1783), p. 31; [Slovtsov], *Istoricheskoye obozrenie Sibiri,* 2 : 355.

28 Chernykh, "Kratkoye istoricheskoye obozrenie," pp. 107–108;

Gagemeister, "Khozyaistvenno-statistichesky obzor Kamchatki," p. 250; Nachalnik Golenishchev and Chinovniki Lazarev and Chernykh, "Izvestiya iz Kamchatki o sredstvakh predprinimayemykh k uluchsheniyu v onoy Selskavo Khozyaistva" ["Information from Kamchatka about the Means Undertaken toward the Improvement of Agriculture There"], *Zemledelchesky zhurnal* . . . , no. 29 (1830), pp. 223–224; Lyubarsky, "Kratkoye izvestie," p. 116; Pallas, "Izvestiya o vvedennom skotovodstve," pp. 31–32; Sgibnev, "Istorichesky ocherk," 103 (July, 1869) : 13; [Slovtsov], *Istoricheskoye obozrenie Sibiri,* 2 : 355–356; Major Von Bem, "O Kamchatskom zemledelii . . ." ["Concerning Kamchatkan Agriculture . . ."], *Prodolzhenie trudov Volnavo ekonomicheskavo obshchestva* . . . , pt. 3 (1783), p. 43.

29 Chernykh, "Kratkoye istoricheskoye obozrenie," p. 108; Gagemeister, "Khozyaistvenno-statistichesky obzor Kamchatki," p. 250.

30 Golenishchev, Lazarev, and Chernykh, "Izvestiya iz Kamchatki," p. 223; [Slovtsov], *Istoricheskoye obozrenie Sibiri,* 2 : 356; Von Bem, "O Kamchatskom zemledelii," p. 43.

31 Rezanov, "Zapiska gorodnichevo Nizhne-Kamchatska Voyevodskovo," fol. 2.

32 *Ibid.,* fol. 1.

33 Von Langsdorff, *Voyages and Travels,* pt. 2, pp. 306–307, 326.

34 Nachalnik Golenishchev, Direktory Rider, Chernykh, and Paderin, and Chinovnik Lazarev, "O deistviyakh Kamchatskoy zemledelcheskoy kompanii" ["Concerning the Activities of the Kamchatka Agricultural Company"], *Zemledelchesky zhurnal* . . . , no. 1 (1833), p. 604; P. Rikord, Timofey Burnashev, Gvardii polkovnik Bronevsky, and Korpusny komandir Kaptsevich, "Pisma iz Kamchatki, Okhotska, Nerchinska i Omska, o sostoyanii Selskavo Khozyaistva v Sibiri i ob uspekhakh onavo" ["Letters from Kamchatka, Okhotsk, Nerchinsk, and Omsk about the Condition of Agriculture in Siberia and about Its Successes"], *Zemledelchesky zhurnal* . . . , 3, no. 8 (1823) : 234.

35 Bulychev, "Ob opytakh zemledeliya," p. 80; Sgibnev, "Istorichesky ocherk," 102 (May, 1869) : 81–82, 103 (August, 1869) : 102.

36 Rezanov, "Zapiska gorodnichevo Nizhne-Kamchatska Voyevodskovo," fol. 1.

37 Beaumont, "Essais d'agriculture," p. 125; Bulychev, "Ob opytakh zemledeliya," p. 85; Chernykh, "Kratkoye istoricheskoye obozrenie," pp. 109–110; Gagemeister, "Khozyaistvenno-statistichesky obzor Kamchatki," p. 250; Golenishchev, Lazarev, and Chernykh, "Izvestiya iz Kamchatki," p. 224; Pervy sibirsky komitet, "O predpolozheniyakh Nachalnika Kamchatki," d. 168, fol. 200ᵛ; Safronov, "Popytki prodvizheniya," p. 525; Semyonov, *Zhivopisnaya Rossiya,* vol. 12, pt. 2, p. 39; Sgibnev, "Istorichesky ocherk," 103 (July, 1869) : 48–49, 68.

38 Ministerstvo gosudarstvennykh imushchestv, Trety departament, "O zanyatiyakh po selskomu khozyaistvu nakhodyashchegosya v Kamchatke 14 klassa Lazareva" ["Concerning the Agricultural Occupa-

tions in Kamchatka of Lazarev of the 14th Class"], TsGIAL, f. 398, op. 1, d. 879, fol. 3.

39 Anonymous, "Opisanie Udskavo ostroga," p. 322; Krasheninnikov, *Opisanie zemli Kamchatki,* p. 783*n;* A. P., "Okhotsk," p. 138; Russia, Pravitelstvuyushchy senat, *Senatsky arkhiv,* 5 : 206.

40 Middendorf, *Puteshestvie na Sibiri,* pt. 1, suppl. 3, p. xiii.

41 Divin, "Vtoraya Sibirsko-tikhookeanskaya ekspeditsiya," p. 163.

42 Semyonov, *Zhivopisnaya Rossiya,* vol. 12, pt. 2, p. 165.

43 *Ibid.,* p. 164; Middendorf, *Puteshestvie na Sibiri,* pt. 1, suppl. 3, p. xiii; Safronov, "Popytki prodvizheniya," pp. 523, 525.

44 Middendorf, *Puteshestvie na Sibiri,* pt. 1, suppl. 3, p. xiii.

45 *Ibid.,* p. xiv; Anonymous, "Opisanie Udskavo ostroga," p. 323; Semyonov, *Zhivopisnaya Rossiya,* vol. 12, pt. 2, p. 164.

46 Middendorf, *Puteshestvie na Sibiri,* pt. 1, suppl. 3, p. xv.

47 *Ibid.;* Semyonov, *Zhivopisnaya Rossiya,* vol. 12, pt. 3, p. 165; Sverbeyev, "Sibirskiya pisma" ["Siberian Letters"], *Vestnik Imperatorskavo russkavo geograficheskavo obshchestva,* vol. 8, pt. 7 (1853), pp. 103–105; F. Bocharov, "Neskolko slov ob Udskom kraye" ["Several Words about Udsk Kray"], *Vostochnoye Pomorye,* no. 20 (October 16/28, 1865), p. 118.

48 Bulychev, "Ob opytakh zemledeliya," p. 78; A. P., "Okhotsk," p. 135; Pallas, "Izvestiya o vvedennom skotovodstve," pp. 27–28; Peizen, "Istorichesky ocherk," p. 23; Shmalev, "Izvestiya Kap. Shmaleva," fol. 38; Shmalev, "Statisticheskiya i Geograficheskiya Primechaniya," fols. 66–67.

49 Alekseyev, *Okhotsk,* p. 67; Minitsky, "Nekotoria izvestiya," p. 91; Minitsky, "Opisanie Okhotskavo porta," p. 214.

50 Anonymous, "Izvestie iz Gizhigi" ["Information from Gizhiga"], *Vostochnoye Pomorye,* no. 10 (August 7/19, 1865), p. 59; Silnitsky, "Mery pravitelstva," p. 28.

51 Shmalev, "Statisticheskiya i Geograficheskiya Primechaniya," fol. 24^v.

52 Krasheninnikov, *Opisanie zemli Kamchatki,* p. 196; Waxell, *Russian Expedition to America,* p. 140.

53 Rikord, Burnashev, Bronevsky, and Kaptsevich, "Pisma iz Kamchatki," p. 232.

54 Krasheninnikov, *Opisanie zemli Kamchatki,* p. 196; Beaumont, "Essais d'agriculture," p. 123.

55 Bulychev, "Ob opytakh zemledeliya," p. 87; Sgibnev, "Istorichesky ocherk," 103 (July, 1869) : 13, 103 (August, 1869) : 102; Shmalev, "Kratkoye opisanie," p. 208.

56 Rikord, Burnashev, Bronevsky, and Kaptsevich, "Pisma iz Kamchatki," p. 233.

57 [G. Golenishchev], "O sostoyanii Kamchatskoy oblasti v 1830 i 1831 godakh" ["Concerning the Condition of Kamchatka Oblast in 1830 and 1831"], *Zhurnal Ministerstva vnutrennikh del,* pt. 10 (1833), pp. 5, 12.

58 Levin and Potapov, *Narody Sibiri,* p. 983; Sgibnev, "Istorichesky ocherk," 103 (August, 1869) : 102.

59 Dobell, *Travels in Kamtchatka and Siberia,* 1 : 49.

60 Cochrane, *Narrative of a Pedestrian Journey,* p. 279.

61 P. K., "O vozmozhnosti uluchsheniya," pp. 302–303; Byvaly, "Pochva i klimat Kamchatki," pp. 183–184; Pallas, "Izvestiya o vvedennom skotovodstve," p. 36; Rikord, Burnashev, Bronevsky, and Kaptsevich, "Pisma iz Kamchatki," p. 232.

62 Otto Von Kotzebue, *A New Voyage Round the World, in the Years 1823, 24, 25, and 26* (London: Henry Colburn and Richard Bentley, 1830), 2 : 6.

63 Beaumont, "Essais d'agriculture," p. 128; Bulychev, "Ob opytakh zemledeliya," p. 87; Gagemeister, "Khozyaistvenno-statistichesky obzor Kamchatki," p. 252; Golenishchev, Rider, Chernykh, Paderin, and Lazarev, "O deistviyakh," p. 604; P. K., "O vozmozhnosti uluchshe-niya," p. 292; [Kapitan Mashin], "Vypiska iz pisma Nachalnika Kam-chatki, g. Mashina, k Nepremennomu sekretaryu V. e. obshchestva" ["Extracts from a Letter of the Commandant of Kamchatka, Mr. Mashin, to the Permanent Secretary of the F. E. Society"], *Trudy Imperatorskavo volnavo ekonomicheskavo obshchestva,* no. 6, pt. 2 (1848), sec. 3, p. 108; Sgibnev, "Istorichesky ocherk," 103 (August, 1869) : 66, 78.

64 [Mashin], "Vypiska iz pisma," p. 108.

65 N. Shchukin, "Ogorodnichestvo Vostochnoy Sibiri" ["Gardening of Eastern Siberia"], *Biblioteka dlya chteniya,* 93 (1849) : 6; Sgibnev, "Istorichesky ocherk," 103 (August, 1869) : 102.

66 Collins, *Siberian Journey,* p. 341.

67 [Slovtsov], *Istoricheskoye obozrenie Sibiri,* 2 : 355; Pallas, "Izvestiya o vvedennom skotovodstve," pp. 28–29; Sgibnev, "Okhotsky port," 105, no. 11 : 56.

68 Sarychev, *Puteshestvie,* p. 59.

69 Shaskolsky, *Geograficheskoye izuchenie Sibiri,* pp. 27–28.

70 Minitsky, "Nekotoria izvestiya," p. 91.

71 Minitsky, "Opisanie Okhotskavo porta," p. 214.

72 Middendorf, *Puteshestvie na Sibiri,* pt. 1, suppl. 3, p. xv; Semyonov, *Zhivopisnaya Rossiya,* vol. 12, pt. 2, p. 165; Shakhovskoy, "Mnenie, o sposobakh prodovolstviya," p. 346; [Slovtsov], *Istoricheskoye obozrenie Sibiri,* 2 : 355; Captain Tebenkov, *Gidrograficheskiya zamechaniya k atlasu severozapadnykh beregov Ameriki . . . [Hydrographical Ob-servations Accompanying the Atlas of the Northwestern Shores of America . . .]* (St. Petersburg: Tipografiya Morskavo kadetskavo korpusa, 1852), p. 143.

73 M. A. Sergeyev, *Narodnoye khozyaistvo Kamchatskovo kraya [The National Economy of Kamchatka Kray]* (Moscow and Leningrad: Izdatelstvo Akademii nauk SSSR, 1936), pp. 542, 546.

74 Von Kruzenstern, *Voyage Round the World,* 1 : 214.

75 Gagemeister, "Khozyaistvenno-statistichesky obzor Kamchatki," pp. 237, 244; P. K., "O vozmozhnosti uluchsheniya," p. 303; Lyubarsky, "Kratkoye izvestie," p. 133*n;* Rikord, Burnashev, Bronevsky, and Kaptsevich, "Pisma iz Kamchatki," p. 235; Von Langsdorff, *Voyages and Travels,* pt. 2, p. 307.
76 Krasheninnikov, *Opisanie zemli Kamchatki,* p. 196.
77 Erman, *Travels in Siberia,* 2 : 398*n.*
78 Divin, "Vtoraya Sibirsko-tikhookeanskaya ekspeditsiya," pp. 163–164; Middendorf, *Puteshestvie na Sibiri,* pt. 2, pp. 551, 551–552*n.*
79 Krasheninnikov, *Opisanie zemli Kamchatki,* p. 158; Rezanov, "Zapiska gorodnichevo Nizhne-Kamchatska Voyevodskovo," fol. 3.
80 Shaskolsky, *Geografícheskoye izuchenie Sibiri,* p. 28.
81 Sgibnev, "Okhotsky port," 105, no. 11 : 56; Minitsky, "Opisanie Okhotskavo porta," p. 217; Anonymous, "Opisanie Irkutskoy gubernii," fols. 51ᵛ–52; Erman, *Travels in Siberia,* 2 : 398; Vtoroy sibirsky komitet, "Kopiya s otchyota," fol. 77; Anonymous, "Izvestie iz Gizhigi," p. 59.

Chapter 12: AGRICULTURAL PROBLEMS

1 Bulychev, "Ob opytakh zemledeliya," pp. 77, 85; Cochrane, *Narrative of a Pedestrian Journey,* p. 288; Lyubarsky, "Kratkoye izvestie," p. 126; Pallas, "Izvestiya o vvedennom skotovodstve," p. 29; Sarychev, *Puteshestvie,* p. 59; Sgibnev, "Istorichesky ocherk," 102 (May, 1869) : 80, 103 (August, 1869) : 78.
2 Pervy sibirsky komitet, "O predpolozheniyakh Nachalnika Kamchatki," d. 167, fol. 23ᵛ.
3 Sarychev, *Puteshestvie,* p. 59; Byvaly, "Pochva i klimat Kamchatki," p. 192; Middendorf, *Puteshestvie na Sibiri,* pt. 1, suppl. 3, p. xiii; Safronov, "Popytki prodvizheniya," p. 523.
4 [Bering], "Donesenie flota kapitana Beringa," p. 73.
5 Krasheninnikov, *Opisanie zemli Kamchatki,* p. 197.
6 Shmalev, "Statisticheskiya i Geograficheskiya Primechaniya," fol. 22.
7 Von Bem, "O Kamchatskom zemledelii," p. 44.
8 Byvaly, "Pochva i klimat Kamchatki," p. 189; Lyubarsky, "Kratkoye izvestie," p. 134*n;* Russia, Ministerstvo vnutrennikh del, *Statisticheskoye obozrenie Sibiri,* p. 353; Shmalev, "Kratkoye o Kamchatke obyasnenie," fol. 4ᵛ.
9 Alaska History Research Project, *Documents Relative to Alaska,* 3 : 241; Gagemeister, "Khozyaistvenno-statisticheskoy obzor Kamchatki," p. 252; Lyubarsky, "Kratkoye izvestie," p. 127; Russia, Ministerstvo vnutrennikh del, *Statisticheskoye obozrenie Sibiri,* pp. 353–354; Shmalev, "Statisticheskiya i Geograficheskiya Primechaniya," fol. 24; William Tooke, *View of the Russian Empire, During the Reign of Catherine the Second, and to the Close of the Eighteenth Century,* 2d ed. (London: T. N. Longman and O. Rees, 1800), 3 : 152; Von Bem, "O Kamchatskom zemledelii," pp. 44–45.

10 Safronov, "Popytki prodvizheniya," p. 520.

11 Chernykh, "Kratkoye istoricheskoye obozrenie," p. 112.

12 Lyubarsky, "Kratkoye izvestie," pp. 117, 131.

13 Minitsky, "Ob Okhotskom porte," *Severnaya pochta*, no. 49, p. [4].

14 Sgibnev, "Okhotsky port," 105, no. 12 : 43.

15 *Ibid.*, no. 11 : 56; Middendorf, *Puteshestvie na Sibiri*, pt. 1, suppl. 3, pp. xii–xiv; Rowand, *Notes of a Journey*, p. 21; Tebenkov, *Gidrograficheskiya zamechaniya*, p. 144.

16 Pallas, "Izvestiya o vvedennom skotovodstve," p. 28.

17 Simpson, *Narrative of a Journey Round the World*, 2 : 249–250.

18 De Semenov, *La Russie Extra-Européene et Polaire*, p. 91; A. C. Hildreth, J. R. Magness, and John W. Mitchell, "Effects of Climatic Factors on Growing Plants," in *Climate and Man*, Yearbook of Agriculture (Washington, D.C.: U. S. Government Printing Office, 1941), p. 294; P. I. Koloskov, "Klimatichesky ocherk poluostrova Kamchatki," ["Climatic Survey of the Kamchatka Peninsula"], *Izvestiya Dalnevostochnovo geofizicheskovo instituta*, no. 2 (1932), p. 134.

19 Shteller, "Opisanie strany Kamchatki," pp. 80–81.

20 Waxell, *Russian Expedition to America*, p. 140.

21 *Ibid.*

22 [Golovnin], *Sochineniya i perevody*, 5 : 110

23 Sauer, *Account of an Expedition*, p. 40.

24 Anonymous, "Okhotsky kray," no. 23, p. 135.

25 Middendorf, *Puteshestvie na Sibiri*, pt. 1, suppl. 3, p. xv.

26 Cochrane, *Narrative of a Pedestrian Journey*, p. 288.

27 Lyubarsky, "Kratkoye izvestie," p. 127.

28 Anonymous, "Opisanie Udskavo ostroga," pp. 322–323; Divin, "Vtoraya Sibirsko-tikhookeanskaya ekspeditsiya," p. 172*n*.

29 Middendorf, *Puteshestvie na Sibiri*, pt. 1, suppl. 3, p. xii; Semyonov, *Zhivopisnaya Rossiya*, vol. 12, pt. 2, p. 164.

30 Middendorf, *Puteshestvie na Sibiri*, pt. 1, suppl. 3, pp. xviii–xix; Safronov, *Okhotsko-Kamchatsky kray*, p. 78.

31 Izbekova, "Materialy o razvitii khlebopashestva," p. 81; Middendorf, *Puteshestvie na Sibiri*, pt. 1, suppl. 3, pp. xiv, xviii–xix; Safronov, *Okhotsko-Kamchatsky kray*, p. 78.

32 Beaumont, "Essais d'agriculture," p. 118; Divin, "Vtoraya Sibirsko-tikhookeanskaya ekspeditsiya," pp. 163–164; Sauer, *Account of an Expedition*, p. 290; Shchukin, "Udskoye selenie," 35, no. 114 : 456.

33 Pervy sibirsky komitet, "O predpolozheniyakh Nachalnika Kamchatki," d. 167, fol. 24^{v}.

34 *Ibid.*, fol. 25.

35 Krasheninnikov, *Opisanie zemli Kamchatki*, pp. 208–210.

36 *Ibid.*, pp. 207, 210; Semyonov, *Zhivopisnaya Rossiya*, vol. 12, pt. 2, p. 5; Sgibnev, "Istorichesky ocherk," 103 (July, 1869) : 39*n*.

37 Alekseyev, *Okhotsk*, pp. 84–85.

38 Anonymous, "Poluostrov Kamchatka," no. 92, p. 368; Cochrane, *Narrative of a Pedestrian Journey*, p. 288; Cook [and King], *Voyage to the*

Pacific Ocean, 3 : 327; Gagemeister, "Khozyaistvenno-statistichesky obzor Kamchatki," p. 237; Krasheninnikov, *Opisanie zemli Kamchatki*, pp. 158, 196; Minitsky, "Nekotoria izvestiya," p. 99; Sgibnev, "Istorichesky ocherk," 103 (July, 1869) : 26–27.

39 Shmalev, "Primechanie uchinyonnoye Kapitanom Timofeiyem Shmalevym," fol. 8ᵛ; Shmalev, "Nachalo izyskaniya novavo trakta," fol. 6.

40 Anonymous, "Opisanie Udskavo ostroga," p. 325; Tebenkov, *Gidrograficheskiya zamechaniya*, p. 144.

41 Middendorf, *Puteshestvie na Sibiri*, pt. 2, p. 552.

42 Semyonov, *Zhivopisnaya Rossiya*, vol. 12, pt. 2, p. 165.

43 Middendorf, *Puteshestvie na Sibiri*, pt. 1, suppl. 3, pp. xvi–xvii, xix.

44 *Ibid.*, p. xx.

45 Rezanov, "Zapiska gorodnichevo Nizhne-Kamchatska Voyevodskovo," fol. 3.

46 Sergeyev, *Narodnoye khozyaistvo*, p. 544; Shmalev, "Statisticheskiya i Geograficheskiya Primechaniya," fol. 16ᵛ.

47 Sergeyev, *Narodnoye khozyaistvo*, pp. 544, 547–548; Levin and Potapov, *Narody Sibiri*, p. 984; Shmalev, "Kratkoye opisanie," p. 209.

48 Anonymous, "Opisanie Udskavo ostroga," p. 325; Middendorf, *Puteshestvie na Sibiri*, pt. 2, p. 553.

49 Middendorf, *Puteshestvie na Sibiri*, pt. 1, suppl. 3, p. xiii; Semyonov, *Zhivopisnaya Rossiya*, vol. 12, pt. 2, p. 164.

50 Simpson, *Narrative of a Journey*, 2 : 250; De Lesseps, *Travels in Kamtschatka*, 2 : 224–225n.

51 Sauer, *Account of an Expedition*, p. 41.

52 *Ibid.;* Pallas, "Izvestiya o vvedennom skotovodstve," p. 40; Sgibnev, "Okhotsky port," 105, no. 11 : 56; Middendorf, *Puteshestvie na Sibiri*, pt. 1, suppl. 3, p. xvi, pt. 2, p. 552, 552n.

53 Levin and Potapov, *Narody Sibiri*, p. 984; Sergeyev, *Narodnoye khozyaistvo*, pp. 543–544.

54 Krasheninnikov, *Opisanie zemli Kamchatki*, p. 247.

55 Shteller, "Opisanie strany Kamchatki," pp. 142, 147.

56 [Khlebnikov], "Pisma o Kamchatke," fol. 11ᵛ.

57 Sgibnev, "Istorichesky ocherk," 103 (August, 1869) : 34; Anonymous, "Vzglyad na torgovlyu," pp. 33–34; Dobell, *Travels in Kamtchatka and Siberia*, 1 : 79.

58 Shteller, "Opisanie strany Kamchatki," p. 166; Cochrane, *Narrative of a Pedestrian Journey*, p. 289; De Lesseps, *Travels in Kamtschatka*, 1 : 115–116; Krasheninnikov, *Opisanie zemli Kamchatki*, p. 253; Cook [and King], *Voyage to the Pacific Ocean*, 3 : 215; Pallas, "Izvestiya o vvedennom skotovodstve," p. 39; Golovnin, *Puteshestvie na shlyupe "Diana,"* p. 276; Gagemeister, "Khozyaistvenno-statistichesky obzor Kamchatki," p. 245.

59 Shchukin, "Udskoye selenie," *Russky invalid*, 35, no. 115 : 460; Shchukin, "Udskoye selenie," *Zhurnal Ministerstva vnutrennikh del*, p. 180.

60 Pallas, "Izvestiya o vvedennom skotovodstve," p. 37.
61 Shchukin, "Udskoye selenie," *Russky invalid*, 35, no. 114 : 456; Shchukin, "Udskoye selenie," *Zhurnal Ministerstva vnutrennikh del*, p. 179; Anonymous, "Opisanie Udskavo ostroga," p. 324.
62 Divin, "Vtoraya Sibirsko-tikhookeanskaya ekspeditsiya," pp. 163–164; Levin and Potapov, *Narody Sibiri*, p. 984; [Mashin], "Vypiska iz pisma," p. 109; Pallas, "Izvestiya o vvedennom skotovodstve," p. 39; Sgibnev, "Istorichesky ocherk," 103 (July, 1869) : 51.
63 Tikhmenev, *Supplement of Documents*, p. 276.
64 Shmalev, "Kratkoye o Kamchatke obyasnenie," fols. 4ᵛ–5; Shmalev, "Kratkoye opisanie," p. 211; [Slovtsov], *Istoricheskoye obozrenie Sibiri*, 2 : 355.
65 Von Bem, "O Kamchatskom zemledelii," p. 43.
66 De Lesseps, *Travels in Kamtschatka*, 1 : 174.
67 Rezanov, "Zapiska gorodnichevo Nizhne-Kamchatska Voyevodskovo," fols. 1, 5; Von Langsdorff, *Voyages and Travels*, pt. 2, p. 306; Sgibnev, "Istorichesky ocherk," 103 (August, 1869) : 37; Lyubarsky, "Kratkoye izvestie," p. 134n; Spassky, "O peremenakh," pp. 333, 337; [Golenishchev], "O sostoyanii Kamchatksoy oblasti," p. 2; Pervy sibirsky komitet, "O predpolozheniyakh Nachalnika Kamchatki," d. 167, fols. 2, 8, d. 168, fols. 147–147ᵛ; Vagin, *Istoricheskiya svedeniya*, 2 : 43; Sauer, *Account of an Expedition*, p. 306.
68 Andriyevich, *Sibir v XIX stoletii*, pt. 2, pp. 75–76.
69 Golenishchev, Lazarev, and Chernykh, "Izvestiya iz Kamchatki," pp. 224–225.
70 [Khlebnikov], "Pisma o Kamchatke," fol. 11.
71 Nachalnik Golenishchev and Direktory Nadezhin and Sakharov, "Otchyot Kamchatskoy zemledelcheskoy kompanii za 1833-ye leto" ["Report of the Kamchatka Agricultural Company for 1833"], *Zemledelchesky zhurnal . . .* , no. 4 (1834), pp. 586–587.
72 *Ibid.;* [Mashin], "Vypiska iz pisma," pp. 109–111.
73 Rezanov, "Zapiska gorodnichevo Nizhne-Kamchatska Voyevodskovo," fol. 3; Safronov, *Okhotsko-Kamchatsky kray*, p. 102; Sgibnev, "Istorichesky ocherk," 103 (July, 1869) : 48.
74 Rezanov, "Opisanie morskavo berega," fol. 2.
75 Minitsky, "Nekotoria izvestiya," pp. 93–94; Minitsky, "Opisanie Okhotskavo porta," p. 216.
76 Sgibnev, "Okhotsky port," 105, no. 12 : 49; Shchukin, "Udskoye selenie," *Russky invalid*, 35, no. 114 : 456; Shchukin, "Udskoye selenie," *Zhurnal Ministerstva vnutrennikh del*, p. 177.
77 De Lesseps, *Travels in Kamtschatka*, 1 : 94, 128; [Khlebnikov], "Pisma o Kamchatke," fol. 26; Bulychev, "Ob opytakh zemledeliya," pp. 82–83; Sauer, *Account of an Expedition*, p. 307.
78 De Lesseps, *Travels in Kamtschatka*, 1 : 199.
79 [Khlebnikov], "Pisma o Kamchatke," fol. 26.
80 Cochrane, *Narrative of a Pedestrian Journey*, pp. 268, 270, 274, 280.

81 Divin, "Vtoraya Sibirsko-tikhookeanskaya ekspeditsiya," p. 172n; Krasheninnikov, *Opisanie zemli Kamchatki*, pp. 241, 244; Lyubarsky, "Kratkoye izvestie," pp. 131–132.

82 [Golovnin], *Sochineniya i perevody*, 5 : 28.

83 Minitsky, "Opisanie Okhotskavo porta," p. 217.

84 Middendorf, *Puteshestvie na Sibiri*, pt. 1, suppl. 3, p. xiii; Semyonov, *Zhivopisnaya Rossiya*, vol. 12, pt. 2, p. 164.

85 Krasheninnikov, *Opisanie zemli Kamchatki*, p. 256.

86 *Ibid.*, pp. 163, 198.

87 Shteller, "Opisanie strany Kamchatki," p. 65.

88 Alkor and Grekov, *Kolonialnaya politika Moskovskovo gosudarstva*, doc. 133, p. 194; V. N. Skalon, *Russkie zemleprokhodtsy—issledovateli Sibiri XVII veka [Russian Landsmen—Explorers of Siberia of the XVIIth Century]* (Moscow: Moskovskoye obshchestvo ispytateley prirody, 1951), p. 94.

89 Von Krusenstern, *Voyage Round the World*, 2 : 244–245.

90 De Lesseps, *Travels in Kamtschatka*, 1 : 174.

91 Sauer, *Account of an Expedition*, pp. 291–292.

92 Dobell, *Travels in Kamtchatka and Siberia*, 1 : 51.

93 [Khlebnikov], "Pisma o Kamchatke," fol. 11ᵛ.

94 Lyubarsky, "Kratkoye izvestie," p. 133n.

95 Dobell, *Travels in Kamtchatka and Siberia*, 1 : 38–39, 51.

96 Sgibnev, "Okhotsky port," 105, no. 11 : 53.

97 Al. Sk., "Opis Udskavo berega," p. 62.

98 Middendorf, *Puteshestvie na Sibiri*, pt. 2, p. 553.

99 Dobell, *Travels in Kamtchatka and Siberia*, 1 : 74.

100 *Ibid.*, 1 : 51–52.

101 *Ibid.*, 2 : 23.

102 *Ibid.*

103 Shteller, "Opisanie strany Kamchatki," pp. 60–61.

104 Sauer, *Account of an Expedition*, p. 291.

105 Middendorf, *Puteshestvie na Sibiri*, pt. 1, suppl. 3, p. xiv; Pallas, "Izvestiya o vvedennom skotovodstve," pp. 36–37.

106 Blum, *Lord and Peasant in Russia*, p. 328.

107 Semyonov, *Zhivopisnaya Rossiya*, vol. 12, pt. 2, p. 165.

Chapter 13: REACTIONS

1 Alkor and Drezen, *Kolonialnaya politika tsarizma*, doc. 53, p. 146.

2 *Ibid.*

3 Bulychev, "Ob opytakh zemledeliya," pp. 78–79; Sgibnev, "Istoriche-sky ocherk," 102 (May, 1869) : 81.

4 Bulychev, "Ob opytakh zemledeliya," p. 79; Sgibnev, "Istorichesky ocherk," 102 (May, 1869) : 80–81.

5 Bulychev, "Ob opytakh zemledeliya," p. 79; Strelov, *Akty arkhivov Yakutskoy oblasti*, vol. 1, doc. 46, p. 216.

6 Bulychev, "Ob opytakh zemledeliya," p. 79.

7 *Ibid.;* Sgibnev, "Istorichesky ocherk," 102 (May, 1869) : 82.

8 Izbekova, "Materialy o razvitii khlebopashestva," p. 81.

9 Strelov, *Akty arkhivov Yakutskoy oblasti,* vol. 1, doc. 46, p. 212.

10 Shmalev, "Kratkoye opisanie," pp. 209, 211.

11 Safronov, "Popytki prodvizheniya," p. 522; Sgibnev, "Istorichesky ocherk," 102 (May, 1869) : 81–82.

12 Russia, *Polnoye sobranie zakonov,* 1st ser., vol. 15, doc. 11,193, p. 634; Strelov, *Akty arkhivov Yakutskoy oblasti,* vol. 1, doc. 46, pp. 212–213.

13 Russia, *Polnoye sobranie zakonov,* 1st ser., vol. 15, doc. 11,193, p. 633.

14 *Ibid.,* p. 634; Strelov, *Akty arkhivov Yakutskoy oblasti,* vol. 1, doc. 46, p. 213.

15 Russia, *Polnoye sobranie zakonov,* 1st ser., vol. 15, doc. 11,193, p. 634; Strelov, *Akty arkhivov Yakutskoy oblasti,* vol. 1, doc. 46, p. 214.

16 Safronov, "Popytki prodvizheniya," p. 522; Safronov, *Okhotsko-Kamchatsky kray,* p. 72.

17 Safronov, "Popytki prodvizheniya," p. 524.

18 *Ibid.,* pp. 522–523; Safronov, *Okhotsko-Kamchatsky kray,* p. 73; Sgibnev, "Istorichesky ocherk," 102 (May, 1869) : 82; Strelov, *Akty arkhivov Yakutskoy oblasti,* vol. 1, doc. 46, pp. 211–219.

19 Divin, "Vtoraya Sibirsko-tikhookeanskaya ekspeditsiya," p. 169.

20 *Ibid.,* pp. 170–172.

21 Bulychev, "Ob opytakh zemledeliya," pp. 80–81; Safronov, "Popytki prodvizheniya," p. 524.

22 Bulychev, "Ob opytakh zemledeliya," p. 81; Lyubarsky, "Kratkoye izvestie," p. 112; Sgibnev, "Istorichesky ocherk," 102 (June, 1869) : 45.

23 Beaumont, "Essais d'agriculture," pp. 122–123; Bulychev, "Ob opytakh zemledeliya," p. 81; Chernykh, "Kratkoye istoricheskoye obozrenie," p. 107; Lyubarsky, "Kratkoye izvestie," p. 113; Sgibnev, "Istorichesky ocherk," 103 (July, 1869) : 6.

24 Beaumont, "Essais d'agriculture," p. 123.

25 Bulychev, "Ob opytakh zemledeliya," p. 83; Sgibnev, "Istorichesky ocherk," 102 (June, 1869) : 50–51.

26 Sgibnev, "Istorichesky ocherk," 103 (July, 1869) : 6–7.

27 Bulychev, "Ob opytakh zemledeliya," p. 84; Chernykh, "Kratkoye istoricheskoye obozrenie," p. 108; Sgibnev, "Istorichesky ocherk," 103 (July, 1869) : 13; Von Bem, "O Kamchatskom zemledelii," p. 42.

28 Von Bem, "O Kamchatskom zemledelii," p. 41.

29 Sgibnev, "Istorichesky ocherk," 103 (July, 1869) : 26; Chernykh, "Kratkoye istoricheskoye obozrenie," p. 109; Bulychev, "Ob opytakh zemledeliya," p. 84; Beaumont, "Essais d'agriculture," p. 125.

30 Sgibnev, "Istorichesky ocherk," 103 (July, 1869) : 26–27.

31 *Ibid.;* Beaumont, "Essais d'agriculture," pp. 124–125; Bulychev, "Ob opytakh zemledeliya," p. 84; Sauer, *Account of an Expedition,* p. 310.

32 Bulychev, "Ob opytakh zemledeliya," pp. 84–85.

33 Von Langsdorff, *Voyages and Travels,* pt. 2, p. 256.

34 Sarychev, *Puteshestvie*, p. 121.

35 Pallas, "Izvestiya o vvedennom skotovodstve," pp. 34–35.

36 Alaska History Research Project, *Documents Relative to Alaska*, 3 : 241; Pervy sibirsky komitet, "O predpolozheniyakh Nachalnika Kamchatki," d. 167, fol. 20; Rezanov, "Zapiska gorodnichevo Nizhne-Kamchatska Voyevodskovo," fols. 2–4; Sgibnev, "Istorichesky ocherk," 103 (July, 1869) : 48.

37 Pervy sibirsky komitet, "O predpolozheniyakh Nachalnika Kamchatki," d. 167, fols. 20–20ᵛ.

38 Sgibnev, "Istorichesky ocherk," 103 (July, 1869) : 49.

39 *Ibid.*

40 Pervy sibirsky komitet, "O predpolozheniyakh Nachalnika Kamchatki," d. 167, fols. 20ᵛ–21.

41 Sgibnev, "Istorichesky ocherk," 103 (July, 1869) : 49.

42 *Ibid.*, pp. 50–51; Pervy sibirsky komitet, "O predpolozheniyakh Nachalnika Kamchatki," d. 167, fols. 21, 22ᵛ–23, 24ᵛ–25.

43 Pervy sibirsky komitet, "O predpolozheniyakh Nachalnika Kamchatki," d. 167, fols. 23ᵛ–24, 25–25ᵛ, 40–40ᵛ; Sgibnev, "Istorichesky ocherk," 103 (July, 1869) : 51–52, 76, 94.

44 Chernykh, "Kratkoye istoricheskoye obozrenie," p. 109; Sgibnev, "Istorichesky ocherk," 103 (July, 1869) : 54; Lyubarsky, "Kratkoye izvestie," pp. 121–123.

45 Sgibnev, "Istorichesky ocherk," 103 (July, 1869) : 54.

46 Tikhmenev, *Supplement of Documents*, p. 275.

47 Beaumont, "Essais d'agriculture," p. 125; Bulychev, "Ob opytakh zemledeliya," p. 85; Sgibnev, "Istorichesky ocherk," 103 (July, 1869) : 68, 94.

48 Sgibnev, "Istorichesky ocherk," 103 (July, 1869) : 74–75.

49 *Ibid.*, p. 80.

50 Captain F. W. Beechey, *Narrative of a Voyage to the Pacific and Beering's Strait* . . . (London: Henry Colburn and Richard Bentley, 1831), 2 : 246–247; Lyubarsky, "Kratkoye izvestie," pp. 125–126.

51 Pervy sibirsky komitet, "O predpolozheniyakh Nachalnika Kamchatki," d. 166, fols. 1ᵛ–4, 20–21, 43–44ᵛ, 46–47ᵛ, 145–146ᵛ, 148ᵛ–150; Sgibnev, "Istorichesky ocherk," 103 (August, 1869) : 53.

52 Golenishchev, Rider, Chernykh, Paderin, and Lazarev, "O deistviyakh," p. 603; Pervy sibirsky komitet, "O predpolozheniyakh Nachalnika Kamchatki," d. 168, fols. 253–254, 261ᵛ; Sgibnev, "Istorichesky ocherk," 103 (August, 1869) : 52, 55–56; Shcheglov, *Kronologichesky perechen*, p. 497.

53 Golenishchev, Lazarev, and Chernykh, "Izvestiya iz Kamchatki," pp. 222–223; Ministerstvo gosudarstvennykh imushchestv, Trety departament, "O zanyatiyakh po selskomu khozyaistvu," fols. 2, 12ᵛ–13, 14.

54 Ministerstvo gosudarstvennykh imushchestv, Trety departament, "O zanyatiyakh po selskomu khozyaistvu," fol. 2ᵛ.

55 Chernykh, "Kratkoye istoricheskoye obozrenie," p. 110; Nachalnik

Golenishchev, "Ob otkrytii v Kamchatke zemledelcheskoy kompanii" ["Concerning the Opening of an Agricultural Company in Kamchatke"], *Zemledelchesky zhurnal . . .* , no. 1 (1833), pp. 94–96, 99; [Golenishchev], "O sostoyanii Kamchatskoy oblasti," pp. 8–9; Golenishchev, Nadezhin, and Sakharov, "Otchyot Kamchatskoy zemledelcheskoy kompanii," pp. 577, 581–582; Golenishchev, Rider, Chernykh, Paderin, and Lazarev, "O deistviyakh," pp. 585–586, 590, 597–600, 602; Sgibnev, "Istorichesky ocherk," 103 (August, 1869) : 56; Shcheglov, *Kronologichesky perechen,* p. 497.

56 Chernykh, "Kratkoye istoricheskoye obozrenie," p. 111.
57 Golenishchev, Rider, Chernykh, Paderin, and Lazarev, "O deistviyakh," pp. 586, 593.
58 Sgibnev, "Istorichesky ocherk," 103 (August, 1869) : 56–57.
59 *Ibid.,* p. 57.
60 *Ibid.,* pp. 63, 69–70.
61 *Ibid.,* p. 70.
62 *Ibid.,* p. 71.
63 *Ibid.*
64 *Ibid.,* p. 72.
65 Sergeyev, *Narodnoye khozvaistvo,* pp. 541, 552.
66 Safronov, *Okhotsko-Kamchatsky kray,* pp. 96–97.
67 Sgibnev, "Istorichesky ocherk," 103 (August, 1869) : 102.
68 *Ibid.;* Barsukov, *Graf Nikolay Nikolayevich Muravyov-Amursky,* vol. 1, pt. 1, pp. 220–221; Sergeyev, *Narodnoye khozvaistvo,* pp. 542, 552.

Chapter 14: SUMMARY AND CONCLUSION

1 Islenyev, "Perechen dnevnoy zapiski," p. 14; Shmalev, "Kratkoye opisanie," pp. 205–206, 209; [Slovtsov], *Istoricheskoye obozrenie Sibiri,* 2 : 339–340; De Lesseps, *Travels in Kamtschatka,* 1 : 84; Erman, *Travels in Siberia,* 2 : 145; Al. Sk., "Opis Udskavo berega," unpaginated suppl.; A. V., "Neskolko slov o noveishikh opytakh ko vvedeniyu v Kamchatke khlebopashestva i obrabotaniya ogorodnykh rasteny" ["Several Words about the Latest Attempts at Introducing Grain Cultivation and the Cultivation of Garden Plants in Kamchatka"], *Russky invalid,* no. 134 (May 28/April 9, 1832), p. 536.
2 Silnitsky, "Mery pravitelstva," p. 28; Vagin, *Istoricheskiya svedeniya,* vol. 2, suppl., p. 417.
3 Shmalev, "Kratkoye opisanie," p. 196; Anonymous, "Poluostrov Kamchatka," no. 94, p. 375; [Golovnin], *Sochineniya i perevody,* vol. 3, pt. 1, p. 83; P. K., "O vozmozhnosti uluchsheniya," pp. 300–301; Krasheninnikov, *Opisanie zemli Kamchatki,* p. 299; Lindenau, "Opisanie sukhoputnovo puteshestviya," fol. 16; Minitsky, "Nekotoria izvestiya," p. 91; Minitsky, "Ob Okhotskom porte," *Severnaya pochta,* no. 49, p. [4]; Minitsky, "Opisanie Ohkotskavo porta," pp. 216–217; Minitsky, "Prodolzhenie izvesty," p. 146; Sarychev, *Puteshestvie,* pp. 54–55;

Sauer, *Account of an Expedition,* p. 41; Savin, "Okhotsk," p. 158; Shaskolsky, *Geograficheskoye izuchenie Sibiri,* pp. 27–28, 34; Shmalev, "Primechanie uchinyonnoye Kapitanom Timofeiyem Shamlevym," fol. 8ᵛ; Vagin, *Istoricheskiya svedeniya,* vol. 2, suppl., pp. 416–417.

 4 Sarychev, *Puteshestvie,* p. 54.
 5 Shaskolsky, *Geograficheskoye izuchenie Sibiri,* p. 27.
 6 Hill, *Travels in Siberia,* 2 : 322.
 7 A., "Myorzly kray," p. 254; Bulychev, *Puteshestvie po Sibiri,* pt. 1, p. 117.
 8 Cook [and King], *Voyage to the Pacific Ocean,* 3 : 231.
 9 Pallas, *Puteshestvie po raznym provintsiyam,* vol. 3, pt. 1, pp. 184, 207; Urness, *Naturalist in Russia,* p. 113.
10 Silnitsky, "Mery pravitelstva," pp. 62–63*n.*
11 Quoted by Pierre Rondière, *Siberia,* trans. Charles Duff (New York: Ungar, 1967), p. 7.
12 Quoted by A. I. Stepanchenko, *Gordost nasha Sibir (Our Pride Is Siberia)* (Irkutsk: Vostochno-Sibirskoye knizhnoye izdatelstvo, 1964), p. 5.
13 For example, see Hugh McLean, "Leskov and the Russian Superman," *Midway,* 8, no. 4 (Spring, 1968) : 105–123.
14 V. O. Klyuchevsky, *Sochineniya [Works]* (Moscow: Gosudarstvennoye izdatelstvo politicheskoy literatury, 1956), 1 : 311.
15 Ye. Shmurlo, "Solovyov," *Entsiklopedichesky slovar,* 60 (1900) : 799–800.

BIBLIOGRAPHY

Most of the written records for this study have been published; it is not based primarily on archival documents, despite their allure. The published sources vary considerably both in kind and in quality, ranging from spare decrees to elaborate reports and from scientific treatises to impressionistic travel accounts. Some sources, like Krasheninnikov's *Opisanie zemli Kamchatki* (*Description of the Land of Kamchatka*), are classic authorities; and many of the travel accounts are reliable, since their authors—such as Simpson, Davydov, and Erman—were, despite personal prejudices, well-educated, intelligent, perceptive observers. Some of the secondary sources are in effect primary sources, since they incorporate documentary material now lost or destroyed; for example, Sgibnev's invaluable series of articles on Okhotsk and Kamchatka were based on local archives that were subsequently burned. Few archival records remain, and most of the pertinent remnants are found in the "Muller portfolios" (TsGADA), which contain material collected by the father of Siberian history.

Several valuable documents, such as Chirikov's 1746 report to the Admiralty College on the economic development of the Russian Far East (Tsentralny gosudarstvenny arkhiv Voyenno-Morskovo flota, f. Golovina, d. 1) and the Yakutsk archivist's report (ca. 1830) on state transport between Yakutsk and Okhotsk (Tsentralny gosudarstvenny arkhiv Yakutskoy ASSR, f. 12, op. 1, d. 49), were unavailable because I was refused permission to use their depositories and was unable to obtain microfilm copies. Most of the relevant Soviet archives, however, as well as all the relevant Soviet libraries, admitted me during a ten-month sojourn in the U.S.S.R. Regrettably, a couple of available documents were overlooked, including the reports by Governor Soimonov of Siberia on agriculture in Kamchatka (TsGADA, f. 214, op. 18, no. 2,724) and on the provisionment of Okhotsk from Yakutsk (Gosudarstvenny istorichesky muzey, Otdal pismennikh istochnikov, f. 395, n. 5). Pre-nineteenth-century documents, which were often difficult to read, necessitated work in paleography—the Faculty of History of Moscow State University kindly gave me free lessons in this—in metrology and in chronology. Almost all published sources are available in the Lenin Library in Moscow and in the Public Library in Leningrad; however, before entering the Soviet Union I had already used most of these sources in the Library of Congress, the New York Public Library, and the Helsinki University Library via visitation, interlibrary loan, or photoduplication.

Most of the sources, published and unpublished alike, reflect the views of officials, officers, merchants, and scientists, not of commoners. There are no records by Kamchatkan peasants or by Yakut transporters, and this lack has undoubtedly biased the study, although the peasants and the transporters had some literate sympathizers whose views were publicized.

SOURCES

A. "Myorzly kray. Ocherki severo-vostochnoy Sibiri" ["The Frozen Kray. Sketches of Northeastern Siberia"], *Vsemirny puteshestvennik,* 12 (December, 1877) : 237–260.

Akademiya nauk Soyuza Sovetskikh Sotsialisticheskikh Respublik (SSSR). *Pamyati Dekabristov [Remembrances of the Decembrists].* Leningrad: Izdatelstvo Akademii nauk SSSR, 1926. Vol. 2.

Akademiya nauk SSSR. Institut geografii. *Vostochnaya Sibir: ekonomiko-geograficheskaya kharakteristika [Eastern Siberia: Economico-geographical Character].* Moscow: Gosudarstvennoye izdatelstvo geograficheskoy literatury, 1963.

————. Institut istorii. *S. V. Bakhrushin: nauchnie trudy [S. V. Bakhrushin: Scientific Works].* Moscow: Izdatelstvo Akademii nauk SSSR, 1952–59. Vol. 3.

————. Institut literatury (Pushkinsky dom). *A. N. Radishchev: polnoye sobranie sochineny [A. N. Radishchev: Complete Collection of Works].* Moscow and Lenigrad: Izdatelstvo Akademii nauk SSSR, 1938–52. Vols. 2–3.

————. Institut yazyka, literatury i istorii Yakutskovo filiala AN SSSR. *Istoriya Yakutskoy ASSR [History of the Yakut ASSR].* Moscow: Izdatelstvo Akademii nauk SSSR, 1957. Vol. 2.

Alaska History Research Project. *Documents Relative to the History of Alaska.* College: University of Alaska, 1938. Vol. 3.

Alekseyev, A. I. *Okhotsk—kolybel russkovo Tikhookeanskovo flota [Okhotsk—Cradle of the Russian Pacific Fleet].* Khabarovsk: Khabarovskoye knizhnoye izdatelstvo, 1958.

Alkor, Ya. P., and Drezen, A. K., eds. *Kolonialnaya politika tsarizma na Kamchatke i Chukotke v XVIII veke [Colonial Policy of Tsarism in Kamchatka and Chukotka in the XVIIIth Century].* Leningrad: Izdatelstvo Instituta narodov severa TsIK SSSR, 1935.

Alkor, Ya. P., and Grekov, B. D., eds. *Kolonialnaya politika Moskovskovo gosudarstva v Yakutii XVII v. [Colonial Policy of the Muscovite*

State in Yakutia of the XVIIth Century]. Leningrad: Izdatelstvo Instituta narodov severa TsIK SSSR imeni P. G. Smidovicha, 1936.

Andreyev, A. I., ed. *Russian Discoveries in the Pacific and in North America in the Eighteenth and Nineteenth Centuries.* Trans. Carl Ginsburg. Ann Arbor: J. W. Edwards, 1952.

————, ed. *Russkie otkrytiya v Tikhom okeane i Severnoy Amerike v XVIII veke* [*Russian Discoveries in the Pacific Ocean and in North America in the XVIIIth Century*]. Moscow: Gosudarstvennoye izdatelstvo geograficheskoy literatury, 1948.

Andriyevich, V. K. *Sibir v XIX stoletii* [*Siberia in the XIXth Century*]. 2 pts. St. Petersburg: Tipografiya V. V. Komarova, 1889.

Anonymous. "Chernovie opisi kazyonnikh stroyeny g. Gizhiginska i svedeniya o chisle zhiteley" ["Rough Inventories of the State Buildings of the Town of Gizhiga and Information about the Number of Inhabitants"]. TsGADA, f. 1,096, op. 1, d. 53.

————. "Delo o osvidetelstvovanii novoy i staroy dorogi ot Yakutska do Okhotska i mesta dlya postroiki gor. Aldana" ["File on the Examination of the New and the Old Road from Yakutsk to Okhotsk and the Places for the Construction of the Town of Aldan"]. TsGADA, f. 416, op. 1, d. 16.

————. "Delo o zapiske v prikhod kazyonnovo provianta 1784 goda" ["File Noting the Arrival of State Provisions of 1784"]. TsGADA, f. 1,096, op. 1, d. 47.

————. "Delo po predlozheniyu . . . Irkutskovo gubernatora . . . o sostoyanii zdeshnevo vedomstva 1782 goda aprelya 16 chislo" ["File on the Proposal . . . of the Irkutsk Governor . . . about the Condition of the Local Department, April 16, 1782"]. TsGADA, f. 416, op. 1, d. 24.

————. "Iskhodyashchy zhurnal Gizhiginskoy kreposti za 1767 god" ["Outgoing Journal of Gizhiga Fortress for 1767"]. TsGADA, f. 1,096, op. 1, d. 24.

————. "Iskhodyashchy zhurnal Gizhiginskoy kreposti za 1774 god" ["Outgoing Journal of Gizhiga Fortress for 1774"]. TsGADA, f. 1,096, op. 1, d. 29.

————. "Izvestie iz Gizhigi" ["Information from Gizhiga"], *Vostochnoye Pomorye,* no. 10 (August 7/19, 1865), pp. 58–59.

————. "Materialy dlya istorii Kamchatskavo kraya" ["Materials for the History of Kamchatka Kray"], *Severnaya pchela,* no. 252 (November 4/16, 1844), p. 1,008.

————. "Okhotsky kray" ["Okhotsk Kray"], *Vostochnoye Pomorye,* no. 22 (October 30/November 11, 1865), p. 128, and no. 23 (November 6/18, 1865), pp. 134–135.

————. "Opisanie Irkutskoy gubernii" ["Description of Irkutsk Province"]. TsGIAL, f. 1,350, op. 312, d. 239.

————. "Opisanie Udskavo ostroga" ["Description of Udsk Ostrog"], *Moskovsky telegraf,* pt. 1 (1825), pp. 321–329.

————. "Opisanie Yakutskoy provintsii" ["Description of Yakutsk Province"]. GPB OR, Ermitazhnoye sobranie, no. 238 6-f.

————. "Poluostrov Kamchatka" ["The Kamchatka Peninsula"], *Rusky invalid,* no. 92 (November 17/29, 1815), pp. 367–368, and no. 94 (November 24/December 6, 1815), pp. 375–376.

————. "Razniya izvestiya iz Okhotska ot 30 noyabrya po 17 dekabre 1775 g." ["Various Information from Okhotsk from November 30 until December 17 of 1775"]. TsGADA, f. 199, port. 528, pt. 1, d. 24.

————. "Reyester s vedomostyami o kazyonnykh veshchakh, nakhodivshchikhsya pri Gizhiginskoy kreposti (ne polnoye delo) 1766 goda" ["Register with Lists on State Belongings at Gizhiga Fortress (Incomplete File) 1766"]. TsGADA, f. 1,096, op. 1, d. 14.

————. "Vkhodyashchaya kniga Gizhiginskoy kreposti s priobshchyonnymi k ney vedomostyami o sostoyanii Gizhiginskovo proviantskovo magazina . . ." ["Incoming Book of Gizhiga Fortress with Attached Lists on the Condition of the Gizhiga Provision Magazine . . ."]. TsGADA, f. 1,096, op. 1, d. 56.

————. "Vzglyad na torgovlyu, proizvodimuyu chrez Okhotsky port" ["A Glance at the Trade Conducted through Okhotsk Port"], *Severny arkhiv,* pt. 7 (1823), pp. 28–45.

————. "Zapiski o Chukotskom narode . . . iz imeyushchikhsya v Senatskom sekretnom Arkhive svedeny" ["Notes on the Chukot People . . . from Information Available in the Senate's Secret Archive"], *Chteniya v Obshchestve istorii i drevnostey rossiiskikh pri Moskovskom universitete,* bk. 4, pt. 5 (1858), pp. 101–108.

Arktichesky nauchno-issledovatelsky institut. *Istorichesky pamyatnik russkovo arkticheskovo moreplavaniya XVII veka [Historical Memorial of Russian Arctic Navigation of the XVIIth Century].* Moscow and Leningrad: Izdatelstvo Glavsevmorputi, 1951.

[Avdeyeva, Yekaterina]. *Zapiski i zamechaniya o Sibiri [Notes and Remarks about Siberia].* Moscow: Tipografiya Nikolaya Stepanova, 1837.

Bagrov, L. S. *Karty Aziatskoy Rossii [Maps of Asiatic Russia].* Petrograd: Articheskoye zavedenie T-va A. F. Marksa, 1914.

Bakhrushin, S. V., and Tokarev, S. A., eds. *Yakutiya v XVII veke [Yakutia in the XVIIth Century].* Yakutsk: Yakutskoye knizhnoye izdatelstvo, 1953.

Barbashev, N. I. *K istorii morekhodnovo obrazovaniya v Rossii [Toward a History of Naval Education in Russia].* Moscow: Izdatelstvo Akademii nauk SSSR, 1959.

Barsukov, I. *Graf Nikolay Nikolayevich Muravyov-Amursky . . . [Count Nikolay Nikolayevich Muravyov-Amursky . . .].* 2 vols. Moscow: Sinodalnaya tipografiya, 1891.

————. *Pisma Innokentiya mitropolita Moskovskavo i Kolomenskavo 1828–1853 [Letters of Metropolitan Innokenty of Moscow and Kolomna 1828–1853].* St. Petersburg: Sinodalnaya tipografiya, 1897. Bk. 1.

Basharin, G. P. *Istoriya agrarnykh otnosheny v Yakutii (60-ye gody XVIII– seredina XIX v. [History of Agrarian Relations in Yakutia (1760's to the Middle of the XIXth Century)].* Moscow: Izdatelstvo Akademii nauk SSSR, 1956.

Baskin, Semyon, ed. " 'Bolshoy chertyozh Kamchadalskoy zemli' " [" 'The Great Map of the Kamchadal Land' "], *Izvestiya Vsesoyuznovo geograficheskovo obshchestva* 81, no. 2 (March–April, 1949) : 226–238.

Beaumont, H. "Essais d'agriculture dans le Kamtchatka" ["Attempts at Agriculture in Kamchatka"], *Memoires de la Société de Géographie de Genève* 1 (1860) : 117–131.

Beazley, Raymond; Forbes, Nevill; and Birkett, G. A. *Russia from the Varangians to the Bolsheviks.* Oxford: The Clarendon Press, 1918.

Beechey, Captain F. W. *Narrative of a Voyage to the Pacific and Beering's Strait* . . . . London: Henry Colburn and Richard Bentley, 1831. Vol. 2.

Belov, M. I. *Arkticheskoye moreplavanie s drevneishikh vremen do serediny XIX veka* [*Arctic Navigation from Antiquity until the Middle of the XIXth Century*]. Vol. 1 of *Istoriya otkrytiya i osvoyeniya Severnovo morskovo puti.* Ed. Ya. Ya. Gakkel, A. P. Okladnikov, and M. B. Chernenko. Moscow: Izdatelstvo "Morskoy transport," 1956.

―――. "Novie dannie o sluzhbakh Vladimira Atlasova i pervykh pokhodakh russkikh na Kamchatku" ["New Information on the Services of Vladimir Atlasov and on the First Russian Campaigns to Kamchatka"], *Letopis Severa* 2 (1957) : 89–106.

―――., comp. *Russkie morekhody v Ledovitom i Tikhom okeanakh: sbornik dokumentov* . . . [*Russian Seafarers in the Arctic and the Pacific Oceans: A Collection of Documents* . . .]. Leningrad and Moscow: Izdatelstvo Glavsevmorputi, 1952.

Berg, L. S. *Natural Regions of the U.S.S.R.* Trans. Olga Adler Titelbaum. New York: The Macmillan Company, 1950.

―――. *Ocherki po istorii russkikh geograficheskikh otkryty* [*Sketches on the History of Russian Geographical Discoveries*]. 2d ed. Moscow and Leningrad: Izdatelstvo Akademii nauk SSSR, 1949.

―――. *Otkrytie Kamchatki i ekspeditsii Beringa* [*The Discovery of Kamchatka and the Expeditions of Bering*]. 3d ed. Moscow and Leningrad: Izdatelstvo Akademii nauk SSSR, 1946.

[Bering, Vitus]. "Donesenie flota kapitana Beringa ob ekspeditsii yevo k vostochnym beregam Sibiri" ["Report of Fleet Captain Bering about his Expedition to the Eastern Shores of Siberia"], *Zapiski Voyenno-topograficheskavo depo,* vol. 10, pt. 1 (1847), 2d suppl., pp. 69–75.

Berkh, Vasily. *The Chronological History of the Discovery of the Aleutian Islands* . . . . Trans. Dimitri Krenov. Seattle: Works Progress Administration, 1938.

―――. "Izvestie o mekhovoy torgovle, proizvodimoy rossiyanami pri ostrovakh Kurilskikh, Aleutskikh i severozapadnom beregu Ameriki" ["Information on the Fur Trade Conducted by the Russians along the Kurile and Aleutian Islands and the Northwestern Coast of America"], *Syn otechestva,* pt. 88, no. 39 (1823), pp. 243–264, pt. 89, no. 43 (1823), pp. 97–106, and pt. 89, no. 44 (1823), p. 165 and table between pp. 178 and 179.

―――. *Pervoye morskoye puteshestvie rossiyan* . . . [*The First Sea Voyage of a Russian* . . .]. St. Petersburg: Imperatorskaya akademiya nauk, 1823.

Bilbasov, V. A., ed. *Arkhiv grafov Mordvinovykh* [*Archive of the Counts Mordvinov*]. St. Petersburg: Tipografiya I. N. Skorokhodova, 1901–3. Vol. 3.

Blair, Russell. "The Food Habits of the East Slavs." Ph.D. dissertation, University of Pennsylvania, Department of Slavic and Baltic Studies, 1956.

Blum, Jerome. *Lord and Peasant in Russia from the Ninth to the Nineteenth Century.* Princeton: Princeton University Press, 1961.

Bocharov, F. "Neskolko slov ob Udskom kraye" ["Several Words about Udsk Kray"], *Vostochnoye Pomorye,* no. 20 (October 16/28, 1865), pp. 118–119.

Borisov, Ivan. "Vedomost sochineniya v Yakutskoy voyevodskoy kantselyarii po trebovaniyu Akademii Nauk professora Gerarda Fridrikha Gospodina Millera o sostoyanii goroda Yakutska i Yakutskovo vedomstva . . ." ["List of Works in the Yakutsk Gubernatorial Office Relating to the Request of Professor of the Academy of Sciences Mr. Gerhard Friedrich Muller about the Condition of the Town of Yakutsk and Yakutsk Province . . ."]. TsGADA, f. 199, port. 528, pt. 7, d. 481.

Bulychev, I. "Ob opytakh zemledeliya v Kamchatke" ["Concerning Agricultural Experiments in Kamchatka"], *Vestnik Imperatorskavo russkavo geograficheskavo obshchestva,* pt. 8 (1853), pp. 75–88.

———. *Puteshestvie po Vostochnoy Sibiri* [*Journey through Eastern Siberia*]. St. Petersburg: n.p., 1856. Pt. 1.

Bush, Richard J. *Reindeer, Dogs, and Snow-Shoes* . . . . New York: Harper & Brothers, 1871.

Byvaly. "Pochva i klimat Kamchatki" ["The Soil and Climate of Kamchatka"], *Zemledelchesky zhurnal* . . . , no. 2 (1836), pp. 183–196.

Campbell, Archibald. *A Voyage Round the World from 1806 to 1812* . . . . Honolulu: University of Hawaii Press, 1967.

Cederberg, A. R., ed. "Heinrich Fick. Ein Beitrag zur russischen Geschichte des XVIII. Jahrhunderts" ["Heinrich Fick. A Contribution to Russian History of the XVIIIth Century"], *Acta et Commentationes Universitatis Tartuensis (Dorpatensis),* ser. B, 17 (1930) : i–160.

Chappe D'Auteroche, M. L'Abbé. *A Journey into Siberia, Made by the Order of the King of France.* 2d ed. London: Faden and Jefferys, 1774.

Chekhov, Anton. *The Island: A Journey to Sakhalin.* Trans. Luba and Michael Terpak. New York: Washington Square Press, 1967.

Chernykh, D. K. "Kratkoye istoricheskoye obozrenie zemledeliya v Kamchatke" ["A Brief Historical Review of Agriculture in Kamchatka"], *Zemledelchesky zhurnal* . . . , no. 1 (1833), pp. 106–112.

Cochrane, Capt. John Dundas. *Narrative of a Pedestrian Journey through Russia and Siberian Tartary* . . . . Philadephia: H. C. Carey, I. Lea, and A. Small, 1824.

Collins, Perry McDonough. *Siberian Journey: Down the Amur to the Pacific,*

1856–1857. Ed. Charles Vevier. Madison: University of Wisconsin Press, 1962.

Cook, Captain James [and King, Captain James]. *A Voyage to the Pacific Ocean* . . . . London: G. Nicol and T. Cadell, 1784. Vol. 3.

Cottrell, Charles Herbert. *Recollections of Siberia* . . . . London: John W. Parker, 1842.

Cowdin, Elliot C. "The Northwest Fur Trade," *Hunt's Merchants' Magazine* 14 (June, 1846): 532–539.

Culin, Stewart, ed. "The Wonderful News of the Circumnavigation," *Asia* 20 (1920) : 365–372, 436, 505–512, 583–588, 704–711, 807–814.

Dal, Vladimir. *Tolkovy slovar zhivovo velikorusskovo yazyka* [*Explanatory Dictionary of the Living Great Russian Language*]. Moscow: Gosudarstvennoye izdatelstvo inostrannykh i natsionalnykh slovarey, 1955. Vols. 2–3.

Davydov, G. I. *Dvukratnoye puteshestvie v Ameriku morskikh ofitserov Khvostova i Davydova* [*Double Voyage to America of the Naval Officers Khvostov and Davydov*]. St. Petersburg: Morskaya tipografiya, 1810. Vol. 1.

De Benyowsky, Mauritius Augustus Count. *Memoirs and Travels* . . . . Dublin: P. Wogan, L. White, P. Byrne et al., 1790. Vol. 1.

De Humboldt, Alexander. *Political Essay on the Kingdom of New Spain.* Trans. John Black. London: Longman, Hurst, Rees, Orme, and Brown and H. Colburn, 1811. Vol. 2.

De La Perouse, J. F. G. *A Voyage Round the World* . . . . London: J. Johnson, 1798. Vol. 3.

De Lesseps, M. *Travels in Kamtschatka, during the Years 1787 and 1788.* 2 vols. London: J. Johnson, 1790.

De Semenov, M. P. *La Russie Extra-Européene et Polaire.* Paris: Paul Dupont, 1900.

Divin, V. A. *Veliky russky moreplavatel A. I. Chirikov* [*The Great Russian Navigator A. I. Chirikov*]. Moscow: Gosudarstvennoye izdatelstvo geograficheskoy literatury, 1953.

————. "Vtoraya Sibirsko-tikhookeanskaya ekspeditsiya i voprosy khozyaistvennavo osvoyeniya Dalnevo Vostoka" ["The Second Siberia–Pacific Ocean Expedition and Questions of the Economic Development of the Far East"], *Letopis Severa* 2 (1957) : 157–175.

Dobell, Peter. *Travels in Kamtchatka and Siberia* . . . . 2 vols. London: Henry Colburn and Richard Bentley, 1830.

Doklad komiteta ob ustroistve russkikh amerikanskikh kolony [*Report of the Committee on the Organization of the Russian American Colonies*]. St. Petersburg: Tipografiya Departamenta vneshney torgovli, 1863–64. Pt. 1.

Dossick, Jesse J. *Doctoral Research on Russia and the Soviet Union.* New York: New York University Press, 1960.

Dostoyevsky, F. *Notes From A Dead House.* Trans. L. Navrozov and Y. Guralsky. Moscow: Foreign Languages Publishing House, n.d.

Du Halde, J. B. *Description Geographique, Historique, Chronologique, Politique, et Physique de l'Empire de la Chine et de la Tartarie Chinoise* . . . . 2d ed. La Haye: Henri Scheurleer, 1736. Vol. 2.

D'Wolf, Captain John. *A Voyage to the North Pacific and A Journey through Siberia* . . . . Cambridge, Mass.: Welch, Bigelow, and Company, 1861.

Dzhuliyani, Yu. "O Yakutakh" ["Concerning the Yakuts"], pt. 2, *Syn otechestva,* vol. 4, pt. 178 (1836), pp. 138–159.

E. [E. I. Stogov]. "Ssylno-katorzhnie v Okhotskom solevarennom zavode" ["Hard-Labor Exiles at the Okhotsk Saltworks"], *Russkaya starina* 22 (June, 1878) : 301–315, and 22 (August, 1878) : 616–632.

Ellison, Herbert J. "Peasant Colonization of Siberia." Ph.D. dissertation, University of London, 1955.

Erman, Adolph. *Travels in Siberia* . . . . Trans. W. D. Cooley. 2 vols. Philadelphia: Lea and Blanchard, 1850.

Firsov, N. N. "Istoricheskaya zapiska o Kamchatke" ["An Historical Note on Kamchatka"], *Izvestiya Obshchestva arkheologii, istorii i etnografii pri Kazanskom gosudarstvennom universitete* 33 (1926) : 175–187.

Fisher, Raymond H. *The Russian Fur Trade 1550–1700.* "University of California Publications in History," vol. 31. Berkeley and Los Angeles: University of California Press, 1943.

Gagemeister, Yu. A. "Khozyaistvenno-statistichesky obzor Kamchatki" ["Economico-statistical Survey of Kamchatka"], *Zhurnal Ministerstva vnutrennikh del,* pt. 42 (1853), pp. 228–255.

————. *Statisticheskoye obozrenie Sibiri* [*Statistical Survey of Siberia*]. 3 pts. St. Petersburg: Tipografiya II otdeleniya Sobstvennoy Yevo Imperatorskavo Velichestva Kantselyarii, 1854.

Gapanovich, I. I. *Rossiya v Severo-Vostochnoy Azii* [*Russia in Northeastern Asia*]. Peiping: Tipografiya Pekinskoy russkoy missii, 1933. Pt. 1.

Gedenstrom, M. *Otryvki o Sibiri* [*Excerpts on Siberia*]. St. Petersburg: Ministerstvo vnutrennikh del, 1830.

German, K. F. "Statisticheskiya svedeniya o lovle zverey i ptits v Rossii i Sibiri" ["Statistical Information on the Catching of Animals and Birds in Russia and Siberia"], *Sibirsky vestnik,* pt. 11, bk. 8 (1820), pp. 41–60, and pt. 11, bk. 9 (1820), pp. 82–95.

Gmelin, [Johann Georg]. *Voyage en Siberie* . . . . Paris: Desaint, 1767. Vol. 1.

Gmelini, Johannis Georgii. *Reliquias quae supersunt commercii epistolici* . . . [*Fragments concerning Letters of Commerce* . . .]. Stuttgartiae: Typis C. F. Heringianis, 1861.

Goldenberg, L. A. *Fyodor Ivanovich Soimonov (1692–1780).* Moscow: Izdatelstvo "Nauka," 1966.

Golder, Frank A. *Bering's Voyages.* New York: American Geographical Society, 1922–25. Vol. 2.

————. "A Survey of Alaska, 1743–1799," *Washington Historical Quarterly* 4, no. 2 (April, 1913) : 83–95.

[Golenishchev, G.]. "O sostoyanii Kamchatskoy oblasti v 1830 i 1831 go-dakh" ["Concerning the Condition of Kamchatka Oblast in 1830 and 1831"], *Zhurnal Ministerstva vnutrennikh del*, pt. 10 (1833), pp. 1–29.

————. "Ob otkrytii v Kamchatke zemledelcheskoy kompanii" ["Concerning the Opening of an Agricultural Company in Kamchatka"], *Zemledelchesky zhurnal . . .*, no. 1 (1833), pp. 93–105.

Golenishchev, Nachalnik, and Lazarev and Chernykh, Chinovniki. "Izvestiya iz Kamchatki o sredstvakh predprinimayemykh k uluchsheniyu v onoy Selskavo Khozyaistva" ["Information from Kamchatka about the Means Undertaken toward the Improvement of Agriculture There"], *Zemledelchesky zhurnal . . .*, no. 29 (1830), pp. 219–246.

Golenishchev, Nachalnik, and Nadezhin and Sakharov, Direktory. "Otchyot Kamchatskoy zemledelcheskoy kompanii za 1833-ye leto" ["Report of the Kamchatka Agricultural Company for 1833"], *Zemledelchesky zhurnal . . .*, no. 4 (1834), pp. 577–588.

Golenishchev, Nachalnik; Rider, Chernykh, and Paderin, Direktory; and Lazarev, Chinovnik. "O deistviyakh Kamchatskoy zemledelcheskoy kompanii" ["Concerning the Activities of the Kamchatka Agricultural Company"], *Zemledelchesky zhurnal . . .*, no. 1 (1833), pp. 579–606.

Golman, V. "Zametki o konevodstve v Yakutskoy oblasti" [Notes on Horse-breeding in Yakutsk Oblast"], *Pamyatnaya knizhka Yakutskoy oblasti na 1871 god*. St. Petersburg: Yakutsky oblastnoy statistichesky komitet, 1877.

Golovnin, Flot Leitenant. *Puteshestvie na shlyupe "Diana" iz Kronshtadta v Kamchatku . . . [Voyage on the Sloop "Diana" from Kronstadt to Kamchatka . . .]*. Moscow: Gosudarstvennoye izdatelstvo geograficheskoy literatury, 1961.

[————.]. *Sochineniya i perevody Vasiliya Mikhailovicha Golovnina [The Writings and the Translations of Vasily Mikhailovich Golovnin]*. St. Petersburg: Tipografiya Morskavo ministerstva, 1864–65. Vols. 3, 5.

Goncharov, I. A. *Sobranie sochineny [Collected Works]*. Moscow: Gosudarstvennoye izdatelstvo khudozhestvennoy literatury, 1952–53. Vol. 3.

Gorip, P., ed. "Iz istorii osvoyeniya Severnovo morskovo puti" ["From the History of the Opening of the Northern Sea Route"], *Krasny arkhiv* 71 (1935) : 137–169.

Gorskov, G. P., and Popov, V. V. "A Short Review of the Seismicity of the Kamchatka Peninsula," *Bulletin of the Kamchatka Volcanological Station*, no. 4 (1938), pp. 21–29.

Grachev, V. A. *Obzor istochnikov po istorii Priamurya i Okhotsko-Kamchatskovo kraya [A Review of the Sources on the History of Preamuria and Okhotsk-Kamchatka Kray]*. No. 1. "Trudy Gosudarstvennovo dalnevostochnovo universiteta," 3d ser., no. 5. Vladivostok: Tipografiya Gosudarstvennovo dalnevostochnovo universiteta, 1927.

Granik, G. I. "Letopis sudokhodstva na rekakh Yakutii" ["A Chronicle of Navigation on the Rivers of Yakutia"], *Letopis Severa* 3 (1962) : 211–222.

Gribanovsky, N. N. *Bibliografiya Yakutii [Bibliography of Yakutia]*. 2 pts.

Moscow and Leningrad: Akademiya nauk SSSR i Yakutsky Gosizdat, 1932–35.

Gromov, Prokopy. "Istoriko-statisticheskoye opisanie Kamchatskikh tser-kvey" ["An Historico-statistical Description of Kamchatkan Churches"], pt. 1, *Trudy Kiyevskoy dukhovnoy akademii* 1 (1860) : 28–50.

————. "Put ot Irkutska v Kamchatku" ["The Route from Irkutsk to Kam-chatka"], *Pribavleniya k Irkutskim yeparkhialnym vedomostyam* 7, no. 4 (1869) : pp. 41–47; no. 5, pp. 56–63; no. 6, pp. 75–80; no. 7, pp. 81–87; no. 9, pp. 105–114; no. 12, pp. 145–149; no. 16, pp. 193–201; nos. 17–18, pp. 216–222; and no. 20, pp. 249–257.

Hellman, Lillian, ed. *The Selected Letters of Anton Chekhov*. Trans. Sidonie Lederer. New York: Farrar, Straus and Company, 1955.

Hildreth, A. C.; Magness, J. R.; and Mitchell, John W. "Effects of Climatic Factors on Growing Plants," in *Climate and Man,* Yearbook of Agricul-ture. Washington, D.C.: U. S. Government Printing Office, 1941.

Hill, S. S. *Travels in Siberia*. London: Longman, Brown, Green, and Long-mans, 1854. Vol. 2.

Holman, James. *Travels through Russia, Siberia, Poland, Austria, Saxony, Prussia, Hanover* . . . . London: George B. Whittaker, 1825. Vol. 2.

Ilimskaya voyevodskaya kantselyariya. "Delo o splavke khleba, semen i go-rokha v Yakutsk i v kamchatskuyu ekspeditsiyu" ["File about the Shipping of Grain, Seed, and Peas to Yakutsk and to the Kamchatka Expedition"]. TsGADA, f. 494, op. 2, d. 172, sv. 17.

————. "Sbornik del, tom I" ["Collection of Files, Volume I"]. TsGADA, f. 494, op. 2, d. 285, sv. 39.

————. "Splav khleba" ["Shipping of Grain"]. TsGADA, f. 494, op. 2, d. 279, sv. 28.

————. "Splav po Lene i na Kamchatku, tom I" ["Shipping along the Lena and to Kamchatka, Volume 1"]. TsGADA, f. 494, op. 2, d. 297, sv. 30.

Imperatorskaya akademiya nauk. *Atlas rossiiskoy* . . . *[Russian Atlas* . . .]. St. Petersburg: Imperatorskaya akademiya nauk, 1745.

Imperatorskoye russkoye istoricheskoye obshchestvo. *Protokoly, zhurnaly i ukazy Verkhovnavo tainavo soveta, 1726–1730* [*Minutes, Journals and Decrees of the Supreme Privy Council, 1726–1730*]. Vol. 63 of *Sbornik Imperatorskavo russkavo istoricheskavo obshchestva*. St. Petersburg: Im-peratorskoye russkoye istoricheskoye obshchestvo, 1888.

Ionina, A. A. *Noviya danniya k istorii Vostochnoy Sibiri XVII veka* [*New Data on the History of Eastern Siberia of the XVIIth Century*]. Irkutsk: Tipo-litografiya P. I. Makushkina, 1895.

Islenyev, Ivan. "Perechen dnevnoy zapiski g. Islenyeva" ["List of the Daily Notes of Mr. Islenyev"], *Novia yezhemesyachnia sochineniya,* pt. 23 (May, 1788), pp. 3–15.

Izbekova, A. "Materialy o razvitii khlebopashestva v Yakutii v XVIII–XIX vekakh" ["Materials on the Development of Grain Cultivation in Yakutia in the XVIIIth–XIXth Centuries"], *Uchyonie zapiski Instituta yazyka, li-teratury i istorii Yakutskovo filiala Akademii nauk SSSR,* no. 3 (1955), pp. 73–94.

Jelavich, Barbara. *A Century of Russian Foreign Policy, 1814–1914.* Philadelphia and New York: J. B. Lippincott Company, 1964.

K., P. "O vozmozhnosti uluchsheniya Selskavo Khozyaistva v Kamchatke i bliz Tigilskoy kreposti" ["Concerning the Possibility of Improving Agriculture in Kamchatka and Near Tigilsk Fortress"], *Zemledelchesky zhurnal . . . ,* no. 2 (1833), pp. 285–305.

Kalinin, V. "Severnie mestnie porody loshadey" ["Northern Local Breeds of Horses"], in *Selskokhozyaistvennaya entsiklopediya.* 3d ed. Moscow: Gosudarstvennoye izdatelstvo selskokhozyaistvennoy literatury, 1955. Vol. 4.

Kanagev. "Okhotsk," *Severnoye obozrenie* 3 (1850) : 363–384.

Kashik, O. I. "Torgovlya v Vostochnoy Sibiri v XVII–nachale XVIII vv." ["Trade in Eastern Siberia in the XVIIth–to the Beginning of the XVIIIth Centuries"], in *Voprosy istorii Sibiri i Dalnevo Vostoka.* Ed. Akademiya nauk SSSR, Sibirskoye otdelenie. Novosibirsk: Izdatelstvo Sibirskovo otdeleniya AN SSSR, 1961.

Kerner, Robert J. "The Russian Eastward Movement: Some Observations on Its Historical Significance," *Pacific Historical Review* 17, no. 5 (May, 1948) : 135–148.

———. "Russian Expansion to America, Its Bibliographical Foundations," *Papers of the Bibliographical Society of America* 25 (1931) : 111–129.

———. *The Urge to the Sea.* Berkeley and Los Angeles: University of California Press, 1946.

Khersonsky. "Neskolko slov o proshlom i nastoyashchem g. Okhotska" ["Several Words about the Past and the Present of the Town of Okhotsk"], *Priamurskiya vedomosti,* no. 39 (September 25/October 7, 1894), pp. 11–13.

[Khlebnikov, K. T.]. "Pisma o Kamchatke" ["Letters about Kamchatka"]. GPB OR, f. IV, no. 815.

Kilberger, I. F. *Kratkoye izvestie o russkoy torgovle, kakim obrazom onaya proizvodilas chrez vsyu Rossiyu v 1674 godu [Brief Information on Russian Trade and on the Way It Is Conducted throughout Russia in 1674].* St. Petersburg: Tipografiya Departamenta narodnavo prosveshcheniya, 1820.

Kiselev, Stefan. "Zamechaniya uchinyonnia na puti iz Yakutska v Okhotsk, o perevozke tovarov Yakutami" ["Observations Made on the Route from Yakutsk to Okhotsk about the Transport of Goods by the Yakuts"], *Trudy Volnavo ekonomicheskavo obshchestva,* vol. 52, pt. 3 (1798), pp. 130–139.

Klyuchevsky, V. *Kurs russkoy istorii [The Course of Russian History].* Moscow: Gosudarstvennoye sotsialno-ekonomicheskoye izdatelstvo, 1937. Vol. 1.

———. *Sochineniya [Works].* Moscow: Gosudarstvennoye izdatelstvo politicheskoy literatury, 1956. Vol. 1.

Koloskov, P. I. "Klimatichesky ocherk poluostrova Kamchatki" ["Climatic Survey of the Kamchatka Peninsula"], *Izvestiya Dalnevostochnovo geofizicheskovo instituta,* no. 2 (1932), pp. 119–145.

Komitet Severa pri Russkom geograficheskom obshchestve i Severnaya ko-

Ionizatsionnaya ekspeditsiya. *Ocherki po istorii kolonizatsii Severa i Sibiri* [*Sketches on the History of the Colonization of the North and Siberia*]. 2d ed. Petrograd: Redaktsionno-izdatelsky komitet Narodnovo komissariata zemledeliya, 1922.

Kopylov, A. N. "Yeniseisky zemledelchesky raion v seredine XVII v. i yevo znachenie dlya snabzheniya Vostochnoy Sibiri khlebom" ["The Yeniseisk Agricultural Region in the Middle of the XVIIth Century and Its Significance for the Supply of Eastern Siberia with Grain"], *Trudy Moskovskovo gosudarstvennovo istoriko-arkhivnovo instituta* 10 (1957) : 115–134.

Kozmin, N. N. *Ocherki proshlavo i nastoyashchavo Sibiri* [*Sketches of Past and Present Siberia*]. St. Petersburg: Tipografiya "Pechatny trud," 1910.

[Krasheninnikov, Stepan P.] *The History of Kamtschatka, and the Kurilski Islands, with the Countries Adjacent.* Trans. James Grieve. London: T. Jefferys, 1764.

———. *Opisanie zemli Kamchatki* [*Description of the Land of Kamchatka*]. Moscow and Leningrad: Izdatelstvo Glavsevmorputi, 1949.

Kruzenshtern, I. F. *Puteshestvie vokrug sveta . . .* [*Voyage around the World . . .*]. Moscow: Gosudarstvennoye izdatelstvo geograficheskoy literatury, 1950. For English translation, see Von Krusenstern below.

Kuzmishchev, Pavel. "O lesakh i kustarnikakh, rastushchikh v Kamchatke" ["Concerning the Trees and Shrubs Growing in Kamchatka"], *Lesnoy zhurnal . . .* 4 (1836) : 117–131.

Langsdorff, Dr. "Remarques sur le Kamtschatka et sur ses productions naturelles" ["Remarks on Kamchatka and on Its Natural Productions"], *Memoires de la Société Impériale des Naturalistes de Moscou* 3 (1812) : 97–102.

Lantzeff, George V. "Russian Eastward Expansion before the Mongol Invasion," *American Slavic and East European Review* 6, nos. 18–19 (December, 1947) : 1–10.

———. *Siberia in the Seventeenth Century.* "University of California Publications in History," vol. 30. Berkeley and Los Angeles: University of California Press, 1943.

Lauridsen, Peter. *Vitus Bering: The Discoverer of Bering Strait.* Trans. Julius E. Olson. Chicago: S. C. Griggs & Company, 1889.

Ledyard, John. *John Ledyard's Journal of Captain Cook's Last Voyage.* Ed. James Kenneth Munford. Corvallis: Oregon State University Press, 1963.

Levin, M. G., and Potapov, L. P., eds. *Istoriko-etnografichesky atlas Sibiri* [*Historico-ethnographical Atlas of Siberia*]. Moscow and Leningrad: Izdatelstvo Akademii nauk SSSR, 1961.

———. *Narody Sibiri* [*Peoples of Siberia*]. Moscow and Leningrad: Izdatelstvo Akademii nauk SSSR, 1956.

Lin, T. C. "The Amur Frontier Question between China and Russia, 1850–1860," *Pacific Historical Review* 3 (1934) : 1–27.

Lindenau, Jacob. "Opisanie sukhoputnovo puteshestviya iz Yakutska v Okhotsk 1741 g." ["Description of a Land Journey from Yakutsk to Okhotsk of 1741"] (in German). TsGADA, f. 199, port. 511, pt. 1, d. 1.

Lobanov-Rostovsky, A. *Russia and Asia*. Ann Arbor: The George Wahr Publishing Co., 1951.

Lyashchenko, Peter I. *History of the National Economy of Russia to the 1917 Revolution*. Trans. L. M. Herman. New York: The Macmillan Company, 1949.

————. *Istoriya narodnovo khozyaistva SSSR* [*History of the National Economy of the USSR*]. 4th ed. Moscow: Gosudarstvennoye izdatelstvo politicheskoy literatury, 1956. Vol. 1.

Lyubarsky, M. "Kratkoye izvestie o Kamchatskom zemledelii" ["Brief Information about Kamchatkan Agriculture"], *Severny arkhiv*, pt. 6 (1823), pp. 109–135.

Lyubimova, Ye. L. *Kamchatka*. Moscow: Gosudarstvennoye izdatelstvo geograficheskoy literatury, 1961.

McLean, Hugh. "Leskov and the Russian Superman," *Midway* 8, no. 4 (Spring, 1968) : 105–123.

Maikov, L. N. *Razskazy Nartova o Petre velikom* [*Nartov's Narrations about Peter the Great*]. St. Petersburg: Tipografiya Imperatorskoy akademii nauk, 1891.

Mainov, I. I. *Russkie krestyane i osedlie inorodtsy Yakutskoy oblasti* [*Russian Peasants and Settled Natives of Yakutsk Oblast*]. "Zapiski Imperatorskavo russkavo geograficheskavo obshchestva po Otdeleniyu statistiki," vol. 12. St. Petersburg: Tipografiya V. F. Kirshbauma, 1912.

Makarova, R. V. "Ekspeditsii russkikh promyshlennykh lyudey v Tikhom okeane v XVIII veke" ["Expeditions of Russian Promyshlenniks in the Pacific Ocean in the XVIIIth Century"], *Voprosy geografii*, no. 17 (1950), pp. 23–42.

————. *Russkie na Tikhom okeane vo vtoroy polovine XVIII v.* [*Russians on the Pacific Ocean in the Second Half of the XVIIIth Century*]. Moscow: Izdatelstvo "Nauka," 1968.

Mamyshev, V. "Amerikanskiya vladeniya Rossii" ["Russia's American Possessions"], *Biblioteka dlya chteniya*, vol. 130, pts. 3–4 (March–April, 1855), pp. 205–292.

Markov, Al. *Russkie na Vostochnom okeane* [*Russians on the Eastern Ocean*]. 2d ed. St. Petersburg: Tipografiya A. Dmitriyeva, 1856.

Marlinsky, A. *Polnoye sobranie sochineny* [*Complete Collection of Works*]. St. Petersburg: Tipografiya N. Grecha, 1832. Vol. 1.

Martos, Aleksey. *Pisma o Vostochnoy Sibiri* [*Letters about Eastern Siberia*]. Moscow: Universitetskaya tipografiya, 1827.

Martov, K. B., ed. *Atlas istorii geograficheskikh otkryty i issledovany* [*Atlas of the History of Geographical Discoveries and Explorations*]. Moscow: Glavnoye upravlenie geodezii i kartografii SSSR, 1959.

[Mashin, Kapitan]. "Vypiska iz pisma Nachalnika Kamchatki, g. Mashina, k Nepremennomu sekretaryu V. e. obshchestva" ["Extracts from a Letter of the Commandant of Kamchatka, Mr. Mashin, to the Permanent Secretary of the F. E. Society"], *Trudy Imperatorskavo volnavo ekonomicheskavo obshchestva*, no. 6, pt. 2 (1848), sec. 3, pp. 106–111.

Masterson, James R., and Brower, Helen. *Bering's Successors 1745–1780*. Seattle: University of Washington Press, 1948.

Mezhov, V. I. *Sibirskaya bibliografiya* [*Siberian Bibliography*]. 3 vols. St. Petersburg: A. S. Semyonov i Syn, 1903.

Michell, Robert, and Forbes, Nevill, eds. *The Chronicle of Novgorod 1016–1471*. "Camden Third Series," vol. 25. London: Camden Society, 1914.

Middendorf, A. *Puteshestvie na severe i vostoke Sibiri* [*Journey in the North and the East of Siberia*]. St. Petersburg: Tipografiya Imperatorskoy akademii nauk, 1867. Pts. 1–2.

Miller [Muller], G. F. *Istoriya Sibiri* [*History of Siberia*]. 2 vols. Moscow and Leningrad: Izdatelstvo Akademii nauk SSSR, 1937–41.

Miller, Ivan. "Moy put iz Irkutska v Kirensk (v 1814 godu)" ["My Route from Irkutsk to Kirensk (in 1814)"], *Kazanskaya izvestiya*, no. 52 (June 28/July 10, 1816), pp. 258–260.

Ministerstvo gosudarstvennykh imushchestv, Trety department. "O zanyatiyakh po selskomu khozyaistvu nakhodyashchegosya v Kamchatke 14 klassa Lazareva" ["Concerning the Agricultural Occupations in Kamchatka of Lazarev of the 14th Class"]. TsGIAL, f. 398, op. 1, d. 879.

Ministerstvo inostrannykh del SSSR. *Vneshnyaya politika Rossii XIX i nachala XX veka* [*The Foreign Policy of Russia of the XIXth and Beginning of the XXth Centuries*]. 1st ser. Moscow: Izdatelstvo politicheskoy literatury, 1960. Vol. 1.

Minitsky, Kapitan-Leitenant. "Nekotoria izvestiya ob Okhotskom porte i uyezde onavo, dostavlennia Kapitan-Leitenantom Minitskim v 1809 godu" ["Some Information about Okhotsk Port and Its Uyezd, Supplied by Captain-Lieutenant Minitsky in 1809"], *Zapiski, izdavayemia Gosudarstvennym admiralteiskim departamentom*, pt. 3 (1815), pp. 87–103.

———. "Ob Okhotskom porte" ["Concerning Okhotsk Port"], *Severnaya pochta*, no. 49 (June 19/July 1, 1812), pp. [3–4], and no. 50 (June 20/July 2, 1812), p. [4].

———. "Ob Okhotskom porte" ["Concerning Okhotsk Port"], *Zapiski, izdavayemia Gosudarstvennym admiralteiskim departamentom*, pt. 7 (1824), pp. 86–97.

———. "Opisanie Okhotskavo porta" ["Description of Okhotsk Port"], *Syn otechestva i severny arkhiv* 5 (1829) : 136–153, 206–221.

———. "Opisanie Yakutskoy oblasti" ["Description of Yakutsk Oblast"], *Zhurnal Ministerstva vnutrennikh del*, bk. 6 (1830), pp. 147–176.

———. "Prodolzhenie izvesty ob Okhotskom porte, dostavlennykh Kapitan-Leitenantom Minitskim v 1811 godu" ["Continuation of Information about Okhotsk Port, Supplied by Captain-Lieutenant Minitsky in 1811"], *Zapiski, izdavayemia Gosudarstvennym admiralteiskim departamentom*, pt. 3 (1815), pp. 137–150.

Moskvin, I. S. "Voyevody i Nachalniki g. Yakutska i ikh deistviya" ["Governors and Commandants of the Town of Yakutsk and Their Activities"], in *Pamyatnaya knizhka Yakutskoy oblasti za 1863 god*. St. Petersburg: Yakutsky oblastnoy statistichesky komitet, 1864.

Muller, G. F. "Geografiya ili nyneshnoye sostoyanie zemli Kamchatki 1737 goda" ["The Geography or the Present Condition of the Land of Kamchatka of 1737"]. TsGADA, f. 199, port. 527, d. 3.

[————.] "Izvestie o torgakh sibirskikh" ["Information on Siberian Trade"], *Yezhemesyachnia sochineniya* . . . 2 (September, 1755): 195–250; 2 (December, 1755) : 525–537; 3 (February, 1756) : 180–191; 3 (March, 1756) : 195–226; 3 (April, 1756) : 339–360; and 3 (May, 1756) : 387–421.

————. "Opisanie reki Leny ot Verkholenskavo ostroga vniz do goroda Yakutska" ["Description of the Lena River from Verkholensk Ostrog Downstream to the Town of Yakutsk"]. TsGADA, f. 199, port. 517, pt. 1, d. 20.

Muller, G. P. [*sic:* G. F.] *Voyages et découvertes faites par les Russes* . . . . Trans. C. G. F. Dumas. Amsterdam: Marc Michel Rey, 1766. Vol. 1.

Muller, S. [*sic:* G. F.] *Voyages from Asia to America* . . . . London: T. Jefferys, 1761.

Muller, G. F., and Pallas, Peter Simon. *Conquest of Siberia, and the History of the Transactions, Wars, Commerce, etc. etc. Carried on Between Russia and China, from the Earliest Period.* London: Smith, Elder, and Co., 1842.

Myatlev, Vasily. "Instruktsiya ot General-Leitenanta, Kavelera i Sibirskavo Gubernatora Myatleva opredelyonnomu v Okhotsk Glavnomu Komandiru Kollezhskomu Sovetniku Shapilovu 22 fevr. 1757 g." ["Instructions from General-Lieutenant, Cavalier and Siberian Governor Myatlev Appointing Collegiate Councillor Shapilov Chief Commander at Okhotsk Feb. 22, 1757"]. TsGADA, f. 199, port. 528, pt. 1, d. 2.

Naumov, G. V. *Yakutskaya loshad i yeyo khozyaistvennoye znachenie* [*The Yakut Horse and Its Economic Significance*]. Yakutsk: Yakutskoye knizhnoye izdatelstvo, 1953.

Nolde, Boris. *La formation de l'Empire russe: études, notes et documents.* "Collection historique de l'Institut d'Etudes slaves," vol. 15. Paris: Institut d'Etudes slaves, 1952. Vol. 1.

Ogden, Adele. *The California Sea Otter Trade 1784–1848.* "University of California Publications in History," vol. 26. Berkeley and Los Angeles: University of California Press, 1941.

Ogloblin, N. "Dve 'skaski' Vl. Atlasova ob otkrytii Kamchatki" ["Vl. Atlasov's Two 'Tales' about the Discovery of Kamchatka"], *Chteniya v Imperatorskom obshchestve istorii i drevnostey rossiiskikh pri Moskovskom universitete,* bk. 3, pt. 1 (1891), pp. 1–18.

————. *Obozrenie stolbtsov i knig Sibirskavo prikaza (1592–1768 gg.)* [*Survey of the Rolls and the Books of the Siberian Office (1592–1768)*]. Moscow: Universitetskaya tipografiya, 1895. Pt. 1.

Ogorodnikov, V. I. *Ocherk istorii Sibiri do nachala XIX st.* [*A Sketch of the History of Siberia up to the Beginning of the XIXth Century*]. Irkutsk: n.p., 1921. Pt. 2, no. 3.

————. *Tuzemnoye i russkoye zemledelie na Amure v XVII v.* [*Aboriginal and Russian Agriculture on the Amur in the XVIIth Century*]. "Trudy Gosudarstvennovo dalnevostochnovo universiteta," 3rd ser., no. 4. Vladivostok: Tipografiya Gosudarstvennovo dalnevostochnovo universiteta, 1927.

Okun, S. B. *Ocherki po istorii kolonialnoy politiki tsarizma v Kamchatskom kraye* [*Sketches on the History of the Colonial Policy of Tsarism in Kamchatka Kray*]. Leningrad: Ogiz, 1935.

Orlova, N. S., comp. *Otkrytiya russkikh zemleprokhodtsev i polyarnykh morekhodov XVII veka na severo-vostoke Azii: sbornik dokumentov* [*Discoveries of Russian Landsmen and Polar Seafarers of the XVIIth Century in the North-East of Asia: A Collection of Documents*]. Moscow: Gosudarstvennoye izdatelstvo geograficheskoy literatury, 1951.

P., A. [Polonsky, A. S.] "Okhotsk," *Otechestvennia zapiski,* no. 6, pt. 8 (June, 1850), pp. 133–148.

———. "Pervaya kamchatskaya ekspeditsiya Beringa 1725–1729 goda" ["The First Kamchatka Expedition of Bering 1725–1729"], *Otechestvennia zapiski,* vol. 75, pt. 8 (1851), pp. 1–24.

Pallas, P. "Izvestiya o vvedennom skotovodstve i zemlepashestve v Kamchatke i okolo Okhotska, pri Udskom ostroge lezhashchem podle Okhotskavo morya" ["Information about Stockbreeding and Cultivation Introduced into Kamchatka and around Okhotsk, Lying alongside the Okhotsk Sea near Udsk Ostrog"], *Prodolzhenie trudov Volnavo ekonomicheskavo obshchestva . . . ,* pt. 3 (1783), pp. 26–40.

———. *Puteshestvie po raznym provintsiyam rossiiskavo gosudarstva* [*Journey through Various Provinces of the Russian State*]. Trans. Vasily Zuyev. St. Petersburg: Imperatorskaya Akademiya nauk, 1788. Vol. 3, pt. 1.

Pavlinov, D. M.; Vitashevsky, N. A.; and Levental, L. G. *Materialy po obychnomu pravu i po obshchestvennomu bytu Yakutov* [*Materials on the Customary Law and on the Social Life of the Yakuts*]. "Trudy Komissii po izucheniyu Yakutskoy Avtonomnoy Sovetskoy Sotsialisticheskoy Respubliki," vol. 4. Leningrad: Izdatelstvo Akademii nauk SSSR, 1929.

Pavlov, P. N., ed. *K istorii Rossiisko-Amerikanskoy kompanii: sbornik dokumentalnykh materialov* [*Concerning the History of the Russian-American Company: A Collection of Documentary Materials*]. Krasnoyarsk: Krasnoyarsky krayevoy gosudarstvenny arkhiv i Krasnoyarsky gosudarstvenny pedagogichesky institut, 1957.

Peizen, G. "Istorichesky ocherk kolonizatsii Sibiri" ["Historical Sketch of the Colonization of Siberia"], *Sovremennik,* vol. 77, no. 9 (1859), pp. 9–46.

Pekarsky, Pyotr. *Istoriya Imperatorskoy akademii nauk* [*History of the Imperial Academy of Sciences*]. St. Petersburg: Tipografiya Imperatorskoy akademii nauk, 1870. Vol. 1.

Pervy sibirsky komitet. "O predpolozheniyakh Nachalnika Kamchatki ob ustroistve sevo kraya" ["Concerning the Proposals of the Commandant of Kamchatka on the Organization of This Kray"], TsGIAL, f. 1,264, op. 1, ds. 166–168.

Pisarev, V. E. "K voprosu o proiskhozhdenii zemledeliya i polevykh kultur Vostochnoy Sibiri" ["Concerning the Question about the Origin of Agriculture and Field Cropping of Eastern Siberia"], in *Materialy po istorii zemledeliya SSSR.* Ed. B. D. Grekov. Moscow and Leningrad: Izdatelstvo Akademii nauk SSSR, 1956. Collection 2.

Platonov, S. F. *Proshloye russkovo severa* [*The Past of the Russian North*]. Peterburg: Izdatelstvo "Vremya," 1923.

Pokrovsky, A., ed. *Ekspeditsiya Beringa: sbornik dokumentov* [*Bering's Expedition: A Collection of Documents*]. Moscow: Glavnoye arkhivnoye upravlenie NKVD SSSR, 1941.

Priklonsky, V. L. *Materialy dlya bibliografii Yakutskoy oblasti* [*Materials for a Bibliography of Yakutsk Oblast*]. Irkutsk: K. I. Vitkovsky, 1893.

Pushkin, A. S. *A. S. Pushkin: polnoye sobranie sochineny v shesti tomakh* [*A. S. Pushkin: Complete Collection of Works in Six Volumes*]. Moscow and Leningrad: Academia, 1935. Vol. 5.

Raeff, Marc. *Siberia and the Reforms of 1822.* Seattle: University of Washington Press, 1956.

Rezanov, N. P. "Opisanie morskavo berega ot Okhotska do rechki Ulkan, s pokazaniem glubin farvaterov i opisaniem flory i fauny po rekam, predstavlennoye Britovym i Ocheredinym" ["Description of the Coast from Okhotsk to the Ulkan River, with an Indication of the Depths of Channels and a Description of the Flora and Fauna along the Rivers, Submitted by Britov and Ocheredin"]. TsGADA, f. 796, op. 1, d. 284.

———. "Pismo Bukharina Ivana neustanovlennomu litsu s opisaniem sostoyaniya transportnikh sudov v Okhotske; zapiska neustanovlennovo litsa o deyatelnosti Bukharina Ivana" ["A Letter of Ivan Bukharin to an Unidentified Person with a Description of the Condition of the Transport Vessels at Okhotsk; Note of an Unidentified Person about the Activities of Ivan Bukharin"]. TsGADA, f. 796, op. 1, d. 290.

———. "Zapiska gorodnichevo Nizhne-Kamchatska Voyevodskovo o sostoyanii Kamchatki i vygodnosti yeyo ekspluatatsii dlya kazny" ["Note of Mayor Voyevodsky of Nizhne-Kamchatsk on the Condition of Kamchatka and the Advantages of Its Exploitation for the State"]. TsGADA, f. 796, op. 1, d. 285.

Rikord, Flot Kapitan. "O sostoyanii poluostrova Kamchatki i o blagotvoritelnykh zavedeniyakh v onoy uchrezhdayemykh" ["Concerning the Condition of the Peninsula of Kamchatka and the Charitable Institutions Founded in It"], *Zhurnal Imperatorskavo chelovekolyubivavo obshchestva* 8 (April, 1819) : 8–18.

Rikord, Lyudmila. "Pismo k g. Predsedatelyu Obshchestva" ["A Letter to Mr. President of the Society"], *Trudy Vsyochaishe utverzhdennavo Volnavo obshchestva lyubiteley rossiiskoy slovesnosti,* pt. 23 (1823), pp. 94–106.

———. "Vospominaniya L. I. Rikord" ["Recollections of L. I. Rikord"], *Russkaya starina* 24 (January, 1879): 41–48.

Rikord, P.; Burnashev, Timofey; Bronevsky, Gvardii polkovnik; and Kaptsevich, Korpusny komandir. "Pisma iz Kamchatki, Okhotska, Nerchinska i Omska, o sostoyanii Selskavo Khozyaistva v Sibiri i ob uspekhakh onavo" ["Letters from Kamchatka, Okhotsk, Nerchinsk, and Omsk about the Condition of Agriculture in Siberia and about Its Successes"], *Zemledelchesky zhurnal* . . . 3, no. 8 (1823) : 229–266.

Romanov, D. "Prisoyedinenie Amura k Rossii" ["The Annexation of the Amur to Russia"], *Russkoye slovo* 6 (June, 1859) : 329–388.

Rondière, Pierre. *Siberia.* Trans. Charles Duff. New York: Ungar, 1967.

Rossiisko-Amerikanskaya kompaniya. *Otchyot Rossiisko-Amerikanskoy kompanii Glavnavo pravleniya* [*Report of the Main Administration of the Russian-American Company*]. St. Petersburg: Tipografiya Fishera, 1845.

———. "Po predstavleniyu Glavnavo Pravleniya Rossiisko-Amerikanskoy Kompanii o predpolozheniyakh onoy Kompanii ustanovit put iz Yakutska k Okhotskomu moryu i o promyshlennosti na Shantarskikh Ostrovakh" ["Concerning the Company's Proposals to Establish a Route from Yakutsk to the Okhotsk Sea and Concerning Business on the Shantar Islands, According to the Representation of the Main Administration of the Russian-American Company"]. TsGIAL, f. 18, op. 5, d. 1,288.

Rowand, Alexander. *Notes of a Journey in Russian America and Siberia.* . . . Edinburgh [?] : n.p., n.d.

Rozhdestvenskaya, K. "Dorogi v Sibir" ["Roads to Siberia"], *Uralsky sovremennik* 9 (1944) : 105–112.

Rumyantsov, Graf Nikolay, et al. "Doklad ob ustroyenii Kamchatki i Okhotska" ["Report on the Organization of Kamchatka and Okhotsk"], *Sanktpeterburgsky zhurnal,* no. 5 (May, 1804), pp. 35–52.

Russia. *Polnoye sobranie zakonov rossiiskoy imperii* [*Complete Collection of Laws of the Russian Empire*]. 1st ser. (1649–1825). St. Petersburg: Kantselyariya Yevo Imperatorskavo Velichestva, 1830. Vols. 8, 15–16, 29, 32–33, and 35.

———. *Polnoye sobranie zakonov rossiiskoy imperii* [*Complete Collection of Laws of the Russian Empire*]. 2d ser. (1825–1881). St. Petersburg: Kantselyariya Yevo Imperatorskavo Velichestva, 1830–84. Vols. 11, 31.

———. Arkheograficheskaya kommissiya. *Akty istoricheskie* [*Historical Acts*]. St. Petersburg: Tipografiya Vtorovo otdeleniya Sobstvennoy Ye. I. V. Kantselyarii, 1841–42. Vols. 2 and 5.

———. Arkheograficheskaya kommissiya. *Dopolneniya k Aktam istoricheskim* . . . [*Supplements to Historical Acts* . . .]. St. Petersburg: Tipografiya Eduarda Pratsa, 1846–72. Vols. 3–7 and 10.

———. Arkheograficheskaya kommissiya. *Pamyatniki sibirskoy istorii XVIII veka* [*Memorials of Siberian History of the XVIIIth Century*]. 2 vols. St. Petersburg: Tipografiya Ministerstva vnutrennikh del, 1882–85.

———. Arkheograficheskaya kommissiya. *Russkaya istoricheskaya biblioteka* [*Russian Historical Library*]. St. Petersburg: Tipografiya Br. Panteleyevykh, 1872–1927. Vol. 2.

———. Arkheograficheskaya kommissiya. *Sibirskiya letopisi* [*Siberian Chronicles*]. St. Petersburg: Tipografiya I. N. Skorokhodova, 1907.

———. Gosudarstvenny sovet. *Arkhiv Gosudarstvennavo soveta* [*Archive of the State Council*]. St. Petersburg: Tipografiya Vtoravo otdeleniya Sobstvennoy Ye. I. V. Kantselyarii, 1869–1904. Vol. 1.

————. Ministerstvo vnutrennikh del. *Statisticheskoye obozrenie Sibiri* [*Statistical Survey of Siberia*]. St. Petersburg: Tipografiya Shnora, 1810.

————. Pravitelstvuyushchy senat. *Senatsky arkhiv* [*Senate Archive*]. St. Petersburg: Tipografiya Pravitelstvuyushchavo senata, 1892–1901. Vols. 5 and 8–9.

Safronov, F. G. *Gorod Yakutsk v XVII–nachale XIX vekov* [*The Town of Yakutsk in the XVIIth–to the Beginning of the XIXth Centuries*]. Yakutsk: Yakutskoye knizhnoye izdatelstvo, 1957.

————. *Okhotsko-Kamchatsky kray* (*Puti soobshcheniya, naselenie, snabzhenie i zemledelie do revolyutsii*) [*Okhotsk-Kamchatka Kray* (*Routes of Communication, Population, Supply and Agriculture before the Revolution*)]. Yakutsk: Yakutskoye knizhnoye izdatelstvo, 1958.

————. "Popytki prodvizheniya granitsy sibirskovo zemledeliya do beregov Tikhovo okeana v XVIII v." ["Attempts at the Extension of the Boundary of Siberian Agriculture up to the Shores of the Pacific Ocean in the XVIIIth Century"], *Izvestiya Vsesoyuznovo geograficheskovo obshchestva,* vol. 86, no. 6 (1954), pp. 515–525.

————. *Russkie krestyane v Yakutii* (*XVII–nachalo XX vv.*) [*Russian Peasants in Yakutia* (*XVIIth–to the Beginning of the XXth Centuries*)]. Yakutsk: Yakutskoye knizhnoye izdatelstvo, 1961.

Sarychev, G. A. *Puteshestvie flota kapitana Sarycheva . . .* [*Voyage of Fleet Captain Sarychev . . .*]. St. Petersburg: Tipografiya Shnora, 1802.

————. *Puteshestvie po severo-vostochnoy chasti Sibiri, Ledovitomu moryu i Vostochnomu okeanu* [*Journey through the Northeastern Part of Siberia, the Arctic Sea and the Eastern Ocean*]. Moscow: Gosudarstvennoye izdatelstvo geograficheskoy literatury, 1952.

Sauer, Martin. *An Account of a Geographical and Astronomical Expedition to the Northern Parts of Russia . . . .* London: T. Cadell, Jr. and W. Davies, 1802.

Savin. "Okhotsk," *Zapiski Gidrograficheskavo departamenta Morskavo ministerstva,* pt. 9 (1851), pp. 148–161.

[Semivsky, Nikolay V.]. *Noveishiya, lyubopytnia i dostovernia povestvovaniya o Vostochnoy Sibiri . . .* [*The Latest Interesting and Authentic Accounts about Eastern Siberia . . .*]. St. Petersburg: Voyennaya tipografiya Glavnavo shtaba, 1817.

Semyonov, P. P., ed. *Zhivopisnaya Rossiya* [*Picturesque Russia*]. St. Petersburg and Moscow: Izdanie Tovarishchestva M. O. Volf, 1895. Vol. 12, pt. 2.

Semyonov, Yuri. *The Conquest of Siberia.* Trans. E. W. Dickes. London: George Routledge & Sons Ltd., 1944.

Sergeyev, M. A. *Narodnoye khozyaistvo Kamchatskovo kraya* [*The National Economy of Kamchatka Kray*]. Moscow and Leningrad: Izdatelstvo Akademii nauk SSSR, 1936.

Sgibnev, A. "Amurskaya ekspeditsiya 1854 goda" ["The Amur Expedition of 1854"], *Drevnyaya i novaya Rossiya* 4, no. 11 (November, 1878) : 214–233, and 4, no. 12 (December, 1878) : 309–322.

————. "Bolshoy kamchatsky naryad" ["The Great Kamchatka Detail"], *Morskoy sbornik,* vol. 99, pt. 2 (December, 1868), pp. 131–139.

————. "Istorichesky ocherk glavneishikh sobyty v Kamchatke" ["Historical Sketch of the Main Events in Kamchatka"], *Morskoy sbornik* 101 (April, 1869) : 65–142; 102 (May, 1869) : 53–84; 102 (June, 1869) : 37–69; 103 (July, 1869) : 1–129; and 103 (August, 1869) : 33–110.

————. "Navigatskiya shkoly v Sibiri" ["Navigational Schools in Siberia"], *Morskoy sbornik* 87, no. 11 (1866) : 3–44.

————. "Okhotsky port s 1649 po 1852 g." ["Okhotsk Port from 1649 to 1852"], *Morskoy sbornik* 105, no. 11 (November, 1869) : 1–92, and 105, no. 12 (December, 1869) : 1–63.

————. "Skornyakov-Pisarev i Devyer v Sibiri" ["Skornyakov-Pisarev and Devier in Siberia"], *Russkaya starina* 15, no. 2 (February, 1876) : 444–450.

Shakhovskoy, Aleksandr. "Izvestiya o Gizhiginskoy kreposti" ["Information about Gizhiga Fortress"], *Severny arkhiv,* pt. 4 (1822), pp. 283–312.

————. "Mnenie, o sposobakh prodovolstviya zhiteley Okhotskavo i Gizhiginskavo uyezdov" ["Opinion on the Ways of Provisioning the Inhabitants of Okhotsk and Gizhiga Uyezds"], *Severny arkhiv,* pt. 5 (1823), pp. 345–352.

————. "O nachale postroyeniya Gizhiginskoy kreposti" ["Concerning the Beginning of the Construction of Gizhiga Fortress"], *Vestnik Yevropy,* no. 24, pt. 102 (December, 1818), pp. 280–285.

Shaskolsky, I. P., ed. *Geograficheskoye izuchenie Sibiri XVII–XIX v.v.* [*The Geographical Study of Siberia of the XVIIth–XIXth Centuries*]. "Materialy Otdeleniya istorii geograficheskikh znany Geograficheskovo obshchestva Soyuza SSR," no. 1. Leningrad: Geograficheskoye obshchestvo SSSR, 1962.

Shcheglov, I. V. *Kronologichesky perechen vazhneishikh dannykh iz istorii Sibiri 1032–1882 gg.* [*Chronological List of the Major Facts from the History of Siberia 1032–1882*]. Irkutsk: Tipografiya Shtaba Vostochnavo Sibirskavo voyennavo okruga, 1883.

Shch. [Shchukin], N. *Poyezdka v Yakutsk* [*Journey to Yakutsk*]. St. Petersburg: Tipografiya Konrada Vingebera, 1833.

Shchukin, N. "Ogorodnichestvo Vostochnoy Sibiri" ["Gardening of Eastern Siberia"], *Biblioteka dlya chteniya* 93 (1849) : 1–14.

————. "Udskoye selenie" ["Udsk Settlement"], *Russky invalid,* 35, no. 114 (May 25/June 6, 1848) : 456, and 35, no. 115 (May 26/June 7, 1848) : 460.

————. "Udskoye selenie" ["Udsk Settlement"], *Zhurnal Ministerstva vnutrennikh del,* pt. 22 (1848), pp. 174–186.

Shemelin, Fyodor. *Zhurnal pervavo puteshestvie rossiyan vokrug zemnavo shara . . .* [*Journal of the First Voyage of a Russian around the Globe . . .*]. St. Petersburg: Meditsinskaya tipografiya, 1818. Pt. 2.

Sherstoboyev, V. N. *Ilimskaya pashnya* [*The Ilimsk Plowland*]. 2 vols.

Irkutsk: Irkutskoye oblastnoye gosudarstvennoye izdatelstvo and Irkutskoye knizhnoye izdatelstvo, 1949–57.

———. "Zemledelie severnovo Predbaikalya v XVII–XVIII vv." ["Agri-
culture of Northern Prebaikalia in the XVIIth–XVIIIth Centuries"], in
Materialy po istorii zemledeliya SSSR. Ed. B. D. Grekov. Moscow and
Leningrad: Izdatelstvo Akademii nauk SSSR, 1952. Collection 1.

Shmalev, Timofey. "Izvestiya Kapitana Shmaleva ob Okhotskom porte; o
stroyenii sudov i o pr." ["Captain Shmalev's Information about Okhotsk
Port; about Shipbuilding, etc."]. TsGADA, f. 199, port. 539, pt. 1, d.
12.

———. "Izvestiya Kap. Shmaleva o byvshikh prezhde v Sibirskikh otdalyonnykh mestakh sukhoputnykh i vodnykh soobshcheniyakh" ["Capt. Shmalev's Information about Former Land and Water Communications in
Remote Siberian Places"]. TsGADA, f. 199, port. 539, pt. 1, d. 13.

———. "Kratkoye o Kamchatke obyasnenie uchinyonnoye Kapitanom
Timofeiyem Shmalevym" ["Brief Explanation about Kamchatka Made by
Captain Timofey Shmalev"]. TsGADA, f. 199, port. 539, pt. 1, d. 8.

———. "Kratkoye opisanie o Kamchatke . . ." ["Brief Description of
Kamchatka . . ."], *Opyt trudov Volnavo rossiiskavo sobraniya pri Imperatorskom moskovskom universitete*, pt. 1 (1774), pp. 195–215.

———. "Pribavlenie, uchinyonnoye Kap. T. Shmalevym, kasayushchusya do
raznykh proisshestvy v Okhotskom porte, Kamchatke i okolo onykh
otdalyonnykh mest" ["Supplement Made by Capt. T. Shmalev Concerning Various Occurrences in Okhotsk Port and Kamchatka and Remote
Places near Them"]. TsGADA, f. 199, port. 528, pt. 1, d. 12.

———. "Primechanie uchinyonnoye Kapitanom Timofeiyem Shmalevym
k ne sposobnomu vpred bytyu Okhotskavo Porta . . ." ["Comment Made
by Captain Timofey Shmalev Concerning the Insupportable Existence of
Okhotsk Port in the Future . . ."]. TsGADA, f. 199, port. 539, pt. 1, d. 9.

———. "Statisticheskiya i Geograficheskiya Primechaniya Kapitana Tim.
Shmaleva ob otdalyonnykh onykh mest krepostyakh, o khlebopashestve i
pr. s pribavleniyami" ["Statistical and Geographical Notes of Captain
Tim Shmalev about the Fortresses, Grain Cultivation, etc. of the Aforementioned Remote Places with Supplements"]. TsGADA, f. 199, port.
528, pt. 1, d. 19.

———. "Ukaz i Instruktsiya opredelyonnomu v Okhotsk Glavnym Komandirom Grigoryu Pisarevu 1 Aprel 1732 goda" ["Decree and Instructions
Appointing Grigory Pisarev Chief Commander of Okhotsk on April 1,
1732"]. TsGADA, f. 199, port. 528, pt. 1, d. 1.

———. "Vedomost o nakhodyashchemsya proviante v Okhotskom porte"
["List of Provisions Found at Okhotsk Port"]. TsGADA, f. 199, port.
528, pt. 1, d. 13.

———. "Vypiski o raspolozhenii v Sibirskoy Gubernii vnov yasak" ["Excerpts on the Re-establishment of Yasak in the Province of Siberia"].
TsGADA, f. 199, port. 528, pt. 1, d. 18.

Shmalev, Vasily. "Nachalo izyskaniya novavo trakta ot Yakutska k Okhotsku" ["The Beginning of the Search for a New Track from Yakutsk toward Okhotsk"]. TsGADA, f. 199, port. 528, pt. 1, d. 9.

――――. "Ukazy i raporty ob Okhotskom porte s prilozhennym planom" ["Decrees and Reports about Okhotsk Port with an Appended Plan"]. TsGADA, f. 199, port. 528, pt. 1, d. 11.

Shteller. "Opisanie strany Kamchatki" ["Description of the Country of Kamchatka"]. AIE, f. K-II, op. 1, d. 304.

Shunkov, V. I. "Geograficheskoye razmeshchenie sibirskovo zemledeliya v XVII veke" ["Geographical Distribution of Siberian Agriculture in the XVIIth Century"], *Voprosy geografii*, no. 20 (1950), pp. 203–238.

――――. "Geografiya khlebnykh tsen Sibiri XVII v." ["Geography of the Grain Prices of Siberia of the XVIIth Century"], *Voprosy geografii*, no. 31 (1953), pp. 169–205.

――――. "K voprosu o kharaktere khlebooborota Sibiri v XVII v." ["Concerning the Question of the Character of Siberia's Grain Turnover in the XVIIth Century"], in *Voprosy sotsialno-ekonomicheskoy istorii i istochnikovedeniya perioda feodalizma v Rossii*. Ed. Akademiya nauk SSSR, Institut istorii. Moscow: Izdatelstvo Akademii nauk SSSR, 1961.

――――. *Ocherki po istorii zemledeliya Sibiri (XVII vek)* [*Sketches on the History of the Agriculture of Siberia (XVIIth Century)*]. Moscow: Izdatelstvo Akademii nauk SSSR, 1956.

――――. " 'Opyt' v selskom khozyaistve Sibiri XVII veka" [" 'Experimentation' in the Agriculture of Siberia of the XVIIth Century"], in *Materialy po istorii zemledeliya SSSR*. Ed. B. D. Grekov. Moscow and Leningrad: Izdatelstvo Akademii nauk SSSR, 1952. Collection 1.

Sibirskaya sovetskaya entsiklopediya [*Siberian Soviet Encyclopedia*]. 3 vols. Novosibirsk: Zapadno-Sibirskoye otdelenie Ogiz, 1929–32.

Sibirskie goroda. Materialy dlya ikh istorii XVII i XVIII stolety. Nerchinsk. Selenginsk. Yakutsk. [*Siberian Towns. Materials for Their History of the XVIIth and XVIIIth Centuries. Nerchinsk. Selenginsk. Yakutsk.*]. Moscow: Tipografiya M. G. Volchaninova, 1886.

Sibirsky prikaz. TsGADA, f. 214, st. 1,424.

Silnitsky, A. "Mery pravitelstva dlya podnyatiya blagosostoyaniya Gizhiginskavo kraya, s 1819–1840 g." ["Measures of the Government for Improving the Well-Being of Gizhiga Kray, 1819–1840"], *Zapiski Priamurskavo otdela Imperatorskavo russkavo geograficheskavo obshchestva* 4, no. 1 (1898) : 27–73.

Simpson, Sir George. *Narrative of a Journey Round the World . . . .* 2 vols. London: Henry Colburn, 1847.

Sirotkin, V. G. "Dokumenty o politike Rossii na Dalnem Vostoke v nachale XIX v." ["Documents on the Policy of Russia in the Far East in the Beginning of the XIXth Century"], *Istorichesky arkhiv* 6 (November–December, 1962) : 85–99.

Sk., Al. [Sokolov, A.] "Opis Udskavo berega i Shantarskikh ostrovov, poruchika Kozmina" ["Lieutenant Kozmin's Inventory of the Udsk Coast and the Shantar Islands"], *Zapiski Gidrograficheskavo departamenta*, pt. 4 (1846), pp. 1–78.

Skalon, V. N. *Russkie zemleprokhodtsy—issledovateli Sibiri XVII veka* [*Russian Landsmen—Explorers of Siberia of the XVIIth Century*]. Moscow: Moskovskoye obshchestvo ispytateley prirody, 1951.

Skornyakov-Pisarev, Grigory. "Promemoriya is kantselyarii Okhotskovo porta blagorodnomu Gospodinu Akademii Nauk professoru Gerardu Fridrikhu Milleru . . ." ["Memorandum from the Office of Okhotsk Port to Professor of the Academy of Sciences Noble Mr. Gerhard Friedrich Muller . . ."]. TsGADA, f. 199, port. 528, pt. 7, d. 481.

[Slovtsov, P. A.] *Istoricheskoye obozrenie Sibiri* [*Historical Survey of Siberia*]. 2 vols. St. Petersburg: Tipografiya I. N. Skorokhodova, 1886.

[Soimonov, F. I.]. "Drevnyaya poslovitsa Sibir zolotoye dno" ["The Old Proverb Siberia Is a Gold Mine"], *Sochineniya i perevody . . .* 14 (November, 1761) : 449–467, and *Yezhemesyachnia sochineniya . . .* , 11 (January, 1764) : 44–59.

Sokolov, A. "Severnaya ekspeditsiya 1733–43 godu" ["The Northern Expedition 1733–43"], *Zapiski Gidrograficheskavo departamenta* 9 (1851) : 190–469 and appendix.

[———.] "Zaliv Ayan" ["Ayan Bay"], *Zapiski Gidrograficheskavo departamenta*, pt. 4 (1846), pp. 79–85.

Spassky, Grigory. "Izvestie o Kamchatskoy dukhovnoy missii" ["Information about the Kamchatka Ecclesiastical Mission"], *Sibirsky vestnik*, pt. 17 (1822), pp. 89–98.

———. "O peremenakh, proizshedshikh na Kamchatke so vremeni opisaniya onoy Krasheninnikovym" ["Concerning the Changes Wrought in Kamchatka since the Time of Its Description by Krasheninnikov"], *Sibirsky vestnik*, pt. 4, bks. 19–24 (1824), pp. 331–353.

Stary pochtalion. "Vospominaniya Lenskavo pochtaliona" ["Reminiscences of a Lena Postman"], *Sibirskaya gazeta*, no. 24 (June 13/25, 1882), pp. 584–586.

Stejneger, Leonhard. *Georg Wilhelm Steller . . . .* Cambridge, Mass.: Harvard University Press, 1936.

Stepanchenko, A. I. *Gordost nasha Sibir* [*Our Pride Is Siberia*]. Irkutsk: Vostochno-Sibirskoye knizhnoye izdatelstvo, 1964.

Strelov, Ye. D. *Akty arkhivov Yakutskoy oblasti* (*s 1650 g. do 1800 g.*) [*Archival Acts of Yakutsk Oblast* (*from 1650 to 1800*)]. Yakutsk: Yakutskaya oblastnaya uchyonaya arkhivnaya kommissiya, 1916. Vol. 1.

Struve, V. V. *Vospominaniya o Sibiri, 1848–1854* [*Reminiscences about Siberia, 1848–1854*]. St. Petersburg: Tipografiya Tovarishchestva "Obshchestvennaya polza," 1889.

Sushkov, N. V. "O sibirskikh solyanykh promyslakh" ["Concerning the Siberian Salt Industries"], *Sibirsky vestnik*, pt. 15, bk. 7 (July, 1821), pp. 71–94.

Suslov, S. P. *Physical Geography of Asiatic Russia*. Trans. Noah D. Gershevsky. San Francisco and London: W. H. Freeman and Company, 1961.

Sverbeyev, N. "Sibirskiya pisma" ["Siberian Letters"], *Vestnik Imperatorskavo russkavo geograficheskavo obshchestva,* vol. 8, pt. 7 (1853), pp. 95–109.

Tebenkov, Captain. *Gidrograficheskiya zamechaniya k atlasu severozapadnykh beregov Ameriki . . . [Hydrographical Observations Accompanying the Atlas of the Northwestern Shores of America . . .].* St. Petersburg: Tipografiya Morskavo kadetskavo korpusa, 1852.

Teplov, S. N., ed. *Atlas SSSR [Atlas of the USSR].* Moscow: Glavnoye upravlenie geodezii i kartografii Ministerstva geologii i okhrany nedr SSSR, 1962.

Termin, Major. "Kratkoye obozrenie reki Leny i sudokhodstva po onoy" ["Brief Survey of the Lena River and of Navigation on It"], *Zhurnal putey soobshcheniya,* no. 32 (1835), pp. 73–91.

Tikhmenev, P. *Supplement of some Historical Documents to the Historical Review of the Formation of the Russian-American Company . . . .* Trans. Dimitri Krenov. Seattle: Works Progress Administration, 1938.

————. *The Historical Review of Formation of the Russian-American Company . . . .* Trans. Dimitri Krenov. 2 pts. Seattle: Works Progress Administration, 1939–40.

Titov, A., ed. *Sibir v XVII veke [Siberia in the XVIIth Century].* Moscow: G. Yudin, 1890.

Tokarev, S. A. *Etnografiya narodov SSSR [Ethnography of the Peoples of the USSR].* Moscow: Izdatelstvo Moskovskovo universiteta, 1958.

————. *Ocherk istorii yakutskovo naroda [Sketch of the History of the the USSR].* Moscow: Izdatelstvo Moskovskovo universiteta, 1958.

————. *Ocherk istorii yakutskovo naroda [Sketch of the History of the Yakut People].* Moscow: Gosudarstvennoye sotsialno-ekonomicheskoye izdatelstvo, 1940.

Tolstoy, Graf M. "Missionerskaya deyatelnost pokoinavo mitropolita Innokentiya" ["The Missionary Activity of the Late Metropolitan Innokenty"], *Russky arkhiv,* vol. 17, bk. 2 (1879), pp. 273–303.

Tomashevsky, V. V. *Materialy k bibliografii Sibiri i Dalnevo Vostoka (XV–pervaya polovina XIX veka) [Materials toward a Bibliography of Siberia and the Far East (XVth to the First Half of the XIXth Century)].* Vladivostok: Akademiya nauk Soyuza SSR, Dalnevostochny filial, 1957.

Tooke, William. *View of the Russian Empire, During the Reign of Catherine the Second, and to the Close of the Eighteenth Century.* 2d ed. London: T. N. Longman and O. Rees, 1800. Vol. 3.

Tronson, J. M. *Personal Narrative of a Voyage to Japan, Kamtschatka, Siberia, Tartary . . . .* London: Smith, Elder & Co., 1859.

United States. Congress. Senate. *Proceedings of the Alaskan Boundary Tribunal . . . .* Washington: Government Printing Office, 1904. Vols. 2–3.

————. Congress. Senate. *Russian Administration of Alaska and the Status of the Alaskan Natives.* 81st Congress, 2d Session, 1950. Senate Document 152.

Urness, Carol. ed. *A Naturalist in Russia*. Minneapolis: The University of Minnesota Press, 1967.

V., A. "Neskolko slov o noveishikh opytakh ko vvedeniyu v Kamchatke khlebopashestva i obrabotaniya ogorodnykh rasteny" ["Several Words about the Latest Attempts at Introducing Grain Cultivation and the Cultivation of Garden Plants in Kamchatka"], *Russky invalid*, no. 134 (May 28/April 9, 1832), pp. 534–536.

Vagin, V. *Istoricheskiya svedeniya o deyatelnosti grafa M. M. Speranskavo v Sibiri s 1819 po 1822 god* [*Historical Information about the Activities of Count M. M. Speransky in Siberia from 1819 to 1822*]. 2 vols. St. Petersburg: Tipografiya Vtoravo otdeleniya Sobstvennoy Ye. I. V. Kantselyarii, 1872.

Vakhtin, V. *Russkie truzheniki morya* [*Russian Toilers of the Sea*]. St. Petersburg: Tipografiya Morskavo ministerstva, 1890.

Vaksel, Sven. *Vtoraya kamchatskaya ekspeditsiya Vitusa Beringa* [*Vitus Bering's Second Kamchatka Expedition*]. Leningrad and Moscow: Izdatelstvo Glavsevmorputi, 1940.

Veselago, F. *Kratkaya istoriya russkavo flota* [*Brief History of the Russian Fleet*]. St. Petersburg: Tipografiya V. Demakova, 1893. Pt. 1.

———, ed. *Materialy dlya istorii russkavo flota* [*Materials for the History of the Russian Fleet*]. St. Petersburg: Tipografiya Morskavo ministerstva, 1880–1904. Vols. 8 and 17.

[———.] *Russkoy morskoy istorii* [*Of Russian Naval History*]. St. Petersburg: Tipografiya Demakova, 1875. Pt. 1.

Von Bem, Major. "O Kamchatskom zemledelii . . ." ["Concerning Kamchatkan Agriculture . . ."], *Prodolzhenie trudov Volnavo ekonomicheskavo obshchestva . . .* , pt. 3 (1783), pp. 41–45.

Von Kotzebue, Otto. *A New Voyage Round the World, in the Years 1823, 24, 25, and 26*. London: Henry Colburn and Richard Bentley, 1830. Vol. 2.

Von Krusenstern, Captain A. J. *Voyage Round the World in the Years 1803, 1804, 1805, & 1806*. Trans. Richard Belgrave Hoppner. London: John Murray, 1813. Vol. 2.

Von Langsdorff, G. H. *Bemerkungen auf einer Reise um die Welt in den Jahren 1803 bis 1807* [*Notes of a Voyage Around the World in the Years 1803 to 1807*]. Frankfurt am Mayn: F. Williams, 1812. Vol. 2.

———. *Voyages and Travels in Various Parts of the World . . . .* London: Henry Colburn, 1814. Pt. 2.

Von Strahlenburg, Philip J. *An Historico-Geographical Description of the North and Eastern Parts of Europe and Asia . . . .* London: W. Innys and R. Manby, 1738.

Von Wrangell, Ferdinand. *Narrative of an Expedition to the Polar Sea . . . .* London: James Madden and Co., 1840.

Vrangel, F. "Putevia zapiski admirala barona F. P. Vrangelya" ["Travel Notes of Admiral Baron F. P. Wrangel"], *Istorichesky vestnik* 18 (1884) : 162–180.

Vtoroy sibirsky komitet. "Kopiya s otchyota Yakutskavo grazhdanskavo gubernatora o sostoyanii Yakutskoy oblasti za 1854 god" ["A Copy from the Report of the Civil Governor of Yakutsk on the Condition of Yakutsk Oblast for 1854"]. TsGIAL, f. 1,265, op. 4, d. 109.

Waxell, Sven. *The Russian Expedition to America.* Trans. M. A. Michael. New York: Collier Books, 1962.

Yanitsky, N. "Torgovlya pushnym tovarom v XVII v." ["The Fur Trade in the XVIIth Century"], *Universitetskiya izvestiya* 52, no. 2 (September, 1912) : 1–33.

Yefimov, A. V., ed. *Atlas geograficheskikh otkryty v Sibiri i v Severo-Zapadnoy Amerike XVII–XVIII vv.* [*Atlas of Geographical Discoveries in Siberia and Northwestern America of the XVIIth–XVIIIth Centuries*]. Moscow: Izdatelstvo "Nauka," 1964.

Yefimov, A. V., and Tokarev, S. A., eds. *Narody Ameriki* [*Peoples of America*]. Moscow: Izdatelstvo Akademii nauk SSSR, 1959. Vol. 1.

Zagoskin, L. A. *Puteshestviya i issledovaniya leitenanta Lavrentiya Zagoskina v Russkoy Amerike v 1842–1844 g.g.* [*Travels and Explorations of Lieutenant Lavrenty Zagoskin in Russian America in the Years 1842–1844*]. Moscow: Gosudarstvennoye izdatelstvo geograficheskoy literatury, 1956.

Zagoskin, N. P. *Russkie vodnie puti i sudovoye delo v do-Petrovskoy Rossii* [*Russian Waterways and Shipping in Pre-Petrine Russia*]. Kazan: Lito-tipografiya I. N. Kharitonova, 1910.

Zavalishin, D. I. *Zapiski Dekabrista* [*Notes of a Decembrist*]. St. Petersburg: Tipografiya "Sirius," 1906.

Zoologichesky institut Akademii nauk SSSR. *Atlas okhotnichikh i promyslo-vykh ptits i zverey SSSR* [*Atlas of Game Birds and Animals of the USSR*]. Moscow: Izdatelstvo Akademii nauk SSSR, 1950–53. Vol. 2.

INDEX

Aborigines. *See* Natives

Abyshtov, Captain: founds Captain's Clearing, 81

Admiralty College: orders shipbuilding at Okhotsk, 103; on causes of shipwrecks, 132; orders disuse of Lopatka Channel, 135; orders sending of cats to Petropavlovsk, 140; mentioned, 134, 172

Agricultural implements: Kamchatka's imports of, 204; Udsk's imports of, 204

Agricultural settlement in Siberia: methods of, 155; inducements to, 156; organization of, 157; numbers in, 157; success of, 157; regions of, 157, 159

—on Okhotsk Seaboard and Kamchatka Peninsula: causes of, 160; more necessary in Kamchatka than at Okhotsk, 160; beginnings of, 160–61; monastic, 160–62; state, 162–68; livestock for, 164, 165, 167; peasants for, 164–68; numbers in, 168

Agriculture in Siberia: causes of, 155

—on Okhotsk Seaboard and Kamchatka Peninsula: causes of, 155; perspective of, 159; organization and type of, 169–70; production of, 171–84; abandonment of, 176, 196–97, 198–99; physical problems of, 185–92; conflicts with fishing, 190, 195,

197, 199, 203; cultural problems of, 192–201; conflicts with trapping, 197, 199; neglect of, 197–98, 203, 208, 210; discouraged by officials, 199–200, 200; lax supervision of, 200, 202; Kamchatka's attempts at improvement of, 202–15; summary of, 221

Ainus. *See* Kurilians

Alachak Portage, 143

Alaska: fur trade in, xv; occupation of, 23–24; transshipment to, 96; mentioned, xvii, xvii*n*, 17, 24, 25, 27, 31, 32, 33, 93, 96, 102, 115, 128, 132, 135, 148, 186*n*, 219

Albazin: founding of, 9

Aldan Basin, 115

Aldan Okrug: cattle raising in, 70

Aldan River: ferry charges on, 93; founding of Yakut town along, 142; mentioned, 8, 9, 79, 82, 87, 101, 115, 116, 117, 119, 123, 124, 143, 144, 145, 149, 150

Aldan Track. *See* Yakutsk-Okhotsk Track

Aldoma River, 144, 145

Aleutian Islands, 17, 23, 30, 32, 33, 51*n*, 131, 133

Aleuts: exploitation of, 31; mentioned, 32

Allakh-Yun: size of, 146; mentioned, 145